New Perspectives on

Microsoft® Office WITHDRAWN
Word 2007

Introductory

New Perspectives on

Microsoft® Office Word 2007

Introductory

S. Scott Zimmerman
Brigham Young University

Beverly B. Zimmerman
Brigham Young University

Ann Shaffer

Katherine T. Pinard

THOMSON

COURSE TECHNOLOGY

Australia • Canada • Mexico • Singapore • Spain • United Kingdom • United States

THOMSON
™
COURSE TECHNOLOGY

New Perspectives on Microsoft Office Word 2007—Introductory

is published by Thomson Course Technology.

Acquisitions Editor:
Kristina Matthews

Senior Product Manager:
Kathy Finnegan

Product Manager:
Erik Herman

Associate Product Manager:
Brandi Henson

Editorial Assistant:
Leigh Robbins

Senior Marketing Manager:
Joy Stark

Marketing Coordinator:
Jennifer Hankin

Developmental Editor:
Mary Kemper

Senior Content Project Manager:
Catherine G. DiMassa

Composition:
GEX Publishing Services

Text Designer:
Steve Deschene

Cover Designer:
Elizabeth Paquin

Cover Art:
Bill Brown

Preface

The New Perspectives Series' critical-thinking, problem-solving approach is the ideal way to prepare students to transcend point-and-click skills and take advantage of all that Microsoft Office 2007 has to offer.

In developing the New Perspectives Series for Microsoft Office 2007, our goal was to create books that give students the software concepts and practical skills they need to succeed beyond the classroom. We've updated our proven case-based pedagogy with more practical content to make learning skills more meaningful to students.

With the New Perspectives Series, students understand *why* they are learning *what* they are learning, and are fully prepared to apply their skills to real-life situations.

"I really love the Margin Tips, which add 'tricks of the trade' to students' skills package. In addition, the Reality Check exercises provide for practical application of students' knowledge. I can't wait to use them in the classroom when we adopt Office 2007."

—Terry Morse Colucci
Institute of Technology, Inc.

About This Book

This book provides thorough, hands-on coverage of the new Microsoft Office Word 2007 software, and includes the following:

- A new "Getting Started with Microsoft Office 2007" tutorial that familiarizes students with the new Office 2007 features and user interface
- Complete coverage of Word 2007 basics, including creating, editing, and formatting documents; working with multi-page documents; and simple desktop publishing
- Expanded and in-depth coverage of higher level skills, including working with templates, styles, and tables of contents; customizing document themes; performing a mail merge; revising and merging documents with tracked changes; and creating Web pages
- Guidance in using the new themes and Quick Styles to create professional-looking documents quickly and easily, and in exploring styles for document elements using the new Live Preview feature
- Instruction in using the new SmartArt feature to create and modify diagrams that illustrate concepts, such as processes and organizational structures
- New business case scenarios throughout, which provide a rich and realistic context for students to apply the concepts and skills presented

System Requirements

This book assumes a typical installation of Microsoft Office Word 2007 and Microsoft Windows Vista Ultimate with the Aero feature turned off (or Windows Vista Home Premium or Business edition). Note that you can also complete the tutorials in this book using Windows XP; you will notice only minor differences if you are using Windows XP. Refer to the tutorial "Getting Started with Microsoft Office 2007" for Tips noting these differences. The browser used in this book for any steps that require a browser is Internet Explorer 7.

The New Perspectives Approach

Context
Each tutorial begins with a problem presented in a "real-world" case that is meaningful to students. The case sets the scene to help students understand what they will do in the tutorial.

Hands-on Approach
Each tutorial is divided into manageable sessions that combine reading and hands-on, step-by-step work. Colorful screenshots help guide students through the steps. **Trouble?** tips anticipate common mistakes or problems to help students stay on track and continue with the tutorial.

InSight

InSight Boxes
New for Office 2007! InSight boxes offer expert advice and best practices to help students better understand how to work with the software. With the information provided in the InSight boxes, students achieve a deeper understanding of the concepts behind the software features and skills.

Tip

Margin Tips
New for Office 2007! Margin Tips provide helpful hints and shortcuts for more efficient use of the software. The Tips appear in the margin at key points throughout each tutorial, giving students extra information when and where they need it.

Reality Check

Reality Checks
New for Office 2007! Comprehensive, open-ended Reality Check exercises give students the opportunity to practice skills by creating practical, real-world documents, such as resumes and budgets, which they are likely to use in their everyday lives at school, home, or work.

Review

In New Perspectives, retention is a key component to learning. At the end of each session, a series of Quick Check questions helps students test their understanding of the concepts before moving on. Each tutorial also contains an end-of-tutorial summary and a list of key terms for further reinforcement.

Apply

Assessment
Engaging and challenging Review Assignments and Case Problems have always been a hallmark feature of the New Perspectives Series. Colorful icons and brief descriptions accompany the exercises, making it easy to understand, at a glance, both the goal and level of challenge a particular assignment holds.

Reference Window

Task Reference

Reference
While contextual learning is excellent for retention, there are times when students will want a high-level understanding of how to accomplish a task. Within each tutorial, Reference Windows appear before a set of steps to provide a succinct summary and preview of how to perform a task. In addition, a complete Task Reference at the back of the book provides quick access to information on how to carry out common tasks. Finally, each book includes a combination Glossary/Index to promote easy reference of material.

Our Complete System of Instruction

Brief

Introductory

Comprehensive

Coverage To Meet Your Needs

Whether you're looking for just a small amount of coverage or enough to fill a semester-long class, we can provide you with a textbook that meets your needs.

- Brief books typically cover the essential skills in just 2 to 4 tutorials.
- Introductory books build and expand on those skills and contain an average of 5 to 8 tutorials.
- Comprehensive books are great for a full-semester class, and contain 9 to 12+ tutorials.

So if the book you're holding does not provide the right amount of coverage for you, there's probably another offering available. Go to our Web site or contact your Thomson Course Technology sales representative to find out what else we offer.

Student Online Companion

This book has an accompanying online companion Web site designed to enhance learning. This Web site includes:

- Internet Assignments for selected tutorials
- Student Data Files
- PowerPoint presentations

COURSECASTS

CourseCasts – Learning on the Go. Always available…always relevant.

Want to keep up with the latest technology trends relevant to you? Visit our site to find a library of podcasts, CourseCasts, featuring a "CourseCast of the Week," and download them to your mp3 player at http://coursecasts.course.com.

Our fast-paced world is driven by technology. You know because you're an active participant—always on the go, always keeping up with technological trends, and always learning new ways to embrace technology to power your life.

Ken Baldauf, host of CourseCasts, is a faculty member of the Florida State University Computer Science Department where he is responsible for teaching technology classes to thousands of FSU students each year. Ken is an expert in the latest technology trends; he gathers and sorts through the most pertinent news and information for CourseCasts so your students can spend their time enjoying technology, rather than trying to figure it out. Open or close your lecture with a discussion based on the latest CourseCast.

Visit us at http://coursecasts.course.com to learn on the go!

Instructor Resources

We offer more than just a book. We have all the tools you need to enhance your lectures, check students' work, and generate exams in a new, easier-to-use and completely revised package. This book's Instructor's Manual, ExamView testbank, PowerPoint presentations, data files, solution files, figure files, and a sample syllabus are all available on a single CD-ROM or for downloading at www.course.com.

Skills Assessment and Training

SAM 2007 helps bridge the gap between the classroom and the real world by allowing students to train and test on important computer skills in an active, hands-on environment.

SAM 2007's easy-to-use system includes powerful interactive exams, training or projects on critical applications such as Word, Excel, Access, PowerPoint, Outlook, Windows, the Internet, and much more. SAM simulates the application environment, allowing students to demonstrate their knowledge and think through the skills by performing real-world tasks.

Designed to be used with the New Perspectives Series, SAM 2007 includes built-in page references so students can print helpful study guides that match the New Perspectives textbooks used in class. Powerful administrative options allow instructors to schedule exams and assignments, secure tests, and run reports with almost limitless flexibility.

Blackboard

Online Content

Blackboard is the leading distance learning solution provider and class-management platform today. Thomson Course Technology has partnered with Blackboard to bring you premium online content. Content for use with *New Perspectives on Microsoft Office Word 2007, Introductory* is available in a Blackboard Course Cartridge and may include topic reviews, case projects, review questions, test banks, practice tests, custom syllabi, and more.

Thomson Course Technology also has solutions for several other learning management systems. Please visit http://www.course.com today to see what's available for this title.

Acknowledgments

Thanks to Kristina Matthews, the fearless leader of the New Perspective Series. To Kathy Finnegan, amazing and resourceful project manager, thank you for the great ideas and much-needed encouragement. Thanks, also, to Brandi Henson, Associate Product Manager, and Leigh Robbins, Editorial Assistant, for their support during the development of this text. My thanks to Mary Kemper, Developmental Editor extraordinaire, who made this a far better book than it would have been without her careful edits. A special thanks to Kitty Pinard and Lisa Ruffolo for their patient advice and explanations at all hours of the day and night. Thank you to Cathie DiMassa, our hard-working Production Editor, who managed the million details involved in transforming the manuscript into a printed book. As always, I relied on the ace Manuscript Quality Assurance testers at Thomson Course Technology, who provided detailed comments on every tutorial, at several stages in the process. Many thanks to Christian Kunciw, MQA Project Leader, and to the following QA testers for their help and suggestions: John Freitas, Serge Palladino, Danielle Shaw, Marianne Snow, and Susan Whalen.

Finally, I'm extremely grateful to our reviewers, who provided valuable insights into the needs of their students: Carla Jones, Middle Tennessee State University; Pamela Silvers, Asheville-Buncombe Technical Community College; and Monique Sluymers, Kaplan University.

–Ann Shaffer

We likewise want to thank all those who made this book possible. We especially want to thank Ann Shaffer, our co-author, for her expertise, hard work, and creative talents. Special thanks also go to Mary Kemper for her dedication and expertise as Developmental Editor in bringing this new edition to fruition.

–Beverly and Scott Zimmerman
–Katherine T. Pinard

Brief Contents

Table of Contents

Tutorial 2 Editing and Formatting a Document
Preparing a Handout on Choosing a Design Style . . . .*WD 45*

Tutorial 3 Creating a Multiple-Page Report
Writing a Recommendation . . . .*WD 97*

Tutorial 4 Desktop Publishing and Mail Merge
Creating a Newsletter, Cover Letter, and Blog Post . . . . .WD 147

Tutorial 5 Working with Templates and Outlines
Creating a Site Selection Report . . . . .WD 201

Tutorial 6 Using Mail Merge
Creating a Form Letter, Mailing Labels, and a List

Tutorial 7 Collaborating with Others and Creating Web Pages
Writing a Program Description

Objectives

- Explore the programs that comprise Microsoft Office
- Start programs and switch between them
- Explore common window elements
- Minimize, maximize, and restore windows
- Use the Ribbon, tabs, and buttons
- Use the contextual tabs, Mini toolbar, and shortcut menus
- Save, close, and open a file
- Use the Help system
- Print a file
- Exit programs

Getting Started with Microsoft Office 2007

Preparing a Meeting Agenda

Case | Recycled Palette

Recycled Palette, a company in Oregon founded by Ean Nogella in 2006, sells 100 percent recycled latex paint to both individuals and businesses in the area. The high-quality recycled paint is filtered to industry standards and tested for performance and environmental safety. The paint is available in both 1 gallon cans and 5 gallon pails, and comes in colors ranging from white to shades of brown, blue, green, and red. The demand for affordable recycled paint has been growing each year. Ean and all his employees use Microsoft Office 2007, which provides everyone in the company with the power and flexibility to store a variety of information, create consistent files, and share data. In this tutorial, you'll review how the company's employees use Microsoft Office 2007.

Starting Data Files

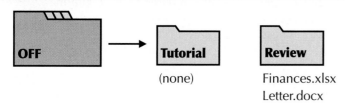

OFF → Tutorial
(none)

Review
Finances.xlsx
Letter.docx

Exploring Microsoft Office 2007

Microsoft Office 2007, or **Office**, is a collection of Microsoft programs. Office is available in many suites, each of which contains a different combination of these programs. For example, the Professional suite includes Word, Excel, PowerPoint, Access, Outlook, and Publisher. Other suites are available and can include more or fewer programs (for additional information about the available suites, go to the Microsoft Web site). Each Office program contains valuable tools to help you accomplish many tasks, such as composing reports, analyzing data, preparing presentations, compiling information, sending e-mail, and planning schedules.

Microsoft Office Word 2007, or **Word**, is a computer program you use to enter, edit, and format text. The files you create in Word are called **documents**, although many people use the term *document* to refer to any file created on a computer. Word, often called a word processing program, offers many special features that help you compose and update all types of documents, ranging from letters and newsletters to reports, brochures, faxes, and even books—all in attractive and readable formats. You can also use Word to create, insert, and position figures, tables, and other graphics to enhance the look of your documents. For example, the Recycled Palette employees create business letters using Word.

Microsoft Office Excel 2007, or **Excel**, is a computer program you use to enter, calculate, analyze, and present numerical data. You can do some of this in Word with tables, but Excel provides many more tools for recording and formatting numbers as well as performing calculations. The graphics capabilities in Excel also enable you to display data visually. You might, for example, generate a pie chart or a bar chart to help people quickly see the significance of and the connections between information. The files you create in Excel are called **workbooks** (commonly referred to as spreadsheets), and Excel is often called a spreadsheet program. The Recycled Palette accounting department uses a line chart in an Excel workbook to visually track the company's financial performance.

Microsoft Office Access 2007, or **Access**, is a computer program used to enter, maintain, and retrieve related information (or data) in a format known as a database. The files you create in Access are called **databases**, and Access is often referred to as a database or relational database program. With Access, you can create forms to make data entry easier, and you can create professional reports to improve the readability of your data. The Recycled Palette operations department tracks the company's inventory in a table in an Access database.

Microsoft Office PowerPoint 2007, or **PowerPoint**, is a computer program you use to create a collection of slides that can contain text, charts, pictures, sound, movies, multimedia, and so on. The files you create in PowerPoint are called **presentations**, and PowerPoint is often called a presentation graphics program. You can show these presentations on your computer monitor, project them onto a screen as a slide show, print them, share them over the Internet, or display them on the World Wide Web. You can also use PowerPoint to generate presentation-related documents such as audience handouts, outlines, and speakers' notes. The Recycled Palette marketing department has created an effective slide presentation with PowerPoint to promote its paints to a wider audience.

Microsoft Office Outlook 2007, or **Outlook**, is a computer program you use to send, receive, and organize e-mail; plan your schedule; arrange meetings; organize contacts; create a to-do list; and jot down notes. You can also use Outlook to print schedules, task lists, phone directories, and other documents. Outlook is often referred to as an information management program. The Recycled Palette staff use Outlook to send and receive e-mail, plan their schedules, and create to-do lists.

Although each Office program individually is a strong tool, their potential is even greater when used together.

Integrating Office Programs

One of the main advantages of Office is **integration**, the ability to share information between programs. Integration ensures consistency and accuracy, and it saves time because you don't have to reenter the same information in several Office programs. The staff at Recycled Palette uses the integration features of Office daily, including the following examples:

- The accounting department created an Excel bar chart on the previous two years' fourth-quarter results, which they inserted into the quarterly financial report created in Word. They included a hyperlink in the Word report that employees can click to open the Excel workbook and view the original data.
- The operations department included an Excel pie chart of sales percentages by paint colors on a PowerPoint slide, which is part of a presentation to stockholders.
- The marketing department produced a mailing to promote its recycled paints to local contractors and designers by combining a form letter created in Word with an Access database that stores the names and addresses of these potential customers.
- A sales representative wrote a letter in Word about an upcoming promotion for new customers and merged the letter with an Outlook contact list containing the names and addresses of prospective customers.

These are just a few examples of how you can take information from one Office program and integrate it with another.

Starting Office Programs

You can start any Office program by clicking the Start button on the Windows taskbar, and then selecting the program you want from the All Programs menu. As soon as the program starts, you can immediately begin to create new files or work with existing ones. If an Office program appears in the most frequently used programs list on the left side of the Start menu, you can click the program name to start the program.

Starting Office Programs	Reference Window

- Click the Start button on the taskbar.
- Click All Programs.
- Click Microsoft Office.
- Click the name of the program you want to start.

or

- Click the name of the program you want to start in the most frequently used programs list on the left side of the Start menu.

You'll start Excel using the Start button.

To start Excel and open a new, blank workbook:

▶ **1.** Make sure your computer is on and the Windows desktop appears on your screen.

Trouble? If your screen varies slightly from those shown in the figures, your computer might be set up differently. The figures in this book were created while running Windows Vista with the Aero feature turned off, but how your screen looks depends on the version of Windows you are using, the background settings, and so forth.

Windows XP Tip

The Start button is the green button with the word "start" on it, located at the bottom left of the taskbar.

2. Click the **Start** button on the taskbar, and then click **All Programs** to display the All Programs menu.

3. Click **Microsoft Office** on the All Programs list, and then point to **Microsoft Office Excel 2007**. Depending on how your computer is set up, your desktop and menu might contain different icons and commands.

   Trouble? If you don't see Microsoft Office on the All Programs list, click Microsoft Office Excel 2007 on the All Programs list. If you still don't see Microsoft Office Excel 2007, ask your instructor or technical support person for help.

4. Click **Microsoft Office Excel 2007**. Excel starts, and a new, blank workbook opens. See Figure 1.

Figure 1	New, blank Excel workbook

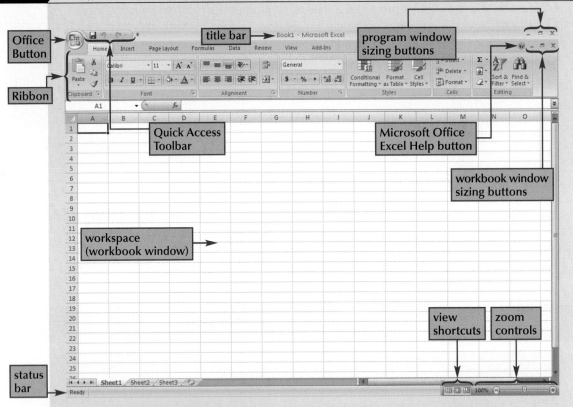

Trouble? If the Excel window doesn't fill your entire screen, the window is not maximized, or expanded to its full size. You'll maximize the window shortly.

You can have more than one Office program open at once. You'll use this same method to start Word and open a new, blank document.

To start Word and open a new, blank document:

1. Click the **Start** button on the taskbar, click **All Programs** to display the All Programs list, and then click **Microsoft Office**.

   Trouble? If you don't see Microsoft Office on the All Programs list, click Microsoft Office Word 2007 on the All Programs list. If you still don't see Microsoft Office Word 2007, ask your instructor or technical support person for help.

2. Click **Microsoft Office Word 2007**. Word starts, and a new, blank document opens. See Figure 2.

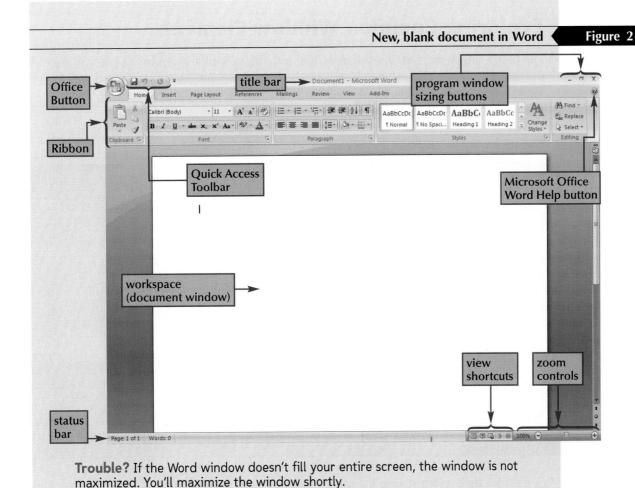

New, blank document in Word ◀ **Figure 2**

Trouble? If the Word window doesn't fill your entire screen, the window is not maximized. You'll maximize the window shortly.

Switching Between Open Programs and Files

Two programs are running at the same time—Excel and Word. The taskbar contains buttons for both programs. When you have two or more programs running or two files within the same program open, you can use the taskbar buttons to switch from one program or file to another. The button for the active program or file is darker. The employees at Recycled Palette often work in several programs at once.

To switch between Word and Excel files:

▶ **1.** Click the **Microsoft Excel – Book1** button on the taskbar. The active program switches from Word to Excel. See Figure 3.

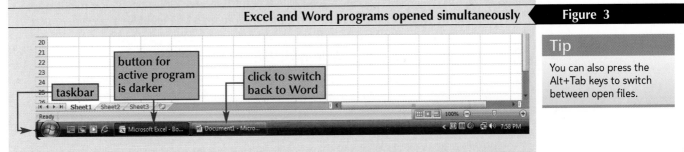

Excel and Word programs opened simultaneously ◀ **Figure 3**

Tip

You can also press the Alt+Tab keys to switch between open files.

▶ **2.** Click the **Document1 – Microsoft Word** button on the taskbar to return to Word.

Exploring Common Window Elements

The Office programs consist of windows that have many similar features. As you can see in Figures 1 and 2, many of the elements in both the Excel program window and the Word program window are the same. In fact, all the Office programs have these same elements. Figure 4 describes some of the most common window elements.

Figure 4	Common window elements

Element	Description
Office Button	Provides access to document-level features and program settings
Quick Access Toolbar	Provides one-click access to commonly used commands, such as Save, Undo, and Repeat
Title bar	Contains the name of the open file, the program name, and the sizing buttons
Sizing buttons	Resize and close the program window or the workspace
Ribbon	Provides access to the main set of commands organized by task into tabs and groups
Microsoft Office Help button	Opens the Help window for that program
Workspace	Displays the file you are working on (Word document, Excel workbook, Access database, or PowerPoint slide)
Status bar	Provides information about the program, open file, or current task as well as the view shortcuts and zoom controls
View shortcuts	Change how a file is displayed in the workspace
Zoom controls	Magnify or shrink the content displayed in the workspace

Because these elements are the same in each program, after you've learned one program, it's easy to learn the others. The next sections explore these common features.

Resizing the Program Window and Workspace

There are three different sizing buttons. The Minimize button ▬, which is the left button, hides a window so that only its program button is visible on the taskbar. The middle button changes name and function depending on the status of the window—the Maximize button ▫ expands the window to the full screen size or to the program window size, and the Restore Down button ⧉ returns the window to a predefined size. The Close button ✕, on the right, exits the program or closes the file. Excel has two sets of sizing buttons. The top set controls the program window and the lower set controls the workspace. The workspace sizing buttons look and function in exactly the same way as the program window sizing buttons, except the button names change to Minimize Window and Restore Window when the workspace is maximized.

Most often, you'll want to maximize the program window and workspace to take advantage of the full screen size you have available. If you have several files open, you might want to restore down their windows so that you can see more than one window at a time, or you might want to minimize programs or files you are not working on at the moment. You'll try minimizing, maximizing, and restoring down windows and workspaces now.

To resize windows and workspaces:

▶ **1.** Click the **Minimize** button ▭ on the Word title bar. The Word program window reduces to a taskbar button. The Excel program window is visible again.

▶ **2.** If necessary, click the **Maximize** button ▢ on the Excel title bar. The Excel program window expands to fill the screen.

▶ **3.** Click the **Restore Window** button ▢ in the lower set of Excel sizing buttons. The workspace is resized and is now smaller than the full program window. See Figure 5.

Resized Excel window and workspace | **Figure 5**

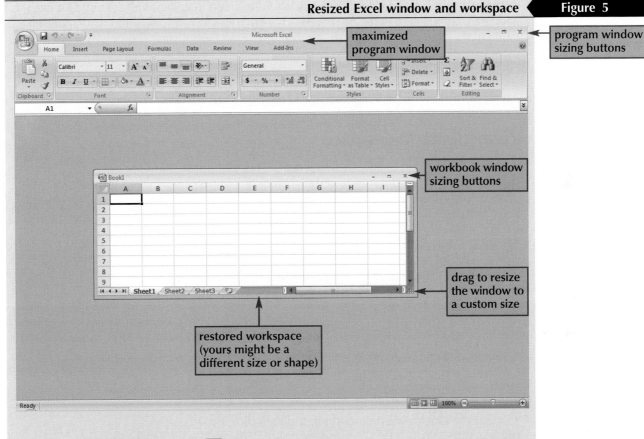

4. Click the **Maximize** button ▢ on the Excel workbook window title bar. The Excel workspace expands to fill the program window.

5. Click the **Document1 - Microsoft Word** button on the taskbar. The Word program window returns to its previous size.

6. If necessary, click the **Maximize** button ▢ on the Word title bar. The Word program window expands to fill the screen.

The sizing buttons give you the flexibility to arrange the program and file windows on your screen to best fit your needs.

Getting Information from the Status Bar

The **status bar** at the bottom of the program window provides information about the open file and current task or selection. It also has buttons and other controls for working with the file and its content. The status bar buttons and information displays are specific to the individual programs. For example, the Excel status bar displays summary information about a selected range of numbers (such as their sum or average), whereas the Word status bar shows the current page number and total number of words in a document. The right side of the status bar includes buttons that enable you to switch the workspace view in Word, Excel, PowerPoint, and Access as well as zoom the workspace in Word, Excel, and PowerPoint. You can customize the status bar to display other information or hide the **default** (original or preset) information.

Switching Views

Each program has a variety of views, or ways to display the file in the workspace. For example, Word has five views: Print Layout, Full Screen Reading, Web Layout, Outline, and Draft. The content of the file doesn't change from view to view, although the presentation of the content will. In Word, for example, Page Layout view shows how a document would appear as the printed page, whereas Web Layout view shows how the document would appear as a Web page. You can quickly switch between views using the shortcuts at the right side of the status bar. You can also change the view from the View tab on the Ribbon. You'll change views in later tutorials.

Zooming the Workspace

Zooming is a way to magnify or shrink the file content displayed in the workspace. You can zoom in to get a closer look at the content of an open document, worksheet, or slide, or you can zoom out to see more of the content at a smaller size. There are several ways to change the zoom percentage. You can use the Zoom slider at the right of the status bar to quickly change the zoom percentage. You can click the Zoom level button to the left of the Zoom slider in the status bar to open the Zoom dialog box and select a specific zoom percentage or size based on your file. You can also change the zoom settings using the Zoom group in the View tab on the Ribbon.

Reference Window | Zooming the Workspace

- Click the Zoom Out or Zoom In button on the status bar (or drag the Zoom slider button left or right) to the desired zoom percentage.
  or
- Click the Zoom level button on the status bar.
- Select the appropriate zoom setting, and then click the OK button.
  or
- Click the View tab on the Ribbon, and then in the Zoom group, click the zoom setting you want.

The figures shown in these tutorials are zoomed to enhance readability. You'll zoom the Word and Excel workspaces.

To zoom the Word and Excel workspaces:

  ▶ **1.** On the Zoom slider on the Word status bar, drag the **slider button** to the left until the Zoom percentage is **10%**. The document reduces to its smallest size, which makes the entire page visible but unreadable. See Figure 6.

Word document zoomed to 10% ◀ Figure 6

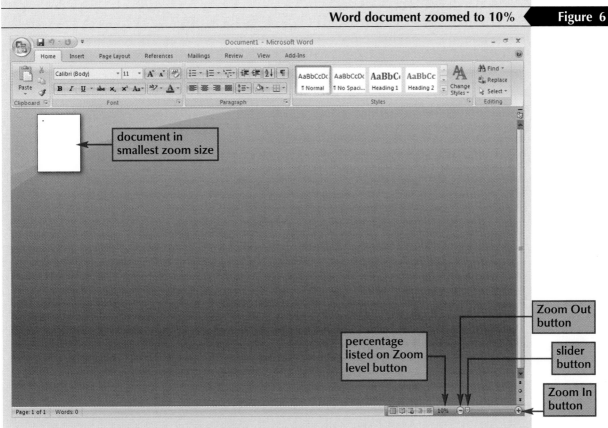

You'll zoom the document so its page width fills the workspace.

▶ **2.** Click the **Zoom level** button `10%` on the Word status bar. The Zoom dialog box opens. See Figure 7.

Zoom dialog box ◀ Figure 7

▶ **3.** Click the **Page width** option button, and then click the **OK** button. The Word document magnifies to its page width to match the rest of the Word figures shown in these tutorials.

Now, you'll zoom the workbook to 120%.

4. Click the **Microsoft Excel – Book1** button on the taskbar. The Excel program window is displayed.

5. Click the **Zoom In** button ⊕ on the status bar two times. The workspace magnifies to 120%. This is the zoom percentage that matches the rest of the Excel figures shown in these tutorials.

6. Click the **Document1 – Microsoft Word** button on the taskbar. The Word program window is displayed.

Using the Ribbon

The **Ribbon** at the top of the program window just below the title bar is the main set of commands that you click to execute tasks. The Ribbon is organized into tabs. Each **tab** has commands related to particular activities. For example, in Word, the Insert tab on the Ribbon provides access to all the commands for adding objects such as shapes, pages, tables, illustrations, text, and symbols to a document. Although the tabs differ from program to program, the first tab in each program, called the Home tab, contains the commands for the most frequently performed activities, including cutting and pasting, changing fonts, and using editing tools. In addition, the Insert, Review, View, and Add-Ins tabs appear on the Ribbon in all the Office programs except Access, although the commands they include might differ from program to program. Other tabs are program specific, such as the Design tab in PowerPoint and the Datasheet tab in Access.

To use the Ribbon tabs:

1. In Word, point to the **Insert** tab on the Ribbon. The Insert tab is highlighted, though the Home tab with the options for using the Clipboard and formatting text remains visible.

2. Click the **Insert** tab. The Ribbon displays the Insert tab, which provides access to all the options for adding objects such as shapes, pages, tables, illustrations, text, and symbols to a document. See Figure 8.

Figure 8	Insert tab on the Ribbon

3. Click the **Home** tab on the Ribbon. The Ribbon displays the Home options.

Clicking Button Icons

Each **button**, or icon, on the tabs provides one-click access to a command. Most buttons are labeled so that you can easily find the command you need. For the most part, when you click a button, something happens in your file. If you want to repeat that action, you click the button again. Buttons for related commands are organized on a tab in **groups**. For example, the Clipboard group on the Home tab includes the Cut, Copy, Paste, and Format Painter buttons—the commands for moving or copying text, objects, and formatting.

Buttons can be toggle switches: one click turns on the feature and the next click turns off the feature. While the feature is on, the button remains colored or highlighted to remind you that it is active. For example, in Word, the Show/Hide button on the Home tab in the Paragraph group displays the nonprinting screen characters when toggled on and hides them when toggled off.

Some buttons have two parts: a button that accesses a command and an arrow that opens a menu of all the commands available for that task. For example, the Paste button on the Home tab includes the default Paste command and an arrow that opens the menu of all the Paste commands—Paste, Paste Special, and Paste as Hyperlink. To select a command on the menu, you click the button arrow and then click the command on the menu.

The buttons and groups change based on your monitor size, your screen resolution, and the size of the program window. With smaller monitors, lower screen resolutions, and reduced program windows, buttons can appear as icons without labels and a group can be condensed into a button that you click to display the group options. The figures in these tutorials were created using a screen resolution of 1024 × 768 and, unless otherwise specified, the program and workspace windows are maximized. If you are using a different screen resolution or window size, the button icons on the Ribbon might show more or fewer button names, and some groups might be condensed into buttons.

You'll type text in the Word document, and then use the buttons on the Ribbon.

To use buttons on the Ribbon:

1. Type **Recycled Palette**, and then press the **Enter** key. The text appears in the first line of the document and the insertion point moves to the second line.

   Trouble? If you make a typing error, press the Backspace key to delete the incorrect letters, and then retype the text.

2. In the Paragraph group on the Home tab, click the **Show/Hide** button ¶ . The nonprinting screen characters appear in the document, and the Show/Hide button remains toggled on. See Figure 9.

   Trouble? If the nonprinting characters are removed from your screen, the Show/Hide button ¶ was already selected. Repeat Step 2 to show the nonprinting screen characters.

Button toggled on | Figure 9

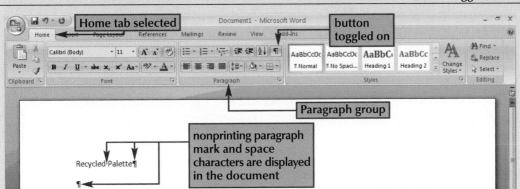

Home tab selected · button toggled on · Paragraph group · nonprinting paragraph mark and space characters are displayed in the document · Recycled·Palette¶

3. Drag to select all the text in the first line of the document (but not the paragraph mark).

4. In the Clipboard group on the Home tab, click the **Copy** button . The selected text is copied to the Clipboard.

▶ **5.** Press the ↓ key. The text is deselected and the insertion point moves to the second line in the document.

▶ **6.** In the Clipboard group on the Home tab, point to the top part of the **Paste** button. Both parts of the Paste button are highlighted, but the icon at top is darker to indicate it will be clicked if you press the mouse button.

▶ **7.** Point to the **Paste button arrow**. The button arrow is now darker.

▶ **8.** Click the **Paste button arrow**. A menu of paste commands opens. See Figure 10. To select one of the commands on the list, you click it.

| Figure 10 | Two-part Paste button |

▶ **9.** Click **Paste**. The menu closes, and the text is duplicated in the second line of the document.

As you can see, you can quickly access commands and turn features on and off with the buttons on the Ribbon.

InSight | **Using Keyboard Shortcuts and Key Tips**

Keyboard shortcuts can help you work faster and more efficiently. A **keyboard shortcut** is a key or combination of keys you press to access a tool or perform a command. To quickly access options on the Ribbon, the Quick Access Toolbar, and the Office Button without removing your hands from the keyboard:

1. Press the Alt key. Key Tips appear that list the keyboard shortcut for each Ribbon tab, each Quick Access Toolbar button, and the Office Button.
2. Press the key for the tab or button you want to use. An action is performed or Key Tips appear for the buttons on the selected tab or the commands for the selected button.
3. Continue to press the appropriate key listed in the Key Tip until the action you want is performed.

You can also use keyboard shortcuts to perform specific commands. For example, Ctrl+S is the keyboard shortcut for the Save command (you hold down the Ctrl key while you press the S key). This type of keyboard shortcut appears in ScreenTips next to the command's name. Not all commands have this type of keyboard shortcut. Identical commands in each Office program use the same keyboard shortcut.

Using Galleries and Live Preview

A button can also open a **gallery**, which is a grid or menu that shows a visual representation of the options available for that command. For example, the Bullet Library gallery in Word shows an icon of each bullet style you can select. Some galleries include a More button that you click to expand the gallery to see all the options in it. When you hover the pointer over an option in a gallery, **Live Preview** shows the results you would achieve in your file if you clicked that option. To continue the bullets example, when you hover over a bullet style in the Bullet Library gallery, the current paragraph or selected text previews that bullet style. By moving the pointer from option to option, you can quickly see the text set with different bullet styles; you can then select the style that works best for your needs.

To use a gallery and Live Preview:

▶ **1.** In the Paragraph group on the Home tab, click the **Bullets button arrow** ⊞ ▾. The Bullet Library gallery opens.

▶ **2.** Point to the **check mark bullet** style. Live Preview shows the selected bullet style in your document, so you can determine if you like that bullet style. See Figure 11.

Live Preview of bullet style ◀ **Figure 11**

▶ **3.** Place the pointer over each of the remaining bullet styles and preview them in your document.

You don't want to add bullets to your document right now, so you'll close the Bullet Library gallery and deselect the Bullets button.

▶ **4.** Press the **Esc** key on the keyboard. The Bullet Library gallery closes and the Bullets button is deselected.

▶ **5.** Press the **Backspace** key on the keyboard to delete the text "Recycled Palette" on the second line.

Galleries and Live Preview let you quickly see how your file will be affected by a selection.

Opening Dialog Boxes and Task Panes

The button to the right of the group names is the **Dialog Box Launcher**, which you click to open a task pane or dialog box that provides more advanced functionality for that group of tasks. A **task pane** is a window that helps you navigate through a complex task or feature. For example, the Clipboard task pane allows you to paste some or all of the items that have been cut or copied from any Office program during the current work session and the Research task pane allows you to search a variety of reference resources from within a file. A **dialog box** is a window from which you enter or choose settings for how you want to perform a task. For example, the Page Setup dialog box in Word contains options for how you want a document to look. Some dialog boxes organize related information into tabs, and related options and settings are organized into groups, just as they are on the Ribbon. You select settings in a dialog box using option buttons, check boxes, text boxes, lists, and other controls to collect information about how you want to perform a task.

In Excel, you'll use the Dialog Box Launcher for the Page Setup group to open the Page Setup dialog box.

To open the Page Setup dialog box using the Dialog Box Launcher:

▶ 1. Click the **Microsoft Excel – Book1** button on the taskbar to switch from Word to Excel.

▶ 2. Click the **Page Layout** tab on the Ribbon.

▶ 3. In the Page Setup group, click the **Dialog Box Launcher**, which is the small button to the right of the Page Setup group name. The Page Setup dialog box opens with the Page tab displayed. See Figure 12.

Figure 12 | **Page tab in the Page Setup dialog box**

click a tab to view a group of related controls

click the Dialog Box Launcher to open a dialog box

click an option button to select that option in the group

click the up or down spin arrow to increase or decrease the number

click the list arrow and click an option in the list

click in the text box and type an entry

click a button to open another dialog box or window

click to accept the changes and close the dialog box

click to close the dialog box without making any changes

▶ 4. Click the **Landscape** option button. The workbook's page orientation changes to a page wider than it is long.

▶ 5. Click the **Sheet** tab. The dialog box displays options related to the worksheet. You can click a check box to turn an option on (checked) or off (unchecked). You can check more than one check box in a group, whereas you can select only one option button in a group.

▶ 6. In the Print group, click the **Gridlines** check box and the **Row and column headings** check box. Check marks appear in both check boxes, indicating that these options are selected.

You don't want to change the page setup right now, so you'll close the dialog box.

▶ 7. Click the **Cancel** button. The dialog box closes without making any changes to the page setup.

Using Contextual Tools

Some tabs, toolbars, and menus come into view as you work. Because these tools become available only as you might need them, the workspace on your screen remains more open and less cluttered. However, tools that appear and disappear as you work can be distracting and take some getting used to.

Displaying Contextual Tabs

Any object that you can select in a file has a related contextual tab. An **object** is anything that appears on your screen that can be selected and manipulated as a whole, such as a table, a picture, a text box, a shape, a chart, WordArt, an equation, a diagram, a header, or a footer. A **contextual tab** is a Ribbon tab that contains commands related to the selected object so you can manipulate, edit, and format that object. Contextual tabs appear to the right of the standard Ribbon tabs just below a title label. For example, Figure 13 shows the Table Tools contextual tabs that appear when you select a table in a Word document. Although the contextual tabs appear only when you select an object, they function in the same way as standard tabs on the Ribbon. Contextual tabs disappear when you click elsewhere on the screen and deselect the object. Contextual tabs can also appear as you switch views. You'll use contextual tabs in later tutorials.

Table Tools contextual tabs ◀ **Figure 13**

Accessing the Mini Toolbar

The **Mini toolbar** is a toolbar that appears next to the pointer whenever you select text, and it contains buttons for the most commonly used formatting commands, such as font, font size, styles, color, alignment, and indents that may appear in different groups or tabs on the Ribbon. The Mini toolbar buttons differ in each program. A transparent version of the Mini toolbar appears immediately after you select text. When you move the pointer over the Mini toolbar, it comes into full view so you can click the appropriate formatting button or buttons. The Mini toolbar disappears if you move the pointer away from the toolbar, press a key, or press a mouse button. The Mini toolbar can help you format your text faster, but initially you might find that the toolbar disappears unexpectedly. All the commands on the Mini toolbar are also available on the Ribbon. Be aware that Live Preview of selected styles does not work in the Mini toolbar.

You'll use the Mini toolbar to format text you enter in the workbook.

Tip

You can turn off the Mini toolbar and Live Preview in Word, Excel, and PowerPoint. Click the Office Button, click the Options button at the bottom of the Office menu, uncheck the first two check boxes in the Popular category, and then click the OK button.

To use the Mini toolbar to format text:

▶ **1.** If necessary, click cell **A1** (the rectangle in the upper-left corner of the worksheet).

▶ **2.** Type **Budget**. The text appears in the cell.

▶ **3.** Press the **Enter** key. The text is entered in cell A1 and cell A2 is selected.

▶ **4.** Type **2008**, and then press the **Enter** key. The year is entered in cell A2 and cell A3 is selected.

You'll use the Mini toolbar to make the word in cell A1 boldface.

▶ **5.** Double-click cell **A1** to place the insertion point in the cell. Now you can select the text you typed.

▶ **6.** Double-click **Budget** in cell A1. The selected text appears white in a black background, and the transparent Mini toolbar appears directly above the selected text. See Figure 14.

Figure 14 Transparent Mini toolbar

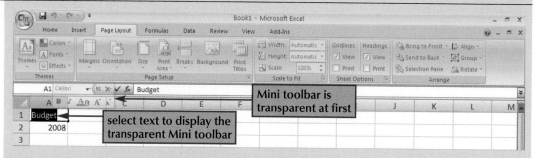

▶ **7.** Move the pointer over the Mini toolbar. The Mini toolbar is now completely visible, and you can click buttons.

Trouble? If the Mini toolbar disappears, you probably moved the pointer to another area of the worksheet. To redisplay the Mini toolbar, repeat Steps 5 through 7, being careful to move the pointer directly over the Mini toolbar in Step 7.

▶ **8.** Click the **Bold** button **B** on the Mini toolbar. The text in cell A1 is bold and the Mini toolbar remains visible so you can continue formatting the selected text. See Figure 15.

Tip

You can redisplay the Mini toolbar if it disappears by right-clicking the selected text.

Figure 15 Mini toolbar with the Bold button selected

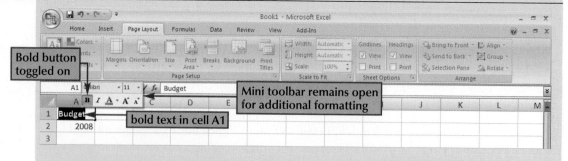

You don't want to make any other changes, so you'll close the Mini toolbar.

▶ **9.** Press the **Enter** key. The Mini toolbar disappears and cell A2 is selected.

Opening Shortcut Menus

A **shortcut menu** is a list of commands related to a selection that opens when you click the right mouse button. Each shortcut menu provides access to the commands you'll most likely want to use with the object or selection you right-click. The shortcut menu includes commands that perform actions, commands that open dialog boxes, and galleries of options that provide Live Preview. The Mini toolbar also opens when you right-click. If you click a button on the Mini toolbar, the rest of the shortcut menu closes while the Mini toolbar remains open so you can continue formatting the selection. Using a shortcut menu provides quick access to the commands you need without having to access the tabs on the Ribbon. For example, you can right-click selected text to open a shortcut menu with a Mini toolbar, text-related commands, such as Cut, Copy, and Paste, as well as other program-specific commands.

You'll use a shortcut menu in Excel to delete the content you entered in cell A1.

To use a shortcut menu to delete content:

▶ **1.** Right-click cell **A1**. A shortcut menu opens, listing commands related to common tasks you'd perform in a cell, along with a Mini toolbar. See Figure 16.

Shortcut menu with Mini toolbar ◀ **Figure 16**

- Mini toolbar appears above the shortcut menu
- click a command with ellipsis to open a dialog box
- click a command to perform an action
- point to an arrow to open a submenu of additional options
- shortcut menu

You'll use the Clear Contents command to delete the bold text from cell A1.

▶ **2.** Click **Clear Contents** on the shortcut menu. The shortcut menu closes, the Mini toolbar disappears, and the formatted text is removed from cell A1.

You'll use the Clear Contents command again to delete the year from cell A2.

▶ **3.** Right-click cell **A2**, and then click **Clear Contents** on the shortcut menu. The year is removed from cell A2.

Tip

Press the Esc key to close an open menu, shortcut menu, list, gallery, and so forth without selecting an option.

Shortcut menus enable you to quickly access commands that you're most likely to need in the context of the task you're performing.

Working with Files

The most common tasks you perform in any Office program are to create, open, save, and close files. The processes for these tasks are basically the same in all the Office programs. In addition, there are several methods for performing most tasks in Office. This flexibility enables you to use Office in a way that best fits how you like to work.

The **Office Button** provides access to document-level features, such as creating new files, opening existing files, saving files, printing files, and closing files, as well as the most common program options, called **application settings**. The **Quick Access Toolbar** is a collection of buttons that provide one-click access to commonly used commands, such as Save, Undo, and Repeat.

To begin working in a program, you need to create a new file or open an existing file. When you start Word, Excel, or PowerPoint, the program opens along with a blank file—ready for you to begin working on a new document, workbook, or presentation. When you start Access, the Getting Started with Microsoft Access window opens, displaying options for creating a new database or opening an existing one.

Ean has asked you to continue working on the agenda for the stockholder meeting. You already started typing in the document that opened when you started Word. Next, you will enter more text in the Word document.

Tip

You can add buttons you use frequently to the Quick Access Toolbar. Click the Customize Quick Access Toolbar button, and then click a button name on the menu.

To enter text in the Word document:

▶ 1. Click the **Document1 – Microsoft Word** button on the taskbar to activate the Word program window.

▶ 2. Type **Meeting Agenda** on the second line of the document, and then press the **Enter** key. The text you typed appears in the document.

   Trouble? If you make a typing error, press the Backspace key to delete the incorrect letters, and then retype the text.

Saving a File

As you create and modify Office files, your work is stored only in the computer's temporary memory, not on a hard disk. If you were to exit the programs without saving, turn off your computer, or experience a power failure, your work would be lost. To prevent losing work, save your file to a disk frequently—at least every 10 minutes. You can save files to the hard disk located inside your computer, a floppy disk, an external hard drive, a network storage drive, or a portable storage disk, such as a USB flash drive.

Reference Window | **Saving a File**

To save a file the first time or with a new name or location:
- Click the Office Button, and then click Save As (or for an unnamed file, click the Save button on the Quick Access Toolbar or click the Office Button, and then click Save).
- In the Save As dialog box, navigate to the location where you want to save the file.
- Type a descriptive title in the File name box, and then click the Save button.

To resave a named file to the same location:
- Click the Save button on the Quick Access Toolbar (or click the Office Button, and then click Save).

The first time you save a file, you need to name it. This **filename** includes a descriptive title you select and a file extension assigned by Office. You should choose a descriptive title that accurately reflects the content of the document, workbook, presentation, or database, such as "Shipping Options Letter" or "Fourth Quarter Financial Analysis." Your descriptive title can include uppercase and lowercase letters, numbers, hyphens, and spaces in any combination, but not the following special characters: ? " / \ < > * | and :. Each filename ends with a **file extension**, a period followed by several characters that Office adds to your descriptive title to identify the program in which that file was created. The default file extensions for Office 2007 are .docx for Word, .xlsx for Excel, .pptx for PowerPoint, and .accdb for Access. Filenames (the descriptive title and the file extension) can include a maximum of 255 characters. You might see file extensions depending on how Windows is set up on your computer. The figures in these tutorials do not show file extensions.

You also need to decide where to save the file—on which disk and in what folder. A **folder** is a container for your files. Just as you organize paper documents within folders stored in a filing cabinet, you can organize your files within folders stored on your computer's hard disk or a removable disk, such as a USB flash drive. Store each file in a logical location that you will remember whenever you want to use the file again. The default storage location for Office files is the Documents folder; you can create additional storage folders within that folder or navigate to a new storage location.

You can navigate the Save As dialog box by clicking a folder or location on your computer in the Navigation pane along the left side of the dialog box, and then double-clicking folders in the file list until you display the storage location you want. You can also navigate to a storage location with the Address bar, which displays the current file path. Each location in the file path has a corresponding arrow that you can click to quickly select a folder within that location. For example, you can click the Documents arrow in the Address bar to open a list of all the folders in the Documents folder, and then click the folder you want to open. If you want to return to a specific spot in the file hierarchy, you click that folder name in the Address bar. The Back and Forward buttons let you quickly move between folders.

Tip

Office adds the correct file extension when you save a file. Do not type one in the descriptive title, or you will create a duplicate (such as Meeting Agenda. docx.docx).

Windows XP Tip

The default storage location for Office files is the My Documents folder.

Saving and Using Files with Earlier Versions of Office | InSight

The default file types in Office 2007 are different from those used in earlier versions. This means that someone using Office 2003 or earlier cannot open files created in Office 2007. Files you want to share with earlier Office users must be saved in the earlier formats, which use the following extensions: .doc for Word, .xls for Excel, .mdb for Access, and .ppt for PowerPoint. To save a file in an earlier format, open the Save As dialog box, click the Save as type list arrow, and then click the appropriate 97-2003 format. A compatibility checker reports which Office 2007 features or elements are not supported by the earlier version of Office, and you can choose to remove them before saving. You can use Office 2007 to open and work with files created in earlier versions of Office. You can then save the file in its current format or update it to the Office 2007 format.

The lines of text you typed are not yet saved on disk. You'll do that now.

To save a file for the first time:

▶ **1.** Click the **Save** button 🔲 on the Quick Access Toolbar. The Save As dialog box opens because you have not yet saved the file and need to specify a storage location and filename. The default location is set to the Documents folder, and the first few words of the first line appear in the File name box as a suggested title.

▶ **2.** In the Navigation pane, click the link for the location that contains your Data Files, if necessary.

Trouble? If you don't have the starting Data Files, you need to get them before you can proceed. Your instructor will either give you the Data Files or ask you to obtain them from a specified location (such as a network drive). In either case, make a backup copy of the Data Files before you start so that you will have the original files available in case you need to start over. If you have any questions about the Data Files, see your instructor or technical support person for assistance.

▶ **3.** Double-click the **OFF** folder in the file list, and then double-click the **Tutorial** folder. This is the location where you want to save the document.

Next, you'll enter a more descriptive title for the filename.

▶ **4.** Type **Meeting Agenda** in the File name box. See Figure 17.

Figure 17 ▶ **Completed Save As dialog box**

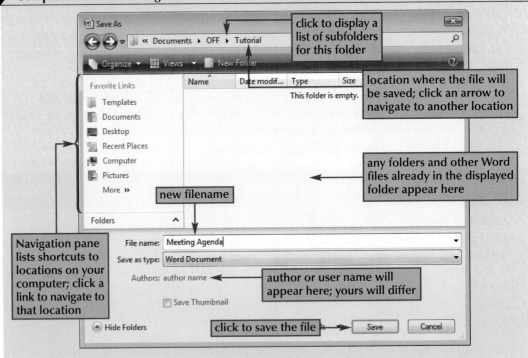

Trouble? If the .docx file extension appears after the filename, your computer is configured to show file extensions. Continue with Step 5.

▶ **5.** Click the **Save** button. The Save As dialog box closes, and the name of your file appears in the title bar.

The saved file includes everything in the document at the time you last saved it. Any new edits or additions you make to the document exist only in the computer's memory and are not saved in the file on the disk. As you work, remember to save frequently so that the file is updated to reflect the latest content of the document.

Because you already named the document and selected a storage location, the Save As dialog box doesn't open whenever you save the document again. If you want to save a copy of the file with a different filename or to a different location, you reopen the Save As dialog box by clicking the Office Button, and then clicking Save As. The previous version of the file remains on your disk as well.

You need to add your name to the agenda. Then, you'll save your changes.

To modify and save the Word document:

▶ **1.** Type your name, and then press the **Enter** key. The text you typed appears on the next line.

▶ **2.** Click the **Save** button 🖫 on the Quick Access Toolbar to save your changes.

Closing a File

Although you can keep multiple files open at one time, you should close any file you are no longer working on to conserve system resources as well as to ensure that you don't inadvertently make changes to the file. You can close a file by clicking the Office Button and then clicking the Close command. If that's the only file open for the program, the program window remains open and no file appears in the window. You can also close a file by clicking the Close button in the upper-right corner of the title bar or double-clicking the Office Button. If that's the only file open for the program, the program also closes.

As a standard practice, you should save your file before closing it. However, Office has an added safeguard: If you attempt to close a file without saving your changes, a dialog box opens, asking whether you want to save the file. Click the Yes button to save the changes to the file before closing the file and program. Click the No button to close the file and program without saving changes. Click the Cancel button to return to the program window without saving changes or closing the file and program. This feature helps to ensure that you always save the most current version of any file.

You'll add the date to the agenda. Then, you'll attempt to close it without saving.

To modify and close the Word document:

▶ **1.** Type today's date, and then press the **Enter** key. The text you typed appears below your name in the document.

▶ **2.** In the upper-left corner of the program window, click the **Office Button** 🔵. A menu opens with commands for creating new files, opening existing files, saving files, printing files, and closing files.

▶ **3.** Click **Close**. A dialog box opens, asking whether you want to save the changes you made to the document.

▶ **4.** Click the **Yes** button. The current version of the document is saved to the file, and then the document closes. Word is still running.

After you have a program open, you can create additional new files for the open program or you can open previously created and saved files.

Opening a File

When you want to open a blank document, workbook, presentation, or database, you create a new file. When you want to work on a previously created file, you must first open it. Opening a file transfers a copy of the file from the storage disk (either a hard disk or a portable disk) to the computer's memory and displays it on your screen. The file is then in your computer's memory and on the disk.

Reference Window | **Opening an Existing File or Creating a New File**

- Click the Office Button, and then click Open.
- In the Open dialog box, navigate to the storage location of the file you want to open.
- Click the filename of the file you want to open.
- Click the Open button.

or

- Click the Office Button, and then click a filename in the Recent Documents list.

or

- Click the Office Button, and then click New.
- In the New dialog box, click Blank Document, Blank Workbook, Blank Presentation, or Blank Database (depending on the program).
- Click the Create button.

Ean asks you to print the agenda. To do that, you'll reopen the file.

To open the existing Word document:

▶ **1.** Click the **Office Button** (🔵), and then click **Open**. The Open dialog box, which works similarly to the Save As dialog box, opens.

▶ **2.** Use the Navigation pane or the Address bar to navigate to the **OFF\Tutorial** folder included with your Data Files. This is the location where you saved the agenda document.

▶ **3.** Click **Meeting Agenda** in the file list. See Figure 18.

| Figure 18 | ▶ | Open dialog box |

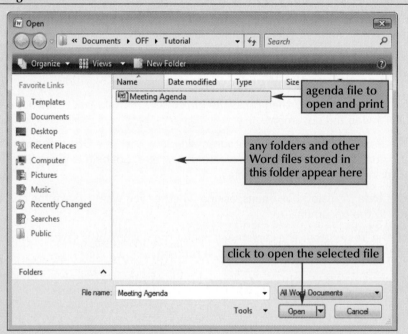

▶ **4.** Click the **Open** button. The agenda file opens in the Word program window.

Next, you'll use Help to get information about printing files in Word.

Getting Help

If you don't know how to perform a task or want more information about a feature, you can turn to Office itself for information on how to use it. This information, referred to simply as **Help**, is like a huge encyclopedia available from your desktop. You can get Help in ScreenTips, from the Help window, and in Microsoft Office Online.

Viewing ScreenTips

ScreenTips are a fast and simple method you can use to get help about objects you see on the screen. A **ScreenTip** is a box with the button's name, its keyboard shortcut if it has one, a description of the command's function, and, in some cases, a link to more information. Just position the mouse pointer over a button or object to view its ScreenTip. If a link to more information appears in the ScreenTip, press the F1 key while the Screen-Tip is displayed to open the Help window with the appropriate topic displayed.

To view ScreenTips:

▶ 1. Point to the **Microsoft Office Word Help** button 🔘. The ScreenTip shows the button's name, its keyboard shortcut, and a brief explanation of the button. See Figure 19.

ScreenTip for the Help button ◀ **Figure 19**

▶ 2. Point to other buttons on the Ribbon to display their ScreenTips.

Using the Help Window

For more detailed information, you can use the **Help window** to access all the Help topics, templates, and training installed on your computer with Office and available on Microsoft Office Online. **Microsoft Office Online** is a Web site maintained by Microsoft that provides access to the latest information and additional Help resources. For example, you can access current Help topics, templates of predesigned files, and training for Office. To connect to Microsoft Office Online, you need Internet access on your computer. Otherwise, you see only those topics stored locally.

Reference Window | Getting Help

- Click the Microsoft Office Help button (the button name depends on the Office program).
- Type a keyword or phrase in the "Type words to search for" box, and then click the Search button.
- Click a Help topic in the search results list.
- Read the information in the Help window. For more information, click other topics or links.
- Click the Close button on the Help window title bar.

You open the Help window by clicking the Microsoft Office Help button 🔘 located below the sizing buttons in every Office program. Each program has its own Help window from which you can find information about all the Office commands and features as well as step-by-step instructions for using them. You can search for information in the Help window using the "Type words to search for" box and the Table of Contents pane.

The "Type words to search for" box enables you to search the Help system using keywords or phrases. You type a specific word or phrase about a task you want to perform or a topic you need help with, and then click the Search button to search the Help system. A list of Help topics related to the keyword or phrase you entered appears in the Help window. If your computer is connected to the Internet, your search results come from Microsoft Office Online rather than only the Help topics stored locally on your computer. You can click a link to open a Help topic with step-by-step instructions that will guide you through a specific procedure and/or provide explanations of difficult concepts in clear, easy-to-understand language. For example, if you type "format cell" in the Excel Help window, a list of Help topics related to the words you typed appears in the Help window. You can navigate through the topics you've viewed using the buttons on the Help window toolbar. These buttons—including Back, Forward, Stop, Refresh, Home, and Print—are the same as those in the Microsoft Internet Explorer Web browser.

You'll use the "Type words to search for" box in the Help window to obtain more information about printing a document in Word.

To use the "Type words to search for" box:

▶ 1. Click the **Microsoft Office Word Help** button 🔘 . The Word Help window opens.

▶ 2. Click the **Type words to search for** box, if necessary, and then type **print document**. You can set where you want to search.

▶ 3. Click the **Search button arrow**. The Search menu shows the online and local content available.

▶ **4.** If your computer is connected to the Internet, click **All Word** in the Content from Office Online list. If your computer is not connected to the Internet, click **Word Help** in the Content from this computer list.

▶ **5.** Click the **Search** button. The Help window displays a list of topics related to your keywords. See Figure 20.

Search results displaying Help topics ◀ **Figure 20**

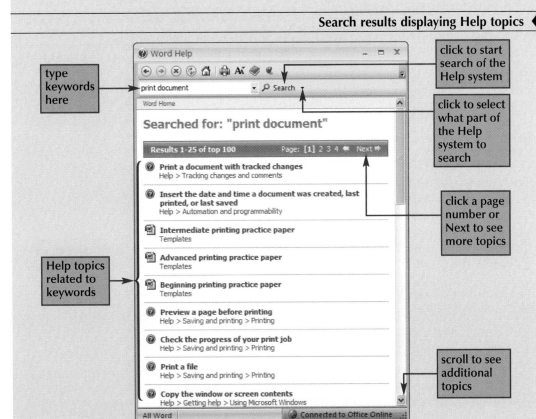

type keywords here

click to start search of the Help system

click to select what part of the Help system to search

click a page number or Next to see more topics

Help topics related to keywords

scroll to see additional topics

Trouble? If your search results list differs from the one shown in Figure 20, your computer is not connected to the Internet or Microsoft has updated the list of available Help topics since this book was published. Continue with Step 6.

▶ **6.** Scroll through the list to review the Help topics.

▶ **7.** Click **Print a file**. The Help topic is displayed in the Help window so you can learn more about how to print a document. See Figure 21.

Figure 21	Print a file Help topic

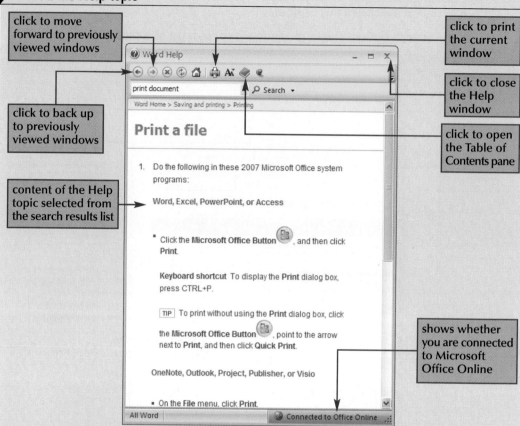

click to move forward to previously viewed windows

click to back up to previously viewed windows

content of the Help topic selected from the search results list

click to print the current window

click to close the Help window

click to open the Table of Contents pane

shows whether you are connected to Microsoft Office Online

Word Help

print document   🔎 Search ▾

Word Home > Saving and printing > Printing

Print a file

1. Do the following in these 2007 Microsoft Office system programs:

   Word, Excel, PowerPoint, or Access

   ▪ Click the **Microsoft Office Button**, and then click **Print**.

   Keyboard shortcut To display the **Print** dialog box, press CTRL+P.

   TIP To print without using the **Print** dialog box, click the **Microsoft Office Button**, point to the arrow next to **Print**, and then click **Quick Print**.

   OneNote, Outlook, Project, Publisher, or Visio

   ▪ On the **File** menu, click **Print**.

All Word   🌐 Connected to Office Online

Trouble? If you don't see the Print a file Help topic on page 1, its current location might be on another page. Click the Next link to move to the next page, and then scroll down to find the Print a file topic, repeating to search additional pages until you locate the topic.

▶ **8.** Read the information.

Another way to find information in the Help system is to use the Table of Contents pane. The Show Table of Contents button on the Help window toolbar opens a pane that displays a list of the Help system content organized by subjects and topics, similar to a book's table of contents. You click main subject links to display related topic links. You click a topic link to display that Help topic in the Help window. You'll use the Table of Contents to find information about getting help in Office.

To use the Help window table of contents:

▶ **1.** Click the **Show Table of Contents** button 🔘 on the Help window toolbar. The Table of Contents pane opens on the left side of the Help window.

▶ **2.** Click **Getting help** in the Table of Contents pane, scrolling up if necessary. The Getting help "book" opens, listing the topics related to that subject.

▶ **3.** Click the **Work with the Help window** topic, and then click the **Maximize** button 🔲 on the title bar. The Help topic is displayed in the maximized Help window, and you can read the text to learn more about the various ways to obtain help in Word. See Figure 22.

Table of Contents pane in the Help window | **Figure 22**

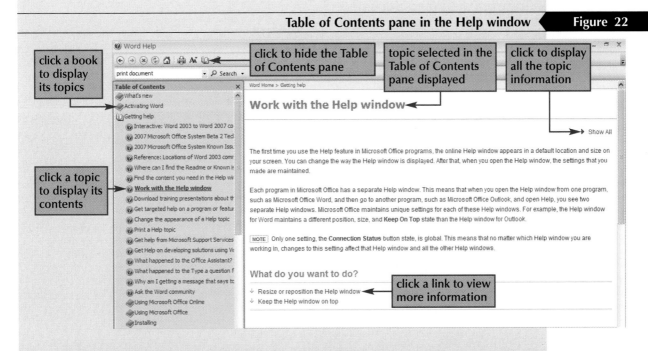

Trouble? If your search results list differs from the one shown in Figure 22, your computer is not connected to the Internet or Microsoft has updated the list of available Help topics since this book was published. Continue with Step 4.

4. Click **Using Microsoft Office Online** in the Table of Contents pane, click the **Get online Help, templates, training, and additional content** topic to display information about that topic, and then read the information.

5. Click the links within this topic and read the information.

6. Click the **Close** button ☒ on the Help window title bar to close the window.

Printing a File

At times, you'll want a paper copy of your Office file. The first time you print during each session at the computer, you should use the Print command to open the Print dialog box so you can verify or adjust the printing settings. You can select a printer, the number of copies to print, the portion of the file to print, and so forth; the printing settings vary slightly from program to program. If you want to use the same default settings for subsequent print jobs, you can use the Quick Print button to print without opening the dialog box.

Printing a File		Reference Window

- Click the Office Button, and then click Print.
- Verify the print settings in the Print dialog box.
- Click the OK button.

or

- Click the Office Button, point to Print, and then click Quick Print.

Now that you know how to print, you'll print the agenda for Ean.

To print the Word document:

▶ **1.** Make sure your printer is turned on and contains paper.

▶ **2.** Click the **Office Button** 🔵, and then click **Print**. The Print dialog box opens. See Figure 23.

Figure 23 ▶ Print dialog box

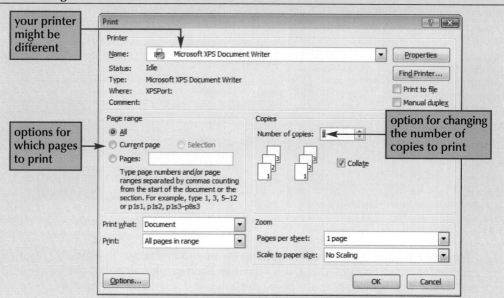

your printer might be different

options for which pages to print

option for changing the number of copies to print

Trouble? If a menu of Print commands opens, you clicked the Print button arrow on the two-part Print button. Click Print on the menu to open the Print dialog box.

▶ **3.** Verify that the correct printer appears in the Name box in the Printer group. If necessary, click the **Name** arrow, and then click the correct printer from the list of available printers.

▶ **4.** Verify that **1** appears in the Number of copies box.

▶ **5.** Click the **OK** button to print the document.

Trouble? If the document does not print, see your instructor or technical support person for help.

Exiting Programs

When you finish working with a program, you should exit it. As with many other aspects of Office, you can exit programs with a button or a command. You'll use both methods to exit Word and Excel. You can use the Exit command to exit a program and close an open file in one step. If you haven't saved the final version of the open file, a dialog box opens, asking whether you want to save your changes. Clicking the Yes button saves the open file, closes the file, and then exits the program.

To exit the Word and Excel programs:

▶ **1.** Click the **Close** button ☒ on the Word title bar to exit Word. The Word document closes and the Word program exits. The Excel window is visible again.

> **Trouble?** If a dialog box opens, asking if you want to save the document, you might have inadvertently made a change to the document. Click the No button.
>
> **2.** Click the **Office Button** 🔘, and then click **Exit Excel**. A dialog box opens, asking whether you want to save the changes you made to the workbook. If you click the Yes button, the Save As dialog box opens and Excel exits after you finish saving the workbook. This time, you don't want to save the workbook.
>
> **3.** Click the **No** button. The workbook closes without saving a copy, and the Excel program exits.

Exiting programs after you are done using them keeps your Windows desktop uncluttered for the next person using the computer, frees up your system's resources, and prevents data from being lost accidentally.

Quick Check | Review

1. What Office program would be best to use to create a budget?
2. How do you start an Office program?
3. Explain the difference between Save and Save As.
4. How do you open an existing Office file?
5. What happens if you open a file, make edits, and then attempt to close the file or exit the program without saving the current version of the file?
6. What are two ways to get Help in Office?

Tutorial Summary | Review

You have learned how to use features common to all the programs included in Microsoft Office 2007, including starting and exiting programs; resizing windows; using the Ribbon, dialog boxes, shortcut menus, and the Mini toolbar; opening, closing, and printing files; and getting Help.

Key Terms

Access	Help window	Office Button
application settings	integration	Outlook
button	keyboard shortcut	PowerPoint
contextual tab	Live Preview	presentation
database	Microsoft Office 2007	Quick Access Toolbar
default	Microsoft Office Access 2007	Ribbon
dialog box	Microsoft Office Excel 2007	ScreenTip
Dialog Box Launcher	Microsoft Office Online	shortcut menu
document	Microsoft Office	status bar
Excel	Outlook 2007	tab
file extension	Microsoft Office	task pane
filename	PowerPoint 2007	Word
folder	Microsoft Office Word 2007	workbook
gallery	Mini toolbar	zoom
group	object	
Help	Office	

| Practice | **Review Assignments** |

Practice the skills you learned in the tutorial.

Data Files needed for the Review Assignments: Finances.xlsx, Letter.docx

You need to prepare for an upcoming meeting at Recycled Palette. You'll open and print documents for the presentation. Complete the following:

1. Start PowerPoint.
2. Use the Help window to search Office Online for the PowerPoint demo "Demo: Up to Speed with PowerPoint 2007." (*Hint*: Use "demo" as the keyword to search for, and make sure you search All PowerPoint in the Content from Office Online list. If you are not connected to the Internet, continue with Step 3.) Open the Demo topic, and then click the Play Demo link to view it. Close Internet Explorer and the Help window when you're done.
3. Start Excel.
4. Switch to the PowerPoint window using the taskbar, and then close the presentation but leave open the PowerPoint program. (*Hint:* Click the Office Button and then click Close.)
5. Open a new, blank PowerPoint presentation from the New Presentation dialog box.
6. Close the PowerPoint presentation and program using the Close button on the PowerPoint title bar; do not save changes if asked.
7. Open the **Finances** workbook located in the OFF\Review folder included with your Data Files.
8. Use the Save As command to save the workbook as **Recycled Palette Finances** in the OFF\Review folder.
9. Type your name, press the Enter key to insert your name at the top of the worksheet, and then save the workbook.
10. Print one copy of the worksheet using the Print button on the Office Button menu.
11. Exit Excel using the Office Button.
12. Start Word, and then open the **Letter** document located in the OFF\Review folder included with your Data Files.
13. Use the Save As command to save the document with the filename **Recycled Palette Letter** in the OFF\Review folder.
14. Press and hold the Ctrl key, press the End key, and then release both keys to move the insertion point to the end of the letter, and then type your name.
15. Use the Save button on the Quick Access Toolbar to save the change to the Recycled Palette Letter document.
16. Print one copy of the document, and then close the document.
17. Exit the Word program using the Close button on the title bar.

Assess | SAM Assessment and Training

If you have a SAM user profile, you may have access to hands-on instruction, practice, and assessment of the skills covered in this tutorial. Log in to your SAM account (**http://sam2007.course.com**) to launch any assigned training activities or exams that relate to the skills covered in this tutorial.

Review | Quick Check Answers

1. Excel
2. Click the Start button on the taskbar, click All Programs, click Microsoft Office, and then click the name of the program you want to open.
3. Save updates a file to reflect its latest contents using its current filename and location. Save As enables you to change the filename and storage location of a file.
4. Click the Office Button, and then click Open.
5. A dialog box opens asking whether you want to save the changes to the file.
6. Two of the following: ScreenTips, Help window, Microsoft Office Online

Ending Data Files

Meeting Agenda.docx

Recycled Palette Finances.xlsx
Recycled Palette Letter.docx

Reality Check

At home, school, or work, you probably complete many types of tasks, such as writing letters and balancing a checkbook, on a regular basis. You can use Microsoft Office to streamline many of these tasks.

Note: Please be sure *not* to include any personal information of a sensitive nature in the documents you create to be submitted to your instructor for this exercise. Later on, you can update the documents with such information for your own personal use.

1. Start Word, and open a new document, if necessary.
2. In the document, type a list of all the personal, work, and/or school tasks you do on a regular basis.
3. For each task, identify the type of Office file (document, workbook, presentation, or database) you would create to complete that task. For example, you would create a Word document to write a letter.
4. For each file, identify the Office program you would use to create that file, and explain why you would use that program. For example, Word is the best program to use to create a document for a letter.
5. Save the document with an appropriate filename in an appropriate folder location.
6. Use a Web browser to visit the Microsoft Web site at *www.microsoft.com* and research the different Office 2007 suites available. Determine which suite includes all the programs you need to complete the tasks on your list.
7. At the end of the task list you created in your Word document, type which Office suite you decided on and a brief explanation of why you chose that suite. Then save the document.
8. Double-click the Home tab on the Ribbon to minimize the Ribbon to show only the tab names and extend the workspace area. At the end of the Word document, type your opinion of whether minimizing the Ribbon is a helpful feature. When you're done, double-click the Home tab to display the full Ribbon.
9. Print the finished document, and then submit it to your instructor.

Objectives

Session 1.1
- Plan a document
- Identify the components of the Word window
- Set up the Word window
- Create a new document

Session 1.2
- Scroll a document and move the insertion point
- Correct errors and undo and redo changes
- Enter the date with AutoComplete
- Change a document's line and paragraph spacing
- Save, preview, and print a document
- Create an envelope

Creating a Document

Writing a Business Letter

Case | Carlyle University Press

Carlyle University Press is a nonprofit book publisher associated with Carlyle State University in Albany, New York. The Press, as it is referred to by both editors and authors, publishes scholarly books, with an emphasis on history and literature. When a new author signs a contract for a book, he or she receives the *Author's Guide*, a handbook describing the process of creating a manuscript. In this tutorial, you will help one of the editors, Andrew Suri, create a cover letter to accompany a copy of the *Author's Guide*.

You will create the letter using **Microsoft Office Word 2007** (or simply **Word**), a popular word-processing program. Before you begin typing the letter, you will learn how to start the Word program, identify and use the elements of the Word window, and adjust some Word settings. Next, you will create a new Word document, type the text of the cover letter, save the letter, and then print the letter. In the process of entering the text, you'll learn several ways to correct typing errors. Finally, you will create an envelope for the letter.

Starting Data Files

There are no starting Data Files needed for this tutorial.

Session 1.1

Four Steps to a Professional Document

With Word, you can create polished, professional documents in a minimal amount of time. You can type a document in Word, adjust margins and spacing, create columns and tables, add graphics, and then quickly make revisions and corrections. The most efficient way to produce a document is to follow these four steps: (1) planning, (2) creating and editing, (3) formatting, and (4) printing or distributing online.

In the long run, planning saves time and effort. First, you should determine what you want to say. State your purpose clearly and include enough information to achieve that purpose without overwhelming or boring your reader. Be sure to organize your ideas logically. Decide how you want your document to look as well. In this case, your letter will take the form of a standard business letter, in the block style.

Figure 1-1 shows what the completed, block style letter will look like when it is printed on Carlyle University Press letterhead. You will create the letter in this tutorial by following detailed steps. Throughout the tutorial, you might want to refer back to Figure 1-1 for help locating the various parts of a block style letter.

| Figure 1-1 | Completed block style letter |

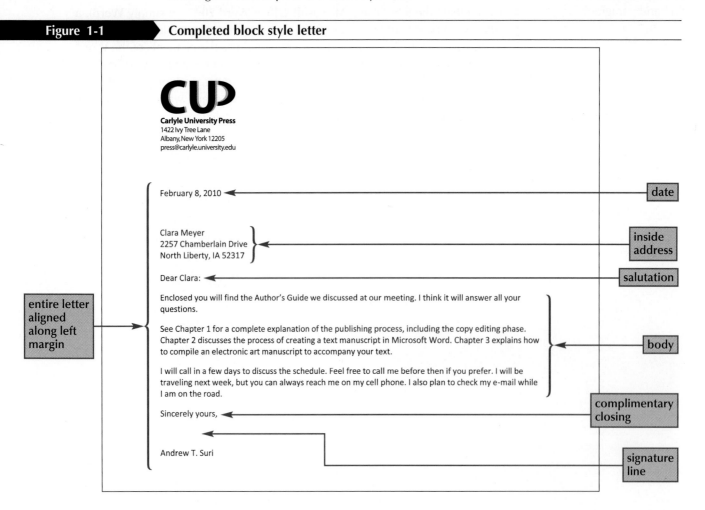

Writing a Business Letter | InSight

There are several accepted styles for business letters. The main differences among them have to do with how parts of the letter are indented from the left margin. In the block style, which you will use to create the letter in this tutorial, each line of text starts at the left margin. In other words, nothing is indented. Another style is to indent the first line of each paragraph. The choice of style is largely a matter of personal preference, or it can be determined by the standards used in a particular business or organization.

After you plan your document, you can create and edit it using Word. Creating the document generally means typing the text of your document. Editing consists of reading the document you've created; correcting, adding, deleting, or moving text to make the document easy to read; and finally, correcting your errors.

To make your document visually appealing, you need to format it. Formatting—for example, adjusting margins, setting line spacing, and using bold and italic—can help make your document easier to read.

Finally, you will usually want to print your document so that you can give it to other people, or you might want to distribute it via e-mail. Whether you print the document yourself or e-mail it to others, it is important to preview it first to make sure it is suitable for printing.

Exploring the Word Window

Before you can apply these four steps to produce a letter in Word, you need to start Word and learn about the general organization of the Word window. You'll do that now.

To start Microsoft Word:

▶ **1.** Click the **Start** button 🔵 on the taskbar, click **All Programs**, click **Microsoft Office**, and then click **Microsoft Office Word 2007**. The Word window opens. See Figure 1-2.

Figure 1-2   Maximized Word window

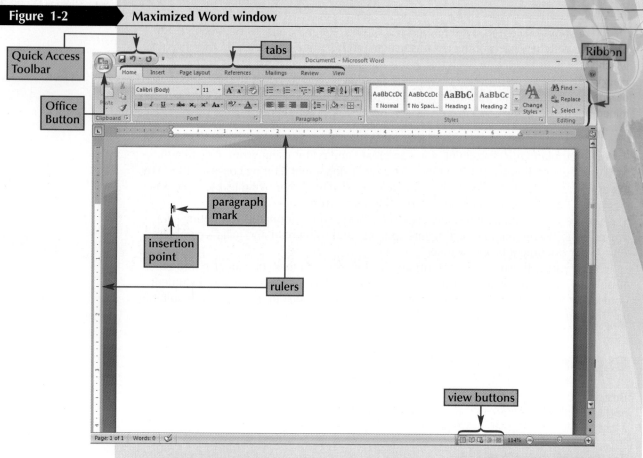

> **Trouble?** If you don't see the Microsoft Office Word 2007 option on the Microsoft Office submenu, look for it in a different submenu or as an option on the All Programs menu. If you still can't find the Microsoft Office Word 2007 option, ask your instructor or technical support person for help.

▶ **2.** If the Word window does not fill the entire screen, click the **Maximize** button ☐ in the upper-right corner of the Word window. Your screen should now resemble Figure 1-2.

> **Trouble?** If your screen looks slightly different from Figure 1-2, just continue with the steps. You will learn how to change the appearance of the Word window shortly.

> Word is now running and ready to use. Don't be concerned if you don't see everything shown in Figure 1-2. You'll learn how to adjust the appearance of the Word window soon.

The Word window is made up of a number of elements, which are described in Figure 1-3. You might be familiar with some of these elements, such as the Office Button and the Ribbon, because they are common to all Microsoft Office 2007 programs.

Parts of the Word window | Figure 1-3

Window Element	Description
Office Button	Provides access to the Word Options dialog box and to commands that control what you can do with a document that you have created, such as saving, printing, and so on
Ribbon	Provides access to commands that are grouped according to the tasks you perform in Word
Tabs	Provide one-click access to the groups of commands on the Ribbon; the tabs you see change depending on the task you are currently performing
Quick Access Toolbar	Provides access to common commands you use frequently, such as Save
Rulers	Show page margins, tab stops, row heights, and column widths
Insertion point	Shows where characters will appear when you start typing
Paragraph mark	Marks the end of a paragraph
View buttons	Allow you to change the way the document is displayed

If at any time you would like to learn more about an item on the Ribbon, position your mouse pointer over the item without clicking anything. A **ScreenTip**, a small box with information about the item, will appear.

Opening a New Document

You'll begin by opening a new blank document (in case you accidentally typed something in the current page while you were examining the Word window).

To open a new document:

▶ **1.** Click the **Office Button** in the upper-left corner of the Word window and view the menu of commands that opens. These commands are all related to working with Word documents. See Figure 1-4.

Microsoft Office menu | Figure 1-4

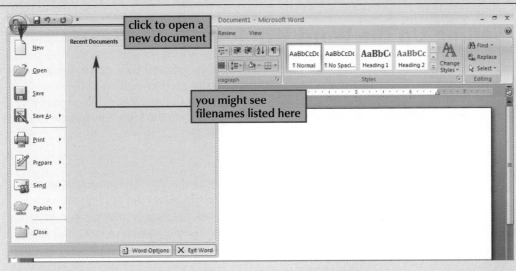

> **2.** Click **New**. The New Document dialog box opens. See Figure 1-5. In this dialog box, you can choose from several different types of documents. In this case, you simply want a new, blank document, which is already selected for you, as in Figure 1-5.

Figure 1-5   **New Document dialog box**

> **3.** Verify that the **Blank document** option is selected (that is, highlighted in orange), and then click the **Create** button at the bottom of the dialog box. The New Document dialog box closes and a new document (named Document2) opens. Later in this tutorial, you'll choose a more descriptive name for this document.

Setting Up the Word Window

To make it easier to follow the steps in these tutorials, you should take care to arrange your window to match the tutorial figures. The rest of this section explains what your window should look like and how to make it match those in the tutorials. After you've set up your window to match the figures, you'll begin writing the letter for Andrew.

Selecting Print Layout View

You can use the View buttons in the lower-right corner of the Word window to change the way your document is displayed. You will learn how to select the appropriate view for a document as you gain more experience with Word. For now, you want your letter displayed in Print Layout view because this view most closely resembles how your letter will look when you print it.

To make sure Print Layout view is selected:

▶ **1.** Click the **Print Layout** button 🗏 , as shown in Figure 1-6. If your window was not in Print Layout view, it changes to Print Layout view now. The Print Layout button is now highlighted in orange, indicating that it is selected. See Figure 1-6.

Selecting Print Layout view | **Figure 1-6**

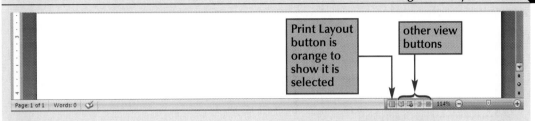

Displaying the Rulers and Selecting the Home Tab

Depending on the choices made by the last person to use your computer, you might not see the rulers. The options controlling the rulers are located on the Ribbon's View tab. When Word opens, the Home tab is typically displayed, so to display the rulers, you need to switch to the View tab. Even if the rulers are currently displayed on your computer, perform the following steps to get some practice moving among the tabs on the Ribbon.

Displaying the Rulers | Reference Window

- Click the View tab.
- In the Show/Hide group, click the Ruler check box to display a check mark.

To display the rulers:

▶ **1.** At the top of the Word window, click the **View** tab. This tab contains buttons and commands related to displaying the document.

▶ **2.** In the Show/Hide group on the View tab, locate the Ruler check box. If it already contains a check mark, the rulers are already displayed on your screen. If the Ruler check box is empty, click it to insert a check mark. You should now see a vertical ruler on the left side of the document and a horizontal ruler below the Ribbon. See Figure 1-7.

Figure 1-7 ▶ **Displaying the rulers**

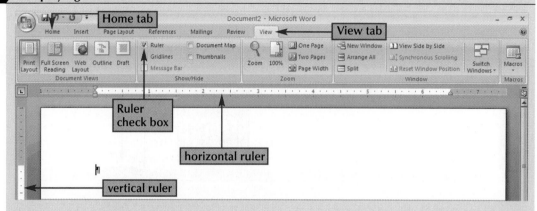

> **3.** Click the **Home** tab. The Ribbon changes to show Word's basic text-editing options, as shown earlier in Figure 1-2.

Displaying Nonprinting Characters

Nonprinting characters are symbols that appear on the screen but are not visible on the printed page; they help you see details that you might otherwise miss. For example, one nonprinting character (¶) marks the end of a paragraph, and another (•) marks the space between words. It is helpful to display nonprinting characters so you can see whether you've typed an extra space, ended a paragraph, and so on.

Depending on how your computer is set up, nonprinting characters might be displayed automatically when you start Word. In Figure 1-8, you can see the paragraph symbol (¶) in the blank document window. Also, the Show/Hide ¶ button is highlighted on the Ribbon. Both of these indicate that nonprinting characters are displayed. If they are not displayed on your screen, you need to perform the following step.

To display nonprinting characters:

> **1.** In the Paragraph group on the Home tab, click the **Show/Hide ¶** button ¶ if it is not already selected. A paragraph mark (¶) appears at the top of the document window. Your screen should match Figure 1-8.

Figure 1-8 ▶ **Nonprinting characters displayed**

Trouble? If the Show/Hide ¶ button was already highlighted before you clicked it, you turned off nonprinting characters instead of turning them on. Click the Show/Hide ¶ button a second time to select it.

Checking the Font and Font Size

Next, you need to make sure the correct font and font size are selected. The term **font** refers to the shape of the characters in a document. **Font size** refers to the size of the characters. You'll learn more about fonts in Tutorial 2. For now, you just need to make sure that the font and font size selected on your computer match those selected in the figures in this book. The figures in this book were created using the default font and font size. (The term **default** refers to settings that are automatically selected.)

To verify that the correct font is selected:

▶ **1.** In the Font group on the Home tab, locate the **Font** and **Font Size** boxes. See Figure 1-9.

Font settings | Figure 1-9

The setting in the Font box should read "Calibri (Body)" as in Figure 1-9. If you see something else in your Font box, click the **Font** list arrow, and then click **Calibri (Body)**.

Trouble ? If you see just "Calibri" in your font box instead of "Calibri (Body)" you should still perform Step 1.

▶ **2.** The setting in your Font Size box should read "11." If you see something else in your Font size box, click the **Font Size** list arrow, and then click **11**.

Checking the Zoom Setting

Next, you'll take care of the document **Zoom level**, which controls the document's on-screen magnification. A Zoom level of 100% shows the document as if it were printed on paper. It is often helpful to increase the Zoom level to more than 100% (zoom in) to make the text easier to read. Other times, you may want to decrease the Zoom level to less than 100% (zoom out) so that you can see more of the document at a glance. To make your screen match the figures in this tutorial, you need to set the Zoom level to **Page width**, a setting that shows the entire width of the document on your screen. You can change the Zoom level by using the Zoom buttons in the lower-right corner of the Word window.

Tip

Changing the zoom affects only the way the document is displayed on the screen; it does not affect the document itself.

To check your Zoom setting:

▶ **1.** In the lower-right corner of the Word window, locate the current Zoom level, the Zoom Out button, the Zoom In button, and the Zoom slider. In Figure 1-10, the current Zoom setting is 114%, but yours might be higher or lower. In the next two steps you'll practice zooming in and zooming out. Then you will select the Page width setting.

| Figure 1-10 | Options for changing the Zoom setting |

Zoom Out button
Zoom slider
Zoom level; yours might differ
Zoom In button

Page: 1 of 1   Words: 0   114%

Tip

You can also drag the Zoom slider button left or right to change the Zoom level.

▶ **2.** Click the **Zoom In** button ⊕ several times to increase the document magnification. The Zoom level increases and the Zoom slider moves to the right.

▶ **3.** Click the **Zoom Out** button ⊖ several times to decrease the document magnification. The Zoom level decreases and the Zoom slider button moves to the left.

▶ **4.** Click the **Zoom level**. The Zoom dialog box opens. The Zoom level in the Zoom dialog box matches the Zoom level shown in the lower-right corner of the Word window. In Figure 1-11, the current Zoom setting is 110%, but yours might be different.

| Figure 1-11 | Zoom dialog box |

current Zoom level; yours might differ

▶ **5.** Click the **Page width** option button to select it, and then click the **OK** button. The Zoom dialog box closes and the Zoom level adjusts to display the full width of the document page. The exact Zoom level on your computer will depend on the size of your monitor. On a 15-inch monitor, the Zoom level is probably 114%.

To make sure your window always matches the figures in these tutorials, remember to complete the checklist in Figure 1-12 each time you are working in this book.

Word window checklist ◄ **Figure 1-12**

Window Element	Setting
Document view	Print Layout
Nonprinting characters	Displayed
Rulers	Displayed
Word window	Maximized
Zoom	Page width
Font	Identical to setting shown in figures
Font size	Identical to setting shown in figures

Now that you have planned your letter, opened Word, identified screen elements, and adjusted settings, you are ready to begin your letter to Clara Meyer, Carlyle Press's new author.

Beginning a Letter

Before you begin writing, you should insert some blank lines to ensure that you leave enough room for the Carlyle University Press letterhead. The amount of space you leave at the top of a letter depends on the size of the letterhead. In this case, pressing Enter four times should add enough space.

Adjusting Margins vs. Inserting Blank Lines | InSight

As you gain experience with Word, you'll learn how to adjust a document's margin to add blank space at the beginning of a document. (The term **margin** refers to the blank space around the top, bottom, and sides of document.) Adjusting margins is a better method than inserting blank lines, because it ensures that you won't accidentally delete a blank line as you edit the document. However, until you learn more about margins, inserting blank lines is a useful shortcut that enables you to jump right into the task of typing your letter.

To insert blank lines in the document:

► 1. Press the **Enter** key four times. Each time you press the Enter key, a nonprinting paragraph mark appears, and the insertion point moves down to the next line. By default, Word inserts some space between each paragraph mark. You'll learn how to change this setting later in this tutorial. For now, you can ignore this space. On the vertical ruler, you can see that the insertion point is about 1.5 inches from the top margin. Although you might find it hard to see on the ruler, the top margin itself is 1 inch. This means the insertion point is now located a total of 2.5 inches from the top of the page. See Figure 1-13.

Figure 1-13 | **Document window after inserting blank lines**

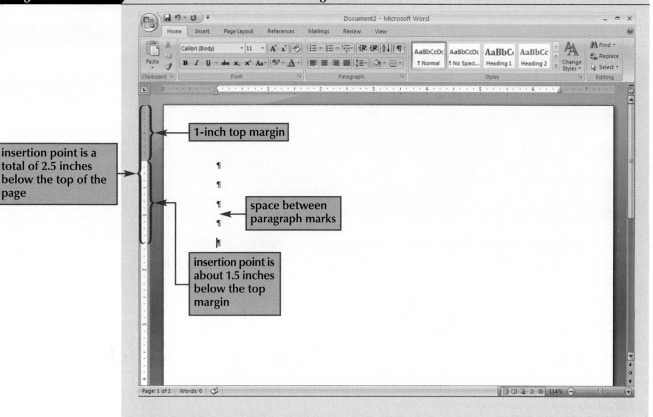

Trouble? If your insertion point is higher or lower on the vertical ruler than in Figure 1-13, don't worry. Different monitors produce slightly different measurements when you press the Enter key.

The insertion point is now low enough in your document to allow room for the letterhead when you print the document. You are ready to start typing.

Entering Text

Normally, you begin a letter by typing the date followed by the inside address. However, typing these two items involves using some specialized Word features. To give you some experience with simply typing text, you'll start with the salutation and the body of the letter. Then you'll go back later to add the date and the inside address.

You'll start by typing the salutation (the "Dear Clara:" text, shown earlier in Figure 1-1). If you make a mistake while typing, press the Backspace key to delete the incorrect character and then type the correct character.

To type the salutation:

▶ 1. Type **Dear Clara:** and then pause to notice the nonprinting character (•) that appears to indicate a space between the two words.

2. Press the **Enter** key to start a new paragraph for the body of the letter. If you have typed a block style business letter before, you might be accustomed to pressing Enter twice between paragraphs. However, because Word is set up to insert extra space between paragraphs by default, you need to press the Enter key only once to start a new paragraph. See Figure 1-14.

Letter with salutation | **Figure 1-14**

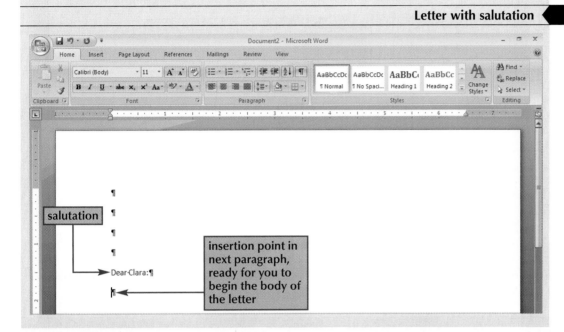

Now you are ready to begin typing the body of the letter (shown earlier in Figure 1-1). As you do, notice that when you reach the end of a line, you can keep typing; the insertion point just moves down to the next line. Depending on the length of the word you are typing when you reach the end of the line, the word will either stay on that line, or if it is long, it will move to the next line. This automatic line breaking is called **word wrap**. You'll see how word wrap works as you begin typing the body of the letter.

To begin typing the body of the letter:

1. Type the following sentence, including the period: **Enclosed you will find the Author's Guide we discussed at our meeting.**

2. Press the **spacebar**.

3. Type the following sentence: **I think it will answer all your questions.**

   Notice how Word moves the insertion point to a new line when the preceding line is full.

4. Press the **Enter** key to end the first paragraph. When you are finished, your screen should look similar to Figure 1-15. Notice that, in addition to inserting space between paragraphs, Word also inserts a smaller amount of space between lines within a paragraph.

Figure 1-15	Completed first main paragraph

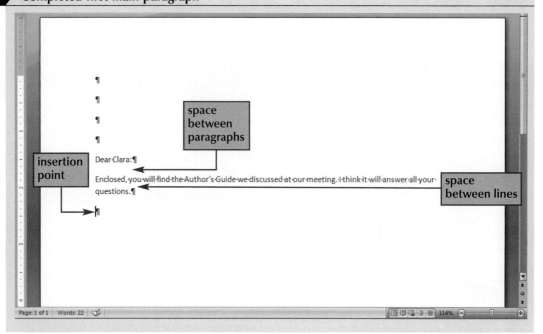

Before you continue with the rest of the letter, you should save what you have typed so far.

Reference Window | **Saving a Document for the First Time**

- Click the Save button on the Quick Access Toolbar.
- Type a name in the File name text box.
- Select the location where you want to save the file.
- Click the Save button at the bottom of the Save As dialog box.

To save the document:

1. On the Quick Access Toolbar, click the **Save** button. The Save As dialog box opens. Note that Word suggests using the first line you typed ("Dear Clara") as the filename. You will replace the suggested filename with something more descriptive.

2. Type **Meyer Letter** in the File name text box, replacing the suggested filename.

   Next, you need to tell Word where you want to save the document. In this case, you want to use the Tutorial subfolder in the Tutorial.01 folder provided with your Data Files.

   Trouble? The Tutorial.01 folder is included with the Data Files for this text. If you don't have the Word Data Files, you need to get them before you can proceed. Your instructor will either give you the Data Files or ask you to obtain them from a specified location (such as a network drive). In either case, be sure that you make a backup copy of your Data Files before you start using them, so that the original files will be available on your copied disk in case you need to start over because of an error or problem. If you have any questions about the Data Files, see your instructor or technical support person for assistance.

▶ **3.** Use the options in the Save As dialog box to select the Tutorial subfolder within the Tutorial.01 folder. See Figure 1-16.

Save As dialog box ◀ **Figure 1-16**

Trouble? If Word adds the .docx extension to your filename, your computer is configured to show file extensions. Just continue with the tutorial.

▶ **4.** Click the **Save** button in the Save As dialog box. The dialog box closes, and you return to the document window. The new document name (Meyer Letter) appears in the title bar.

Note that Word adds the .docx extension to document filenames to identify them as Microsoft Word 2007 documents, whether your computer is set up to display them or not. These tutorials assume that file extensions are hidden, but it is okay if they are displayed.

You've made a good start on the letter, and you've saved your work so far. In the next session, you'll finish typing the letter, and then you'll print it.

Session 1.1 Quick Check | Review

1. In your own words, explain the importance of planning a document.
2. On what tab is the Ruler check box located?
3. Explain how to change the document view to Print Layout.
4. True or False: Nonprinting characters are symbols that can appear on the screen but are not visible on the printed page.
5. True or False: Pressing the Enter key is the only way to insert blank space at the top of a document.
6. What is the file extension for Microsoft Word 2007 documents?

Session 1.2

Scrolling a Document

At this point, unless you are working on a large monitor, your screen probably looks as if it doesn't have enough room to type the rest of Andrew's letter—but of course there is room. As you continue to add text to your document, the text at the top will **scroll** (or shift up) and disappear from the top of the document window. You'll see how scrolling works as you type the second paragraph in the body of the letter.

To observe scrolling while you're typing text:

▶ **1.** If you took a break after the previous session, make sure that Word is running and that the Meyer Letter document is open. Also, review the checklist in Figure 1-12 and verify that your screen is set up to match the figures in this tutorial.

▶ **2.** Make sure the insertion point is positioned to the left of the paragraph symbol below the first paragraph in the body of the letter (as shown earlier in Figure 1-15). If it is not, move the insertion point by clicking in that location now.

▶ **3.** Type the following two paragraphs:

See Chapter 1 for a complete explanation of the publishing process, including the copy editing phase. Chapter 2 discusses the process of creating a text manuscript in Microsoft Word. Chapter 3 explains how to compile an electronic art manuscript to accompany your text.

I will call in a few days to discuss the schedule. Feel free to call me before then if you prefer. I will be traveling next week, but you can always reach me on my cell phone. I also plan to check my e-mail while I am on the road.

Trouble? If you make a mistake while typing, press the Backspace key or the Delete key to delete any incorrect characters, and then type the correct characters.

▶ **4.** Press the **Enter** key.

▶ **5.** Type **Sincerely yours,** (including the comma) to enter the complimentary closing.

▶ **6.** Press the **Enter** key 10 times so you can see the document scroll up to accommodate the blank paragraphs. You're doing this only to demonstrate how a document scrolls up. You'll delete the extra blank paragraphs shortly.

As you pressed the Enter key repeatedly, the upper part of the document probably scrolled off the top of the document window. Exactly when this happens depends on the size of your monitor. See Figure 1-17.

Part of the document scrolled off the window ◄ **Figure 1-17**

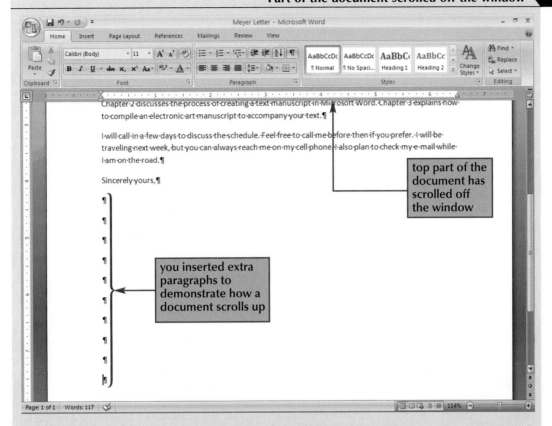

You don't really want all those blank paragraph marks after the complimentary closing, so you need to delete them.

▶ **7.** Press the **Backspace** key eight times. When you finish, you should see two paragraph marks below the complimentary closing, with the insertion point blinking to the left of the bottom one. This allows enough space for a signature.

▶ **8.** Type **Andrew Suri**, and then press the **Enter** key. A wavy red line appears below "Suri." In Word, such lines indicate possible spelling errors. Because Andrew's last name is not in the Word dictionary, Word suggests that it might be spelled incorrectly. You'll learn more about Word's error-checking features in a moment. For now, you can ignore the wavy red line.

You've completed most of the letter, so you should save your work.

▶ **9.** On the Quick Access Toolbar, click the **Save** button 🔚 . Word saves your letter with the same name and in the same location you specified earlier. Don't be concerned about any typing errors. You'll learn how to correct them later in this tutorial.

In the previous set of steps, you watched paragraph marks and text at the top of your document move off the window. Anytime you need to see the beginning of the letter, you can scroll this hidden text back into view. When you do, the text at the bottom of the window will scroll out of view. There are three ways to scroll the document window: click the up or down arrows in the vertical scroll bar, click anywhere in the vertical scroll bar, or drag the scroll box. See Figure 1-18.

Figure 1-18 Scrolling the document window

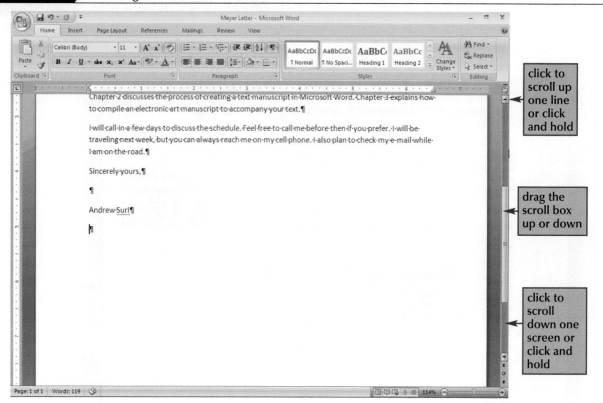

To practice scrolling the document using the vertical scroll bar:

1. Position the mouse pointer over the arrow at the top of the vertical scroll bar. Press and hold the mouse button to scroll the text. When the text stops scrolling, you have reached the top of the document and can see the beginning of the letter. Note that scrolling does not change the location of the insertion point in the document.

2. Click the down arrow on the vertical scroll bar several times. The document scrolls down one line at a time.

3. Click anywhere in the vertical scroll bar below the scroll box. The document scrolls down one full screen.

4. Drag the scroll box up to the top of the scroll bar, so you can see the beginning of the letter.

5. Continue practicing these steps until you feel comfortable scrolling up and down. When you are finished, scroll the document so you can see the complimentary closing at the end of the letter.

Andrew asks you to include his middle initial in the signature line. Performing this task will give you a chance to practice moving the insertion point around the document.

Moving the Insertion Point Around a Document

When you scroll a document, you change the part of the document that is displayed on the screen. But to change the location in the document where new text will appear when you type, you need to move the insertion point. One way to move the insertion point is to scroll up or down and then click where you want to insert new text. However, it is often more efficient to use the keyboard so you don't have to move your hand to the mouse, move the insertion point, and then move your hand back to the keyboard to type. You can use the arrow keys, ←, ↑, →, and ↓, to move the insertion point one character at a time to the left or right or one line at a time up or down. In addition, you can press a variety of key combinations to move the insertion point from one paragraph to another, to the beginning or end of the document, and so on. As you become more experienced with Word, you'll learn which methods you prefer.

Before you add Andrew's middle initial to the signature line, you'll take some time to practice moving the insertion point around the document.

To move the insertion point with keystrokes:

▶ **1.** Press the **Ctrl+Home** keys (that is, press the Ctrl key and hold it down while you press the Home key). The insertion point moves to the beginning of the document.

▶ **2.** Press the **Page Down** key to move the insertion point down to the next screen.

▶ **3.** Press the ↑ key several times to move the insertion point up one line at a time, and then press the → key several times to move the insertion point to the right one character at a time.

▶ **4.** Press the **Ctrl+End** keys. The insertion point moves to the end of the document.

▶ **5.** Use the arrow keys to position the insertion point to the right of the "w" in "Andrew." Now you can add Andrew's middle initial.

▶ **6.** Press the **spacebar**, and then type the letter **T** followed by a period so that the signature line reads "Andrew T. Suri."

Figure 1-19 summarizes the keystrokes you can use to move the insertion point around a document.

Keystrokes for moving the insertion point ◀ **Figure 1-19**

To move the insertion point	Press
Left or right one character at a time	← or →
Up or down one line at a time	↑ or ↓
Left or right one word at a time	Ctrl+ ← or Ctrl+ →
Up or down one paragraph at a time	Ctrl+ ↑ or Ctrl+ ↓
To the beginning or to the end of the current line	Home or End
To the beginning or to the end of the document	Ctrl+Home or Ctrl+End
To the previous screen or to the next screen	Page Up or Page Down
To the top or to the bottom of the document window	Alt+Ctrl+Page Up or Alt+Ctrl+Page Down

Using the Undo and Redo Commands

To undo (or reverse) the last thing you did in a document, you can click the **Undo button** on the Quick Access Toolbar. If you want to restore your original change, the **Redo button** reverses the action of the Undo button (or redoes the undo). To undo more than your last action, you can click the Undo button arrow on the Quick Access Toolbar. A list will open that shows your most recent actions.

Andrew asks you to undo the addition of his middle initial, to see how the signature line looks without it.

To undo the addition of the "T.":

▶ **1.** On the Quick Access Toolbar, place the mouse pointer over the **Undo** button 🔄 , but don't click it. The ScreenTip "Undo Typing (Ctrl + Z)" appears, indicating that your most recent action involved typing. The item in parentheses is the keyboard shortcut for the Undo command. See Figure 1-20.

Figure 1-20	Using the Undo button

▶ **2.** Click the **Undo** button 🔄 on the Quick Access Toolbar. The letter "T," the period, and the space you typed earlier are deleted.

Trouble? If something else changes, you probably made another edit or change to the document between the addition of Andrew's middle initial and the undo action. Click the Undo button on the Quick Access Toolbar until the letter "T," the period, and the space following it are deleted. If a list of possible changes appears under the Undo button, you clicked the arrow next to the Undo button rather than the Undo button itself. Press the Esc key to close the list.

Andrew decides that he does want to include his middle initial after all. Instead of retyping it, you'll redo the undo.

▶ **3.** On the Quick Access Toolbar, place the mouse pointer over the **Redo** button and observe the "Redo Typing (Ctrl + Y)" ScreenTip.

▶ **4.** Click the **Redo** button 🔄 on the Quick Access Toolbar. Andrew's middle initial (along with the period and an additional space) are reinserted into the signature line.

▶ **5.** Click the **Save** button 💾 on the Quick Access Toolbar to save your changes to the document.

Correcting Errors

If you notice a typing error as soon as you make it, you can press the Backspace key, which deletes the characters and spaces to the left of the insertion point one at a time. Backspacing erases both printing and nonprinting characters. After you erase the error, you can type the correct character(s). You can also press the Delete key, which deletes characters to the right of the insertion point one at a time.

In many cases, however, Word's **AutoCorrect** feature will do the work for you. Among other things, AutoCorrect automatically corrects common typing errors, such as typing "adn" for "and." For example, you might have noticed AutoCorrect at work if you forgot to capitalize the first letter in a sentence as you typed the letter. AutoCorrect can automatically correct this error as you type the rest of the sentence. You'll learn more about using AutoCorrect as you become a more experienced Word user. For now, just keep in mind that AutoCorrect corrects certain typing errors automatically. Depending on how your computer is set up, some or all AutoCorrect features might be turned off. You'll learn how to turn AutoCorrect on in the following steps.

Whether or not AutoCorrect is turned on, you can always rely on Word's **spelling checker**. By default, this feature continually checks your document against Word's built-in dictionary. If you type a word that doesn't match the correct spelling in Word's dictionary, or if a word is not in the dictionary at all (as is the case with Andrew's last name, Suri), a wavy red line appears beneath the word. A wavy red line also appears if you type duplicate words (such as "the the"). Word also includes a grammar checker, which is turned off by default. You will learn how to use the grammar checker in Tutorial 2.

Before you can practice using AutoCorrect and the spelling checker, you need to verify that you have the correct settings in the Word Options dialog box.

To verify the spelling checker and AutoCorrect settings:

▶ **1.** Click the **Office Button** 🗋 , and then (at the bottom of the Office menu) click the **Word Options** button. The Word Options dialog box opens.

▶ **2.** In the left pane, click **Proofing**. Options related to proofing a document are displayed in the right pane.

▶ **3.** Verify that the **Check spelling as you type** check box contains a check mark.

▶ **4.** Verify that the **Mark grammar errors as you type** check box does *not* contain a check mark. (This option is typically turned off by default.)

▶ **5.** Near the top of the right pane, click the **AutoCorrect Options** button. The AutoCorrect: English (United States) dialog box opens.

▶ **6.** Locate the **Capitalize first letter of sentences** check box and the **Replace text as you type** check box. If they are not already checked, click them to insert check marks now. (It is okay if other check boxes have check marks.) See Figure 1-21.

Figure 1-21 ▶ **Selecting AutoCorrect options**

7. Click the **OK** button to close the AutoCorrect English (United States) dialog box, and then click the **OK** button again to close the Word Options dialog box.

The easiest way to see how these features work is to make some intentional typing errors.

To correct intentional typing errors:

▶ **1.** Use the arrow keys to move the insertion point to the left of the last paragraph mark in the document.

▶ **2.** Carefully and slowly type the following sentence exactly as it is shown, including the spelling errors: **notice how microsoft Word corects teh commen typing misTakes you make**. See Figure 1-22.

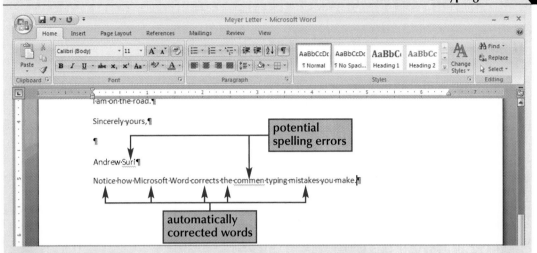

Trouble? If you see wavy green underlines, the grammar checker is turned on and you made a mistake not included in Step 2. Delete the text you just typed, repeat Steps 1–4 in the preceding set of steps to turn the grammar checker off, click the OK button to close the Word Options dialog box, and then begin these steps again with Step 1.

When you pressed the spacebar after the word "commen," a wavy red line appeared beneath it, indicating that the word might be misspelled. Also, Word automatically capitalized the word "Notice" (because it is the first word in the sentence) and "Microsoft" (because it is a proper noun). And, when you pressed the spacebar after the words "corects," "teh," and "misTakes," Word automatically corrected the typing errors.

Correcting Spelling Errors

After you verify that AutoCorrect made the changes you want, you should review your document for red wavy underlines, which indicate potential spelling errors. In the following steps, you will learn a quick way to correct such errors.

To correct spelling and grammar errors:

▶ **1.** Position the I-beam pointer over the word "commen," and then click the right mouse button. A shortcut menu appears with suggested spellings. You also see the Mini toolbar, which provides easy access to some of the most commonly used options in the Home tab for the object you've right-clicked. You'll learn more about the Mini toolbar as you gain more experience with Word. See Figure 1-23.

Figure 1-23 | **Shortcut menu with suggested spellings**

Trouble? If the shortcut menu doesn't appear, repeat Step 1, making sure you click the right mouse button, not the left one. If you see a different menu from the one shown in Figure 1-23, you didn't right-click exactly on the word "commen." Press the Esc key to close the menu, and then repeat Step 1.

▶ **2.** Click **common** in the shortcut menu. The menu closes (along with the Mini toolbar), and the correct spelling appears in your document. Notice that the wavy red line disappears after you correct the error.

Proofreading the Letter

You can see how quick and easy it is to correct common typing errors with AutoCorrect and the spelling checker. Remember, however, to proofread each document you create thoroughly. AutoCorrect will not catch words that are spelled correctly but used improperly (such as "your" for "you're"). Before you can proofread your letter, you need to delete the practice sentence.

To delete the practice sentence:

▶ **1.** Make sure the insertion point is to the right of "common" in the sentence you just typed, and then press the **Delete** key repeatedly to delete any spaces and characters to the right of the insertion point.

▶ **2.** Press the **Backspace** key repeatedly until the insertion point is located just left of the paragraph mark below Andrew's name. There should only be one paragraph mark below his name. If you accidentally delete part of the letter, retype it, using Figure 1-1 as a guide.

Now you can proofread the letter for any typos. You can also get rid of the wavy red underline below Andrew's last name.

To proofread the document:

▶ 1. Be sure the signature line is visible. Because Word doesn't recognize "Suri" as a word, it is marked as a potential error. You need to tell Word to ignore this name wherever it occurs in the letter.

▶ 2. Right-click **Suri**. A shortcut menu and the Mini toolbar open.

▶ 3. Click **Ignore All** on the shortcut menu. This tells Word to ignore the word "Suri" each time it occurs in this document. The wavy red underline disappears from below Andrew's last name.

▶ 4. Scroll up to the beginning of the letter and proofread it for typing errors. If a word has a wavy red underline, right-click it and choose an option on the shortcut menu. To correct other errors, click to the right or left of the error, use the Backspace or Delete key to remove it, and then type a correction.

▶ 5. On the Quick Access Toolbar, click the **Save** button 🔲 . Word saves your letter with the same name and to the same location you specified earlier.

Next, you need to return to the beginning of the document and insert the date. In the process, you'll learn how to use Word's AutoComplete feature.

Inserting a Date with AutoComplete

The advantage of using a word-processing program such as Microsoft Word is that you can easily make changes to text you have already typed. In this case, you need to insert the current date at the beginning of the letter. Andrew tells you that he wants to send the *Author's Guide* to Clara Meyer on February 8, so you need to insert that date into the letter now.

Before you can enter the date, you need to move the insertion point to the correct location.

To move the insertion point and add some blank lines:

▶ 1. Scroll up to display the top of the document.

▶ 2. Click to the left of the "D" in "Dear Clara" in the salutation, press the **Enter** key twice, then press the ↑ key twice to move the insertion point up to two paragraphs above the salutation. There are now six blank paragraphs before the salutation. The insertion point is located in the second blank paragraph above the salutation. The vertical ruler tells you that the insertion point is located about 1.5 inches from the top margin (that is, the insertion point is now located where the salutation used to be). As you'll recall, the top margin is one inch deep, so the insertion point is now approximately 2.5 inches from the top of the page. This is where you will insert the date. See Figure 1-24.

Figure 1-24 **Insertion point positioned for adding date**

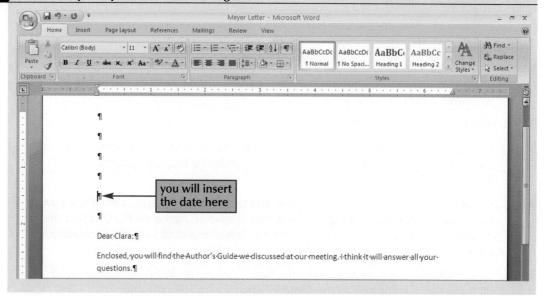

To insert the date, you can take advantage of Word's **AutoComplete** feature, which automatically inserts dates and other regularly used items for you. In this case, you can type the first few characters of the month, and let Word insert the rest.

To insert the date:

▶ 1. Type **Febr** (the first four letters of February). A rectangular box appears above the line, as shown in Figure 1-25. If you wanted to type something other than February, you could continue typing to complete the word. In this case, though, you want to accept the AutoComplete suggestion.

Figure 1-25 **AutoComplete suggestion**

Tip

AutoComplete works for long month names like February, but not shorter ones like May, because "Ma" could be the beginning of many words, not just "May."

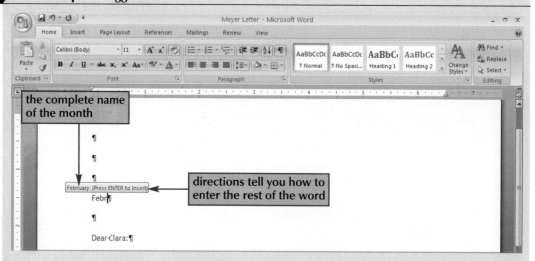

▶ 2. Press the **Enter** key. The rest of the word "February" is inserted in the document.

> ▶ **3.** Press the **spacebar**, type **8, 2010**, and then press the **Enter** key twice. The date is finished, and the insertion point is now located where you want to begin typing the inside address.
>
> **Trouble?** If February happens to be the current month, you will see a second AutoComplete suggestion displaying the current date after you press the spacebar. To ignore that AutoComplete suggestion, continue typing the rest of the date as instructed in Step 3.

You're ready to type the inside address. But first, you need to learn a little more about paragraph and line spacing in Microsoft Word.

Understanding Line and Paragraph Spacing

In Word, any text that ends with a paragraph mark symbol (¶) is a paragraph. A **paragraph** can be a group of words that is many lines long, a single word, or even a blank line, in which case you see a paragraph mark alone on a single line. (Recall that the letter to Clara Meyer includes several blank paragraphs at the beginning of the document.) As you work with paragraphs in a document, you need to be concerned with two types of spacing—line spacing and paragraph spacing.

Line spacing determines the amount of space between lines of text within a paragraph. Lines that are closely positioned one on top of another are said to be single spaced. Technically speaking, single spacing allows for the tallest character in a line of text. All other line spacing options are measured as multiples of single spacing. For example, 1.5 line spacing allows for one and one-half times the space of single spacing. Likewise, double spacing allows for twice the space of single spacing. By default, the line spacing in Word 2007 documents is set to 1.15 times the space allowed in single spacing. This allows for the largest character in a particular line as well as a small amount of extra space.

The other type of spacing you need to be concerned with, **paragraph spacing**, determines the amount of space before and after a paragraph. Paragraph spacing is measured in points; a **point** is approximately $1/72$ of an inch. The default setting for paragraph spacing in Word is 0 points before each paragraph and 10 points after each paragraph.

Although line spacing and paragraph spacing are two different things, it is common to refer to paragraph spacing with the same terms used to refer to line spacing. So, paragraphs that appear very close together, with no space for text in between, are often referred to as single spaced. Paragraphs that have space enough for a single line of text between them are said to be double spaced. The default paragraph spacing in Word (10 points after each paragraph) is designed to look like double spacing (although it is slightly tighter than true double spacing). Figure 1-26 shows the Meyer Letter document zoomed to 90%, so you can see its spacing at a glance.

Figure 1-26 ▶ **Line and paragraph spacing in the letter to Clara Meyer**

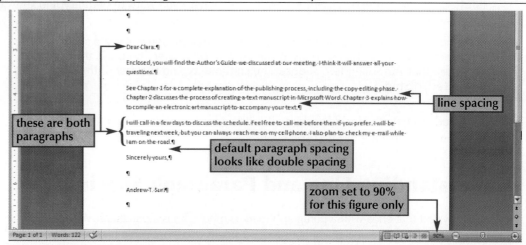

In a block style letter, the inside address (shown earlier in Figure 1-1) should be single spaced. However, with Word's default paragraph spacing, when you press the Enter key to move from the name line in the inside address, to the street address line, and then to the city and state line, Word inserts extra space after each paragraph. This results in an inside address that is double spaced. You'll see how this works in the following steps. Then you'll learn how to correct the problem.

To type the inside address:

▶ 1. Type the following: **Clara Meyer**, press the **Enter** key, type **2257 Chamberlain Drive**, press the **Enter** key, and then type **North Liberty, IA 52317**. Do not press the Enter key after typing the zip code; you should already see one blank paragraph before and after the inside address. See Figure 1-27.

Letter with inside address | Figure 1-27

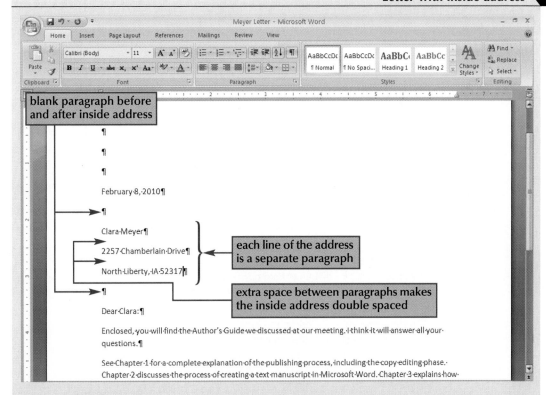

Remember that each line of the inside address is actually a separate paragraph. As you can see in Figure 1-27, the extra space Word inserted between these separate paragraphs results in an inside address that appears to be double spaced.

To correct this problem, you need to **select**, or highlight, the inside address and then change the paragraph spacing. Andrew is also concerned about the document's line spacing. He doesn't really like the extra space between lines, so he asks you to remove it. To change this, you need to select the entire document and then change the line spacing.

Selecting Parts of a Document

You can select one or more paragraphs, one or more words, any other part of a document, or even the entire document, by using the mouse or the keyboard. However, most people find that the mouse is easier and more efficient to use. With the mouse you can quickly select a line or paragraph by clicking the **selection bar** (the blank space in the left margin area of the document window). You can also select text using various combinations of keys. Figure 1-28 summarizes methods for selecting text with the mouse and the keyboard. A notation such as "Ctrl+Shift" means you press and hold the two keys at the same time.

Figure 1-28 Methods for selecting text

To Select	Mouse	Keyboard	Mouse and Keyboard
A word	Double-click the word	Move the insertion point to the beginning of the word, hold down Ctrl+Shift, and then press →	
A line	Click in the selection bar next to the line	Move the insertion point to the beginning of the line, hold down Shift, and then press ↓	
A sentence	Click at the beginning of the sentence, then drag the pointer until the sentence is selected		Press and hold down Ctrl, and then click within the sentence
Multiple lines	Click and drag in the selection bar next to the lines	Move the insertion point to the beginning of the first line, hold down Shift, and then press ↓ until all the lines are selected	
A paragraph	Double-click in the selection bar next to the paragraph, or triple-click within the paragraph	Move the insertion point to the beginning of the paragraph, hold down Ctrl+Shift, and then press ↓	
Multiple paragraphs	Click in the selection bar next to the first paragraph in the group, and then drag in the selection bar to select the paragraphs	Move the insertion point to the beginning of the first paragraph, hold down Ctrl+Shift, and then press ↓ until all the paragraphs are selected	
An entire document	Triple-click in the selection bar	Press Ctrl+A	Press and hold down Ctrl, and then click in the selection bar
A block of text	Click at the beginning of the block, and then drag the pointer until the entire block is selected		Click at the beginning of the block, press and hold down Shift, and then click at the end of the block
Nonadjacent blocks of text	Press and hold down Ctrl, and then drag the mouse pointer to select multiple blocks of nonadjacent text		

You'll practice many of these selection methods in Tutorial 2. For now, you will focus on selecting the multiple paragraphs of the inside address and the entire document. You'll start by selecting the inside address.

To select the inside address:

▶ **1.** Click to the left of the "C" in "Clara Meyer" in the inside address, and then drag the mouse right and down until the entire inside address is selected. Make sure the paragraph mark to the right of the zip code is also selected. See Figure 1-29.

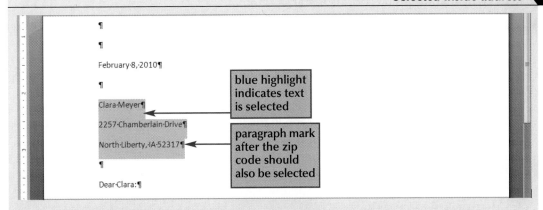

Trouble? If you selected only part of the inside address, or selected a different part of the document, click anywhere in the document to remove the blue highlight, and then begin again with Step 1.

Trouble? Don't be concerned if you see the Mini toolbar hovering over the selected text.

Now that the inside address is selected, you are ready to remove the extra space after each paragraph. You'll also adjust the line spacing, as Andrew requested.

Adjusting Paragraph and Line Spacing

There are several ways to adjust paragraph and line spacing in Word. The quickest method, which you'll use in this tutorial, is to click the Line spacing button in the Paragraph group on the Home tab. (In Tutorial 2, you'll learn another technique that offers more options.)

Clicking the Line spacing button opens a menu with some commonly used line spacing options: single spacing (listed on the Line spacing menu as 1.0), double spacing (listed as 2.0), and so on. The paragraph spacing options offered by the Line spacing button are more streamlined: you can choose to add or remove a default amount of extra space before or after each paragraph. You cannot specify a particular amount of space.

Understanding Spacing Between Paragraphs	InSight

To many people, "to single space between paragraphs" means pressing the Enter key once after each paragraph. Likewise, "to double space between paragraphs" means pressing the Enter key twice after each paragraph. With the default paragraph spacing in Word 2007, however, you only need to press the Enter key once to insert a double space after a paragraph. Keep this in mind if you're used to pressing the Enter key twice; otherwise, you could end up with more space than you want between paragraphs.

Andrew asks you to remove the extra space between the lines within paragraphs. This means you need to change the line spacing from 1.15 to 1.0 (that is, to single spacing). You'll start by adjusting the paragraph spacing in the inside address, and then turn your attention to the line spacing for the entire document.

To adjust the paragraph spacing in the inside address:

▶ **1.** Verify that the inside address is still selected.

▶ **2.** In the Paragraph group on the Home tab, click the **Line spacing** button ⬚. A menu of line spacing options appears, with two paragraph spacing options at the bottom. The current line spacing setting for the selected text (1.15) is indicated by a check mark. Because the line spacing is the same throughout the document, this is also the current line spacing setting for the entire document. At the moment, you are more interested in the paragraph spacing options. Your goal is to remove the extra space after each paragraph in the inside address, so you need to use the last option on the menu, Remove Space After Paragraph. See Figure 1-30.

Figure 1-30 ▶ **Line and paragraph spacing options**

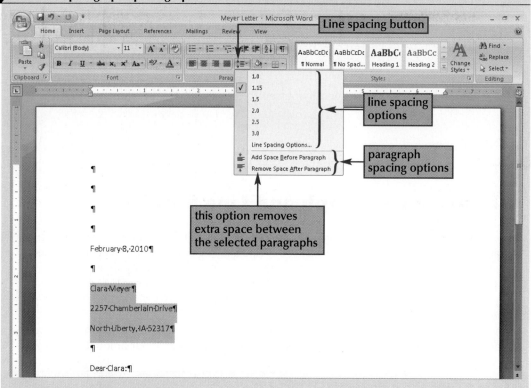

▶ **3.** Click **Remove Space After Paragraph**. The menu closes, and the extra space after each of the three paragraphs of the inside address is removed. The paragraphs are now closer together.

▶ **4.** Click anywhere in the document to deselect the inside address. Notice that the change in paragraph spacing in the inside address did not affect the rest of the document because you had selected only the inside address. The paragraphs in the body of the letter are still separated by extra space, so that they appear to be double spaced.

The three paragraphs of the inside address are closer together, but they don't exactly look single spaced. That's because the default line spacing setting (which you'll recall adds a small amount of space below each line) remains in effect, adding a small amount of extra space below the single line of text in each of the three inside address paragraphs. When you change the line spacing for the entire document to single spaced in the next set of steps, the inside address will finally look single spaced.

To adjust the line spacing for the entire document:

► 1. Press the **Ctrl + A** keys. The entire document is selected, as indicated by the blue highlight.

► 2. In the Paragraph group on the Home tab, click the **Line spacing** button 🔲. The Line spacing menu opens. As you saw earlier, the default line spacing setting of 1.15 is currently selected, as indicated by the check mark. You want to change the setting to single spacing, or 1.0.

► 3. Click **1.0**. The Line spacing menu closes.

► 4. Click anywhere in the document to deselect it. The lines of the entire document move closer together, and the inside address is now single spaced. The lines within the paragraphs in the rest of the document are also single spaced. The double spacing between paragraphs everywhere in the letter except the inside address remains unchanged. See Figure 1-31.

> **Tip**
>
> A line spacing setting of 1.15 is fine for most documents. However, some people prefer a setting of 1.0.

New line spacing in the document ◄ Figure 1-31

Previewing and Printing a Document

Do you think the letter is ready to print? If you print too soon, you risk wasting paper and printer time. For example, if you failed to insert enough space for the company letterhead, you would have to add more space, and then print the letter again. To avoid wasting paper and time, you should first display the document in the **Print Preview window**. By default, the Print Preview window shows you the full page; there's no need to scroll through the document.

To preview the document:

▶ **1.** Proof the document one last time and correct any new errors. Always remember to proof your document immediately before printing it.

▶ **2.** Click to the left of the last paragraph mark in the document (just below Andrew's name), press the **Enter** key and type your first, middle, and last initials in lowercase. In a block style letter, it is customary for the typist to include his or her initials below the signature line. In this case, adding your initials also ensures that you will be able to identify your copy of the letter when you retrieve it from the printer.

▶ **3.** Click the **Office Button** 🔘, point to **Print**, and then click **Print Preview**. The Print Preview window opens and displays a full-page version of your letter, as shown in Figure 1-32. This shows how the letter will fit on the printed page. The Ribbon in Print Preview includes a number of useful options for changing the way the printed page will look.

Figure 1-32	Full page displayed in the Print Preview window

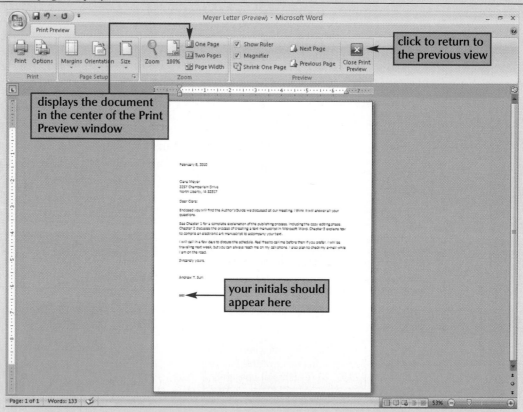

Trouble? If your letter is not centered in the Print Preview window, click the One Page button in the Zoom group on the Print Preview tab.

Trouble? If you don't see a ruler above the document, click the Show Ruler check box in the Preview group on the Print Preview tab to insert a check mark and display the ruler.

▶ **4.** Review your document and make sure its overall layout matches the document in Figure 1-32. If you notice a problem with paragraph breaks or spacing, click the Close Print Preview button in the Preview group on the Print Preview tab, edit the document, and then open the Print Preview window again and check your work.

▶ **5.** In the Preview group on the Print Preview tab, click the **Close Print Preview** button to return to Print Layout view.

▶ **6.** Click the **Save** button 🖫 on the Quick Access Toolbar to save the letter with your newly added initials.

In Andrew's letter, the text looks well spaced, and the letterhead will fit at the top of the page. You are ready to print the letter.

To print a document, click the Office Button, and then click Print. This opens the Print dialog box, where you can adjust various printer settings. Or, if you prefer, you can click the Office Button, point to Print, and then click Quick Print. This prints the document using default settings, without opening a dialog box. In these tutorials, the first time you print, you should check the settings in the Print dialog box and make sure the number of copies is set to 1. After that, you can use the Quick Print command.

To print the letter document:

▶ **1.** Make sure your printer is turned on and contains paper.

▶ **2.** Click the **Office Button** 🔘 , and then click **Print**. The Print dialog box opens.

▶ **3.** Make sure the Printer section of the dialog box shows the correct printer. Also, make sure the number of copies is set to 1.

   Trouble? If the Name list box in the Print dialog box shows the wrong printer, click the Name list arrow, and then select the correct printer from the list of available printers. If you're not sure what the correct printer is, check with your instructor or technical support person.

▶ **4.** Click the **OK** button. Assuming your computer is attached to a printer, the letter prints.

Your printed letter should look similar to Figure 1-1, but without the Carlyle University letterhead. Also, your initials should appear below Andrew's name, on the last line of the letter.

Printing Documents on a Shared Printer		InSight

If your computer is connected to a network, be sure to print only those documents that you need in hard copy format. You should avoid tying up a shared printer with unnecessary printing.

Creating an Envelope

After you print the letter, Andrew asks you to create an envelope in which to mail the *Author's Guide*. Creating an envelope is a simple process because Word automatically uses the inside address from the letter as the address on the envelope. By default, Word does not add extra space between the paragraphs on an envelope, and the line spacing is set to 1.0. As a result, addresses on an envelope are single spaced.

Creating an Envelope

- Click the Mailings tab on the Ribbon.
- In the Create group, click the Envelopes button to open the Envelopes and Labels dialog box.
- Verify that the Delivery address box contains the correct address. If necessary, type a new address or edit the existing one.
- If necessary, type a return address. If you are using preprinted stationery that already includes a return address, click the Omit check box to insert a check mark.
- To print the envelope immediately, insert an envelope in your printer, and then click the Print button.
- To store the envelope along with the rest of the document, click the Add to Document button.
- To print the envelope after you have added it to the document, insert an envelope in your printer, open the Print dialog box, and print the page containing the envelope.

Andrew tells you that your printer is not currently stocked with envelopes. He asks you to create the envelope and add it to the document. Then he will print the envelope later, when he is ready to mail the *Author's Guide* to Clara.

To create an envelope:

▶ 1. Click the **Mailings** tab on the Ribbon.

▶ 2. In the Create group on the Mailings tab, click the **Envelopes** button. The Envelopes and Labels dialog box opens, as shown in Figure 1-33. By default, Word uses the inside address from the letter as the delivery address. Depending on how your computer is set up, you might see an address in the Return address box. Because Andrew will be using his company's printed envelopes, you don't need to print a return address on this envelope.

Figure 1-33 ▶ **Envelopes and Labels dialog box**

address is single spaced

inside address from letter used as delivery address

omits a return address (yours might not be selected)

you might see an address here

▶ 3. If necessary, click the **Omit** check box to insert a check mark.

▶ **4.** Click the **Add to Document** button. The dialog box closes, and you return to the document window. The envelope is inserted at the top of the document, with the address single spaced. The double line with the words "Section Break (Next Page)" indicate how the envelope is formatted, and will not be visible when you print the envelope. The envelope will print in the standard business envelope format. (You'll have a chance to print an envelope in the exercises at the end of this tutorial.)

▶ **5.** Save your changes to the document. You are finished with the letter and the envelope, so you can close the document.

▶ **6.** Click the **Close** button ☒ on the Word program title bar. The Meyer Letter document closes. If you have no other documents open, Word closes also.

Trouble? If you see a dialog box with the message "Do you want to save the changes to 'Meyer Letter?'" click the Yes button.

Congratulations on creating your first letter in Microsoft Word 2007. You'll be able to use the skills you learned in this tutorial to create a variety of professional documents.

Session 1.2 Quick Check | Review

1. True or False: The spelling checker is turned off by default.
2. True or False: To accept an AutoComplete suggestion, such as the name of a month, you need to click a button on the Ribbon.
3. Explain how to correct a misspelled word using a shortcut menu.
4. What's the difference between paragraph spacing and line spacing?
5. Explain how to preview a document before you print it.
6. What tab on the Ribbon do you use to create an envelope?

Tutorial Summary | Review

In this tutorial, you learned how to set up your Word window to match the figures in this book, create a new document from scratch, and type a professional-looking letter. You practiced correcting errors and moving the insertion point around a document. You learned how to undo and redo changes and how to insert a date with AutoComplete. You adjusted paragraph and line spacing, and then you previewed and printed a document. Finally, you created an envelope.

Key Terms

AutoComplete	nonprinting characters	scroll
AutoCorrect	Page width	select
default	paragraph	selection bar
font	paragraph spacing	spelling checker
font size	point	Undo button
line spacing	Print Preview window	Word
margin	Redo button	word wrap
Microsoft Office Word	ScreenTip	Zoom level

Practice the skills you learned in the tutorial using the same case scenario.

There are no Data Files needed for the Review Assignments.

Andrew asks you to write a letter to a local author, Philippa Gallatin, inviting her to an upcoming convention. He also asks you to create an envelope for the letter. You'll create the letter and envelope by completing the following steps. (Note: Text you need to type is shown in bold for ease of reference only; do not bold the text unless otherwise instructed.)

1. Open a new blank document.
2. Compare your screen to the checklist in Figure 1-12, and change any settings if necessary. In particular, make sure that nonprinting characters are displayed.
3. Press the Enter key four times to insert enough space for the company letterhead.
4. Type the date **November 25, 2010** using AutoComplete for "November."
5. Press the Enter key twice, then type the following inside address, using the default paragraph spacing for now:
   Philippa Gallatin
   787 First Street
   Albany, NY 12205
6. Press the Enter key twice, then type the letter's salutation, body, complimentary closing, and signature line, as shown in Figure 1-34. Accept any relevant AutoCorrect suggestions. Use the default line and paragraph spacing; do not insert any extra blank paragraphs.

Figure 1-34

Dear Philippa:

The Albany Visitors Bureau will be hosting the 2011 convention for the National Editorial Association. The convention is scheduled for the first week in March. As a major publishing force in the Albany area, we'd like to make a strong showing at the convention. In particular, we'd like to invite you to attend the opening banquet as our guest. Our own editor-in-chief, Sally Ann Hamilton, will be the keynote speaker.

The complete convention schedule will be posted on the National Editorial Association's Web site after the New Year. I'll e-mail you shortly afterward to confirm your reservation for the opening banquet. At that time, you can tell me if you'll be available to attend any of the afternoon seminars.

Sincerely,

Andrew T. Suri

7. Save your work as **Gallatin Letter** in the Tutorial.01\Review folder provided with your Data Files.
8. Practice using the keyboard to move the insertion point around the document. Use the arrow keys so the insertion point is positioned immediately to the right of the "a" in "Philippa" in the inside address.

9. Press the spacebar and then type **M.**, so the first line of the inside address reads "Philippa M. Gallatin." (Don't forget the period after the middle initial.)

10. Undo the change and then redo it.

11. Scroll to the beginning of the document and proofread your work.

12. Correct any misspelled words marked by wavy red lines. If the correct spelling of a word does not appear in the shortcut menu, close the list, and then make the correction yourself. Remove any red wavy lines below words that are spelled correctly.

13. Click at the end of Andrew's name in the signature line, press the Enter key twice, and type your initials in lowercase.

14. Select the inside address and remove the extra paragraph spacing from the selected paragraphs.

15. Select the entire document and change the line spacing to single spacing.

16. Save your changes to the letter, and then preview and print it.

17. Add an envelope to the document. Use your own address as the delivery address. Do not include a return address.

18. Save your changes and close the document.

| Apply | **Case Problem 1** |

Apply the skills you learned to create a letter about a health-care lecture.

There are no Data Files needed for this Case Problem.

Wingra Family Practice Clinic You are a nurse at Wingra Family Practice Clinic. You have organized a lunchtime lecture series for the clinic staff in which regional medical professionals will discuss topics related to pediatric health care. You have hired your first speaker and need to write a letter confirming your agreement and asking a few questions. Create the letter by completing the following steps. As you type the document, accept the default paragraph and line spacing until you are asked to change them. Because the clinic is currently out of letterhead, you will start the letter by typing a return address. (Note: Text you need to type is shown in bold for ease of reference only; do not bold the text unless otherwise instructed.)

1. Open a new blank document. Compare your screen to the checklist in Figure 1-12, and change any settings if necessary. In particular, make sure that nonprinting characters are displayed.

2. Type your name, press the Enter key, and then type the following return address:
   Wingra Family Practice Clinic
   2278 Norwood Place
   Middleton, WI 52247

3. Press the Enter key twice, and then type **May 8, 2010** as the date.

4. Press the Enter key twice, and then type this inside address:
   Dr. Susanna Trevay
   James Madison Medical Center
   56 Ingersoll Drive
   Madison, WI 53788

5. Press the Enter key twice, type the salutation **Dear Dr. Trevay:** (don't forget the colon), and then press the Enter key once.

6. Type the following paragraph: **Thank you so much for agreeing to lecture about early childhood vaccinations on Friday, May 21. Before I can publicize your talk, I need some information. Please call by Tuesday with your answers to these questions:**

7. Press the Enter key, and then type the following questions as separate paragraphs, using the default paragraph spacing:

   Which vaccines will you cover in detail?

   Will you discuss common immune responses to vaccine antigens?

   Will you provide hand-outs with suggested vaccination schedules?

8. Save the document as **Lecture Series Letter** in the Tutorial.01\Case1 folder provided with your Data Files.

9. Move the insertion point to the beginning of the third question (which begins "Will you provide..."). Insert a new paragraph, and add the following as the new third question in the list: **Would you be willing to take questions from the audience?**

10. Correct any spelling errors indicated by red wavy lines. Because "Wingra" is spelled correctly, use the shortcut menu to remove the wavy red line under the word "Wingra" and prevent Word from marking the word as a misspelling. Repeat this to ignore "Trevay," "Ingersoll," and any other words that are spelled correctly but are marked as misspellings.

11. Insert a new paragraph after the last question, and then type the complimentary closing **Sincerely,** (including the comma).

12. Press the Enter key twice to leave room for your signature, and then type your full name. Press the Enter key and type **Wingra Family Practice Clinic**. Notice that "Wingra" is not marked as a spelling error this time.

13. Select the return address and remove the extra paragraph spacing. Do the same for the inside address. Do not attempt to change them both at the same time by selecting the return address, the date, and the inside address all at once, or you will end up with too little space before and after the date.

14. Select the entire document and change the line spacing to single spacing.

15. Save the document, preview and print it, and then close it.

Apply	Case Problem 2

Apply the skills you learned to create a letter informing a client about a new investment program.

There are no Data Files needed for this Case Problem.

Pear Tree Investment Services As a financial planner at Pear Tree Investment Services, you are responsible for keeping your clients informed about new investment options. You have just learned about a program called HigherEdVest, which encourages parents to save for their children's college educations. You'll write a letter to Joseph Robbins, a client of yours, in which you introduce the program and ask him to call for more information. Create the letter by completing the following steps. (Note: Text you need to type is shown in bold for ease of reference only; do not bold the text unless otherwise instructed.)

1. Open a new blank document. Compare your screen to the checklist in Figure 1-12, and change any settings if necessary. In particular, make sure that nonprinting characters are displayed.

2. To leave room for the company letterhead, press the Enter key until the insertion point is positioned about three inches from the top of the page. (Remember that you can see the exact position of the insertion point, in inches, on the vertical ruler.)

⊕**EXPLORE**

3. Type the current date, accepting any AutoComplete suggestions that appear.

4. Press the Enter key twice and type the inside address: **Joseph Robbins, 5788 Rugby Road, Hillsborough, CO 80732**.

5. Press the Enter key twice, type the salutation **Dear Joseph:**, and then press the Enter key once.

6. Write one paragraph introducing the HigherEdVest program, explaining that you think the client might be interested, and asking him to call your office at (555) 555-5555 for more details.

7. In the next paragraph, type the complimentary closing **Sincerely,**.

8. Press the Enter key twice to leave room for your signature, and then type your name and title.

9. Save the letter as **EdVest Letter** in the Tutorial.01\Case2 folder provided with your Data Files.

10. Reread your letter carefully and correct any errors. Use the keyboard to move the insertion point as necessary.

11. Remove the extra paragraph spacing in the inside address, and then change the entire document to single spacing.

12. Save your changes, and then preview and print the letter.

⊕**EXPLORE**

13. Create an envelope for the letter. Click the Omit check box to deselect it (if necessary), and then, for the return address, type your own address. Add the envelope to the document. If you are asked if you want to save the return address as the new default return address, answer No. If your computer is connected to a printer that is stocked with envelopes, click the Office Button, click Print, click the Pages option button, type **1** in the Pages text box, and then click the OK button.

14. Save and close the document.

| Create | **Case Problem 3** |

Use your skills to create the letter of recommendation shown in Figure 1-35.

There are no Data Files needed for this Case Problem.

Monterrey Mountain Bike Tours   You are the owner of Monterrey Mountain Bike Tours, located in Eugene, Oregon. One of your tour guides, Melissa Coia, has decided to move to the Midwest to be closer to her family. She has applied for a job as a tour guide at Horicon Marsh in Wisconsin, and has asked you to write a letter of recommendation. To create the letter, complete the following steps:

1. Open a new blank document. Compare your screen to the checklist in Figure 1-12, and change any settings if necessary. In particular, make sure that nonprinting characters are displayed.

2. Type the letter shown in Figure 1-35. Assume that you will print the letter on the company's letterhead, with the date positioned about 2.5 inches from the top of the page. Replace "Your Name" with your first and last name.

Figure 1-35

> June 27, 2010
>
>
> Peter Roundtree
> Horicon Marsh Ranger Station
> 9875 Scales Bend Road
> Horicon, Wisconsin 57338
>
>
> Dear Mr. Roundtree:
>
> I am writing on behalf of Melissa Coia, who has applied for a job as a tour guide at Horicon Marsh. I highly recommend that you hire Melissa. She is enthusiastic, energetic, and extremely well organized.
>
> I would be glad to tell you more about Melissa over the phone. You can reach me during business hours at (555) 555-5555.
>
> Sincerely,
>
>
> Your Name

3. Save the document as **Melissa** in the Tutorial.01\Case3 folder provided with your Data Files.
4. Correct any typing errors.
5. Change the paragraph and line spacing so that the entire letter is single spaced, including the inside address.
6. Preview and print the letter.
7. Create an envelope for the letter. Click the Omit check box to deselect it (if necessary), and then, for the return address, type your own address. Add the envelope to the document. If you are asked if you want to save the return address as the new default return address, answer No. If your computer is connected to a printer that is stocked with envelopes, click the Office Button, click Print, click the Pages option button, type **1** in the Pages text box, and then click the OK button.
8. Save the document and close it.

Challenge | Case Problem 4

Go beyond what you've learned to write a fax coversheet for a small engineering company.

There are no Data Files needed for this Case Problem.

Gladstone Engineering   As the office manager for Gladstone Engineering, you are responsible for faxing technical drawings to clients. Along with each set of drawings, you need to include a coversheet that explains what you are faxing, lists the total number of pages, and provides the name and cell phone number of the engineer who created the drawings. The fastest way to create a professional-looking coversheet is to use a template—a special Word document that comes with predefined headings, line and paragraph spacing, and other types of formatting. To create the fax coversheet, perform the following steps. (Note: Text you need to type is shown in bold for ease of reference only; do not bold the text unless otherwise instructed.)

⊕ EXPLORE

1. Click the Microsoft Office Button, and then click New. The New Document dialog box opens. In the Template list (on the left), click Installed Templates.

EXPLORE
2. In the Installed Templates pane (on the right), click Equity Fax, and then click Create. A fax template opens, containing generic text called placeholders that you replace with your own information. (You should always take care to remove any placeholders you don't replace with other text.)

3. Compare your screen to the checklist in Figure 1-12 and change any settings if necessary. In particular, make sure that nonprinting characters are displayed.

EXPLORE
4. Click the text "[Type the recipient name]." The placeholder text appears in a blue box with blue highlighting. The box containing the highlighted text (with the small rectangle attached) is called a document control, or a content control. You can enter text in this document control just as you enter text in a dialog box. You'll learn more about document controls in Tutorial 3.

5. Type **Robert Mason**, and then press the Tab key twice. A document control is now visible to the right of the word "From." If you see a name here, click in the document control (if necessary) and delete the name.

6. Type your first and last name in the document control, and then press the Tab key to highlight the placeholder text "[Type the recipient fax number]."

7. Type **(555) 555-5555**, and then continue using the Tab key as necessary to enter **4** as the number of pages and **(333) 333-3333** as the phone number. If you press the Tab key too many times and skip past a document control, you can click the document control to highlight it. If you make a typing mistake, use the Undo button to reverse the error.

EXPLORE
8. Use the Tab key to select the placeholder text "[Pick the date]," click the list arrow on the document control, click the right facing arrow above the calendar as necessary until you see the calendar for December 2010, and then click 10 in the calendar. The date 12.10.2010 appears in the Date document control.

9. Use the Tab key to select the placeholder text in the "Re:" section, and then press the Delete key to delete the placeholder text. Delete the "CC:" placeholder text as well.

10. Click the box to the left of "Please Reply," and then type an uppercase **X**.

11. Click the placeholder text "[Type comments]," and then type the following message: **Here are the latest drawings, created for you by Matt Xio. After you review them, please call Matt on his cell phone to discuss the next phase of this project. Thank you very much**.

12. Save the coversheet as **Mason Fax** in the Tutorial.01\Case4 folder provided with your Data Files.

EXPLORE
13. Zoom the document out until you can see the entire page on the screen. When you are finished reviewing the document, zoom the document until it returns to its original zoom setting.

14. Review the coversheet and correct any typos. Save the coversheet again, preview it, and then print it.

15. Close the document.

Research | Internet Assignments

Go to the Web to find information you can use to create documents.

The purpose of the Internet Assignments is to challenge you to find information on the Internet that you can use to work effectively with this software. The actual assignments are updated and maintained on the Course Technology Web site. Log on to the Internet and use your Web browser to go to the Student Online Companion for New Perspectives Office 2007 at **www.course.com/np/office2007**. Then navigate to the Internet Assignments for this tutorial.

Assess	SAM Assessment and Training

If you have a SAM user profile, you may have access to hands-on instruction, practice, and assessment of the skills covered in this tutorial. Log in to your SAM account (**http://sam2007.course.com**) to launch any assigned training activities or exams that relate to the skills covered in this tutorial.

Review	Quick Check Answers

Session 1.1

1. Planning a document saves time and effort. It ensures that you include enough information to achieve the document's purpose without overwhelming or boring the reader. It also ensures that the document is organized logically and has the appearance you want.
2. View tab
3. Click the Print Layout button on the bottom-right area of the window.
4. True
5. False
6. .docx

Session 1.2

1. False
2. False
3. Right-click the word, and then click the correct spelling in the shortcut menu.
4. Paragraph spacing controls the amount of space inserted between paragraphs. Line spacing controls the amount of space inserted between lines within a paragraph.
5. Click the Office Button, point to Print, and then click Print Preview. In the Preview group on the Print Preview tab, click the Close Print Preview button to return to the previous view.
6. Mailings tab

Ending Data Files

Tutorial.01	Tutorial	Review	Case1	Case2	Case3	Case4
	Meyer Letter.docx	Gallatin Letter.docx	Lecture Series Letter.docx	EdVest Letter.docx	Melissa.docx	Mason Fax.docx

Tutorial 2

Objectives

Session 2.1
- Check spelling and grammar
- Select and delete text
- Move text within a document
- Find and replace text

Session 2.2
- Change margins
- Change alignment and paragraph indents
- Copy formatting with the Format Painter
- Emphasize points with bullets, numbering, bold, and italic
- Change fonts and adjust font sizes
- Change the document theme
- Preview and print a document

Editing and Formatting a Document

Preparing a Handout on Choosing a Design Style

Case | Pemberly Furniture and Interiors

Natalie Lanci is the lead designer at Pemberly Furniture and Interiors, a design and furniture firm. Over the years, she has found that new customers are often intimidated by the prospect of decorating their homes. To make things easier, she has decided to create a series of handouts about interior styles and furniture. She's just finished a draft of her first handout, "Getting the Look You Want." She has marked up a printed copy of the document with notes about what she wants changed. As her assistant, it's your job to make the necessary changes and reprint the document.

In this tutorial, you will edit the handout according to Natalie's comments. You will open a draft of the document, save it with a different name, and then make the changes Natalie requested. First, you will check the document's grammar and spelling, and then you'll move text using two different methods. You will also use Word's Find and Replace feature to replace one version of the company name with another.

Next, you will change the overall look of the document by changing margins, indenting and justifying paragraphs, and copying the formatting from one paragraph to another. You'll create two bulleted lists and one numbered list. Then you'll make the title and subtitle more prominent by centering them, changing their font, and enlarging them. You'll also change the font of the company name in the body of the document, and you'll add bold to the headings to set them off from the rest of the text. You will experiment with changing the document's theme, and finally, you will preview and print the formatted document.

Starting Data Files

Tutorial.02 → Tutorial — Design.docx

Review — Getting.docx, Staff.docx

Case1 — New.docx

Case2 — Moth.docx

Case3 — Resume.docx

Case4 — Flour.docx

Session 2.1

Reviewing the Document

You'll begin by opening Natalie's first draft of the document, which has the filename Design.

To open the document:

▶ **1.** Start Word.

▶ **2.** On the Quick Access Toolbar, click the **Office Button** 🔘, and then click **Open**. The Open dialog box opens.

▶ **3.** Use the options in the Open dialog box to open the **Tutorial** subfolder within the **Tutorial.02** folder included with your Data Files.

▶ **4.** Click **Design** to select the file, if necessary. The name of the selected file appears in the File name text box. See Figure 2-1.

| Figure 2-1 | Open dialog box |

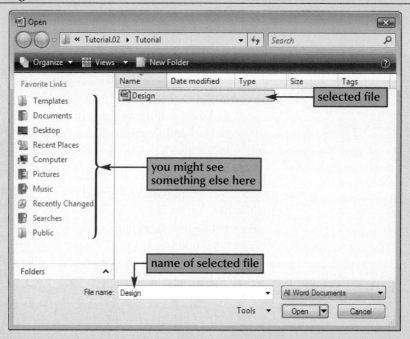

Trouble? If you see "Design.docx" in the folder, it's okay; click Design.docx and continue with Step 5. This just means that Windows is configured to display file extensions. If you can't find the file with or without the file extension, make sure you're looking in the Tutorial subfolder within the Tutorial.02 folder included with your Data Files, and check to make sure the list box next to the File name text box displays All Word Documents or All Files. If you still can't locate the file, ask your instructor or technical support person for help.

▶ **5.** Click the **Open** button. The document opens with the insertion point at the beginning.

Before revising a document for someone else, it's a good idea to familiarize yourself with its overall structure. You'll do that now, and in the process make sure the document is displayed in a way that makes editing it as easy as possible.

To review the document:

▶ **1.** Verify that the document is displayed in Print Layout view, and if necessary, in the Paragraph group, click the **Show/Hide ¶** button ¶ to display nonprinting characters. If the rulers are not visible, switch to the **View** tab, and then click the **Ruler** check box to display the rulers.

▶ **2.** Take a moment to read the document. It consists of a series of headings, with explanatory text below each heading. Right now, the headings (such as "Ask Yourself Some Questions" and "Pick a Style") are hard to spot because they don't look any different from the surrounding text. You'll change that when you format the document. The document also includes some lists; you will format these later in this tutorial to make them easier to read. Natalie used the default font size, 11-point, and the default font, Calibri (Body), for the entire document. She relied on Word's default paragraph spacing to provide a visual separation between paragraphs.

▶ **3.** Scroll down until you can see the line "Stay True to Your Style." The white space after this line is the page's bottom margin. The blue space below the margin indicates a page break. This tells you that the line "Stay True to Your Style" appears on the last line of the first page. Word starts a new page whenever your text fills up a page. The Page box in the lower-left corner of the document window tells you the total number of pages in the document and which page currently contains the insertion point.

Figure 2-2 shows the page break, along with other important elements of the document. Note that in Figure 2-2 the Word window has been zoomed to 80%; this is to make it easy to see several parts of the document at once. At this point, your Zoom setting is probably 100%. To make sure you can see the entire width of the page, you'll select Page width in the Zoom dialog box in the next step.

Document with two pages ◀ **Figure 2-2**

Tip

To hide the blue space between pages, double-click the blue space. To redisplay the blue space, double-click the black line.

► **4.** In the bottom-right corner of the Word window, click the current Zoom setting to open the Zoom dialog box, click **Page width**, and then click the **OK** button to close the Zoom dialog box. Word displays the full width of the document.

Now that you are familiar with Natalie's document, you can turn your attention to the edits she has requested. Natalie's editing marks and notes on the first draft are shown in Figure 2-3.

Figure 2-3 ▶ **Draft of handout with Natalie's edits (page 1)**

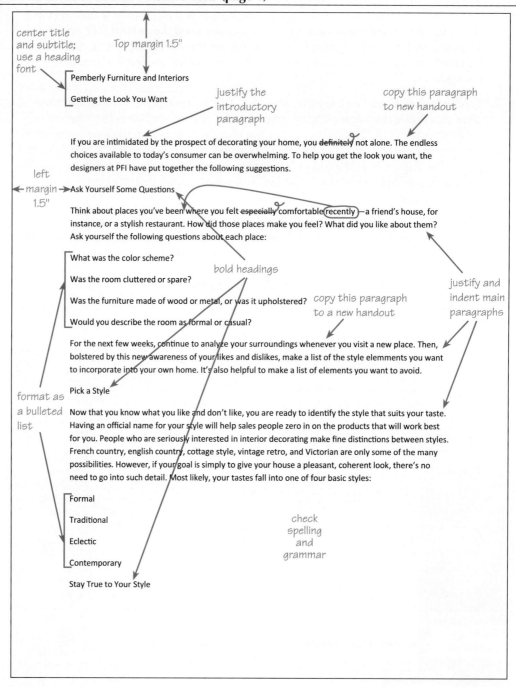

Draft of handout with Natalie's edits (page 2) ◄ **Figure 2-3 (cont.)**

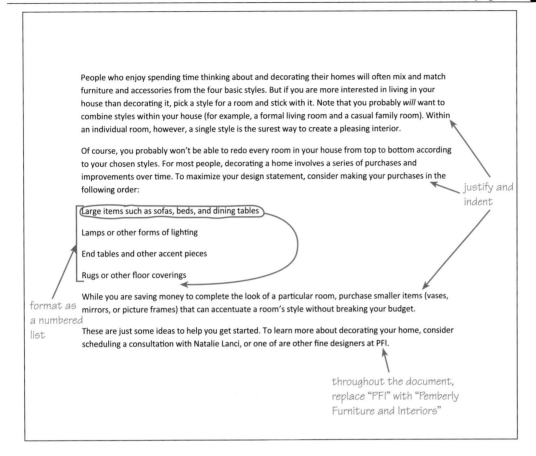

People who enjoy spending time thinking about and decorating their homes will often mix and match furniture and accessories from the four basic styles. But if you are more interested in living in your house than decorating it, pick a style for a room and stick with it. Note that you probably *will* want to combine styles within your house (for example, a formal living room and a casual family room). Within an individual room, however, a single style is the surest way to create a pleasing interior.

Of course, you probably won't be able to redo every room in your house from top to bottom according to your chosen styles. For most people, decorating a home involves a series of purchases and improvements over time. To maximize your design statement, consider making your purchases in the following order:

justify and indent

Large items such as sofas, beds, and dining tables

Lamps or other forms of lighting

End tables and other accent pieces

Rugs or other floor coverings

format as a numbered list

While you are saving money to complete the look of a particular room, purchase smaller items (vases, mirrors, or picture frames) that can accentuate a room's style without breaking your budget.

These are just some ideas to help you get started. To learn more about decorating your home, consider scheduling a consultation with Natalie Lanci, or one of are other fine designers at PFI.

throughout the document, replace "PFI" with "Pemberly Furniture and Interiors"

Before you begin editing the document, you should save it with a new name. Saving the document with a different filename creates a copy of the file and leaves the original file unchanged in case you want to work through the tutorial again.

To save the document with a new name:

► 1. Click the **Office Button** 🔘, and then click **Save As**. The Save As dialog box opens with the current filename highlighted in the File name text box. You could type an entirely new filename, or you could edit the current one.

► 2. Click to the right of the current filename to place the insertion point after the "n" in "Design."

► 3. Press the **spacebar**, and then type **Handout** so that the filename is "Design Handout."

► 4. Verify that the **Tutorial** folder is selected as the location for saving the file.

► 5. Click the **Save** button. The document is saved with the new filename "Design Handout" in the Tutorial folder, and the original Design file closes, remaining unchanged.

Now you're ready to begin working with the document. First, you will check it for spelling and grammatical errors.

Using the Spelling and Grammar Checker

As you type a document, Word marks possible spelling errors with a red wavy underline. When you're working on a document that someone else typed, it's a good idea to start by using the **Spelling and Grammar Checker**, a feature that checks a document word by word for a variety of errors.

Reference Window | **Checking a Document for Spelling and Grammar Errors**

- Move the insertion point to the beginning of the document, click the Review tab on the Ribbon, and then, in the Proofing group, click the Spelling & Grammar button.
- In the Spelling and Grammar dialog box, review any items highlighted in color. Possible grammatical errors appear in green; possible spelling errors appear in red. Review the suggested corrections in the Suggestions list box.
- To accept a suggested correction, click on it in the Suggestions list box, click the Change button to make the correction, and then continue searching the document for errors.
- To skip the current instance of the highlighted text and continue searching the document for errors, click the Ignore Once button.
- Click the Ignore All button to skip all instances of the highlighted text and continue searching the document for errors. Click the Ignore Rule button to skip all instances of a highlighted grammatical error.
- To type your correction directly in the document, click outside the Spelling and Grammar dialog box, make the correction, and then click the Resume button in the Spelling and Grammar dialog box.
- To add an unrecognized word to the dictionary, click the Add to Dictionary button.
- When you see a dialog box informing you that the spelling and grammar check is complete, click the OK button.

You'll see how the Spelling and Grammar Checker works as you check the Design Handout document for mistakes.

To check the Design Handout document for spelling and grammatical errors:

▶ 1. Press the **Ctrl+Home** keys to verify that the insertion point is located at the beginning of the document, to the left of the "P" in "Pemberly Furniture and Interiors."

▶ 2. Click the **Review** tab on the Ribbon, and then, in the Proofing group, click the **Spelling & Grammar** button. The Spelling and Grammar: English (United States) dialog box opens with the word "Pemberly" displayed in red, indicating a possible spelling error. In the document, "Pemberly" is highlighted in blue. Typically, the Suggestions box would contain one or more possible corrections for you to choose from, but in this case, Word doesn't recognize the name of Natalie's company because it is not included in the main dictionary. This isn't really an error. See Figure 2-4.

Spelling and Grammar dialog box Figure 2-4

3. Click the **Ignore All** button. This tells Word to ignore all instances of "Pemberly" throughout the document. Now the first sentence of the document appears in green in the dialog box and in a blue highlight in the document. The Suggestions box tells you that the highlighted text is a sentence fragment. The last part of the sentence should read "you definitely are not alone," but the word "are" is missing. You can fix this problem by clicking outside the Spelling and Grammar dialog box and typing the change directly in the document.

4. Click the blue highlighted sentence outside the Spelling and Grammar dialog box. The blue highlight disappears, and the insertion point appears at the end of the sentence.

   Trouble? If you can't see the entire highlighted sentence, move the mouse pointer over the title bar of the Spelling and Grammar dialog box, press and hold the left mouse button, drag the mouse pointer until the dialog box is out of the way, and then release the mouse button.

5. Click to the left of the "n" in "not," type **are**, and then press the **spacebar**. Verify that the last part of the sentence now reads "you definitely are not alone." (You might notice that the word "definitely" makes the sentence awkward; you will delete this word in the next section.)

You've edited the document to correct the error. Now you need to return to the Spelling and Grammar dialog box to continue checking the document.

To continue checking the document:

1. Click the **Resume** button in the Spelling and Grammar dialog box to continue checking the rest of the document. The misspelled word "elemments" is highlighted in the Spelling and Grammar dialog box and in the document. The correct spelling, "elements," appears in the Suggestions box.

2. Verify that "elements" is highlighted in the Suggestions box, and then click the **Change** button. "Elements" is inserted into the document, and the word "english" is highlighted in the document. This should be "English," with an uppercase "E," instead.

▶ **3.** Verify that "English" is selected in the Suggestions box, and then click the **Change** button. The word "English" is inserted in the document. A message box opens indicating that the spelling and grammar check is complete.

▶ **4.** Click the **OK** button. The Spelling and Grammar dialog box closes. You return to the Design Handout document.

▶ **5.** Click the **Home** tab to display the options related to editing a document again. You'll need to use these options as you continue the tutorial.

Although the Spelling and Grammar Checker is a useful tool, there is no substitute for careful proofreading. Always take the time to read through your document to check for errors the Spelling and Grammar Checker might have missed. Keep in mind that the Spelling and Grammar checker cannot pinpoint phrases that are inaccurate. You'll have to find those yourself. To produce a professional document, you must read it carefully several times. It's a good idea to ask a coworker to read your documents, too.

To proofread the Design Handout document:

▶ **1.** Scroll to the beginning of the document and proofread the document. In the last sentence of the document, notice that the word "are" is used instead of the word "our." You will correct this error in the next section.

▶ **2.** Finish proofreading the Design Handout document, and then click the **Save** button 🖫 on the Quick Access Toolbar to save the changes you've made so far.

Your next job is to delete some text (as shown earlier in Figure 2-3).

Deleting Text

You already have experience using the Backspace and Delete keys to delete a few characters. To delete an entire word or multiple words, it's faster to select the text first. Then you can either replace it with something else by typing over it, or you can delete it by pressing the Delete key. Right now, you need to change the word "are" to "our."

To replace "are" with "our":

▶ **1.** Press the **Ctrl+End** keys. The insertion point moves to the end of the document.

▶ **2.** In the last line of the document, double-click the word **are** (in the phrase "are other fine designers...").

▶ **3.** Type **our**. The selected word is replaced with the correction. The phrase now correctly reads: "...our other fine designers...."

Next, Natalie wants you to delete the word "definitely" in the introductory paragraph at the beginning of the document and the word "especially" in the paragraph below the heading "Ask Yourself Some Questions." You can do this quickly by selecting multiple items and then pressing the Delete key.

To select and delete multiple items:

▶ **1.** Press the **Ctrl+Home** keys. The insertion point is now located at the beginning of the document.

▶ **2.** In the introductory paragraph, which begins "If you are intimidated by...," double-click the word **definitely**. The word and the space following it are selected.

▶ **3.** Press and hold the **Ctrl** key, double-click the word **especially** in the paragraph below the heading "Ask Yourself Some Questions," and then release the **Ctrl** key. At this point the words "definitely" and "especially" should be selected. See Figure 2-5.

Figure 2-5 ◆ **Text to be deleted**

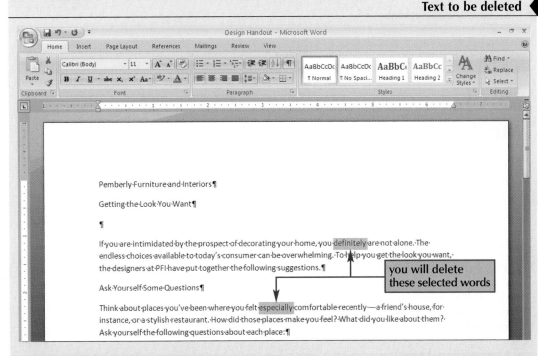

Trouble? If you don't get Step 3 right the first time, click anywhere in the document, and then repeat Steps 2 and 3.

▶ **4.** Press the **Delete** key. The selected items are deleted, and the words around them move in to fill the space. See Figure 2-6.

Figure 2-6 ◆ **Paragraphs after deleting text**

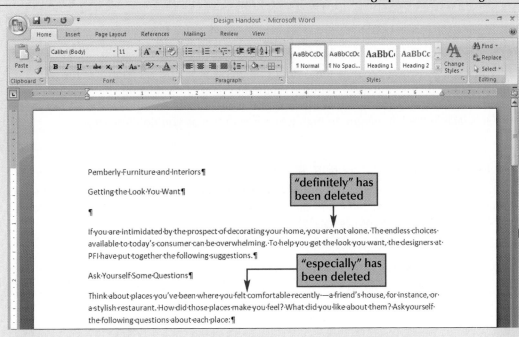

Trouble? If you deleted the wrong text, click the Undo button on the Quick Access Toolbar to reverse your mistake, and then begin again with Step 2.

▶ **5.** Scroll down to display the last line of the document, drag the mouse pointer to select "Natalie Lanci," press the **Delete** key, press the **spacebar** if necessary, and then type your first and last name. This change will make it easier for you to find your document if you print it on a network printer used by other students.

▶ **6.** Save the document.

You have edited the document by replacing "are" with "our" and by removing the text that Natalie marked for deletion. Now you are ready to make the rest of the edits she suggested.

Moving Text in a Document

One of the most useful features of a word-processing program is the ability to move text. For example, Natalie wants to reorder the four points in the section "Stay True to Your Style" on page 2. You could reorder the list by deleting an item and then retyping it at a new location, but it's easier to select and then move the text. Word provides several ways to move text: drag and drop, cut and paste, and copy and paste.

Dragging and Dropping Text

To move text with **drag and drop**, you select the text you want to move, press and hold down the mouse button while you drag the selected text to a new location, and then release the mouse button.

Reference Window | **Dragging and Dropping Text**

- Select the text you want to move.
- Press and hold down the mouse button until the drag-and-drop pointer appears, and then drag the selected text to its new location.
- Use the dotted insertion point as a guide to determine exactly where the text should be inserted.
- Release the mouse button to "drop" the text at the insertion point.

Natalie wants you to change the order of the items in the list on page 2 of the document. You'll use the drag-and-drop method to reorder these items. Because you need to select text before you can move it, you'll get practice using the selection bar (the white space in the left margin) to highlight a line of text as you do these steps.

To move text using drag and drop:

▶ **1.** Scroll up slightly until you see the list of suggested purchases, which begins "Large items such as sofas, beds, and dining tables." Natalie wants you to move the first item to the bottom of the list.

▶ **2.** Move the pointer to the selection bar to the left of the line "Large items such as sofas, beds, and dining tables." The pointer changes to a right-facing arrow ⇗.

▶ **3.** Click in the selection bar to the left of the line "Large items such as sofas, beds, and dining tables." The line is selected. Notice that the paragraph mark at the end of the line is also selected. See Figure 2-7.

Selected text to drag and drop ◀ Figure 2-7

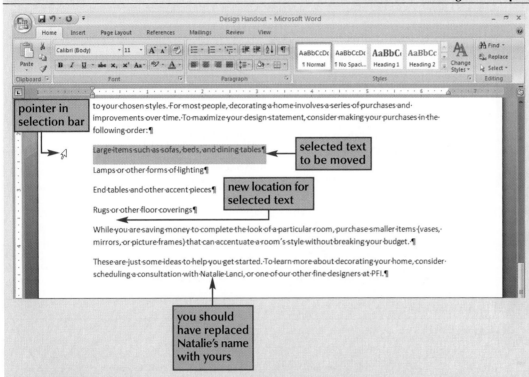

▶ **4.** Position the pointer over the selected text. The pointer changes from a right-facing arrow ⇗ to a left-facing arrow ⇖.

▶ **5.** Press and hold down the mouse button until the drag-and-drop pointer ⇖ appears. Note that a dotted insertion point appears within the selected text. (You may have to move the mouse pointer slightly left or right to see the drag-and-drop pointer or the dotted insertion point.)

▶ **6.** Without releasing the mouse button, drag the selected text down until the dotted insertion point is positioned to the left of the first paragraph below the list (to the left of the "W" in "While you are saving..."). Make sure you use the dotted insertion point, rather than the mouse pointer, to guide the text to its new location. The dotted insertion point indicates exactly where the text will appear when you release the mouse button. See Figure 2-8.

Figure 2-8 **Moving text with drag-and-drop pointer**

7. **Release the mouse button.** The selected text moves to its new location at the end of the list, as shown in Figure 2-9. Near the newly inserted text you might see the Paste Options button, which gives you access to more advanced options related to pasting text. You don't need to use the Paste Options button right now, so you can ignore it. It will disappear when you start performing another task.

Figure 2-9 **Text in new location**

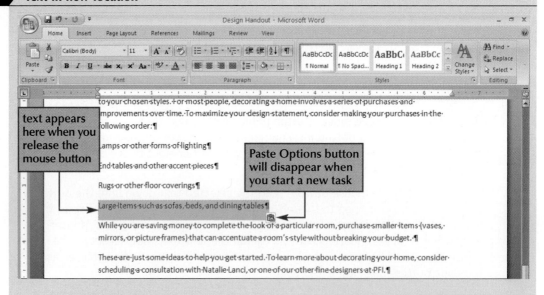

Trouble? If the selected text moves to the wrong location, click the Undo button on the Quick Access Toolbar, and then repeat Steps 2 through 7. Remember to hold down the mouse button until the dotted insertion point appears to the left of the paragraph just below the list.

8. **Deselect** the highlighted text by clicking anywhere in the document, and then save the document.

Dragging and dropping works well if you're moving text a short distance in a document. For moving text longer distances, another method, called cut and paste, works better. You can also use cut and paste to move text short distances, if you find that you prefer it over drag and drop.

Cutting or Copying and Pasting Text

The key to cutting and pasting is the **Clipboard**, a temporary storage area on your computer that holds text or graphics until you need them. To **cut** means to remove something from a document and place it on the Clipboard. Once you've cut something, you can paste it somewhere else. To **paste** means to place a copy of whatever is on the Clipboard into the document; it gets pasted at the insertion point.

To **cut and paste**, you select the text you want to cut (or remove) from the document, click the Cut button, and then use the Paste button to paste (or insert) it into the document in a new location. If you don't want to remove the text from its original location, you can copy it (rather than cutting it), and then paste the copy in a new location. To **copy** means to copy text (or other material, such as pictures) to the Clipboard, leaving the material in its original location.

Note that when you paste an item from the Clipboard into a document, the item also remains on the Clipboard so you can paste it again somewhere else if you want.

Cutting (or Copying) and Pasting Text | Reference Window

- Select the text or graphics you want to cut or copy.
- To remove the text or graphics, click the Cut button in the Clipboard group on the Home tab, or to copy, click the Copy button in the Clipboard group on the Home tab.
- Move the insertion point to the target location in the document.
- Click the Paste button in the Clipboard group on the Home tab.

If you need to keep track of multiple pieces of cut or copied text, it's helpful to open the **Clipboard task pane**, a special part of the Word window that displays the contents of the Clipboard. You open the Clipboard task pane by clicking the Clipboard button on the Home tab. When the Clipboard task pane is not displayed, the Clipboard can hold only one item at a time. (Each newly copied item replaces the current contents of the Clipboard.) However, when the Clipboard task pane is displayed, the Clipboard can store up to 24 items. The last item cut or copied to the Clipboard is the first item listed in the Clipboard task pane.

As indicated in Figure 2-3, Natalie suggested moving the word "recently" (in the paragraph under the heading "Ask Yourself Some Questions") to a new location. You'll use cut and paste to move this word.

To move text using cut and paste:

▶ **1.** Scroll up until you can see the paragraph below the heading "Ask Yourself Some Questions" on page 1.

▶ **2.** Double-click the word **recently**. As you can see in Figure 2-10, you need to move this word to after the phrase "places you've been."

Figure 2-10 **Text to move using cut and paste**

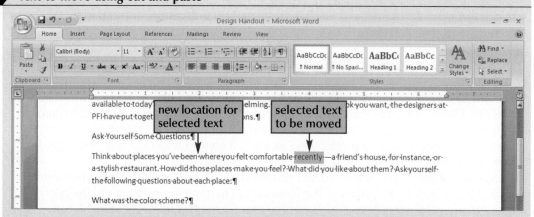

3. In the Clipboard group on the Home tab, click the **Cut** button ✂. The selected text is removed from the document.

    Trouble? If the Clipboard task pane opens, your computer is set up to have it open by default when you click the Cut or Copy buttons. Click its Close button for now. You'll have a chance to use the Clipboard task pane shortly.

    Trouble? If you don't see the Cut button in the Clipboard group, you may have forgotten to switch back to the Home tab earlier. Click the Home tab on the Ribbon and repeat Step 3.

4. In the same line, click to the left of the "w" in "where." The insertion point is now located between the "w" and the blank space after the word "been."

5. In the Clipboard group, click the **Paste** button. The word "recently" appears in its new location. Note that Word also included a space after the word "recently," so that the sentence reads "...places you've been recently where you felt...." See Figure 2-11.

    Trouble? If a menu opens below the Paste button, you clicked the Paste button arrow instead of the Paste button. Press the Esc key to close the menu, and then begin again with Step 5, taking care not to click the arrow below the Paste button.

Figure 2-11 **The word "recently" pasted in new location**

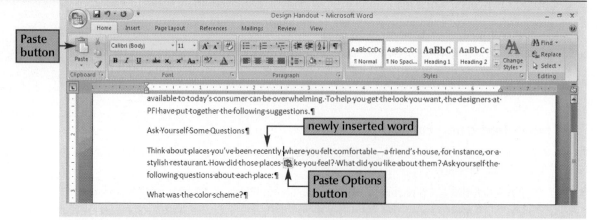

Natalie mentions that she'll be using two paragraphs from the Design Handout document as the basis for a new handout entitled "Formal Designs." She asks you to copy that information and paste it in a new document. You can do this using copy and paste. In the process, you'll have a chance to use the Clipboard task pane.

To copy and paste text into a new document:

▶ **1.** In the Clipboard group, click the **Dialog Box Launcher**. The Clipboard task pane opens on the left side of the document window. It contains the word "recently," which you copied to the Clipboard in the last set of steps. The document zooms out so that you can still see the full width of the page, even though the Clipboard task pane is open. See Figure 2-12. To minimize the clutter on the Clipboard, you will delete its current contents in the next step.

Clipboard task pane | **Figure 2-12**

- Dialog Box Launcher opens the Clipboard task pane
- deletes the contents of the Clipboard
- item just copied to the Clipboard
- Clipboard task pane
- document zooms out to accommodate task pane

▶ **2.** Click the **Clear All** button near the top of the task pane. The current contents of the Clipboard are deleted, and you see the following message on the Clipboard task pane: "Clipboard empty. Copy or cut to collect items."

▶ **3.** Move the mouse pointer to the selection bar and double-click in the margin next to the paragraph that begins "If you are intimidated by the prospect...." The entire paragraph is selected.

▶ **4.** In the Clipboard group, click the **Copy** button 📋. The first part of the paragraph appears in the Clipboard task pane, but a copy of all the text you selected—the whole paragraph—is now stored on the Clipboard.

▶ **5.** If necessary, scroll down until you can see the paragraph below the list of questions, which begins "For the next few weeks, continue...."

▶ **6.** Select the paragraph that begins "For the next few weeks, continue...."

▶ **7.** Click the **Copy** button. The first part of the paragraph appears in the Clipboard task pane, as shown in Figure 2-13.

Tip

To have the Clipboard task pane open each time you cut or copy an item, click Options at the bottom of the Clipboard task pane, and then select Show Office Clipboard Automatically.

Figure 2-13   Items in the Clipboard task pane

Now you can use the Clipboard task pane to insert the copied text into a new document. You'll start by opening a new, blank document.

To insert the copied text into the new document:

▶ 1. Click the **Office Button** (⊞), click **New**, verify that **Blank document** is selected, and then click the **Create** button. A new, blank document opens.

▶ 2. If the Clipboard task pane is not open, click the **Dialog Box Launcher** in the Clipboard group to open it.

▶ 3. In the Clipboard task pane, click the item that begins "**For the next few weeks**...." The text is inserted in the document.

▶ 4. Click the item that begins "**If you are intimidated by**...." The text is inserted as the second paragraph in the document.

▶ 5. Save the document as **Formal Designs** in the Tutorial.02\Tutorial folder.

▶ 6. Close the Formal Designs document. Natalie will be using this document later. You return to the Design Handout document, where the Clipboard task pane is still open. You are finished using the Clipboard task pane. In the next step you will clear the Clipboard so that you can start with an empty Clipboard when you begin work on the Review Assignments and Case Problems at the end of this tutorial.

7. Click the **Clear All** button on the Clipboard task pane. The copied items are removed from the Clipboard.

8. Click the **Close** button ⊠ on the Clipboard task pane. The Clipboard task pane closes.

9. Click anywhere in the document to deselect the highlighted paragraph, and then save the document.

Tip

The Clipboard can hold a total of 24 items. Unless you clear the Clipboard, the items you copy to it will remain there until you close Word.

Finding and Replacing Text

When you're working with a longer document, the quickest and easiest way to locate a particular character, word, or phrase is to use the **Find and Replace dialog box**. This dialog box contains three tabs:

- Find, for finding a word or phrase in a document (for example, you need to know where you referred to "textiles" in a document on interior design)
- Replace, for finding a word or phrase in a document and replacing it with something else (for example, you want to replace "formal design" with "formal style" throughout a document)
- Go To, for moving the cursor directly to a specific part of a document (for example, you want to go directly to page 29)

To open the Find and Replace dialog box, click the Find button or the Replace button (in the Editing group on the Home tab), depending on what you want to do. For example, to find a word or phrase, click the Find button, type the text you want to find in the Find what text box, and then click the Find Next button. The text you type in the Find what text box is known as the **search text**. After you click the Find Next button, Word finds and highlights the first instance of the search text. You continue clicking Find Next to find more occurrences of the search text in your document.

To replace text with something else, click the Replace button, and then type your search text in the Find what text box and the text you want to substitute in the Replace with text box. As with the Find feature, you click the Find Next button to find the next occurrence of the search text; Word stops and highlights each occurrence, allowing you to determine whether or not to substitute the replacement text. If you want to substitute the highlighted occurrence, click the Replace button. If you want to substitute every occurrence of the search text with the replacement text, without locating and reviewing each occurrence, you can click the Replace All button.

Finding and Replacing the Right Words		InSight

When using the Replace All button with single words, keep in mind that the search text might be found within other words. To prevent Word from making incorrect substitutions in such cases, it's a good idea to select the Find whole words only check box. (If you don't see this check box, click the More button to display additional options.) For example, suppose you want to replace the word "figure" with "illustration." Unless you select the Find whole words only check box, Word replaces "figure" in "configure" with "illustration" so the word becomes "conillustration."

Reference Window | Finding and Replacing Text

- Click either the Find button or the Replace button on the Home tab.
- Click the More button to expand the dialog box to display additional options, including the Find whole words only option. If you see the Less button, the additional options are already displayed.
- In the Search list box, select Down if you want to search from the insertion point to the end of the document, select Up if you want to search from the insertion point to the beginning of the document, or select All to search the entire document.
- Type the characters you want to find in the Find what text box.
- If you are replacing text, type the replacement text in the Replace with text box.
- Click the Find whole words only check box to search for complete words.
- Click the Match case check box to insert the replacement text with the same case (upper or lower) as in the Replace with text box. For example, if the Replace with text box contained the words "Pemberly Interiors," this would ensure that Word inserted the text with a capital (uppercase) "P" and a capital (uppercase) "I."
- Click the Find Next button.
- Click the Replace button to substitute the found text with the replacement text and find the next occurrence.
- Click the Replace All button to substitute all occurrences of the found text with the replacement text, without reviewing each occurence.

Throughout the document, Natalie wants to replace the initials "PFI" with the full company name, "Pemberly Furniture and Interiors." You'll use the Replace feature to make this change quickly and easily.

To replace "PFI" with "Pemberly Furniture and Interiors":

▶ 1. Press the **Ctrl+Home** keys to move the insertion point to the beginning of the document.

▶ 2. In the Editing group on the Home tab, click the **Replace** button. The Find and Replace dialog box opens, with the Replace tab displayed.

▶ 3. If you see a **More** button in the lower-left corner of the dialog box, click it to display the additional search options. (If you see a Less button, the additional options are already displayed.) Verify that **All** is selected in the Search list box, so Word will search the entire document.

▶ 4. Click the **Find what** text box if necessary, type **PFI**, press the **Tab** key, and then, in the Replace with text box, type **Pemberly Furniture and Interiors**.

   Trouble? If you already see the text "PFI" and "Pemberly Furniture and Interiors" in your Find and Replace dialog box, someone has recently performed these steps on your computer without closing Word afterward. Skip Step 4 and continue with Step 5.

▶ 5. Click the **Match case** check box to insert a check. This ensures that Word will search only for "PFI" and not "pfi" in the document.

▶ 6. Click the **Find whole words only** check box to insert a check. Your Find and Replace dialog box should look like Figure 2-14.

Find and Replace dialog box ◄ **Figure 2-14**

7. Click the **Replace All** button to replace all occurrences of the search text with the replacement text. When Word finishes making the replacements, you see a message box telling you that two replacements were made.

8. Click the **OK** button to close the message box, and then click the **Close** button in the Find and Replace dialog box to return to the document. The full company name has been inserted near the beginning of the document, as shown in Figure 2-15. If you scroll down to the end of the document, you'll see that it was also inserted in the last sentence.

Document with "Pemberly Furniture and Interiors" inserted ◄ **Figure 2-15**

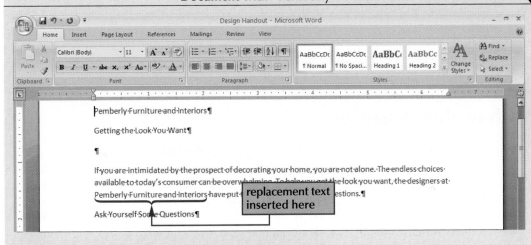

9. Save the document.

InSight | **Searching for Formatting**

You can search for formatting, such as bold or italics, using the Find and Replace dialog box in the same way that you can find text. For example, you might want to check a document to see where you used bold. Or you might need to find where you used a certain font, font size, or style. This is especially useful in long documents where scrolling to look for something would take a long time. To search for formatting, click the Format button at the bottom of the Find and Replace dialog box, click the category of formatting that you want to look for (such as Font, Paragraph, Style, and so on), and then select the formatting you want to find. You can also use the Replace tab to replace formatting in the same way you use it to replace text. To replace formatting, click the Replace tab, and then repeat the previous steps to specify the formatting that should replace the other formatting. Whether you are replacing formatting or not, note that you can look for formatting that occurs only on specific text, or you can look for formatting that occurs anywhere in a document. If you're looking for formatting on certain text (such as all instances of "Contemporary Furniture" that are bold), enter the text in the Find what text box and then specify the formatting you're looking for. To find formatting on any text in a document, leave the Find what text box empty and then specify the formatting.

You have completed the content changes Natalie requested. In the next session, you will make changes that affect the document's appearance.

Review | **Session 2.1 Quick Check**

1. True or False: You should move the insertion point to the beginning of the document before starting the Spelling and Grammar checker.
2. True or False: You need to select text before you can move it.
3. Explain how to drag and drop text.
4. Explain how to cut and paste text.
5. Suppose you want to find a word in a document. How do you open the Find and Replace dialog box?
6. How can you ensure that Word will insert "ZIP code" instead of "zip code" when you use the Find and Replace dialog box?

Session 2.2

Changing Margins

When you **format** a document, you make changes that affect the way the document looks. You'll start formatting Natalie's handout by adjusting the document's margins. By default, the margins for a Word document are one inch on the top, bottom, and sides.

When adjusting a document's margins, you'll find that the rulers are essential. They show you the current margin settings, as well as the amount that individual paragraphs are indented from the margin. On the horizontal ruler, the right edge of the left margin serves as the zero point, with the numbers to the right measuring the distance to the right edge of the page, and the numbers on the left measuring the distance to the left edge of the page. This allows you to see the exact width of the left margin at a glance. See Figure 2-16. The measurements on the vertical ruler work similarly, with the bottom edge of the top margin serving as the zero point from which all other vertical distances are measured.

Using the horizontal ruler to view margins ◄ **Figure 2-16**

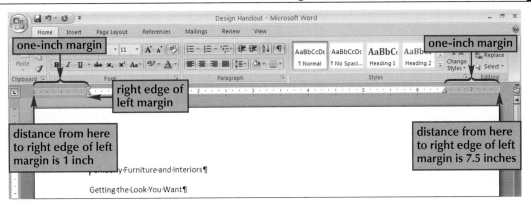

Tip

The Zoom setting affects how much of the margin you can see on the screen. If you zoom in to make the text larger and easier to read, you see less of the margin. If you zoom out, you see more of the margin.

As you'll see in the upcoming steps, you can change the page margins in the Page Setup dialog box. You can also quickly adjust a document's margins in Print Layout view by clicking an option in the Margins menu. You'll have a chance to practice these techniques in the Case Problems at the end of this tutorial.

Changing Margins for a Document | Reference Window

- Make sure no text is selected, and then, in the Page Setup group on the Page Layout tab, click the Dialog Box Launcher. If necessary, click the Margins tab to display the margin settings.
- Use the arrows to change the settings in the Top, Bottom, Left, or Right text boxes, or type a new margin value in each text box.
- Make sure the Apply to list box displays Whole document.
- Click the OK button.
- To choose from groups of predefined margin settings, click the Margins button in the Page Setup group on the Page Layout tab. In the Margins menu, click the group of margin settings that is appropriate for your document.

You need to change the top and left margins of the Design Handout document to 1.5 inches, per Natalie's note in Figure 2-3. The left margin needs to be wider than the right to allow space for holes so that the document can be inserted in a three-ring binder. Also, the top margin needs to be wider than the bottom margin so the document can be printed on the company letterhead. In the next set of steps, you'll change the margins using the Page Setup dialog box.

To change the margins in the Design Handout document:

▶ **1.** Click anywhere in the document to make sure no text is selected.

▶ **2.** Click the **Page Layout** tab on the Ribbon, and then, in the Page Setup group, click the **Margins** button. The Margins menu appears, displaying some common margin settings. The Normal option contains the default margin settings. You can always click Normal to return a document to the default margin settings. The item at the top of the menu, Last Custom Setting, reflects the last margin settings selected in the Page Setup dialog box. See Figure 2-17.

Figure 2-17 | Margins menu

It's possible that the Last Custom Setting option matches the margin settings you want to use in the Design Handout document, but if so, ignore it. Instead, you'll open the Page Setup dialog box in the next step, so you can practice using it. You can open the Page Setup dialog box via the Custom Margins option at the bottom of the Margins menu, or you can use the Dialog Box Launcher in the Page Setup group on the Page Layout tab. You'll try the Custom Margins option now.

3. At the bottom of the Margins menu, click **Custom Margins**. The Page Setup dialog box opens.

4. Click the **Margins** tab, if it is not already selected, to display the margin settings. The Top margin setting is selected. See Figure 2-18. As you complete the following steps, keep an eye on the Preview in the bottom-left part of the dialog box, which changes to reflect changes you make to the margins.

Page Setup dialog box ◄ **Figure 2-18**

- Margins tab selected
- Top margin selected
- preview changes to show the margins you select
- new margin settings will apply to the whole document

▶ **5.** Type **1.5** to change the Top margin setting. (You do not have to type the inches symbol.)

▶ **6.** Press the **Tab** key twice to select the Left text box and highlight the current margin setting. The text area in the Preview box moves down to reflect the larger top margin.

▶ **7.** Verify that the insertion point is in the Left text box, type **1.5**, and then press the **Tab** key. The left margin in the Preview box increases.

▶ **8.** In the Apply to list box, make sure **Whole document** is selected, and then click the **OK** button to return to your document. Notice that the ruler has changed to reflect the new margin settings and the resulting reduced page area. The document text is now 6 inches wide. See Figure 2-19.

Figure 2-19 **Rulers after setting top and left margins to 1.5 inches**

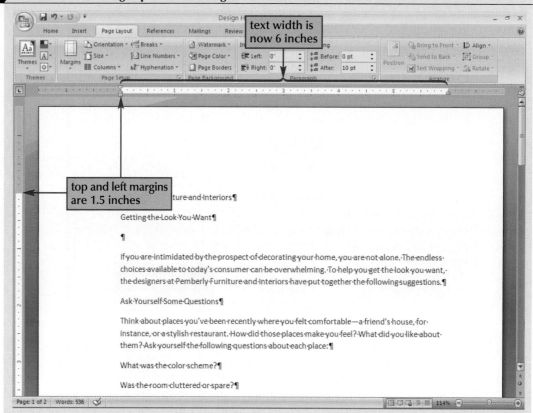

Trouble? If a double-dotted line and the words "Section Break" appear in your document, Whole document wasn't selected in the Apply to list box. If this occurs, click the Undo button on the Quick Access Toolbar and repeat Steps 1 through 8, making sure you select the Whole document option in the Apply to list box.

9. Save the document and then click the **Home** tab.

InSight	**Using Margins to Insert Space**

Recall that in Tutorial 1 you inserted a series of blank paragraphs at the beginning of a document in order to allow room for the company letterhead. Now that you know how to change margins, you should use this method to insert extra space in a document rather than inserting blank paragraphs. Adjusting margins allows you to be more precise, because you can specify an exact amount. Also, if you know you will usually need to use a particular margin setting for your documents, you can click the Default button on the Margins tab of the Page Setup dialog box to make your settings the default for all new documents.

In the next section, you will make some changes that will affect the way certain paragraphs are positioned between the left and right margins.

Aligning Text

The term **alignment** refers to the way a paragraph lines up horizontally between the margins. By default, text is aligned along the left margin and is **ragged**, or uneven, along the right margin. This is called **left alignment**. With **right alignment**, the text is aligned along the right margin and is ragged along the left margin. With **center alignment**, text is centered between the left and right margins and is ragged along both the left and right margins. With **justified alignment**, full lines of text are spaced between both the left and the right margins, and the text is not ragged. Text in newspaper columns is often justified. See Figure 2-20.

Varieties of text alignment ◄ **Figure 2-20**

left alignment If you are intimidated by the prospect of decorating your home, you are not alone. The endless choices available to today's consumer can be overwhelming. To help you get the look you want, the designers at Pemberly Furniture and Interiors have put together the following suggestions.	**right alignment** If you are intimidated by the prospect of decorating your home, you are not alone. The endless choices available to today's consumer can be overwhelming. To help you get the look you want, the designers at Pemberly Furniture and Interiors have put together the following suggestions.
center alignment If you are intimidated by the prospect of decorating your home, you are not alone. The endless choices available to today's consumer can be overwhelming.	**justified alignment** If you are intimidated by the prospect of decorating your home, you are not alone. The endless choices available to today's consumer can be overwhelming. To help you get the look you want, the designers at Pemberly Furniture and Interiors have put together the following suggestions.

The Paragraph group on the Home tab includes a button for each of the four major types of alignment. The Mini toolbar, which appears when you select text in a document, includes just the Center button, which is commonly used to center titles in a document.

To align a single paragraph, click anywhere in that paragraph and then click the appropriate alignment button. To align multiple paragraphs, select the paragraphs first, and then click an alignment button.

Figure 2-3 indicates that the title and subtitle of the Design Handout should be centered and that the main paragraphs should be justified. First, you'll center the title and subtitle using the Center button on the Mini toolbar.

To center-align the title:

▶ **1.** Click and drag in the selection bar to select the title ("Pemberly Furniture and Interiors") and the subtitle ("Getting the Look You Want"). A faint image of the Mini toolbar appears near the selected text. To fully display the Mini toolbar, you need to move the mouse pointer over it.

> **2.** Move the mouse pointer near the Mini toolbar. The Mini toolbar is now fully visible and remains visible until you move the mouse pointer away from it. It contains one alignment button, the Center button. The Align Text Left button on the Home tab is highlighted in orange, indicating that the selected text is currently left-aligned. See Figure 2-21.

Figure 2-21   Mini toolbar visible over selected text

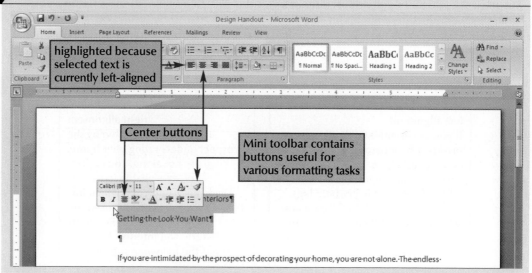

> **3.** On the Mini toolbar, click the **Center** button. The text is centered between the left and right margins. Both Center buttons are now highlighted in orange, indicating that the selected text is centered. The Mini toolbar remains visible until you move the mouse pointer away from it.
>
> **Trouble?** If the Mini toolbar disappears before you click the Center button, click anywhere in the document to deselect the text, and then repeat Steps 1 through 3.

Next, you'll justify the text in the first two main paragraphs.

To justify the first two main paragraphs:

> **1.** Click anywhere in the paragraph that begins "If you are intimidated by...." If the Mini toolbar was still visible, it disappears and the insertion point is now located in the paragraph you want to align. The Align Text Left button in the Paragraph group is highlighted in orange, indicating that the paragraph containing the insertion point is left-aligned.
>
> **2.** In the Paragraph group, click the **Justify** button. The paragraph text spreads out so that it lines up evenly along the left and right margins.
>
> **3.** Scroll down if necessary and click in the paragraph that begins "Think about places you've been recently.... "
>
> **4.** Click the **Justify** button in the Paragraph group again. The text is evenly spaced between the left and right margins. See Figure 2-22.

Justified paragraphs | Figure 2-22

You'll justify the other paragraphs later. But first, you turn your attention to indenting a paragraph.

Indenting a Paragraph

When you **indent** a paragraph, you move the entire paragraph to the right. You can use the indent buttons on the Home tab to increase or decrease paragraph indenting in increments of 0.5 inches. The **indent markers** on the horizontal ruler allow you to see at a glance a paragraph's current indent settings. See Figure 2-23.

Indent markers on horizontal ruler | Figure 2-23

By dragging the indent markers individually, you can create specialized indents, such as a **hanging indent** (where all lines except the first line of the paragraph are indented from the left margin) or a **right indent** (where all lines of the paragraph are indented from the right margin). You'll have a chance to try some of these specialized indents in the Case Problems at the end of this tutorial. In this document, though, you only need to indent the main paragraphs 0.5 inches. When you do a simple indent like this, the three indent markers, shown stacked on top of one another in Figure 2-23, move as a unit along with the paragraphs you are indenting.

To indent a paragraph using the Increase Indent button:

▶ **1.** Verify that the insertion point is still located within the paragraph that begins "Think about places you've been...."

2. In the Paragraph group, click the **Increase Indent** button 📜 twice. (Be careful not to click the Decrease Indent button by mistake.) The entire paragraph and the stacked indent markers in the horizontal ruler move right 0.5 inches each time you click the Increase Indent button. The paragraph is indented 1 inch, which is 0.5 inches more than Natalie wants.

3. Click the **Decrease Indent** button 📜 in the Paragraph group to move the paragraph left 0.5 inches. The paragraph is now indented 0.5 inches from the left margin. Don't be concerned about the list of questions. You will indent this list later, when you format it as a bulleted list. See Figure 2-24.

Figure 2-24	Indented paragraph

You could continue to indent and then justify each paragraph. However, it's faster to use the Format Painter button. With the Format Painter, you can easily copy both the indentation and alignment changes to the remaining paragraphs in the document.

Using the Format Painter

The **Format Painter** makes it easy to copy all the formatting features of one paragraph to other paragraphs (or from one heading to other headings, or from one word to other words). You can use this button to copy formatting to just one item or to multiple items.

Using the Format Painter | Reference Window

- Select the text whose formatting you want to copy. If you are trying to copy the formatting of an entire paragraph, you can just click anywhere in the paragraph.
- To copy formatting to one item, click the Format Painter button in the Clipboard group on the Home tab, and then select the text you want to format, or click anywhere in the paragraph you want to format.
- To copy formatting to multiple items, double-click the Format Painter button in the Clipboard group on the Home tab, and then select, one by one, each text item you want to format, or click anywhere in each paragraph you want to format. When you are finished, click the Format Painter button again to deselect it.

You'll use the Format Painter now to copy the formatting of the second paragraph to the other main paragraphs. The first step is to move the insertion point to the paragraph whose formatting you want to copy.

To copy paragraph formatting with the Format Painter:

▶ **1.** Verify that the insertion point is located in the paragraph that begins "Think about places you've been...."

▶ **2.** In the Clipboard group, double-click the **Format Painter** button 🖌. When you double-click the Format Painter button, it stays selected until you click it again; you can paste the copied formatting as many times as you wish. Also, notice that when you move the pointer over text, the pointer changes to 🖌I to indicate that the format of the paragraph containing the insertion point can be "painted" (or copied) onto another paragraph.

▶ **3.** Scroll down, and then click anywhere in the paragraph that begins "For the next few weeks...." The format of this paragraph changes to match the format of the indented and justified paragraph above it. See Figure 2-25. Two paragraphs are now indented and justified. The Format Painter pointer is still visible, indicating that you can continue formatting paragraphs with it.

Formatting copied with Format Painter ◀ **Figure 2-25**

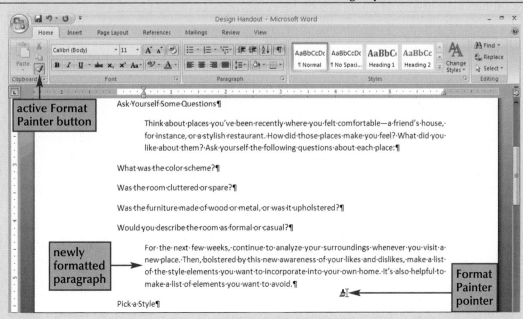

Now you need to continue copying the indented and justified formatting to the main paragraphs of text. You do not want to copy this formatting to the document headings or to the several lists. (You'll format these elements later in this tutorial.)

▶ **4.** Scroll down and click in the paragraph below the "Pick a Style" subheading, which begins "Now that you know what you like...." Also, click the paragraphs that begin "People who enjoy spending time..." and "Of course you probably won't be able...." Finally, click the paragraph that begins "While you are saving money...." Do not click the document title or subtitle, the lists, or the last paragraph of text.

Trouble? If you click a paragraph and the formatting doesn't change to match the indented and justified paragraphs, you single-clicked the Format Painter button rather than double-clicked it. Move the insertion point to a paragraph that has the desired format, double-click the Format Painter button, and then repeat Step 4.

Trouble? If you accidentally click a heading or one line of a list, click the Undo button on the Quick Access Toolbar to return the line to its original formatting. Then select a paragraph that has the desired format, double-click the Format Painter button, and repeat Step 4 to finish copying the format to the desired paragraphs.

▶ **5.** After you are finished formatting paragraphs with the Format Painter pointer, click the **Format Painter** button 🖋 to turn off the feature.

▶ **6.** Save the document.

You've saved considerable time using the Format Painter to format all the main paragraphs in your document with the correct indentation and alignment. Your next job is to make the lists easier to read by adding bullets and numbers.

Adding Bullets and Numbers

You can emphasize a list of items by adding a heavy dot, or **bullet**, before each item in the list. Bulleted lists are usually much easier to read and follow than lists that do not have bullets. For a list of items that have a particular order (such as steps in a procedure), you can use numbers instead of bullets. Natalie's printout requests that you add bullets to the list of questions on page 1 to make them stand out. She also wants you to add bullets to the list of four basic styles on page 1.

To apply bullets to a list of questions:

▶ **1.** Scroll up until you see the list of questions on page 1, which begins "What was the color scheme?"

▶ **2.** Select the four questions in the list.

▶ **3.** In the Paragraph group, click the **Bullets** button 📇. Black circles called bullets appear before each item in the list. Also, the list is indented and the paragraph spacing between the items is reduced. After reviewing the default, circular bullet style in the document, Natalie decides she would prefer square bullets.

Trouble? If no bullets are applied and a menu opens instead, you clicked the Bullets button arrow instead of the Bullets button. Press the Esc key to close the menu, and then repeat Step 3, taking care to click the Bullets button.

▶ **4.** In the Paragraph group, click the **Bullets button arrow** 📇▾ (make sure to click the arrow, not just the button). A gallery of bullet styles opens.

At the top of the gallery of bullet styles is the Recently Used Bullets section; these are the bullet styles that have been used since you started Word. You'll probably see just the round black bullets, which were applied by default when you clicked the Bullets button. However, if you had used several different bullet styles, you would see them here. Below the Recently Used Bullets section is the **Bullet Library**, which offers a variety of bullet styles. For the Design Handout, you want to use a black square, which is an option in the Bullet Library. See Figure 2-26.

Bullets gallery   Figure 2-26

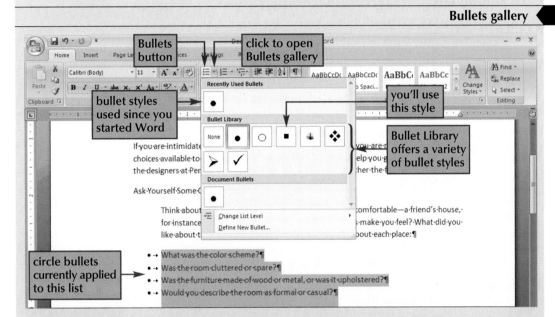

5. Move the mouse pointer over the options in the Bullet Library and observe a live preview of the bullet styles in the document. The blue highlight disappears from the selected list in the document so you can clearly see the live preview.

6. Click the **black square** in the Bullet Library. The round bullets are replaced with square bullets.

7. To align the bullets with the first paragraph, make sure the list is still selected, and then, in the Paragraph group, click the **Increase Indent** button. The bulleted list moves to the right. Figure 2-27 shows the indented bulleted list.

Indented bulleted list   Figure 2-27

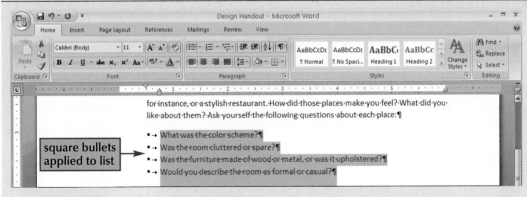

Next, you need to format the list of decorating styles on page 1 with square bullets. When you first start Word, the Bullets button applies the round bullets you saw earlier. But after you select a new bullet style, the Bullets button applies that last bullet style you used. So, to add square bullets to the decorating styles list, you just have to select the list and click the Bullets button.

To add bullets to the list of decorating styles:

▶ **1.** Scroll down and select the list of four basic decorating styles (**Formal**, **Traditional**, **Eclectic**, **Contemporary**) at the bottom of page 1.

▶ **2.** In the Paragraph group, click the **Bullets** button ▤, and then click the **Increase Indent** button ▤. The list is now formatted with square black bullets. The list is also indented, similar to the list of questions shown earlier in Figure 2-27.

Your next step is to format the list of suggested purchases on page 2. Natalie wants you to format this information as a numbered list because it specifies purchases in a sequential order. Adding numbers to a list of items is a quick task thanks to the Numbering button, which numbers selected paragraphs with consecutive numbers. If you insert a new paragraph, delete a paragraph, or reorder the paragraphs, Word adjusts the numbers to make sure they remain consecutive.

To apply numbers to the list of suggested purchases:

▶ **1.** Scroll down and select the list that begins with **Lamps or other forms of lighting** and ends with **Large items such as sofas, beds, and dining tables**.

▶ **2.** In the Paragraph group, click the **Numbering** button ▤. Consecutive numbers appear in front of each item in the list, with a period after each number. As you'll see in the next step, you can choose from more options by clicking the Numbering button arrow instead.

Trouble? If you see a gallery of numbering options, you clicked the Numbering button arrow instead of the Numbering button. Press the Esc key to close the gallery, and then click the Numbering button.

▶ **3.** Make sure the list is still selected in the document, and then click the **Numbering button arrow** ▤▾. A gallery of numbering formats opens. Recently used numbering formats appear at the top of the list. Below the recently used formats you see the **Numbering Library**, which contains a variety of numbering formats. The style currently applied to the numbered list is highlighted in orange. You can move the mouse pointer over the options in the Numbering Library to see a live preview of the other formats in the document. See Figure 2-28.

Numbering Gallery | Figure 2-28

4. Move the mouse pointer over the options in the Numbering Library to display the live preview in the document. The blue highlight disappears from the selected list in the document so you can clearly see the live preview.

5. In the first row of the Numbering Library, click the far-right option, which shows numbers with a parenthesis after each number. The Numbering Gallery closes and each number is now followed by a parenthesis.

6. Make sure the list is still selected, and then in the Paragraph group, click the **Increase Indent** button. The list moves to the right so that the numbers align with the paragraph of text above it.

7. Click anywhere in the document to deselect the text. Figure 2-29 shows the indented and numbered list.

Indented numbered list | Figure 2-29

The text of the document is now properly aligned and indented. The bullets and numbers make the lists easy to read and give readers visual clues about the type of information they contain. Next, you need to adjust the formatting of individual words.

Emphasizing Text Using Bold and Italic

You can emphasize text by formatting it with bold, underline, or italic. These styles help make specific words or phrases stand out. You add bold, underline, or italics by using the corresponding buttons in the Font group on the Home tab. These buttons are **toggle buttons**, which means you can click them once to format the selected text, and click again to remove the formatting from the selected text.

Natalie wants to draw attention to the headings by formatting them in bold.

To format the headings in bold:

▶ 1. On page 1, click in the selection bar to select the heading **Ask Yourself Some Questions**.

▶ 2. In the Font group, click the **Bold** button **B** . The heading is formatted in bold. In the next step, you'll learn a useful method for repeating the task you just performed.

▶ 3. Scroll down and click in the selection bar to select the next heading in the document ("Pick a Style"). Press the **F4** key. The selected heading is formatted in bold. The F4 key repeats your most recent action. It is especially helpful when formatting parts of a document.

▶ 4. Select the last heading, **Stay True to Your Style** (at the bottom of page 1), and then press the **F4** key.

▶ 5. Click anywhere in the document to deselect the text, and then scroll up to return to the beginning of the document. The three headings appear in bold. Two of them are shown in Figure 2-30.

| Figure 2-30 | Formatting headings with bold |

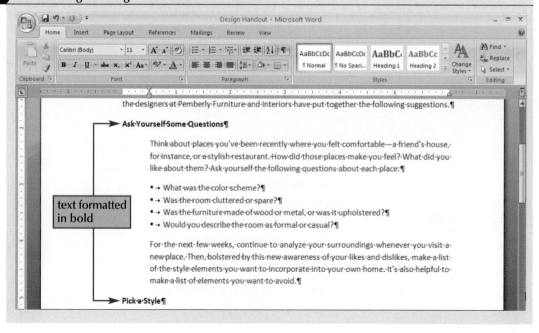

Now that it is formatted in bold, it's easy to see that the last heading, "Stay True to Your Style," is stranded at the bottom of page 1. The handout would look better if the heading was at the top of page 2, just above the first paragraph of the "Stay True to Your Style" section. To fix this problem, you need to tell Word to keep one paragraph (the heading paragraph) on the same page as the next paragraph.

To keep one paragraph with another:

▶ **1.** Scroll down and click anywhere in the heading **Stay True to Your Style**.

▶ **2.** In the Paragraph group, click the **Dialog Box Launcher**, and then, in the Paragraph dialog box, click the **Line and Page Breaks** tab.

▶ **3.** Click the **Keep with next** check box to insert a check mark, and then click the **OK** button. The Paragraph dialog box closes, and the "Stay True to Your Style" heading moves to the top of page 2.

The Underline and Italic buttons on the Home tab work in the same way as the Bold button. You'll try formatting the title and subtitle in italics now, to see how they look.

To format the title and subtitle in italics:

▶ **1.** On page 1, select the title **Pemberly Furniture and Interiors** and the subtitle **Getting the Look You Want**.

▶ **2.** In the Font group, click the **Italic** button $\boxed{I}$. The title and subtitle are italicized, meaning they lean slightly to the right. The Italic button is selected, indicating that the selected text is italicized. See Figure 2-31.

Formatting headings with italics ◀ Figure 2-31

▶ **3.** After reviewing the change, Natalie decides she doesn't care for the italics and asks you to remove them.

▶ **4.** Click the **Italic** button $\boxed{I}$. The italic formatting toggles off. The selected text looks the way it did before you italicized it.

▶ **5.** Save the document, leaving the title and subtitle selected.

Helpful Keyboard Shortcuts

For common tasks, such as applying bold and italics, it's often faster to use a **keyboard shortcut** (a combination of keys pressed at the same time) instead of clicking buttons with the mouse. For each of the keyboard shortcuts listed below, press and hold the Ctrl key, press the indicated number or letter key, and then release both keys.

- Bold selected text: Ctrl+B
- Italicize selected text: Ctrl+I

- Underline selected text: Ctrl+U
- Single-space lines within paragraph that currently contains the insertion point: Ctrl+1
- Double-space lines within paragraph that currently contains the insertion point: Ctrl+2
- Select entire document: Ctrl+A
- Cut selected text: Ctrl+X
- Copy selected text to Clipboard: Ctrl+C
- Paste most recently copied item at location of insertion point: Ctrl+V
- Undo your most recent action: Ctrl+Z

You can also save time by using **KeyTips**, sometimes called access keys, to select buttons and commands. To use KeyTips, press the Alt key and notice the letters that are displayed over each tab. Press the letter for the tab that contains the feature you want. For example, "P" is the KeyTip for the Page Layout tab; pressing it displays the Page Layout tab, with KeyTips showing for each feature on that tab. Press the KeyTip for the feature you want (for example, "B" for the Breaks button), and then notice the KeyTips that appear in the menu or gallery that opens. Press the KeyTip for the option you want. The change you select is applied to your document, and the KeyTips are hidden. You can press the Alt key to display them again for your next task. To hide KeyTips without using them, press the Esc key.

Working with Themes and Fonts

In addition to drawing attention to text with bold, italics, or underlining, you can change the shape and size of the individual letters by changing the font and font size. (As you learned in Tutorial 1, the term "font" refers to the shape of the characters in a document, and "font size" refers to the size of the characters.) You'll learn how to change the font in the Design Handout document soon, but first you need to take a few moments to learn about a related topic, document themes.

The document **theme** controls the variety of fonts, colors, and other visual effects available to you as you format a document. Twenty different themes are included in Word, with each offering a coordinated assortment of fonts, colors, and visual effects. By default, the Office theme is selected in each new Word document, including the Design Handout document you are working on now. You'll learn more about themes as you gain experience with Word. For now, you need to focus only on the relationship between themes and fonts.

One secret to creating a harmonious-looking document is to use no more than two fonts. For this reason, each theme includes only two fonts: one for headings and one for body text (that is, anything that is not a heading). In the Office theme, the heading font is Cambria, and the body font is Calibri. These two fonts were designed specifically for easy reading onscreen as well as on the printed page. A long list of other fonts is available. You can experiment with them and use them in your documents, but take care not to use too many fonts. This will create a document with a cluttered, disjointed appearance.

Applying a New Font and Font Size

To apply a font, select the text you want to format, then in the Font group on the Home tab, click the Font arrow, and click the font you want. The heading and body font for a document's theme are listed first, at the top of the font list.

To select a font size, make sure the text you want to format is selected, then in the Font group, click the Font Size arrow, and click the font size you want. Both the Font and Font Size lists allow you to see a live preview of selections by moving the mouse pointer over a font name or font size.

Natalie typed the entire Design Handout document in the Calibri font, which is intended primarily for body text, and the font size for the entire document is 11-point. She wants you to format the title and the subtitle in Cambria, which is the heading font for the Office theme. She also wants you to increase the size of the title and subtitle to 14-point.

To apply the Cambria heading font to the Design Handout document:

▶ 1. On page 1, verify that the title **Pemberly Furniture and Interiors** and the subtitle **Getting the Look You Want** are selected.

▶ 2. In the Font group, click the **Font** arrow. A list of available fonts appears. The heading and body font for the Office theme (Cambria and Calibri) appear at the top of the list. The intended use of these two fonts (Headings or Body) is specified after each font name. Calibri (Body) is highlighted in orange, indicating that this font is currently applied to the selected text. (Calibri also appears in the Font box, above the list, for the same reason.) Below the heading and body fonts is a list of fonts that have been used recently on your computer, followed by a complete alphabetical list of all available fonts. (You need to scroll the list to see all the fonts.) Each name in the list is formatted with the relevant font. For example, "Cambria" appears in the Cambria font, and "Calibri" appears in the Calibri font. See Figure 2-32.

Font list   Figure 2-32

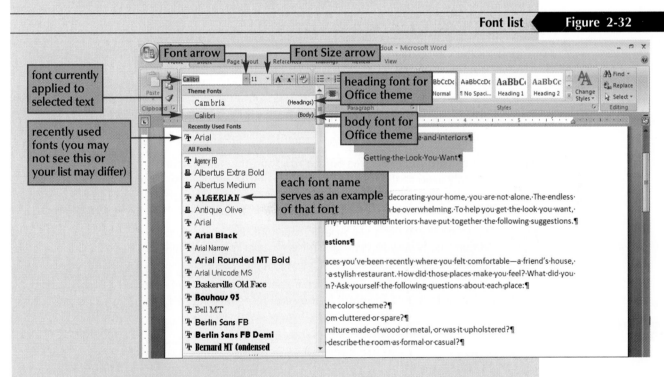

▶ 3. Without clicking, move the mouse pointer over a dramatic-looking font in the font list, such as Algerian or Arial Black, and then drag the pointer over another font. The selected text in the document shows a live preview of the font, changing again to a new font when you drag the mouse pointer to a different font name.

▶ 4. At the top of the list, click **Cambria (Headings)**. Take care to select Cambria (Headings) at the top of the list. Do not click Cambria where it appears farther down, in the alphabetical list of fonts. (The reason for this will become clear in the next section, when you learn more about document themes.) The selected title and subtitle are now formatted in Cambria, and the font list closes. "Cambria (Headings)" appears in the Font box, indicating the font currently applied to the selected text. Next, you need to increase the font size of the selected text from 11 point to 14 point.

> **Trouble?** If you see "Cambria" in the font box rather than "Cambria (Headings)," you selected Cambria where it appears in the alphabetical list of fonts rather than at the top of the list. Begin again with Step 2, taking care to select Cambria (Headings) at the top of the list.

5. Verify that the title and subtitle are still selected, and then in the Font group click the **Font Size** arrow (shown earlier in Figure 2-32). A list of font sizes appears, with the currently selected font size (11) displayed in the Font Size box. Like the Font box, the Font Size box allows you to preview options before selecting one.

6. Drag the mouse pointer over a few font sizes, and notice how the size of the selected text changes accordingly.

7. Click **14**. The Font Size list closes and the selected text increases from 11-point to 14-point Cambria. Click within the title to deselect the text.

You've finished formatting the document's title and subtitle in the Cambria font, the preferred heading font for the Office theme. You could also apply the Cambria font to the headings within the document (such as the heading "Ask Yourself Some Questions"). However, Natalie thinks the bold you applied earlier emphasizes them enough, so you'll leave the headings as they are.

The only remaining font change has to do with the company name. Wherever it appears in the body of the document, Natalie wants to format it in the Arial font, so that it matches the sign outside the company's storefront. Arial is not one of the suggested fonts for the Office theme, and using it breaks the general rule of two fonts per document, but this is a small change that won't affect the overall look of the document.

To format the company name in the Arial font:

1. At the end of the introductory paragraph, select **Pemberly Furniture and Interiors**.

2. In the Font group click the **Font** arrow, and then click **Arial** in either in the Recently used Fonts section of the list or in the All Fonts section. The font for the company name changes from Calibri to Arial. Arial appears in the Font box, indicating that the selected text is formatted in this font.

   Trouble? If you don't see Arial in your font list, choose another font in the All Fonts section that is easy to distinguish from Calibri or Cambria but still looks suitable for a business document.

3. Scroll down to the last paragraph of the document, select **Pemberly Furniture and Interiors**, and format it in the Arial font. See Figure 2-33.

Figure 2-33   **Company name formatted in Arial**

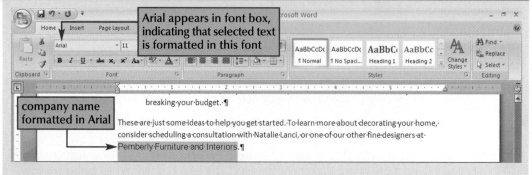

4. Deselect the company name, and then save the document.

You are finished changing the document fonts. In the next section, you'll select a new theme for the document and observe how this affects your font choices.

Changing the Document's Theme

Each document theme is designed to convey a specific look and feel. For example, the Office theme is designed to be appropriate for standard business documents. By contrast, some of the other themes are designed to give documents a more informal look, such as sleek for a new product announcement or earthy for a flyer on environmental news.

The advantage of sticking with a theme's suggested heading and body fonts (the two fonts at the top of the font list) is that if you switch to a different theme, the fonts in the document automatically change to the body and heading fonts for that theme. If you select any fonts on the font list other than the two heading and body fonts at the top of the list, they will remain unchanged in the document as you switch from one theme to another.

Natalie is considering using a different theme for future handouts. She asks you to apply the Metro theme to the Design Handout document to see how it looks.

To change the document's theme:

▶ **1.** Make sure that you saved the document using the current name (Design Handout) at the end of the last section. If you aren't sure, save the document again.

▶ **2.** Save the document as **Design Handout Metro** in the Tutorial folder.

▶ **3.** Press the **Ctrl+Home** keys to move the insertion point up to the headings at the beginning of the document. With the title and subtitle visible, you will more easily be able to see what happens when you change the document's theme.

▶ **4.** Click the **Page Layout** tab, and then click the **Themes** button. The Themes gallery opens. You might have to wait a moment until the various themes appear in the gallery. See Figure 2-34.

Themes gallery | Figure 2-34

► **5.** Without clicking, hold the mouse over the various themes in the gallery, and observe the live preview of each theme in the document. The heading and body fonts change to reflect the fonts associated with the various themes.

► **6.** Click **Metro**. Except for the two instances of the company name (which you formatted earlier in Arial), the text in the Design Handout Metro document changes to the body and heading fonts of the Metro theme. To see exactly what the Metro theme fonts are, you can point to the Theme Fonts button in the Themes group.

► **7.** Point to the **Theme Fonts** button [A▾] in the Themes group. A ScreenTip appears, listing the currently selected theme (Metro), the heading font (Consolas), and the body font (Corbel).

   Trouble? If a menu appears, you clicked the Theme Fonts button instead of pointing to it. Press the Esc key, and then repeat Step 7.

► **8.** Save the document and then close it. You can give the Design Handout Metro file to Natalie later, so she can decide whether or not to use the Metro theme for future handouts. Because you saved the Design Handout document before changing the theme, you can reopen it now and continue with the tutorial.

► **9.** Reopen the Design Handout document, which is formatted with the Office theme.

Tip

To quickly open a document you were recently working on in Word, click the Office Button and then click the document you want in the Recent Documents list.

| InSight | **Changing Fonts by Changing Themes** |

The two fonts at the top of the font list are not actually specific fonts; they are instructions that tell Word to use the heading and body fonts for the currently selected theme. By contrast, the other fonts in the Font list (such as Arial or Calibri where they appear in the alphabetical list of fonts) are more straightforward. When you apply one of these fonts to text in a document, it doesn't change when you change the document theme. The same is true for other kinds of formatting, such as bold, italics, or font size changes. These types of formatting remain unchanged no matter what theme you choose.

Previewing and Printing the Document

You have made all the editing and formatting changes that Natalie requested for the Design Handout document. It's helpful to preview a document after formatting it. The Print Preview window makes it easy to spot things you need to change before printing, such as text that is not aligned correctly.

To preview and print the document:

► **1.** Click the **Office Button** (⊕), point to **Print**, and then click **Print Preview**. The document is displayed in Print Preview.

► **2.** In the Zoom section, click the **Two Pages** button. You see both pages of the document side by side. Review the document's formatting.

   Trouble? If you notice any alignment or indentation errors, click the Close Print Preview button, correct the errors in Print Layout view, save your changes, and then return to the Print Preview window.

► **3.** On the Print Preview tab in the Print group, click the **Print** button, check the print settings, and then click the **OK** button. After a pause, the document prints.

▶ **4.** Click the **Close Print Preview** button. You return to Print Layout view.

▶ **5.** Save the document if necessary and then close it.

You now have a printed copy of the final Design Handout document, as shown in Figure 2-35.

Final version of Design Handout document ◀ **Figure 2-35**

Session 2.2 Quick Check | Review

1. The term _____ refers to the way a paragraph lines up horizontally between the margins.
2. Explain how to indent a paragraph 1 inch or more from the left margin.
3. Explain how to copy formatting to multiple paragraphs.
4. What is the Numbering Library?
5. Explain the effect a theme has on the overall look of a document.
6. Explain how to change a paragraph's font.
7. Explain the relationship between the two items at the top of the Font list and the document's theme.

Tutorial Summary | Review

In this tutorial, you learned how to use the Spelling and Grammar checker, select parts of a document, delete text, and move text within a document. You also learned how to find and replace text. Next, you focused on formatting a document, including changing margins, aligning text, indenting paragraphs, using the Format Painter, and emphasizing text with bold and italics. Finally, you learned how to change the font and font size for selected text and you explored the relationship between fonts and themes.

Key Terms

alignment
bullet
Bullet Library
center alignment
Clipboard
Clipboard task pane
copy
cut
cut and paste
drag and drop
Find and Replace
    dialog box

format
Format Painter
hanging indent
indent
indent markers
justified alignment
keyboard shortcut
Key Tips
left alignment
Numbering Library
paste

ragged
right alignment
right indent
search text
Spelling and Grammar
    checker
theme
toggle buttons

| Practice | | **Review Assignments** |

Apply the skills you learned in the tutorial using the same case scenario.

Data Files needed for the Review Assignments: Getting.docx, Staff.docx

Natalie asks you to work on a document that explains how to get started working with the designers at Pemberly Furniture and Interiors. The document starts by introducing the entire Pemberly design staff and then lists the steps involved in a major home renovation. Natalie also asks you to create a document listing the names of the firm's interior designers and interior decorators.

1. Open the file **Getting** located in the Tutorial.02\Review folder included with your Data Files, and then check your screen to make sure your settings match those in the tutorial.
2. Save the document as **Getting Started** in the same folder.
3. Use the Spelling and Grammar checker to correct any errors in the document. Assume that all names in the document and the term "Feng Shui" are spelled correctly.
4. Proofread the document carefully to check for any additional errors. Look for and correct errors in the last two paragraphs of the document that were not reported when you used the Spelling and Grammar checker.
5. Change the left and top margins to 1.5 inches using the Page Setup dialog box. Make sure to apply the change to the whole document.
6. In the list on the second page of the document, select the paragraph that begins "Interview potential construction..." and move it so that it follows the paragraph that reads "Review the final design plan."
7. Format the heading and subheading in the suggested heading font for the Office theme. Change the font size to 16 point.
8. Make all edits and formatting changes shown in Figure 2-36, and then save your work.

Figure 2-36

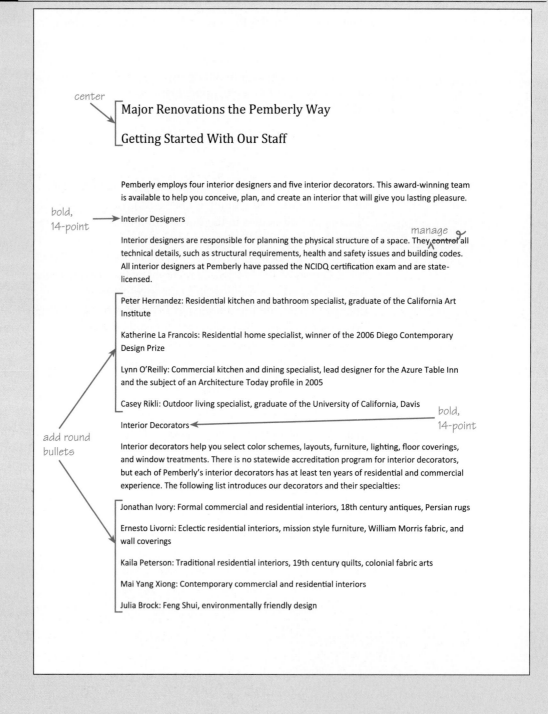

center

Major Renovations the Pemberly Way

Getting Started With Our Staff

Pemberly employs four interior designers and five interior decorators. This award-winning team is available to help you conceive, plan, and create an interior that will give you lasting pleasure.

bold, 14-point → Interior Designers

manage

Interior designers are responsible for planning the physical structure of a space. They control all technical details, such as structural requirements, health and safety issues and building codes. All interior designers at Pemberly have passed the NCIDQ certification exam and are state-licensed.

Peter Hernandez: Residential kitchen and bathroom specialist, graduate of the California Art Institute

Katherine La Francois: Residential home specialist, winner of the 2006 Diego Contemporary Design Prize

Lynn O'Reilly: Commercial kitchen and dining specialist, lead designer for the Azure Table Inn and the subject of an Architecture Today profile in 2005

Casey Rikli: Outdoor living specialist, graduate of the University of California, Davis

bold, 14-point

Interior Decorators ◄

add round bullets

Interior decorators help you select color schemes, layouts, furniture, lighting, floor coverings, and window treatments. There is no statewide accreditation program for interior decorators, but each of Pemberly's interior decorators has at least ten years of residential and commercial experience. The following list introduces our decorators and their specialties:

Jonathan Ivory: Formal commercial and residential interiors, 18th century antiques, Persian rugs

Ernesto Livorni: Eclectic residential interiors, mission style furniture, William Morris fabric, and wall coverings

Kaila Peterson: Traditional residential interiors, 19th century quilts, colonial fabric arts

Mai Yang Xiong: Contemporary commercial and residential interiors

Julia Brock: Feng Shui, environmentally friendly design

Figure 2-36 (cont.)

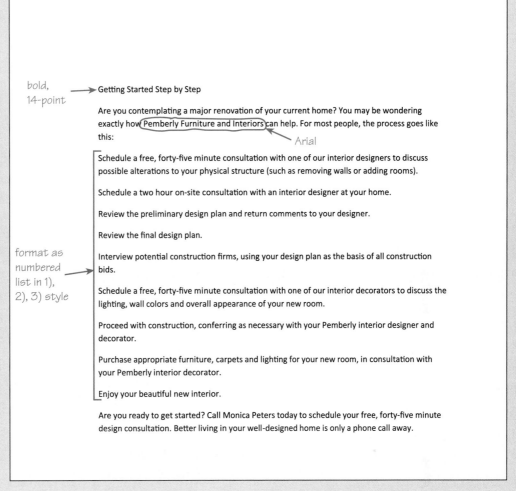

9. In the last paragraph of the document, replace "Monica Peters" with your first and last name.
10. Below the heading "Interior Designers," justify the paragraph that begins "Interior designers are responsible for...." Click the Increase Indent button once. Note that Word indents the justified paragraph slightly to match the bulleted list below it. Click the Increase Indent button again to indent the paragraph a full 0.5 inch. Similarly, justify and indent the paragraph below the heading "Interior Decorators" and the paragraph below the heading "Getting Started Step by Step." Finally, justify and indent the last paragraph in the document, and then indent the two bulleted lists and the numbered list to match the other indented paragraphs. When you are finished, the text and lists below the three boldface headings should all be indented by 0.5 inch. Save the document.
11. If necessary, move the heading "Getting Started Step by Step" to the top of page 2.
12. Display the Clipboard task pane. Copy the list of interior designers and their specialties (starting with Peter Hernandez and ending with Casey Rikli) to the Clipboard. Also copy the list of interior decorators and their specialties (beginning with Jonathan Ivory and ending with Julia Brock) to the Clipboard.
13. Open the file **Staff** located in the Tutorial.02\Review folder included with your Data Files, and save the document as **Pemberly Staff** in the same folder. In the subtitle, insert your first and last name after the word "by."

14. Display the Clipboard task pane. Below the heading "Interior Designers," paste the list of interior designers, which begins "Peter Hernandez." Below the heading "Interior Decorators," paste the list of interior decorators, which begins "Jonathan Ivory." In each case, start by moving the insertion point to the blank paragraph below the heading. Notice that text inserted from the Clipboard retains its original formatting.

15. Clear the contents of the Clipboard task pane, and then print the document.

16. Save the Pemberly Staff document and close it. Close the Clipboard task pane.

17. Save the Getting Started document, deselect any selected text, preview the document, and print it.

18. Save the Getting Started document as **Verve Sample** in the same folder.

19. Select the Verve theme, and then review the newly formatted document and its list of fonts. Check the company name in the paragraph below the heading "Getting Started Step by Step" and make sure it is still formatted in Arial.

20. Save the Verve Sample document, preview it, print it, and close it. Close any other open documents. Submit the finished documents to your instructor, either in printed or electronic form, as requested.

Apply | Case Problem 1

Apply the skills you learned to create a one-page flyer.

Data File needed for this Case Problem: New.docx

Peach Tree School of the Arts Students at Peach Tree School of the Arts, in Savannah, Georgia, can choose from a wide range of after-school classes in fine arts, music, and theater. Amanda Reinhard, the school director, has created a flyer informing parents of some additional offerings. It's your job to format the flyer to make it professional looking and easy to read.

1. Open the file **New** located in the Tutorial.02\Case1 folder included with your Data Files, and save the file as **New Classes** in the same folder.

2. Correct any spelling or grammar errors. Ignore the sentence fragments highlighted by the grammar checker. These fragments will make sense once they are formatted as part of a bulleted list.

3. Proofread for other errors, such as words that are spelled correctly but used incorrectly. Use the Replace command to replace "P.M." with "p.m." throughout the document.

4. Replace "Marcus Cody" with your name.

5. Change the top, left, right, and bottom margins to 1.5 inches, and then save your work.

6. Format everything in the document except the title and subtitle in 12-point Times New Roman font. Format the title and subtitle in Arial, 16 point, bold.

7. Format the list of new classes (which begins "Advanced Drawing") as a bulleted list, using the square bullet style.

8. Move the third bulleted item (which begins "Jazz Dance...") up to make it the first bulleted item in the list.

9. Format the four-step check list near the end of the document as a numbered list, using the default numbering style.

10. Save your work, preview the document, switch back to Print Layout view to make any changes you think necessary, print the document, and then close it. Submit the finished document to your instructor, either in printed or electronic form, as requested.

Apply | Case Problem 2

Use your skills to format the summary document shown in Figure 2-37.

Data File needed for this Case Problem: Moth.docx

Hamilton Polytechnic Institute   Finn Hansen is an associate researcher in the Department of Entomology at Hamilton Polytechnic Institute. He is working on a nationwide program that aims to slow the spread of a devastating forest pest, the gypsy moth. He has created a one-page document that will be used as part of a campaign to inform the public about current efforts to manage gypsy moths in North America. Format the document by completing the following steps.

1. Open the file **Moth** located in the Tutorial.02\Case2 folder included with your Data Files, and then check your screen to make sure your settings match those in the tutorial.
2. Save the file as **Gypsy Moth** in the same folder.
3. Format the document as shown in Figure 2-37.

Figure 2-37

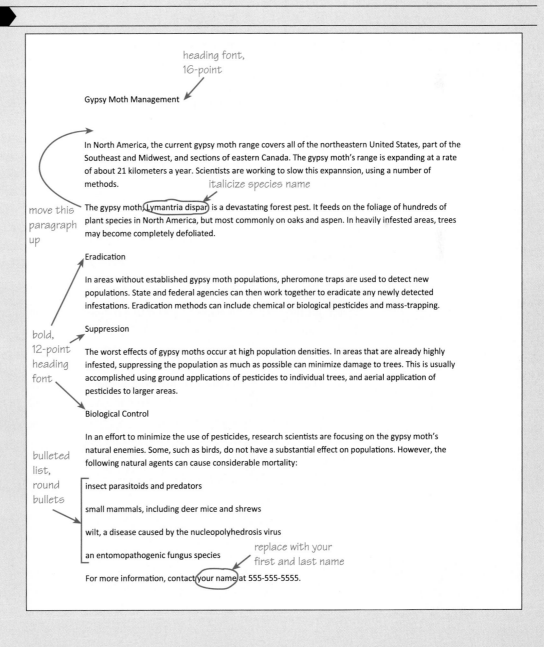

⊕ EXPLORE

4. Use the ruler to indent a paragraph, as follows:

   a. Make sure the horizontal ruler is displayed and the document is in Print Layout view.

   b. Click anywhere in the paragraph below the heading "Eradication."

   c. Position the pointer on the small gray rectangle on the ruler at the left margin (the rectangle is below the two triangles). A ScreenTip with the words "Left Indent" appears.

   d. Press and hold down the mouse button. A vertical dotted line appears in the document window, indicating the current left margin. Drag the Left Indent marker right to the 0.5-inch mark on the ruler, and then release the mouse button.

5. Use the Format Painter to copy the indent to the paragraph below the heading "Suppression" and the heading "Biological Control."

6. Indent the bulleted list so it aligns below the preceding paragraph.

7. Use the Spelling and Grammar checker to make corrections as needed, proofread for additional errors, save, and preview the document.

8. Print the document, and then close it. Submit the finished document to your instructor, either in printed or electronic form, as requested.

Challenge | **Case Problem 3**

Expand your formatting skills to create a resume for an aspiring sales representative.

Data File needed for this Case Problem: Resume.docx

Educational Publishing   Elena Pelliterri has over a decade of experience in education. She worked as a writing teacher and then as a college supervisor of student teachers. Now she would like to pursue a career as a sales representative for a company that publishes textbooks and other educational materials. She has asked you to edit and format her resume. Complete the resume by completing the following steps.

1. Open the file **Resume** located in the Tutorial.02\Case3 folder included with your Data Files, and then check your screen to make sure your settings match those in the tutorial.

2. Save the file as **Elena Resume** in the same folder.

3. Search for the text "your name", and replace it with your first and last name.

4. Replace all occurrences of "Aroyo" with "Arroyo."

5. Use the Spelling and Grammar checker to correct any errors in the document. Note that this document contains lines that the Spelling and Grammar checker might consider sentence fragments but that are acceptable in a resume.

6. Delete the word "traveling" from the sentence below the "OBJECTIVE" heading.

7. Change the document theme to Metro.

8. Format the resume as described in Figure 2-38. Use the Format Painter to copy formatting as necessary.

Figure 2-38

Resume Element	Format
Name "Elena Pelliterri"	16-point, heading font, bold, with underline
Address, phone number, and e-mail address	14-point, heading font, bold
Uppercase headings (OBJECTIVE, EXPERIENCE, etc.)	11-point, heading font, bold
Two subheadings below EXPERIENCE, which begin "Rio Mesa College..." and "Middleton Public Schools..."	11-point, heading font, bold, italic
Lists of teaching experience, educational history, and so on, below the resume headings and subheadings	Bulleted list with square bullets

9. Reorder the two items under the "COMPUTER SKILLS" heading so that the second item becomes the first.

⊕ EXPLORE

10. Open a new, blank document, type some text, and experiment with the Change Case button in the Font group on the Home tab. Close the document without saving it, and then change the name "Elena Pelliterri" at the top of the resume to all uppercase.

11. Save, preview, and print the document.

⊕ EXPLORE

12. Experiment with two special paragraph alignment options: first line and hanging.
    a. Save the document as **Alignment Samples**. Make sure the horizontal ruler is displayed and the document is in Print Layout view.
    b. Select the two bulleted items under the subheading "Middleton Public Schools." Click the Bullets button to remove the bulleted list format.
    c. With the paragraphs still selected, locate the alignment markers on the left side of the horizontal ruler. Position the pointer over the bottom, triangle-shaped alignment marker. A ScreenTip with the words "Hanging Indent" appears. (If you see a different ScreenTip, such as "Left Indent," you don't have the pointer positioned properly.)
    d. Press and hold down the mouse button. A vertical dotted line appears in the document window, indicating the current left margin. Drag the Hanging Indent marker right to the 1-inch mark on the ruler, and then release the mouse button.
    e. Select the two bulleted items under the heading "Educational History" and remove the bulleted list formatting. Position the mouse pointer over the top, triangle-shaped alignment marker until you see the ScreenTip "First Line Indent." Drag the First Line Indent marker right to the 1-inch mark on the ruler, and then release the mouse button.

13. Save, preview, and print the document.

14. Close the document. Close any other open documents. Submit the finished documents to your instructor, either in printed or electronic form, as requested.

Challenge | Case Problem 4

Explore new ways to format an order form for a baking supply company.

Data File needed for this Case Problem: Flour.docx

McElmeel Baking Supply Melissa Martinez is the sales manager for McElmeel Baking Supply, a wholesale distributor of gourmet baking ingredients based in Ames, Iowa. The company is currently offering a special on flour. Melissa has started work on an order form that explains the special offer. She plans to include the form with each invoice sent out next month. It's your job to format the order form to make it easy to use.

1. Open the file **Flour** located in Tutorial.02\Case4 folder included with your Data Files, and save the file as **Flour Form** in the same folder.

EXPLORE

2. When you type Web addresses or e-mail addresses in a document, Word formats them as links. When you click a Web address formatted as a link, Windows opens a Web browser (such as Microsoft Internet Explorer) and, if your computer is connected to the Internet, displays that Web page. Likewise, Word recognizes text that looks like an e-mail address, and formats such text as links as well. If you click an e-mail address formatted as a link, Windows opens a program in which you can type an e-mail message. The address you clicked is included, by default, as the recipient of the e-mail. You'll see how this works as you add a Web address and e-mail address to the order form. At the top of the document, click at the end of the company name, add a new line, and then type the address for the company's Web site: **www.McElmeelBaking.course.com**. (The company is fictitious and does not really have a Web site.) When you are finished, press the Enter key. Word formats the address in blue with an underline, marking it as a link. Move the mouse pointer over the link and read the ScreenTip.

EXPLORE

3. In the line below the Web address, type **McElmeel_Baking@course.com** and then press the Enter key. Word formats the e-mail address as a link. Press and hold the Ctrl key and then click the e-mail link. Your default e-mail program opens, displaying a window where you could type an e-mail message to McElmeel Baking Supply. (If your computer is not set up for email, close any error messages or wizard dialog boxes that open.) Close the e-mail window without saving any changes. The e-mail link is now formatted in a color other than blue, indicating that the link has been clicked.

EXPLORE

4. Right-click the Web site address, and then click Remove Hyperlink in the shortcut menu. Do the same for the e-mail address. The links are now formatted as ordinary text.

5. Delete the phrase "regular clients," and replace it with "loyal customers."

6. Use the Margins menu to change the top and bottom margins to 1 inch and the left and right margins to 2 inches.

7. Format the entire document in the Arial font.

8. At the top of the document, center and single space the company name, Web address, and e-mail address. Remove extra paragraph spacing from all three paragraphs.

9. Change the font size for the company name at the top of the document to 16 points.

10. Near the middle of the document, bold and single space the company address. Remove extra paragraph spacing from all three paragraphs.

11. Format the blank ruled lines at the bottom of the order form as a numbered list.

12. Insert your name in the form to the right of "Name:".

EXPLORE

13. Save your work and preview the document. Click the One Page button on the Print Preview tab to view the entire document on the screen at one time. Print the document and then close the Print Preview window.

⊕ **EXPLORE**

14. The Words box in the bottom, left-hand corner of the document window shows you the number of words in a document. To see more useful statistics, you can use the Word Count dialog box. Click the Words box in the lower-left corner of the document window to open the Word Count dialog box. Note the number of characters (not including spaces), paragraphs, and lines in the document, and then write these statistics in the upper-right corner of the printout. Close the Word Count dialog box.

15. Save and close the document. Submit the finished document to your instructor, either in printed or electronic form, as requested.

| Research | **Internet Assignments** |

Go to the Web to find information you can use to create documents.

The purpose of the Internet Assignments is to challenge you to find information on the Internet that you can use to work effectively with this software. The actual assignments are updated and maintained on the Course Technology Web site. Log on to the Internet and use your Web browser to go to the Student Online Companion for New Perspectives Office 2007 at **www.course.com/np/office2007**. Then navigate to the Internet Assignments for this tutorial.

| Assess | **SAM Assessment and Training** |

If you have a SAM user profile, you may have access to hands-on instruction, practice, and assessment of the skills covered in this tutorial. Log in to your SAM account (**http://sam2007.course.com**) to launch any assigned training activities or exams that relate to the skills covered in this tutorial.

| Review | **Quick Check Answers** |

Session 2.1

1. True
2. True
3. Select the text you want to move. Press and hold down the mouse button until the drag-and-drop pointer appears, and then drag the selected text to its new location. Use the dotted insertion point as a guide to determine exactly where the text will be inserted. Release the mouse button to drop the text at the insertion point.
4. Select the text you want to cut, and then click the Cut button in the Clipboard group on the Home tab. Move the insertion point to the target location in the document, and then click the Paste button in the Clipboard group on the Home tab.
5. Click the Find button in the Editing group on the Home tab.
6. Select the Match case check box.

Session 2.2

1. alignment
2. Click the Increase Indent button in the Paragraph group on the Home tab.
3. Move the insertion point to the paragraph whose formatting you want to copy, double-click the Format Painter button, and then click each paragraph you want to format. When you are finished, click the Format Painter button again to deselect it.
4. A gallery of numbered list styles. To display it (along with other numbered list options), click the Numbering button arrow in the Paragraph group on the Home tab.
5. A theme controls the variety of fonts, colors, and other visual effects available to you as you format a document. Each theme is designed to provide a coordinated, harmonious-looking document.
6. Select the text you want to change. Click the Font arrow in the Font group to display the list of fonts. Move the mouse pointer over the list of font names and observe a preview of the fonts in the selected text. Click the font you want to use.
7. They are the heading and body fonts for the document's theme. They are really instructions that tell Word to use the heading and body fonts for the currently selected theme.

Ending Data Files

Tutorial.02 →

Tutorial
Design Handout.docx
Design Handout Metro.docx
Formal Designs.docx

Review
Getting Started.docx
Pemberly Staff.docx
Verve Sample.docx

Case1
New Classes.docx

Case2
Gypsy Moth.docx

Case3
Alignment Samples.docx
Elena Resume.docx

Case4
Flour Form.docx

Objectives

Session 3.1
- Format headings with Quick Styles
- Insert a manual page break
- Create and edit a table
- Sort rows in a table
- Modify a table's structure
- Format a table

Session 3.2
- Set tab stops
- Create footnotes and endnotes
- Divide a document into sections
- Create a SmartArt graphic
- Create headers and footers
- Insert a cover page

Creating a Multiple-Page Report

Writing a Recommendation

Case | Parkside Housing Coalition

Robin Kinsella is the director of Parkside Housing Coalition, a nonprofit organization that provides low-cost rental housing in Evanston, Illinois, at more than 50 properties it owns and manages in the Evanston area. Robin has been investigating a plan to reduce utility bills for Parkside residents through a process known as an energy audit. Robin has written a multiple-page report for the board of directors at Parkside Housing Coalition summarizing basic information about energy audits. It's your job to finish formatting the report. She also needs some help adding a table to the end of the report.

In this tutorial, you will format headings with Quick Styles and insert a manual page break. Then you will insert a table, select all or part of a table, sort a table's rows, insert and delete rows or columns, change column widths, and format a table to improve its appearance. You will also set tab stops, create footnotes and endnotes, and insert a section break. Finally, you will create a SmartArt graphic, add headers and footers, and insert a cover page.

Starting Data Files

Tutorial.03

Tutorial
Audit.docx

Review
Class.docx

Case1
Textiles.docx

Case2
WiFi.docx

Case3
Clients.docx
Expenses.docx

Case4
(none)

Session 3.1

Planning the Document

Robin saved her draft of the report as a Word document named Audit. In its current form, the report is two pages long. By the time you are finished, it will be five pages long, containing a title page, a table, and an illustration, each on a separate page. Figure 3-1 illustrates the revisions you'll be making to the report.

Figure 3-1 | Revisions planned for Audit document

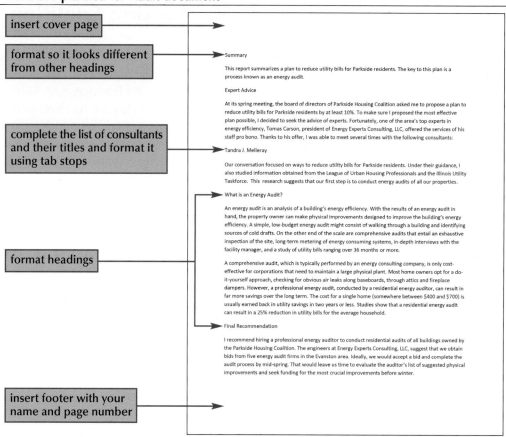

Revisions planned for Audit document (page 2) ◀ **Figure 3-1 (cont.)**

insert header with report title

insert page break

insert table on new page

insert illustration on new page after table

insert footnotes

Now that you have a sense of the revisions you'll be making, you are ready to get started.

To open the document:

▶ **1.** Start Word, and then open the file **Audit** located in the Tutorial.03\Tutorial folder included with your Data Files.

▶ **2.** To avoid altering the original file, save the document as **Audit Report** in the same folder.

▶ **3.** Check your settings to make sure your screen matches the figures in this tutorial. In particular, be sure to display the nonprinting characters, switch to Print Layout view if necessary, display the rulers, and set the zoom so you can see the entire width of the page.

Formatting Headings with Quick Styles

Your first job is to format the headings to make them easier to distinguish from the body text. You already know how to draw attention to text by adding bold, italic, or underline formatting. You also know how to use a heading font. To give a document a really polished look, you can use **Quick Styles**, which allow you to apply an entire set of formatting choices with one click. A Quick Style typically applies many formatting options at once, such as, bold, a specific font, a specific indent setting, and a new color for the text (that is, a new **font color**).

Some Quick Styles apply **paragraph-level formatting**—that is, they are set up to format an entire paragraph (for example, adding space before and after a heading paragraph). Other Quick Styles apply **character-level formatting**—that is, they are set up to format only a few characters or words (for example, formatting a book title in italics).

The Quick Styles gallery on the Home tab gives you access to the document's Quick Styles (or just "styles," as they are sometimes called). One row of the gallery is always visible on the Home tab. When you first open a document, the visible row contains the four most commonly used Quick Styles (Normal, No Spacing, Heading 1, and Heading 2). These are all paragraph-level Quick Styles, so to use one, you place the insertion point anywhere in the paragraph you want to format, and then click one of the four visible styles. To use any other Quick Style, click the More button in the Styles group to display the entire Quick Styles gallery, and then click the Quick Style you want.

The Quick Styles that are available in a given document are controlled by the document's theme. Each theme uses the same names for its Quick Styles (starting with Normal, No Spacing, Heading 1, and Heading 2), but the formatting applied by a given Quick Style depends on the document's theme. For example, in the Office theme (the default theme for new documents), the Heading 1 style applies the Cambria font in blue. But in the Equity theme, the Heading 1 style applies the Franklin Gothic Book font in dark red.

Robin decided that the Office theme (the default) works fine for the Energy Audit document, so you'll be working with the Quick Styles that come with that theme. She would like you to apply the Intense Quote style to the Summary heading and the Heading 1 style to the other headings. As its name suggests, the Intense Quote style is useful for drawing attention to quotations from a document; however, because it indents text, it's also useful for certain types of headings. It applies paragraph-level formatting, so you need to start by moving the insertion point to the paragraph you want to format.

To format the "Summary" heading with the Intense Quote style:

▶ **1.** Click in the paragraph containing the heading **Summary** at the beginning of the document (if necessary), and then on the Home tab, locate the More button in the Styles group, as shown in Figure 3-2.

| Figure 3-2 | ▶ | Locating the More button |

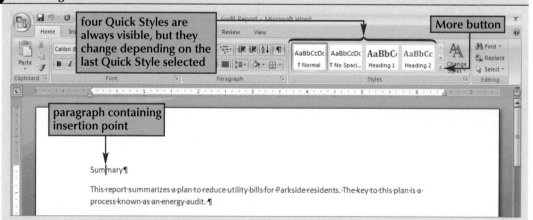

▶ **2.** In the Styles group, click the **More** button. The Quick Styles gallery opens, displaying a total of 16 possible Quick Styles.

▶ **3.** Move the mouse pointer over the styles in the Quick Styles Gallery. When you point to a style, a ScreenTip displays the style's full name, and the text in your document that contains the insertion point is formatted with a preview of that style.

4. Point to (but don't click) the **Intense Quote** style. A preview of the style appears in the document, as shown in Figure 3-3. The Intense Quote style indents text 0.5 inch, inserts a blue line below the text, changes the font color to blue, and adds bold and italic to the text. It does not change the font, which remains 11-point Calibri.

Quick Styles Gallery ◄ Figure 3-3

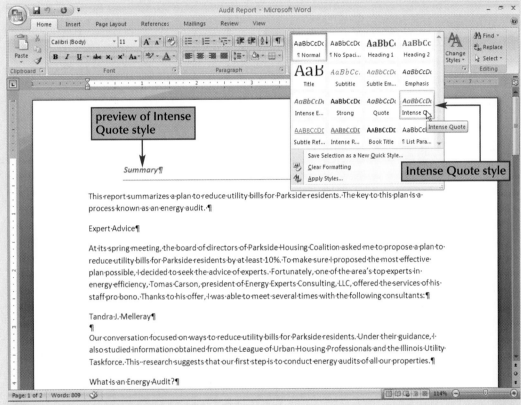

5. Click the **Intense Quote** style. The Quick Style is applied to the paragraph containing the heading "Summary." The row of buttons visible on the Ribbon is now the row containing the Intense Quote style. Next, you need to indent the summary itself so it matches the heading.

6. Click anywhere in the paragraph that begins "The report summarizes..." and then in the Paragraph group, click the **Increase Indent** button ⊞ twice. (Make sure to click it twice.) The summary paragraph indents to match the "Summary" heading.

   Trouble? If the summary paragraph is not indented as far as the "Summary" heading, you probably clicked the Increase Indent button just once. Try clicking it again.

Next, Robin would like you to format the remaining headings in the document with the Heading 1 style. She would also like the table heading at the end of the document to be formatted with the Heading 2 style.

To format the remaining headings with the Heading 1 style:

1. Click the heading **Expert Advice**. The Heading 1 style is no longer visible in the Styles group because when you used the Intense Quote style in the last set of steps, the default row was replaced with the row containing the button you just used. This means that you need to open the Quick Styles gallery again.

▶ **2.** In the Styles group, click the **More** button, and then click the **Heading 1** style in the Quick Styles gallery. The heading is formatted in blue, 14-point Cambria, with bold. The Heading 1 style also inserts some extra space above the heading. The gallery row containing the Heading 1 style is now visible in the Styles group.

▶ **3.** If necessary, scroll down, click the heading **What is an Energy Audit?**, and then press the **F4** key to apply the Heading 1 Quick Style. (Recall that the F4 key repeats your most recent action.) Continue to format these headings with the Heading 1 style: **Final Recommendation**, **Paying for the Energy Audit**, and **Budgeting for Repairs and Upgrades**.

▶ **4.** At the end of the document, click the heading **Probable Expenditures** (the caption for the table that you will create later in this tutorial), and format it with the **Heading 2** Quick Style.

▶ **5.** Save your work. Figure 3-4 shows two headings formatted with the Heading 1 Quick Style and one with the Heading 2 Quick Style.

Figure 3-4	Formatted headings

Next, you need to start working on the table of expenditures. Robin wants the table to appear on its own page (to allow plenty of room for the board of directors to make notes on it), so first you need to insert a page break.

Inserting a Manual Page Break

There are two kinds of page breaks in Word—automatic page breaks and manual page breaks. You've already seen how Word inserts automatic page breaks, by starting a new page every time the current page fills up. A **manual page break** is one you insert at a specific location; it doesn't matter if the previous page is full or not. You insert a manual page break by clicking the Page Break button on the Insert tab or by holding down the Ctrl key and pressing the Enter key. Note that the Page Break button and the Ctrl+Enter keys insert a new page *after* the insertion point. To insert a new page *before* the insertion point, use the Blank Page button (also on the Insert tab).

You need to insert a manual page break just before the table caption. This will ensure that the caption and the table are on their own page.

To insert a manual page break:

▶ **1.** If necessary, scroll down to the bottom of page 2 until you can see the table caption "Probable Expenditures," and then click to the left of the "P" in "Probable."

▶ **2.** Click the **Insert** tab, and then, in the Pages group, click the **Page Break** button. The caption "Probable Expenditures" moves to the top of the new page 3. A dotted line with the words "Page Break" is inserted on page 2, where you positioned the insertion point in Step 1.

> **Trouble?** If you don't see the dotted line with the words "Page Break," check to make sure your document is displayed in Print Layout view and that nonprinting characters are displayed.

You are now ready to insert the table on the new page 3, just below the table caption.

Organizing Information in Tables

A **table** is information arranged in horizontal rows and vertical columns. It's common to organize text or numerical data in a table, but you can also insert graphics, charts, and other kinds of art into tables. You can format text in various ways in different parts of a table, turning some text so it stretches vertically from top to bottom, while centering other text between the left and right margins. You can even insert one table inside another. All of these options make tables extremely useful for setting up complicated documents. You'll have a chance to explore some of the more advanced table features in the Case Problems at the end of this tutorial. Right now, you'll focus on creating the simple table Robin needs for her report. In the process, you'll gain a good understanding of how to work with tables in Word.

When you first insert a table into a document, it appears as a simple grid structure, with black **gridlines** defining the rows and columns. The area where a row and column intersect is called a **cell**. Depending on your needs, you can create a blank table and then insert information into it (as you'll do next), or you can convert existing text into a table (as you'll do in the Case Problems at the end of this tutorial).

Inserting a Blank Table

Figure 3-5 shows a sketch of what Robin wants the table to look like. The top row of the table, called the **header row**, identifies the type of information in each column. Some tables also include a **header column**, which is a column on the left that identifies the type of information in each row.

Table sketch ◀ Figure 3-5

Item	Materials Cost
Weather stripping	$350
High-efficiency water heaters	$8,500
High-efficiency furnaces	$10,000
Insulation	$700

In the following steps, you will insert a blank table by using the Table button on the Insert tab. The Table button allows you to drag the mouse pointer across a blank grid to select the numbers of rows and columns you want to include in your table. A live preview of the table structure appears in the document as you drag the mouse pointer. The table is inserted in the document when you click the mouse button. Keep in mind that the table you insert has the same paragraph and line spacing settings as the paragraph that currently contains the insertion point.

To insert a blank table:

1. Press the **Ctrl+End** keys to move the insertion point to the end of the document (to the blank paragraph below the heading "Probable Expenditures").

2. Make sure the Insert tab is displayed and then, in the Tables group, click the **Table** button. A table grid opens, with a menu at the bottom.

3. Position the pointer in the upper-left cell of the grid, and then drag the pointer down and across the grid until you highlight **two columns** and **five rows**. (The outline of a cell turns orange when it is highlighted.) As you drag the pointer across the grid, Word indicates the size of the table (columns by rows) at the top of the grid. A live preview of the table structure appears in the document. See Figure 3-6.

   Trouble? If the rows of the live preview table are spaced more widely than shown in Figure 3-6, the insertion point is located in a heading, rather than at the end of the document. Press the Esc key to close the Table grid, and begin again with Step 1, taking care to press the Ctrl+End keys as instructed.

Figure 3-6   **Inserting a blank table**

4. When the table size is 2 × 5 (as in Figure 3-6), click the mouse button. An empty table, two columns by five rows, appears below the table caption, with the insertion point in the upper-left cell. The two columns are of equal width. Each cell contains an end-of-cell mark, and each row contains an end-of-row mark, which are important for selecting parts of a table. Two new tabs appear on the Ribbon; the label "Table Tools" identifies them as Table contextual tabs. They are visible only when the table is selected or the insertion point is located inside the table.

   Trouble? If you inserted a table with the wrong number of rows or columns, click the Undo button to remove the table, and then repeat Steps 1 through 4.

5. Move the mouse pointer over the empty table. The Table Move handle appears in the table's upper-left corner, and the Table Resize handle appears in the lower-right corner. See Figure 3-7. You don't need to use either of these handles now, but you should understand their function. To select the entire table quickly, you can click the Table Move handle. Then you can move the entire table by dragging the Table Move handle. To change the size of the entire table, you can drag the Table Resize handle.

Trouble? If you don't see the end-of-cell and end-of-row marks, you need to display nonprinting characters. Click the Show/Hide ¶ button on the Home tab.

Blank table inserted in document | Figure 3-7

The blank table is ready for you to begin entering information. You'll do that next.

Entering Data in a Table

You can enter data in a table by moving the insertion point to a cell and typing. If the data takes up more than one line in the cell, Word automatically wraps the text to the next line and increases the height of that cell (and all the cells in that row). To move the insertion point to another cell in the table, you can click in that cell, use the arrow keys, or use the Tab key.

To enter data into the table:

1. Verify that the insertion point is located in the upper-left cell.

2. Type **Item**. As you type, the end-of-cell mark moves right to accommodate the text.

3. Press the **Tab** key to move to the next cell to the right.

   Trouble? If Word created a new paragraph in the first cell rather than moving the insertion point to the second cell, you pressed the Enter key instead of the Tab key. Press the Backspace key to remove the paragraph mark, and then press the Tab key to move to the second cell in the first row.

4. Type **Materials Cost**, and then press the **Tab** key to move to the first cell in the second row. Notice that when you press the Tab key in the right column, the insertion point moves to the first column in the next row.

You have finished entering the header row—the row that identifies the information in each column. Now you can enter the information about the various expenditures.

To continue entering information in the table:

1. Type **weather stripping**, and then press the **Tab** key to move to the second cell in the second row. Notice that the "w" in "weather stripping" is capitalized, even though you typed it in lowercase. By default, AutoCorrect capitalizes the first letter in a cell entry.

2. Type **$350**, and then press the **Tab** key to move the insertion point to the first cell in the third row.

3. Type the following information to complete the table, pressing the Tab key to move from cell to cell. When you are finished, your table should look like the one in Figure 3-8.

High-efficiency water heaters	**$8,500**
High-efficiency furnaces	**$10,000**
Insulation	**$700**

Figure 3-8   Table with all data entered

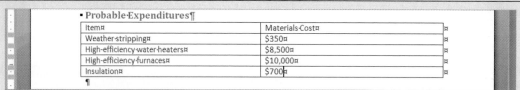

Trouble? If a new row (row 6) appears at the bottom of your table, you pressed the Tab key when the insertion point was in the last cell in the table. Click the Undo button on the Quick Access Toolbar to remove row 6 from the table.

The table you've just created presents information about expenditures in an easy-to-read structure. Your next job is to format the header row in bold so it stands out from the rest of the table. To do that, you need to know how to select a table row.

Selecting Part of a Table

As you have learned, you can select the entire table by clicking the Table Move handle (just above the upper-left corner of the table). You can also click the Select button on the Table Tools Layout tab and then click Select Table.

To select part of a table, you can drag the mouse pointer, just as you would to select regular text in a document—but that's not a good idea, because you can easily miss the end-of-cell mark in a cell or the end-of-row mark at the end of a row. This can produce unpredictable results when you are performing certain formatting or editing tasks. The most foolproof way to select part of a table is to use the Select button on the Table Tools Layout tab. A third method, which is often the most convenient, is to select a row by clicking in the left margin next to the row. Similarly, to select a column, you can click just above the column. After you've selected an entire row or column, you can drag the mouse to select more rows or columns.

You'll get some practice selecting a row in the following steps, as you format the header row in bold. Formatting the header row in bold is helpful for two reasons: (1) it makes it easier to distinguish between the header row and the rest of the data in the table; and (2) when you are using certain table commands, it allows Word to recognize the header row as a special part of the table. Later in this tutorial, you'll apply more elaborate formatting to the table.

To select and format the header row:

▶ **1.** Move the mouse pointer to the left of the table next to the first row (which contains the word "Item"). The pointer changes to a right-facing arrow ⇗.

▶ **2.** Click the left mouse button. The entire header row, including the end-of-cell mark in each cell and the end-of-row mark, is selected. See Figure 3-9. To format this row in bold, you could switch to the Home tab and click the Bold button or use the Mini toolbar, but it's faster to use a keyboard shortcut.

Header row selected ◀ Figure 3-9

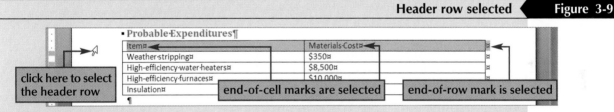

▶ **3.** Press the **Ctrl+B** keys. The headers are formatted in bold.

▶ **4.** Click anywhere in the table to deselect the header row, and then save your work.

You've created a very basic table. Now you can sort the information in the table and improve its appearance.

Sorting Rows in a Table

The term **sort** refers to the process of rearranging information in alphabetical, numerical, or chronological order. You can sort a series of paragraphs, such as a list or the rows of a table.

When you sort a table, you arrange the rows based on the contents of one of the columns. For example, you could sort the table you just created based on the contents of the Item column—either in ascending alphabetical order (from *A* to *Z*) or in descending alphabetical order (from *Z* to *A*). Alternately, you could sort the table based on the contents of the Materials Cost column—either in ascending numerical order (lowest to highest) or in descending numerical order (highest to lowest).

To sort a table, select the table, then, on the Table Tools Layout tab, click the Sort button. This opens the Sort dialog box, which provides a number of options that allow you to fine-tune the sorting process. You'll have to change fewer settings in the Sort dialog box if you first take the time to format the headers in bold, as you just did. That way Word recognizes the bold text as headers and excludes them from the sorting process, leaving them unsorted at the top of the table.

Reference Window | **Sorting the Rows of a Table**

- Format the column headers in bold, and then select the entire table.
- In the Data group on the Table Tools Layout tab, click the Sort button.
- In the Sort dialog box, click the Sort by arrow, and then select the header for the column you want to sort by. For example, if you want to organize the rows in the table according to the contents of the Last Name column, click "Last Name."
- In the Type list box located to the right of the Sort by list box, select the type of information stored in the column you want to sort by. You can choose to sort text, dates, or numbers.
- To sort in alphabetical, chronological, or numeric order, click the Ascending option button. To sort in reverse order, click the Descending option button.
- If you also want to sort by a second column, click the Then by arrow and click a column header. This is useful if, for example, you want to organize the table rows by last name, and then, within each last name, by first name. You can also specify the type of information in the Then by column, and whether you want to sort in ascending or descending order.
- Make sure the Header row option button is selected. This tells Word that the table you want to sort includes a header row that should not be sorted along with the other rows.
- Click the OK button.

Robin would like you to sort the table in ascending alphabetical order, based on the contents of the Item column.

To sort the information in the table:

1. Make sure the insertion point is somewhere in the table, and then click the **Table Tools Layout** tab.

2. In the Table group, click the **Select** button, and then click **Select Table**. The entire table is selected.

3. In the Data group, click the **Sort** button. The Sort dialog box opens, as shown in Figure 3-10. By default, the far-left column heading ("Item") is already selected in the Sort by list box. This tells Word to sort the rows of the table according to the contents of the Item column, which is what you want. Word recognizes the information in the Item column as text, so "Text" is selected by default in the Type list box. (If the column contained dates or numbers, you would see Date or Number in the Type list box instead.) The Ascending option button next to the Sort by list box is selected by default, indicating that Word will sort the contents of the Item column from *A* to *Z*. The Header row option button is selected in the lower-left corner of the dialog box. This indicates that the table contains a header row that should not be sorted along with the rest of the rows. The default settings in the Sort dialog box are all correct, so you can go ahead and complete the sort process.

Sort dialog box ◀ Figure 3-10

► **4.** Click the **OK** button. The Sort dialog box closes.

► **5.** Click anywhere in the table to deselect it. Rows 2 through 5 are now arranged alphabetically according to the text in the Item column, with the "Weather stripping" row now at the bottom. When you sort a table, all the items in a row move together as one entity. In this table, that means the materials cost doesn't become separated from its item during the sort process. Also note that the header row remains in its original position at the top of the table. See Figure 3-11.

Trouble? If the sort was unsuccessful, click the Undo button on the Quick Access Toolbar, and then repeat Steps 1 through 5.

Table after being sorted ◀ Figure 3-11

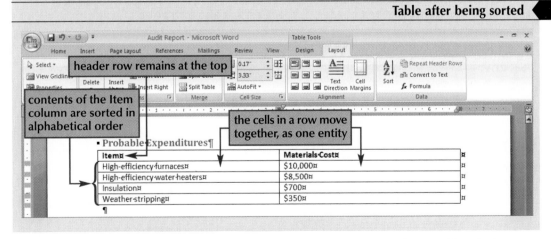

The table looks good, but after reviewing it, Robin decides that she should include an estimate of the labor cost for each item. She asks you to insert a "Labor Cost" column.

Inserting Rows and Columns in a Table

You will often need to modify a table structure by adding or deleting rows and columns. With the buttons in the Rows & Columns group on the Table Tools Layout tab, this is a straightforward task. You'll see how these buttons work in the following steps, as you insert a new column between the Item column and the Materials Cost column. To insert a column, you begin by selecting a column to the left or right of the location where you want to insert a column.

To insert a column in the table:

▶ 1. Click any cell in the Item column, click the **Select** button in the Table group, and then click **Select Column**. The Item column is selected.

▶ 2. In the Rows & Columns group, click the **Insert Right** button. A new, blank column is inserted to the right of the Item column. The three columns in the table are narrower than the original two columns; the overall width of the table does not change.

▶ 3. Click in the top cell of the new column, and enter the following header and data. Use the ↓ key to move the insertion point down through the column.

Labor Cost

$3,000 to $4,500

$2,000 to $3,000

$1,000

$1,500

When you are finished, your table should look like the one in Figure 3-12. Because you selected the entire header row when you formatted the original headers in bold, the newly inserted header, "Labor Cost," is also formatted in bold.

> **Tip**
>
> Word inserts the same number of new columns as are selected. For example, if you had selected two columns in Step 1, Word would have inserted two new columns in the table.

| Figure 3-12 | New Labor Cost column |

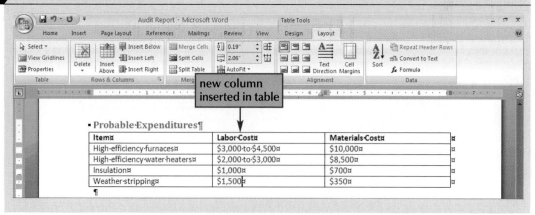

Inserting a row is similar to inserting a column. First, you select a row below the location where you want to insert a row, and then, in the Rows & Columns group, click the Insert Above button. Alternatively, you could select a row above where you want to insert a row, and then click the Insert Below button.

You're almost finished adjusting the structure of the table. But first Robin would like to delete the Insulation row because she's just learned that the costs listed for weather stripping actually cover both weather stripping and insulation.

Deleting Rows and Columns

When you consider deleting a row, you need to be clear about whether you want to delete the *contents* of the row, or the contents and the *structure* of the row. You can delete the *contents* of a row by selecting the row and pressing the Delete key. The same is true for deleting the contents of an individual cell, a column, or the entire table. To delete the *structure* of a row, column, or the entire table—including its contents—you select the row (or column or the entire table) and then use the Delete button in the Rows & Columns group. To delete multiple rows or columns, start by selecting all the rows or columns you want to delete.

Before you delete the Insulation row, you need to edit the bottom row.

To delete the Insulation row:

▶ **1.** In the cell containing the text "Weather stripping," click to the right of the "g," press the **spacebar**, and then type **and insulation**. The cell now reads "Weather stripping and insulation." Next, you can delete the Insulation row, which is no longer necessary.

▶ **2.** Select the Insulation row by clicking to the left of the row in the left margin.

▶ **3.** In the Rows & Columns group, click the **Delete** button. The Delete menu opens, displaying options for deleting cells, columns, rows, or the entire table. See Figure 3-13.

Deleting a row ◀ Figure 3-13

▶ **4.** Click **Delete Rows**. The Insulation row is removed from the table.

▶ **5.** Save your work.

The table now contains all the information Robin wants to include. Your next job is to adjust the widths of the three columns to make the table attractive and easy to read.

Changing Column Widths

Columns that are too wide for the material they contain can make a table hard to read. You can quickly change a column's width by dragging the column's right border to a new position. Or, if you prefer, you can double-click a column border to make the column width adjust automatically to accommodate the widest entry in the column.

You'll adjust the columns in Robin's table by double-clicking the right column borders. You need to start by making sure that no part of the table is selected. Otherwise, when you double-click the border, only the width of the selected part of the table will change.

To change the width of the columns in the table:

▶ **1.** Verify that no part of the table is selected, and then position the mouse pointer over the right border of the Labor Cost column until the pointer changes to ┿╫┿. See Figure 3-14.

| Figure 3-14 | Changing the column width |

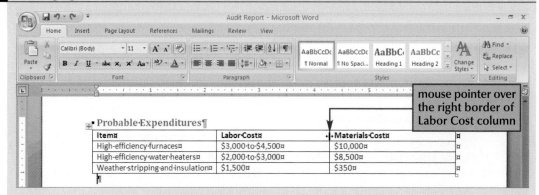

▶ **2.** Double-click the left mouse button. The right column border moves left so that the column is just wide enough to accommodate the widest entry in the column.

▶ **3.** Double-click the right border of the Materials Cost column. The Materials Cost column becomes narrower, leaving just enough room for the widest entry in the column (the column header "Materials Cost").

▶ **4.** Repeat this procedure to adjust the width of the Item column. All three columns in the table are now just wide enough to accommodate their widest entries.

The table is almost finished. Your final job is to add some color and modify the cell borders. As you'll see in the next section, Word's predefined table styles make quick work of these tasks.

Formatting Tables with Styles

Word includes a variety of built-in table styles that you can use to add shading, color, borders, and other design elements with a single click. You can choose a style that includes different formatting for the header row than for the rest of the table. Or you can choose a style that instead applies different formatting to the **first column**, or header column (that is, the far-left column, which sometimes contains headers that identify the type of information in each row). Some styles format the rows in alternating colors, called banded rows, while others format the columns in alternating colors, called banded columns.

At first, the variety of styles available for formatting your tables may seem overwhelming, but once you become familiar with the basic variations (header row formatting, first row formatting, banded rows, banded columns, etc.), you'll grow comfortable with choosing a style that suits your needs. Six table styles are always visible in the Table Styles group on the Table Tools Design tab. To see the complete collection, click the More button in the Table Styles group. After you apply a table style, you can modify it by selecting or deselecting the check boxes in the Table Style Options group on the Table Tools Design tab.

Formatting a Table with a Built-In Table Style | Reference Window

- Click in the table you want to format, and then click the Table Tools Design tab.
- In the Table Styles group, click the More button to display the Table Styles gallery.
- Position the mouse pointer over a style in the Table Styles gallery to see a live preview of the style in the document.
- In the Table Styles gallery, click the style you want.
- To apply or remove style elements (such as special formatting for the header row, banded rows, or banded columns), select or deselect check boxes as necessary in the Table Style Options group.

Robin wants to use a table style that emphasizes the header row with special formatting, that does not include column borders, and that uses color to separate the rows.

To apply a table style to the Probable Expenditures table:

▶ 1. Click anywhere in the table, and then click the **Table Tools Design** tab. Within the six visible styles, the plain black and white grid style is highlighted, indicating that it is the current style of the table in the document. See Figure 3-15.

Table styles visible on the Table Tools Design tab Figure 3-15

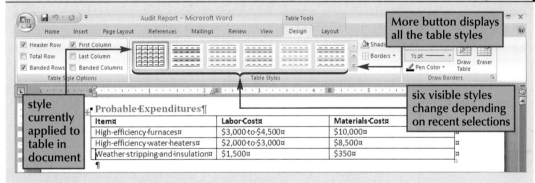

▶ 2. In the Table Styles group, click the **More** button. The Table Styles gallery opens. Now the plain black and white grid style appears at the top of the gallery, under the heading "Plain Tables." The more elaborate Table Styles appear below, in the "Built-In" section of the gallery.

▶ 3. Use the gallery's vertical scroll bar to view the complete collection of table styles. When you are finished looking, scroll up until you can see the Built-In heading again.

▶ 4. Move the mouse pointer over the style located in the fourth row down, second column from the left. See Figure 3-16. A ScreenTip displays the style's official name, "Medium Shading 1 – Accent 1." The style consists of a dark blue heading row, with alternating rows of light blue and white below and no borders between the columns. A live preview of the style is visible in the document, although the size of the Table Styles gallery makes this hard to see.

Figure 3-16 ▶ **Table Styles gallery**

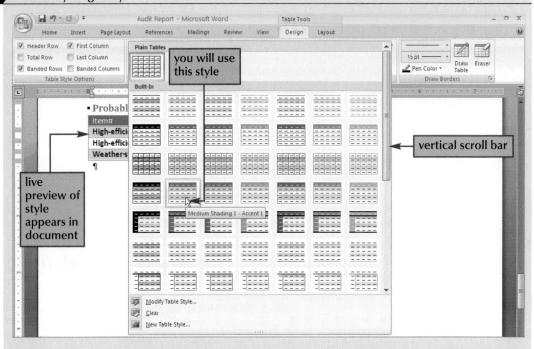

▶ **5.** Click the **Medium Shading 1 – Accent 1** style. The Table Styles gallery closes. The table's header row is formatted with dark blue shading and white text. The rows below are shaded light blue and white.

The only problem with the newly formatted table is that the text in the first column is formatted in bold. In tables where the first column contains headers, bold would be appropriate, but this isn't the case with Robin's table. You'll fix this by deselecting the First Column check box in the Table Style Options group.

To remove the bold formatting from the first column:

▶ **1.** In the Table Style Options group, click the **First Column** check box to remove the check. The bold formatting is removed from the entries in the Item column. Note that the Header Row check box is selected. This indicates that the table's header row is emphasized with special formatting (dark blue shading with white text). The Banded Rows check box is also selected because the table is formatted with banded rows of blue and white. See Figure 3-17.

Figure 3-17 ▶ **Deselecting the First Column check box**

Using Table Styles vs. Manually Formatting a Table		InSight

You can create a table by formatting it "manually" with the buttons on the Table Tools Design tab. For example, you can change the thickness and color of the table borders using the options in the Draw Borders group, and you can add shading using the Shading button in the Table Styles group. However, applying formatting by clicking individual buttons is time consuming. Also, it's easy to make mistakes. For example, you might omit a necessary column border or apply color inconsistently. Instead of formatting a table manually, it's better to start with the built-in table style that most closely resembles the formatting you want. Then you can fine tune the formatting. And remember, if you don't like the selection of table styles available in your document, change the document's theme and look again at the available table styles. Each theme includes a complete set of table styles.

The completed table looks crisp and professional. In the next session, you'll turn your attention to completing the rest of the report.

Session 3.1 Quick Check		Review

1. Explain how to format a heading with a Quick Style.
2. True or False: To insert a manual page break, you can press the Ctrl+End key combination.
3. Explain how to insert a table in a document.
4. What key can you press to move the insertion point from one cell to another in a table?
5. What's the most foolproof way to select part of a table?
6. Explain how to sort a table.
7. True or False: To insert a column, you begin by selecting a column to the left or right of the location where you want to insert a column.

Session 3.2

Setting Tab Stops

A **tab stop** (often called just a **tab**) is a location on the horizontal ruler where the insertion point moves when you press the Tab key. Tab stops are useful for aligning small amounts of data in columns. There are default tab stops every one-half inch on the horizontal ruler, indicated by the small gray tick marks along the bottom edge of the ruler. When you press the Tab key, the insertion point moves to the next tab stop to the right. It's helpful to have the Show/Hide ¶ button selected when you work with tab stops, because then you can see the nonprinting tab character (→) that is inserted when you press the Tab key. A tab is just like any other character you type; you can delete it by pressing the Backspace key or the Delete key.

Text next to tab stops can be aligned in a variety of ways. The five major styles are Left, Center, Right, Decimal, and Bar, as shown in Figure 3-18. The Left style is selected by default and is probably the tab style you'll use most often.

Figure 3-18 ▶ Tab stop alignment styles

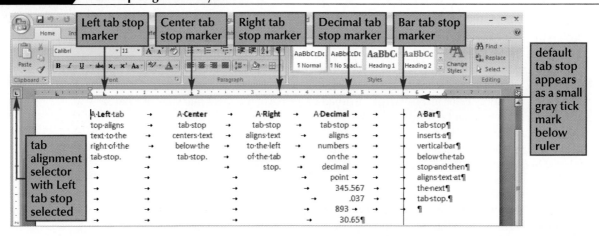

You can set tab stops a few different ways. The simplest is to first select an alignment style from the tab alignment selector, located at the left end of the horizontal ruler, and then click the horizontal ruler where you want the tab stop. When you insert a tab stop in this way, all of the default tab stops to its left are removed. This means you have to press the Tab key only once to move the insertion point to your new tab stop.

Reference Window | **Setting and Clearing Tab Stops**

- To set a tab stop, click the tab alignment selector on the far left of the horizontal ruler until the appropriate tab stop alignment style appears, and then click the horizontal ruler where you want to position the tab stop. Press the Tab key to move the insertion point to the new tab stop.
- To align text that already contains a nonprinting tab character, select the text and then insert a tab stop on the horizontal ruler.
- To remove a tab stop, locate it on the ruler, click it, and drag it off the ruler (into the document window).
- To clear all tab stops in the document or in a selected paragraph, click the Dialog Box Launcher in the Paragraph group, click the Indents and Spacing tab, click the Tabs button, and then click the Clear All button. Click the OK button to close the Tabs dialog box.

In the report, you need to type the list of consultants and their titles. As you type, you'll discover whether Word's default tab stops are appropriate for this document or whether you need to add a new tab stop.

To enter the list of consultants using tabs:

▶ 1. If you took a break after the previous session, make sure Word is running and that the Audit Report document is open. Check that the ruler and nonprinting characters are displayed and that the document is displayed in Print Layout view.

▶ 2. Scroll as necessary to display the Expert Advice section, and then click to the right of the "y" in "Tandra J. Melleray."

▶ 3. Press the **Tab** key. A tab character appears, and the insertion point moves to the first tab stop after the "y" in "Melleray." This tab stop is one of the default tabs and is located at the 1.5-inch mark on the horizontal ruler. See Figure 3-19.

Tab character ◄ **Figure 3-19**

▶ **4.** Type **Associate Engineer**. You've finished typing the first row in the list of consultants. You could press the Enter key now to end the paragraph and start a new paragraph for the next row in the list. However, remember that Word inserts extra space after every paragraph; this will result in a list in which the items are spaced too far apart. Instead, you can use the **Shift+Enter key combination** to insert a manual line break. A **manual line break** moves the insertion point to the next line without actually starting a new paragraph, so no extra space is inserted.

▶ **5.** Press the **Shift+Enter** keys. The insertion point moves to the next line and Word inserts a manual line break nonprinting character. See Figure 3-20.

Starting a new line without starting a new paragraph ◄ **Figure 3-20**

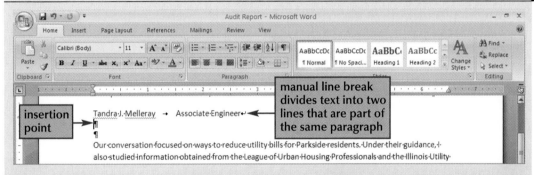

▶ **6.** Type **Susan Tiu** and then press the **Tab** key. The insertion point moves to the first available tab stop, which is another default tab stop, this time located at the 1-inch mark on the horizontal ruler.

▶ **7.** Type **Senior Engineer** and then press the **Shift+Enter** keys to move to the next line.

As you can see, Susan Tiu's title does not align with Tandra J. Melleray's title on the line above it. You'll fix this in a moment by inserting a new tab stop that overrides the default tab stops. But first continue typing the list of names.

▶ **8.** Type **Peter Zaravaggio**, press the **Tab** key, and then type **Community Liaison**. When you are finished, your document should look like the one in Figure 3-21.

Trouble? If you see extra space between the names in your list, you probably forgot to press the Shift+Enter keys at the end of one or more of the lines in the list. Delete the paragraph mark at the end of such a line, and then press the Shift+Enter keys. Repeat for the other lines, if necessary.

Figure 3-21 ▶ List of consultants

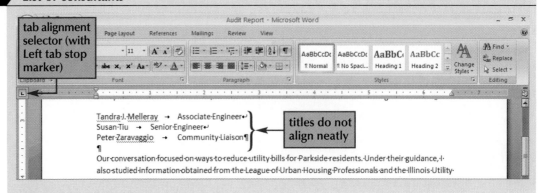

The list of names and titles is not aligned properly. You'll fix this by inserting a new tab stop.

To add a new tab stop to the horizontal ruler:

▶ **1.** Click and drag the mouse pointer to select the list of consultants and their titles.

▶ **2.** Make sure the current tab stop alignment style is Left tab ⎣L⎦, as shown in Figure 3-21. If the Left tab marker is not displayed as in Figure 3-21, click the tab alignment selector one or more times until ⎣L⎦ appears.

▶ **3.** Click the tick mark on the ruler that is at 2.5 inches. Word inserts a Left tab stop at that location and removes the default tab stops to its left. The column of titles shifts to the new tab stop.

▶ **4.** Click anywhere in the list of names and titles. See Figure 3-22.

Figure 3-22 ▶ Titles aligned at the new tab stop

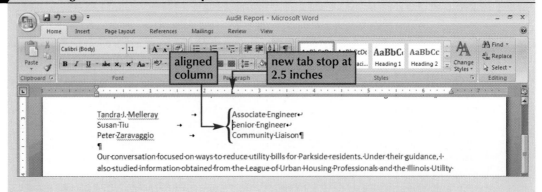

▶ **5.** Save your work.

The two columns of information are now aligned, as Robin requested. In the Case Problems at the end of this tutorial, you'll have a chance to work with tab stops using the Tabs dialog box, which you can open via the Tabs button in the Paragraph dialog box. Among other things, the Tabs dialog box allows you to insert a **dot leader**, which is a row of dots (or other characters) between tabbed text. A dot leader makes it easier to read a long list of tabbed material because the eye can follow the dots from one item to the next.

Choosing Between Tabs and Tables | InSight

What's the best way to align text in columns? It depends. Tabs work well for small amounts of information, such as two columns with three rows, but they become cumbersome when you need to organize a lot of data. For larger amounts of information, tables are better. Unlike with tabbed columns of data, it's easy to add data to tables by inserting columns. Also, you can format tables more elaborately than you can format tabbed columns.

Whatever you do, don't try to align columns of data by adding extra spaces with the spacebar. Although the text might seem precisely aligned on the screen, it might not be aligned when you print the document. Furthermore, if you edit the text, the spaces you inserted to align your columns will be affected by your edits; they get moved just like regular text, ruining your alignment. One of the main advantages of tab stops and tables is that when you edit data, the alignment remains intact.

Your next job is to add two footnotes to the document that provide further information about topics discussed in Robin's report.

Creating Footnotes and Endnotes

A **footnote** is an explanatory comment or reference that appears at the bottom of a page. When you create a footnote, Word inserts a small, superscript number (called a **reference marker**) in the text. The term "superscript" means that the number is raised slightly above the line of text. Word then inserts the same number in the page's bottom margin and positions the insertion point next to it so you can type the text of the footnote. **Endnotes** are similar, except that the text of an endnote appears at the end of a document. Also, by default, the reference marker for an endnote is a lowercase Roman numeral.

Word automatically manages the reference markers for you, keeping them sequential from the beginning of the document to the end, no matter how many times you add, delete, or move footnotes or endnotes. For example, if you move a paragraph containing footnote 4 so that it falls before the paragraph containing footnote 1, Word renumbers all the footnotes in the document to keep them sequential.

Working with Footnotes and Endnotes | Reference Window

- To create a footnote, click where you want to insert a footnote, click the References tab, in the Footnotes group click the Insert Footnote button, and then type the text of the footnote in the bottom margin.
- To create an endnote, click where you want to insert an endnote, click the References tab, in the Footnotes group click the Insert Endnote button, and then type the text of the endnote at the end of the document.
- When you are finished typing the text of a footnote or endnote, click in the body of the document to continue working on it.
- To delete a footnote or endnote, delete its reference marker (the small, superscript number) in the text.
- To edit the text of a footnote or endnote, click in the bottom margin or at the end of the document and edit the note.

Robin asks you to insert a footnote at the end of the paragraph just above the heading "Final Recommendation." The last sentence of this paragraph refers to studies on the effectiveness of residential energy audits. Robin wants a footnote that explains where more information about those studies can be found.

To add a footnote to the report:

▶ **1.** Near the bottom of page 1, locate the paragraph just above the heading "Final Recommendation."

▶ **2.** Click to the right of the period after "household" at the end of the paragraph. The insertion point is now located at the end of the paragraph, where you want the footnote.

▶ **3.** Click the **References** tab, and then in the Footnotes group, click the **Insert Footnote** button. A superscript "1" is inserted to the right of the period after "household." Word also inserts the number "1" in the bottom margin below a separator line. The insertion point is now located next to the number in the bottom margin, ready for you to type the text of the footnote. See Figure 3-23.

Figure 3-23 Inserting a footnote

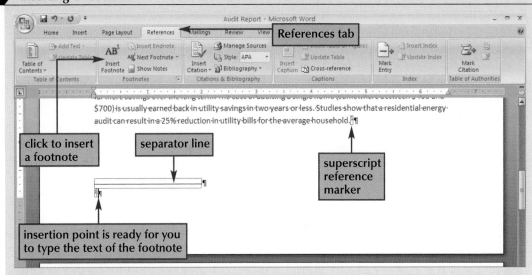

▶ **4.** Type the following footnote text:

For more information, see "A Consumer's Guide to Energy," available at www.course.com/consumer/energy. This helpful Web site is maintained by Course Energy Consultants.

When you press the spacebar after the Web address in the footnote, Word underlines the address and formats it in blue, indicating that it is a live hyperlink, as shown in Figure 3-24. This means people reading the document in Word can open the Web site by pressing the Ctrl key and clicking the link. Because Robin plans to distribute only a hard copy of the report, she asks you to disable the hyperlink.

Figure 3-24 Footnote containing live hyperlink

▶ **5.** Right-click the **hyperlink** and then click **Remove Hyperlink** in the shortcut menu. The disabled hyperlink is formatted to match the surrounding text.

The first footnote is complete. Robin would like you to insert a second footnote explaining more about the cost of a typical residential home energy audit. You start by clicking the location in the main document where you want to insert the footnote's reference marker.

To insert a second footnote:

▶ **1.** In the same paragraph (the paragraph above the heading "Final Recommendation"), locate the second to last sentence, which begins "The cost of auditing a single home…" and then click at the end of the sentence. The insertion point should be positioned to the right of the period after "less."

▶ **2.** In the Footnotes group, click the **Insert Footnote** button. Because this footnote is placed earlier in the document than the one you just created, Word inserts a superscript "1" for this footnote, and the other footnote is now numbered "2." See Figure 3-25.

Inserting a second footnote | Figure 3-25

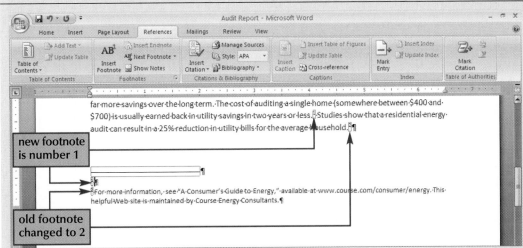

▶ **3.** Type the following footnote text:

While cost varies by auditor, the price of an audit is usually based on a home's square footage.

▶ **4.** Zoom out so you can see the entire page, with the footnotes at the bottom. Note that to make room for the two footnotes, the "Final Recommendation" heading and the paragraph that follows it were moved to the next page. One of the advantages of using Word's heading styles (such as the Heading 1 Quick Style you applied earlier) is that they tell Word to keep the heading and the paragraph that follows it together.

▶ **5.** Zoom back in so you can read the document, and then save your work.

The footnotes will provide helpful information for the board of directors. Next, Robin wants to include a sample of the type of handout she plans to post on community bulletin boards at Parkside, encouraging residents to take part in the energy audit process. Before you can create the handout, you need to divide the document into sections.

Formatting a Document in Sections

Robin wants to format the handout in **landscape orientation**—that is, with the page turned so it is wider than it is tall. The rest of the report is currently formatted in **portrait orientation** (with the page taller than it is wide), which is the default orientation for all Word documents and is appropriate for a report. To format part of a document in an orientation different from the rest of the document, you need to divide the document into sections.

A **section** is a part of a document that can have its own page orientation, margins, headers, footers, and so on. Each section, in other words, is like a document within a document. To divide a document into sections, you insert a **section break**, which appears as a dotted line with the words "Section Break." When you insert a section break, you can choose to have the section start a new page (a Next Page section break) or have the section start at the location of the insertion point, without changing the page flow (a Continuous section break). You insert section breaks with the Breaks button on the Page Layout tab.

To insert a section break below the table:

▶ 1. Press the **Ctrl+End** keys to move the insertion point to the end of the document (to the blank paragraph below the table).

▶ 2. Click the **Page Layout** tab, and then, in the Page Setup group, click the **Breaks** button. The Breaks menu opens, as shown in Figure 3-26. The Page Breaks part of the menu includes options for controlling how the text flows from page to page. The first option, Page, inserts a page break (just like the Page Break button on the Insert tab that you used earlier). The Section Breaks part of the menu includes four types of section breaks. The two you'll use most often are Next Page, which starts a section on a new page, and Continuous, which starts a new section at the location of the insertion point, without starting a new page.

Figure 3-26	Breaks menu

▶ 3. Under "Section Breaks," click **Next Page**. A section break is inserted, and the insertion point moves to the top of the newly inserted page.

4. Scroll up until you can see the double-dotted line and the words "Section Break (Next Page)" below the table. This line indicates that a new section begins on the next page.

Trouble? If you see a single dotted line and the words "Page Break," you inserted a page break rather than a Next Page section break. Click the Undo button on the Quick Access Toolbar, and then repeat Steps 1 through 4.

5. Save your work.

You've created a new page that is a separate section from the rest of the report. The sections are numbered consecutively, so that the first part of the document is section 1 and the new page is section 2. Now you can format section 2 in landscape orientation without affecting the rest of the document.

To format section 2 in landscape orientation:

1. Scroll down if necessary and verify that the insertion point is positioned at the top of the new page 4.

2. Change the zoom setting to 50% (this will allow you to see clearly the page orientation change in the next steps), and then scroll down, if necessary, so you can see the page containing the table and the new page 4, which is blank.

3. In the Page Setup group, click the **Orientation** button. The Orientation menu opens.

4. Click **Landscape**. Section 2, which consists solely of page 4, changes to landscape orientation, as shown in Figure 3-27. Section 1, which consists of pages 1–3, remains in portrait orientation.

Page 4 formatted in landscape orientation ◀ **Figure 3-27**

> **5.** Zoom back in so you can read the document text, and then save your work.

Page 4 is now formatted in landscape orientation, ready for you to create Robin's handout, which will consist of an illustration, or **graphic**, that explains the stages and ultimate goal of the energy audit process. With Word's SmartArt feature, you can quickly create great looking illustrations for a wide variety of purposes.

Creating SmartArt

The **SmartArt** feature allows you to create diagrams and charts to illustrate concepts that would otherwise require several paragraphs of explanation. To begin creating a SmartArt graphic, you switch to the Insert tab and then, in the Illustrations group, click the SmartArt button. This opens the Choose a SmartArt Graphic dialog box, where you can select from seven categories of graphics, including graphics designed to illustrate relationships, processes, and hierarchies. Within each category, you can then choose from numerous designs. Once inserted into your document, a SmartArt graphic contains placeholder text that you replace with something appropriate for your needs. When a SmartArt graphic is selected, the SmartArt tools appear on the Ribbon, with two tabs of editing options. In the following steps, you will begin creating a SmartArt graphic that summarizes the energy audit process.

To create a SmartArt graphic:

> **1.** Verify that the insertion point is located at the top of page 4, which is blank.

> **2.** Click the **Insert** tab, and then, in the Illustrations group, click the **SmartArt** button. The Choose a SmartArt Graphic dialog box opens. This dialog box consists of three panels. The left panel lists the categories of SmartArt Graphics; the middle panel displays the graphics associated with the category selected in the left panel; and the right panel displays a larger image of the graphic that is currently selected in the middle panel, along with an explanation of the graphic's purpose. Currently, All is selected in the left panel. This means you could use the scroll bar in the middle panel to see all of the possible SmartArt graphics.

> **3.** Explore the Choose a SmartArt Graphic dialog box by selecting categories in the left panel and viewing the graphics displayed in the middle panel.

> **4.** In the left panel, click **Relationship**, and then, in the middle panel, click the **Equation** graphic (in the far-left column, fifth row from the top), which shows three circles in an equation. In the right panel, you see an explanation of the Equation graphic, as shown in Figure 3-28.

Tip

To see a detailed view of a graphic, click that graphic in the middle panel and view the details that appear in the right panel.

Selecting a SmartArt graphic ◄ Figure 3-28

5. Click the **OK** button. The Choose a SmartArt Graphic dialog box closes, and the Equation graphic, with placeholder text, is inserted at the top of page 4. The graphic is surrounded by a rectangular border, indicating that it is selected. The SmartArt tools are visible on the Ribbon. To the left or right of the graphic, you might also see the Text Pane, a small window with a title bar that reads "Type your text here."

6. If you do *not* see the Text Pane, click the **left-facing arrow** on the left side of the SmartArt Border, as shown in Figure 3-29.

SmartArt graphic with Text Pane displayed ◄ Figure 3-29

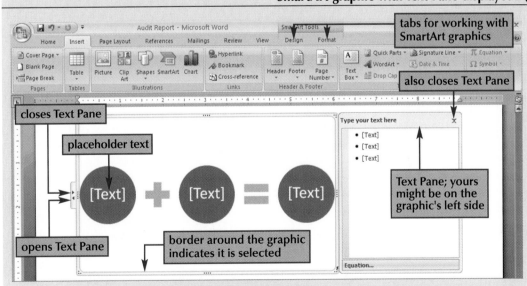

The Text Pane is useful for complicated graphics containing many parts. However, the Equation graphic is simple enough that you can type the text directly in the circles, so you will close the Text Pane in the next step.

Trouble? If you inserted a graphic other than the equation graphic, click the Undo button on the Quick Access Toolbar and start again with Step 1.

Trouble? If you see other elements in your SmartArt graphic, such as a square border around one of the blue circles, or if you see the insertion point blinking inside the Text Pane, don't be concerned. Just continue with the steps.

▶ **7.** Click the **Close** button ⊠ in the upper-right corner of the Text Pane (shown in Figure 3-29). You will type the text directly into the circles.

Now you are ready to begin typing text in the graphic.

To add text to the SmartArt graphic:

▶ **1.** In the blue circle on the left, click the placeholder text (which reads "[Text]"). The placeholder text disappears and the insertion point blinks inside the left circle. (The insertion point might be hard to see on the dark blue background.) The left circle is surrounded by a box consisting of a dotted line, with small white circles on the corners and a small white square in the middle of each side. This box indicates that the blue circle is selected, ready for you to replace the placeholder text with your text. The circles and squares along the border of the box are called **handles**; you can drag them to change the shape of the item inside the box. You'll learn more about dragging handles to change the shape of a graphic in Tutorial 4. For now, you can ignore them. See Figure 3-30.

Trouble? If the circle is selected, but the placeholder text is still visible, you clicked the circle, but not the placeholder text within the circle. Repeat Step 1, but take care to click the placeholder text.

Figure 3-30 ▶ **Entering text in the SmartArt graphic**

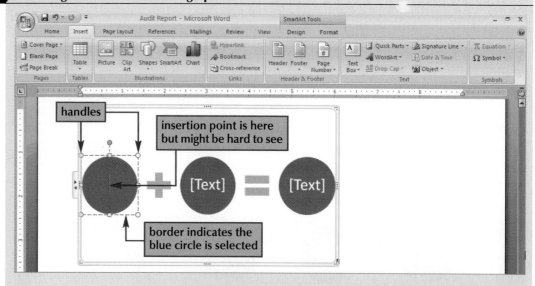

▶ **2.** Type **Energy Audit**. The font size gets smaller as you type, shrinking to accommodate each new letter without increasing the size of the circle.

▶ **3.** Click the placeholder text in the middle circle, type **Repairs and Upgrades**, click the **right circle** to select it, and type **Lower Utility Bills**. The right circle remains selected.

Trouble? If you make a typing mistake, click the circle containing the error and edit the text as you would ordinary text, using the Backspace or Delete keys as necessary.

▶ **4.** Click in the white area inside the SmartArt border to deselect the right circle. The equation now reads "Energy Audit + Repairs and Upgrades = Lower Utility Bills."

The graphic is almost finished. Your last task is to increase its size so it fills the page. To resize the entire SmartArt graphic, you drag the outer border.

To adjust the size of the SmartArt graphic:

▶ **1.** Zoom out so you can see the entire page.

▶ **2.** Position the mouse pointer over the lower-right corner of the SmartArt border. The pointer changes to a diagonal, double-sided arrow ⬉. As you can see on the ruler, the SmartArt border is currently about six inches wide. See Figure 3-31.

Mouse pointer on SmartArt border ◀ **Figure 3-31**

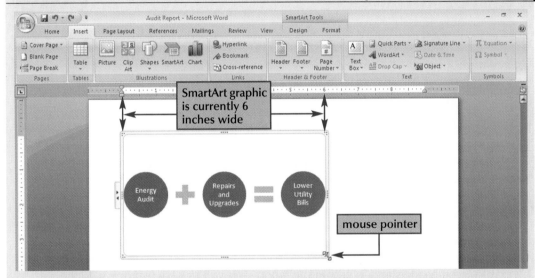

Trouble? If the pointer changes to a four-sided arrow ✥, you haven't positioned the pointer correctly over the lower-right corner. Reposition the pointer until it changes to a diagonal, double-sided arrow, as shown in Figure 3-31.

▶ **3.** Drag the pointer down and to the right. As you drag, the pointer changes to a crosshair ╋. A rectangular outline moves with the pointer, showing how the dimensions of the SmartArt border will appear when you release the mouse button. The size of the graphic won't actually change until you release the mouse button.

Trouble? If the graphic changes size, you released the mouse button too early. Undo the change, and begin again with Step 2.

▶ **4.** Position the pointer in the lower-right corner of the page, so the outline is approximately 9 inches wide and 6.5 inches high, but do *not* release the mouse button yet. Compare your screen to Figure 3-32 to make sure you have the pointer in the correct location.

Figure 3-32 ▸ **Dragging the SmartArt border**

> **5.** Release the mouse button. The SmartArt graphic resizes, so that it is now 9 inches wide and 6.5 inches high, taking up most of the page.

> **6.** Click outside the SmartArt border to view the graphic centered on the page.

The SmartArt graphic is eye-catching and succinctly explains the goal of the energy audit. Robin will add a heading and some text introducing the graphic later. Your next job is to insert headers and footers in the report. This will involve working with the two sections separately.

Adding Headers and Footers

Text that is printed at the top of every page is called a **header**. For example, the information printed at the top of this textbook page is a header. A **footer** is text that is printed at the bottom of every page.

There are two ways to begin inserting a header or footer: (1) you can double-click in the header area (in a page's top margin) or in the footer area (in a page's bottom margin); or (2) you can click the Header button or the Footer button on the Insert tab. Either way, the document switches to **Header and Footer view**, with special tools related to working with headers and footers displayed on the Ribbon. In Header and Footer view, the document text is dimmed, indicating that it cannot be edited while you are in this view.

Some headers and footers also include **document controls**, which are similar to the kinds of controls (text boxes, list boxes, etc.) that you might encounter in a dialog box. Most of the document controls you'll see in headers and footers are text boxes, where you can enter important information such as the document title or the name of the document's author. Any information that you enter in a document control is displayed in the header or footer as ordinary text, but it is also stored in the Word file so that Word can easily reuse it in other parts of the document. For example, later in this tutorial you will create a cover page for the report. Word's predefined cover pages include document controls similar to those found in headers and footers. So if you use a document control to enter the document title in the header, that same document title will show up in the cover page; there's no need to retype it. You'll see how this works shortly.

| **Two Ways to Insert a Header or Footer** | | InSight |

Double-clicking in the top or bottom margin is the simplest way to begin inserting a header or footer. After Word switches to Header and Footer view, you type the text of the header or footer. Three default tab stops allow you to left-align, center, or right-align the text in the header or footer. Many documents require page numbers; you can use the Page Number button on the Insert tab to insert the page number, which Word updates as you add and delete pages from your document.

For a more elaborate header or footer, use the Header and Footer buttons on the Insert tab. These buttons open menus that you can use to select from a number of predefined headers and footers, some of which include page numbers and graphic elements such as horizontal lines or shaded boxes.

You'll create a footer for the whole document (pages 1 through 4) that includes the page number and your name. You'll also create a header for section 1 (pages 1 through 3) that includes the document title and the date. When creating a header or footer for an entire document, you can work in the header or footer area for any page in the document. In the following steps, you'll start on page 1, so you can see how the footer fits below the footnotes at the bottom of the page.

To create a footer for the entire document:

▶ **1.** Zoom back in so you can read the text, and then scroll up until you can see the bottom of page 1.

▶ **2.** Double-click in the bottom margin of page 1, below the footnotes. The document switches to Header and Footer view. On the Ribbon, the Design tab appears below the label "Header & Footer Tools." The insertion point is positioned on the left side of the footer area, ready for you to begin typing. The label "Footer - Section 1" tells you that the insertion point is located in the footer for section 1. The document text (including the footnotes) is gray, indicating that you cannot edit it in Header and Footer view. The header area for section 1 is also visible on top of page 2. The default footer tab stops are visible on the ruler. See Figure 3-33.

| **Figure 3-33** | **Creating a footer** |

Trouble? If the document does not switch to Header and Footer view, you probably did not double-click in the right place in Step 2. Try again.

3. Type your first and last name, and then press the **Enter** key. The insertion point moves to the second line in the footer, on the left margin. This is where you will insert the page number.

4. In the Header & Footer group, click the **Page Number** button. The Page Number menu opens. This menu allows you to insert a page number at the top, bottom, or side of the page. Because the insertion point is already located where you want to insert the page number, you need to use the Current Position option.

5. Point to **Current Position**. A gallery of page number styles opens. The Plain Number style at the top simply inserts a page number, whereas other styles include the word "Page" or design elements such as special shapes or colors. Robin wants to use the Accent Bar 2 style. See Figure 3-34.

Inserting the page number in the footer ◄ Figure 3-34

use this option when the insertion point is located where you want to insert the page number

you will use this page number style

▶ **6.** Scroll down the page number gallery to get a sense of the types of page number styles available, then scroll back up and click the **Accent Bar 2** style (the third from the top). The word "Page," a vertical bar, and the page number are inserted in the document. Next, you'll check to make sure that the footer you just created for section 1 also appears in section 2.

▶ **7.** Scroll down to the end of the document until you can see the footer at the bottom of page 4. Scroll left or right, if necessary, so you can see the entire footer. The label at the top of the footer area on page 4, "Footer – Section 2," tells you that you are looking at the footer for section 2. You see the same text (your name, plus the page number) in this footer as in section 1.

You have successfully created a footer for the entire document. Now you can turn your attention to creating a header for section 1. Robin does not want to include a header in section 2 because it would distract attention from the SmartArt graphic. So your first task is to separate the header for section 1 from the header for section 2.

To separate the headers for section 1 and section 2:

▶ **1.** Click anywhere in the section 2 footer area, at the bottom of page 4. The insertion point moves to the section 2 footer.

▶ **2.** In the Navigation group, click the **Go to Header** button. The insertion point moves to the section 2 header at the top of page 4. Notice that in the Navigation group, the Link to Previous button is selected. This tells you that the section 2 header is linked to the header in the previous section (that is, the section 1 header). In other words, anything you add to the section 1 header will also be added to the section 2 header—but Robin wants the header to appear only in section 1. To make the section 2 header a separate entity, you need to break that link.

3. In the Navigation group, click the **Link to Previous** button to deselect it. Deselecting this button ensures that the header you create in section 1 will not appear in section 2. See Figure 3-35.

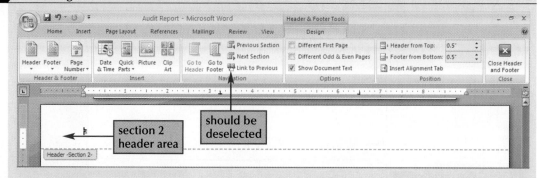

Next, you need to move the insertion point to the section 1 header.

Tip

When you create a header for a section, it doesn't matter what page you're working on, as long as the insertion point is located in a header in that section.

4. In the Navigation group, click the **Previous Section** button. The insertion point moves up to the nearest section 1 header, which is at the top of page 3. The label "Header – Section 1" identifies this as a section 1 header.

5. In the Header & Footer group, click the **Header** button. A gallery of header styles opens. See Figure 3-36.

Figure 3-36 | **Header gallery**

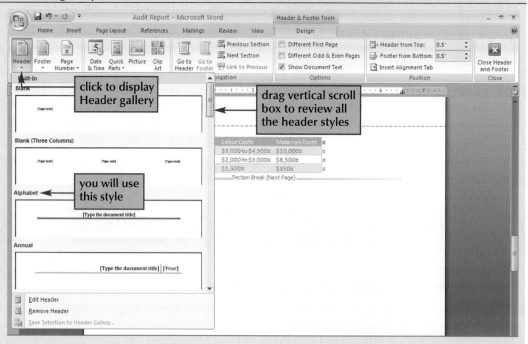

▶ **6.** Scroll down and review the various header styles, and then click the **Alphabet style** (third from the top). A horizontal line is inserted in the document, along with the placeholder text "[Type the document title]." The placeholder text is actually contained within a document control, although right now you can't see anything that would indicate this is anything other than ordinary text.

▶ **7.** Click the placeholder text **[Type the document title]**. The text is highlighted in blue, and a blue label with the word "Title" appears above the highlighted text. The blue highlighting and the blue label indicate that this is a document control. This particular document control is a text box; currently it contains the placeholder text "[Type the document title]." Now that the placeholder text is selected (as indicated by the blue highlight), you can replace it with something appropriate for Robin's report. See Figure 3-37.

Adding a header to section 1 ◀ | **Figure 3-37**

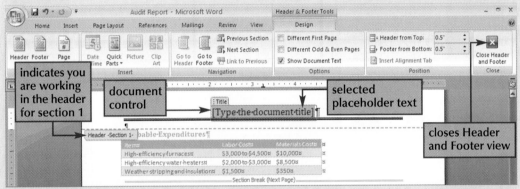

▶ **8.** Type **Parkside Energy Audit**. As soon as you begin typing, the placeholder text and the blue highlight disappear. The new title, "Parkside Energy Audit," is displayed in the document control. You are finished creating the header and footer for Robin's report, so you can close Header and Footer view and return to Print Layout view.

▶ **9.** In the Close group, click the **Close Header and Footer** button, save your work, and then zoom out until you can see all four pages of the document, including the header at the top of pages 1-3 and the footer at the bottom of pages 1-4. See Figure 3-38.

Figure 3-38 **Document with new header and footer**

The header and footer will make it easier for Parkside board members to keep track of the pages of the printed report. This will be especially helpful as Robin adds more pages to the report. Your last job is to create an attractive cover page.

Inserting a Cover Page

A document's cover page typically includes the title and the author of the report. Some writers also prefer to include a summary on the cover page rather than on the first page of the report itself, as Robin chose to do. In addition, you might include the date, the name and possibly the logo of your company or organization, and a subtitle. A cover page should not include the document header or footer.

To create a simple cover page for a report, you can do the following: insert a Next Page section break at the beginning of the document, adjust the header and footer settings for the new section 1 so the header and footer do not appear on the cover page, type the title and other information, and, finally, format the text to add emphasis. To center cover page text between the top and bottom margins, click the Page Layout tab. In the Page Setup group, click the Dialog Box Launcher, click the Layout tab, click the Vertical alignment arrow, and then click Center.

To create a more elaborate cover page—one that includes design elements such as color, lines, and graphics—you can use the Cover Page button on the Insert tab. The Cover Page button inserts a predefined cover page at the beginning of the document.

As with Word's predefined headers and footers, a predefined cover page includes document controls in which you can enter the document title, the document's author, the date, and so on. These document controls are linked to any other document controls in the document. You already entered the document title into a control in the header of Robin's report. You'll see the advantages of that choice in the following steps, as you insert a cover page into Robin's report.

To insert a cover page at the beginning of the report:

▶ **1.** Verify that the document is still zoomed so that you can see all four pages, and then press the **Ctrl+Home** keys. The insertion point moves to the beginning of the document. (You don't have to move the insertion point to the beginning of the document before you insert a cover page, but as a general rule it's a good idea to know where the insertion point is before you start a new task.)

▶ **2.** Click the **Insert** tab, and then, in the Pages group, click the **Cover Page** button. A gallery of cover pages opens. Notice that the names of the cover page styles match the names of the preformatted header styles you saw earlier. For example, the list includes an Alphabet cover page, which is similar in design to the Alphabet header you inserted earlier. To give a document a coherent look, it's helpful to use elements (such as cover pages and headers) with the same name throughout. However, in this case, the Alphabet cover page is more complicated than Robin wants, so you will use the Stacks style instead.

▶ **3.** Scroll down through the gallery to see the choice of cover pages and locate the Stacks cover page, in the left column, bottom row. See Figure 3-39.

Cover Page gallery ◀ **Figure 3-39**

Stacks style

drag the scroll bar to view the cover page choices

▶ **4.** Click the **Stacks** cover page. The new cover page is inserted at the beginning of the document.

▶ **5.** Zoom back in so you can read the document, and then scroll to view the new cover page. The insertion point is positioned in the upper-left corner of the document, just above a page break line. (In pages with complicated formatting, such as this one, a page break line sometimes appears in places you might not expect; you can ignore it.) On the right side of the document, you see controls for the title and the subtitle. Because you already entered "Parkside Energy Audit" in the Title document control in the header, the same text appears in the Title document control in the cover page. The Author document control (for entering the author's name) is located directly below the Subtitle document control. You might not be able to see the Author control. If you can see it, it probably contains a name inserted automatically by Word. See Figure 3-40.

Tip

To delete a cover page that you inserted from the Cover Page gallery, click the Cover Page button in the Pages group, and then click Remove Current Cover Page.

Trouble? If the header is on the new cover page, click the Cover Page button in the Pages group, click Remove Current Cover Page, and then repeat Steps 1 through 5.

Figure 3-40 | Newly inserted cover page

6. Click the text **[Type the document subtitle]**. The text is selected, and the document control label "Subtitle" is visible. The Table Tools contextual tabs appear on the Ribbon because, although you can't tell by looking at them, the document controls are actually organized on the page in a table structure. When you clicked the Subtitle document control, you clicked within the table.

7. Type **A Recommendation Report for the Parkside Housing Coalition Board of Directors**. Word formats the subtitle in a table cell below the title.

8. Press the **Tab** key to display and select the Author control, and then type **Robin Kinsella**. The cover page now includes a title, a subtitle, and Robin's name.

9. Save your work.

Your work on the report is finished. All that remains is to preview it and print it.

To preview and print the report:

▶ 1. Click the **Office Button** 🔘, point to **Print**, and then click **Print Preview**. The document is displayed in the Print Preview window.

▶ 2. On the Print Preview tab, in the Zoom group, click the **Two Pages** button to display the first two pages of the report side by side, and then use the **Next Page** and **Previous Page** buttons in the Preview group to move back and forth among the pages of the report. Make sure that the header is only visible on pages 2–4, and that the footer is visible on pages 2–5. Also, notice that Word renumbered the pages to account for the addition of the cover page, which is the new page 1.

▶ 3. If you need to make any changes to the report, return to Print Layout view, edit the document, and then return to Print Preview.

▶ 4. When you are satisfied with the document, click the **Print** button in the Print group, verify that the printer settings are correct, and then click the **OK** button.

▶ 5. Close the document.

You now have a draft of the Parkside Housing Coalition report, including a cover page, the report text, a nicely formatted table, and the SmartArt graphic (printed in landscape orientation). Eventually, Robin will add more information to the report, including an introduction to the table.

Session 3.2 Quick Check | Review

1. True or False: There are default tab stops every one-half inch on the horizontal ruler.
2. Explain how to create a footnote.
3. What button do you use to insert a section break, and where is it located?
4. How do you know if a SmartArt graphic is selected?
5. Explain two ways to switch to Header and Footer view.
6. True or False: For page numbering purposes, a cover page inserted from the Cover Page gallery is considered page 1.

In this tutorial, you learned how to format headings with Quick Styles and insert a manual page break. Then you learned how to insert a table, select all or part of a table, sort the rows of a table, insert and delete rows or columns, change column widths, and format a table to improve its appearance. You also learned how to set tab stops, create footnotes and endnotes, and insert a section break. Finally, you learned how to create a SmartArt graphic, add headers and footers, and insert a cover page.

Key Terms

cell	handles	reference marker
character-level formatting	header	Shift+Enter key
document controls	Header and Footer view	combination
dot leader	header column	SmartArt
endnote	header row	section
first column	landscape orientation	section break
font color	manual line break	sort
footer	manual page break	tab
footnote	paragraph-level formatting	tab stop
graphic	portrait orientation	table
gridlines	Quick Styles	

| Practice | | **Review Assignments** |

Apply the skills you learned in the tutorial using the same case scenario.

Data File needed for the Review Assignments: Class.docx

In conjunction with a local community college, Robin Kinsella has organized a series of computer training classes for Parkside residents to be held in the Parkside community center. She has begun work on a report for the board that outlines basic information about the classes and introduces the instructors. It's your job to format the report, add a table at the end containing a preliminary schedule, and create a sample graphic that Robin could use in a handout advertising the classes. When you are finished, Robin will expand each section of the report, adding more text to each. (*Note:* Text you need to type is shown in bold for ease of reference only; do not bold the text unless otherwise instructed.) Complete the following:

1. Open the file **Class** located in the Tutorial.03\Review folder included with your Data Files, and then save it as **Class Report** in the same folder.
2. Display the rulers and nonprinting characters and make sure the document is displayed in Print Layout view.
3. Format the document headings with the Heading 2 Quick Style. Use the Intense Quote style for the "Summary" heading and then indent the summary paragraph to match.
4. Click to the left of the heading "Schedule," insert a page break, move the insertion point to the end of the document, and then create the table shown in Figure 3-41.

Figure 3-41

Start Date	Topic
March 17	The Internet
April 21	Spreadsheets
January 13	Computer literacy
May 12	Simple database
June 9	HTML

5. Sort the table by the contents of the Start Date column in ascending order.
6. In the appropriate location, insert a new row for a word-processing class that starts on February 10.
7. Delete the HTML row at the bottom of the table.
8. Modify the widths of both columns to accommodate the widest entry in each.
9. Format the table with banded rows of pink and white and dark red shading for the header row, and then save your work.
10. On page 1, replace the text "[instructor names]" with the following list of instructors and their specialties. Insert a tab after each name, remembering that the list of specialties won't align properly until you complete Step 11. Remember to use the Shift+Enter key combination (instead of just the Enter key) to insert a new line for each name without adding extra space:

    Felicity J. Connelly-Porter   **Word processing**
    Antonio Morales   **Multimedia software**
    Jon Davis   **Web design**
    Amelia Guntz   **Database design and SQL programming**

11. Select the list of instructors and their specialties, and then insert a left tab stop 2.5 inches from the left margin.
12. Below the heading "Equipment Needs," locate the first sentence of the second paragraph, which begins "There are currently five...." At the end of that sentence, insert a footnote that reads **The computers should run either Windows Vista or Windows XP.**

13. Insert a Next Page section break after the table, format the new page 3 in landscape orientation, and then insert a SmartArt graphic that illustrates the advantages of computer classes. Use the Continuous Block Process graphic from the Process category, and, from left to right, include the following text: **Computer Education, Technological Advantage**, and **New Career Prospects**. Size the SmartArt graphic to fill the page.

14. Create a footer for sections 1 and 2 that aligns your name at the left margin. Insert the page number, without any design elements and without the word "Page," below your name.

15. Create a header for just section 1 using the Alphabet header style, enter **Parkside Computer Classes** as the document title, close Header and Footer view, and then save your work.

16. Insert a cover page using the Stacks style, verify that the document title is automatically inserted in the cover page, enter **An Informational Report** for the subtitle, and then enter your name for the author.

17. Save and preview the report, and then submit the finished document to your instructor, either in printed or electronic form, as requested.

| Apply | | **Case Problem 1** |

Apply the skills you learned to create an annual report for a textile store.

Data File needed for this Case Problem: Textiles.docx

Noblewood Textiles, Inc. As an assistant manager of Noblewood Textiles in San Diego, California, you must help prepare an annual report for the board of directors. (*Note*: Text you need to type is shown in bold for ease of reference only; do not bold the text unless otherwise instructed.) Complete the following:

1. Open the file **Textiles** located in the Tutorial.03\Case1 folder included with your Data Files, and then save it as **Textiles Report** in the same folder.

2. Check your screen to make sure your settings match those in the tutorials, with the document displayed in Print Layout view.

3. Format the headings using the Heading 1 Quick Style. (There are 11 headings, beginning with "Introduction" and ending with "Sales Forecast.")

🔷 **EXPLORE**

4. Select the list of members under the heading "Board of Directors," and then click the Page Layout tab. In the Paragraph group, click the Dialog Box Launcher, click the Indents and Spacing tab if necessary, and then click the Tabs button at the bottom of the dialog box. To insert a tab stop with a dot leader at the 4-inch mark, type 4 in the Tab stop position text box, verify that the Left option button is selected in the Alignment section, and then click the 2..... option button in the Leader section. Click the Set button. (Notice the Clear button, which you can use to clear the tab stop you just set, and the Clear All button, which you can use to clear all the custom tab stops from a document.) Click the OK button to close the Tabs dialog box. Notice the tab setting and the dot leaders.

5. On page 2, at the end of the paragraph below the heading "Summer Fiber Art Festival," insert the following endnote: **The Noblewood Web site is currently hosted by NetMind Solutions, but that may change in the coming year.**

6. At the end of the paragraph below the heading "Company Philosophy," insert the following endnote: **Our major, statewide competitor continues to be Boardman Fabrics, which has five retail outlets.**

7. Move the insertion point to the blank paragraph at the end of the Sales Forecast section (above the endnote), and then insert a table consisting of three columns and four rows.

8. Enter the following column headers and data. Format the header row in bold.

Department	January–June	Projected July–December
Yarn	$150,000	$180,000
Quilting	$120,000	$140,000
Garment	$75,000	$100,000

9. Sort the table in ascending order by department.
10. Insert a row above the Garment row and enter the following information:

Embroidery	$100,000	$120,000

11. Adjust the column widths so each column accommodates the widest entry.
12. Format the table using the Light List - Accent 1 table style which applies blue shading to the header row, no shading in the other rows, and no column borders. Save the document.
13. Create a footer for the document that aligns your name at the left margin and the page number (in the Accent Bar 3 style) at the right margin. (*Hint*: Press the Tab key twice to move the insertion point to the right margin before inserting the page number.)

⊕ **EXPLORE**
14. Insert a cover page using the Sideline style. Enter the company name, **Noblewood Textiles**, and the title, **Annual Report**. In the subtitle document control, enter **Prepared by Student Name** (but replace "Student Name" with your first and last name). Click the date document control, click the arrow, and then click the current date in the calendar.
15. Save and preview the document, and then submit the finished document to your instructor, either in printed or electronic form, as requested.

Apply | **Case Problem 2**

Apply the skills you learned to create a report summarizing information on a municipal wireless network.

Data File needed for this Case Problem: WiFi.docx

Report on a Municipal Wireless Network Like many communities, the town of Grand Island, Nebraska, is considering a citywide wireless (or WiFi) network to provide low-cost Internet access for all residents. A task force appointed by the mayor has investigated the issue and summarized its findings in a report. As you format the report in the following steps, you will focus on creating a cover page and a header from scratch, without relying on predefined elements provided by Word. You will also create and edit a SmartArt graphic to illustrate the process of creating the network. (*Note*: Text you need to type is shown in bold for ease of reference only; do not bold the text unless otherwise instructed.) Complete the following:

1. Open the file named **WiFi** located in the Tutorial.03\Case2 folder included with your Data Files, and then save it as **WiFi Report** in the same folder. Check your screen to make sure your settings match those in the tutorials.
2. Replace "Student Name" in the first page with your first and last name.
3. Divide the document into two sections. Begin the second section just before the heading "Summary" and have the second section begin a new page.
4. Position the insertion point somewhere in the page 1 text.

⊕ **EXPLORE**
5. Click the Page Layout tab. In the Page Setup group, click the Dialog Box Launcher, and then click the Layout tab. Click the Vertical alignment arrow, click Center, and then click the OK button. Zoom out so you can see the entire page and review the newly formatted cover page, with the text centered in the middle of the page.

6. Zoom in again so you can read the document text, and format the text of the title and the subtitle using the Title and Subtitle Quick Styles. Leave the line containing your name in Normal style.

7. Format the document headings using the Heading 1 Quick Style.

8. Insert a tab stop at the 2-inch mark in the list of task force members.

9. Change the section 2 header so it is no longer linked to section 1, move the insertion point to the center tab stop in the section 2 header, and then type the header **WiFi Network Report**. Format the header text in italic, 14-point Calibri.

10. Create a footer for just section 2 using the Alphabet style. Replace the placeholder text with your first and last name. Close Header and Footer view. Zoom out and verify that the header and footer appear only in section 2.

11. Move the insertion point to the end of the document, insert a page break, and insert a SmartArt graphic in the new page. In the Process category, select the Upward Arrow graphic. Enter the text **Hire Networking Firm**, **Construct Network**, and **Sell Broadband Rights**.

⊕ EXPLORE

12. In the Create Graphic group, click the Add Shape button (not the Add Shape button arrow), and then type **Sell Network Subscriptions**. Click anywhere in the white area of the SmartArt Graphic, inside the border, to deselect the text.

13. Save the document, preview it, and then submit the finished document to your instructor, either in printed or electronic form, as requested.

| Challenge | **Case Problem 3** |

Go beyond what you've learned to convert text into a table and then use other advanced table options to enhance the table.

Data Files needed for this Case Problem: Clients.docx and Expenses.docx

Contact List for Parson's Graphic Design   Amanda Parson recently launched a new graphic design firm that specializes in creating Web ads for small businesses in the Seattle area. A colleague has just e-mailed her a list of potential clients. The list consists of names, e-mail addresses, and phone numbers. Because it was exported from another program, the information is formatted as simple text, with the pieces of information separated by commas. Amanda asks you to convert this text into a table and then format the table to make it easy to read. When you're finished, she needs you to sum a column of numbers in her Office Expense table. (*Note:* Text you need to type is shown in bold for ease of reference only; do not bold the text unless otherwise instructed.) Complete the following:

1. Open the file named **Clients** located in the Tutorial.03\Case3 folder included with your Data Files, and then save it as **Potential Clients** in the same folder. Check your screen to make sure your settings match those in the tutorials.

⊕ EXPLORE

2. Use Word Help to learn how to convert text to a table. Use what you learned to convert the document to a table. Adjust the column widths to accommodate the widest entry in each column.

3. Insert a header row using the bold headers **Company**, **Contact**, **Phone**, and **E-Mail**.

4. Sort the list alphabetically by Company, and then replace the name "Katherine Shropshire" with your first and last name.

⊕ EXPLORE

5. Change the page orientation to landscape, and then drag the Table Resize handle (located just outside the lower-right corner of the table) until the table is 7 inches wide and 3 inches high. Notice that all the parts of the table increase proportionally.

6. Format the table using a Quick Style that includes row borders but not column borders.

7. Save and preview the document, and then submit the finished document to your instructor, either in printed or electronic form, as requested. Close the document.

8. Open the file named **Expenses** located in the Tutorial.03\Case3 folder included with your Data Files, and then save it as **Office Expenses** in the same folder.

⊕ EXPLORE   9. Use Word Help to learn how to merge cells. Use what you learned to merge the cell containing the word "TOTAL" with the blank cell to its right.

⊕ EXPLORE   10. In the Alignment group, click the Align Top Right button to align the word "TOTAL" on the right side of the new, larger cell. Select the four cells below the Expense header (including the blank cell at the bottom of the Expense column), and then click the Align Top Right button.

⊕ EXPLORE   11. Click the blank cell at the bottom of the Expenses column and then, in the Data group, click the Formula button. The Formula dialog box opens. Make sure the formula "=SUM(ABOVE)" appears in the Formula text box, make sure the other two text boxes are blank, and then click the OK button. Word sums the costs in the Expense column and displays the total ($9587.00) in the selected cell.

12. Save and preview the document, and then submit the finished document to your instructor, either in printed or electronic form, as requested.

| Create | | Case Problem 4 |

Use your table skills to create the instruction sheet shown in Figure 3-42.

There are no Data Files needed for this Case Problem.

Hammond Astronomical Society Sarah Vernon coordinates star-gazing tours for the Hammond Astronomical Society. To ensure that participants can see as well as possible in the night sky, they are asked to follow a set of rules that astronomers refer to as a dark sky protocol. You can use Word table features to create an instruction sheet describing the club's dark sky protocol. Figure 3-42 shows Sarah's sketch. (*Note*: Text you need to type is shown in bold for ease of reference only; do not bold the text unless otherwise instructed.)

Figure 3-42

Hammond Astronomical Society

Dark Sky Protocol

Personal Items

Turn off flashlights.

Shield computers with red foil.

Shield all lights for charts and confine them to the target area.

Vehicle

Turn off all interior lights before arrival.

Turn off headlights.

Park so backup lights are not required upon exit.

Rationale

Most people need 30 minutes to achieve optimum night vision. Accidental exposure to light from cars, computers or flashlights means the period of dark adaption must begin again. Some individuals can tolerate small amounts of red light without significant vision degradation, as long as the light source is dim and does not shine into the eyes. For more information, see Sarah Vernon.

Complete the following steps:

1. Open a new, blank document, and save it as **Dark Sky Protocol** in the Tutorial.03\Case4 folder included with your Data Files.

2. If necessary, zoom out so you can see the entire page, switch to Print Layout view, and display the rulers.

3. Change the document's orientation to landscape.

⊕ **EXPLORE** 4. On the Insert tab, click the Table button, and then click Draw Table at the bottom of the Insert Table menu. The Draw Table pointer (which looks like a pencil) appears. You drag this pointer horizontally or vertically to create a straight line, and diagonally to create a rectangle.

⊕ **EXPLORE** 5. Click in the upper-left corner of the document (near the paragraph mark), and then drag down and to the right to draw a rectangle that stretches to the right and bottom margins. The rectangle should be a little less than nine inches wide and a little more than six inches high. If you make the rectangle too big, Word will insert a second page in the document. In that case, undo the change and redraw the rectangle.

⊕ **EXPLORE** 6. Use the Draw Table pointer to draw the columns and rows shown in Figure 3-42. For example, to draw the column border for the "Dark Sky Protocol" column, click the top of the rectangle where you want the column to begin, and drag down to the bottom of the rectangle. Use the same technique to draw rows. (If you make a mistake, use the Undo button. To delete a border, click the Eraser button on the Table Tools Design tab, click the border you want to erase, and then click the Eraser button again to turn it off. Click the Draw Table button to turn on the Draw Table pointer again.) Don't expect to draw the table perfectly the first time. You may have to practice until you become comfortable with the Draw Table pointer, but once you can use it well, you will find it a helpful tool for creating complex tables.

7. Press the Escape key to turn off the Draw Table pointer.

⊕ **EXPLORE** 8. In the left column, type the text **Dark Sky Protocol**. With the pointer still in that cell, click the Table Tools Layout tab, then in the Alignment group, click the Text Direction button twice to position the text vertically so that it reads from bottom to top. Using the formatting options on the Home tab, format the text in 36-point Cambria. Click the Table Tools Layout tab, and then, in the Alignment group, click the Align Center button. (*Hint*: You will probably have to adjust and readjust the row and column borders throughout these steps, until all the elements of the table are positioned properly.)

9. Type the remaining text, as shown in Figure 3-42. Replace "Sarah Vernon" with your own name. Use bold as shown in Figure 3-42 to draw attention to key elements. Change the font and font sizes as necessary to make your table look like the one in Figure 3-42. Likewise, use the Center Align button on the Table Tools Layout tab as necessary. (*Hint:* For the bottom three cells, use 16-point Cambria for the bold items and 14-point Calibri for the other text.)

⊕ **EXPLORE** 10. Switch to the Insert tab. In the Illustrations group, click the Shapes button and then, under "Stars and Banners," click the 5-Point Star shape. In the blank cell in the top row, position the mouse pointer over the upper-left corner, and then click and drag the mouse pointer down and to the right to draw a five-pointed star. If the star isn't centered neatly in the cell, click the Undo button, and try again until you draw a star that looks similar to the one in Figure 3-42. The star is selected, as indicated by the small squares (called selection handles) that surround it. A new tab, named Format, appears on the Ribbon with a label identifying it as a Drawing Tools contextual tab. On the Drawing Tools Format tab, in the Shape Styles group, click the Shape Fill button arrow and, under "Standard Colors," click the orange square. Click anywhere outside the star to deselect it.

EXPLORE 11. Now that you have organized the information using the Word table tools, you can remove the borders. Select the entire table, click the Table Tools Design tab, click the Borders button arrow (in the Table Styles group) and then click No Border. (You may still see dotted blue gridlines, which will not be visible in the printed document. If you would like to turn off the dotted blue gridlines, click the Table Tools Layout tab, and then click View Gridlines in the Tables group.)

12. Save your work, preview the document, make any necessary adjustments, and then submit the finished document to your instructor, either in printed or electronic form, as requested.

Research | **Internet Assignments**

Go to the Web to find information you can use to create documents.

The purpose of the Internet Assignments is to challenge you to find information on the Internet that you can use to work effectively with this software. The actual assignments are updated and maintained on the Course Technology Web site. Log on to the Internet and use your Web browser to go to the Student Online Companion for New Perspectives Office 2007 at **www.course.com/np/office2007**. Then navigate to the Internet Assignments for this tutorial.

Assess | **SAM Assessment and Training**

If you have a SAM user profile, you may have access to hands-on instruction, practice, and assessment of the skills covered in this tutorial. Log in to your SAM account (**http://sam2007.course.com**) to launch any assigned training activities or exams that relate to the skills covered in this tutorial.

Review | **Quick Check Answers**

Session 3.1

1. Click the paragraph containing the heading; on the Home tab in the Styles group, click the More button; and then click the Quick Style you want. (If the Quick Style you want is already visible in the Styles group, you don't have to click the More button.)
2. False
3. Click where you want to insert the table, click the Insert Tab, in the Tables group click the Tables button, drag the mouse pointer to select the desired number of rows and columns, and then release the mouse button.
4. Tab key
5. Select button on the Table Tools Layout tab
6. In the Data group on the Table Tools Layout tab, click the Sort button. Click the Sort by arrow, and select the header for the column you want to sort by. In the Type list box located to the right of the Sort by list box, select the type of information stored in the column you want to sort by. To sort in alphabetical, chronological, or numeric order, click the Ascending option button. To sort in reverse order, click the Descending option button. If you also want to sort by a second column, click the Then by arrow and click a column header. If the table includes headers, make sure the Header row option button is selected, and then click the OK button.
7. True

Session 3.2

1. True
2. Click where you want to insert a footnote, click the References tab, in the Footnotes group click the Insert Footnote button, and then type the text of the footnote in the bottom margin.
3. The Breaks button on the Page Layout tab
4. The SmartArt graphic appears with a blue border around it.
5. Click in the header area (in a page's top margin) or in the footer area (in a page's bottom margin); or click the Header button or the Footer button on the Insert tab.
6. False

Ending Data Files

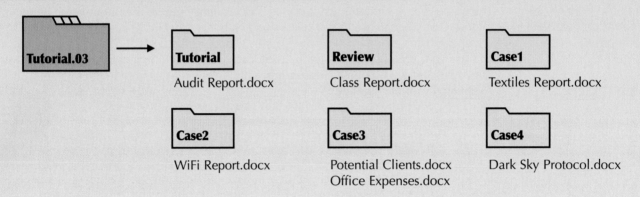

Tutorial.03 →

Tutorial
Audit Report.docx

Review
Class Report.docx

Case1
Textiles Report.docx

Case2
WiFi Report.docx

Case3
Potential Clients.docx
Office Expenses.docx

Case4
Dark Sky Protocol.docx

Desktop Publishing and Mail Merge

Creating a Newsletter, Cover Letter, and Blog Post

Case | Shepherd Bay Medical Center

Joel Conchola, a public outreach specialist at Shepherd Bay Medical Center, needs to create a one-page newsletter that explains the importance of exercise and diet in preventing type II diabetes. He has asked you to help him create the newsletter and a cover letter that will accompany the newsletter. He is also interested in creating a blog for Shepherd Bay Medical and needs your help to create a blog post.

Joel has already written the text of the newsletter. He wants you to transform this text into a publication that is neat, organized, and professional looking. He would like the newsletter to contain headings and an eye-catching headline. He also wants to include a picture that reinforces the newsletter content.

In this tutorial, you'll get acquainted with some desktop publishing features available in Word that you'll use to create the newsletter. You'll format the title as a prominent-looking headline and divide the document into newspaper-style columns to make it easier to read. To add interest and focus to the text, you'll include a graphic. You'll then fine-tune the newsletter layout, give it a more professional appearance with typographic characters, and you'll put a border around the page to give the newsletter a finished look. Next, you will use Word's mail merge feature to insert personalized information into the cover letter that will accompany the newsletter. Finally, you'll experiment with creating a blog post.

Starting Data Files

Tutorial	Review	Case1	Case2	Case3	Case4
Addresses.docx	Addresses.docx	Audio.docx	Island.jpg	Hill.docx	(none)
Letter.docx	Eating.docx		News.docx		
Prevention.docx	Nutrition.docx				

Session 4.1

Elements of Desktop Publishing

Desktop publishing is the process of preparing commercial-quality printed material using a desktop computer system. In addition to newsletters, you can desktop-publish brochures, posters, and other documents that include text and graphics.

The following elements are commonly associated with desktop publishing:

- Columns and other page layout features—Columns of text, pull quotes (small portions of text pulled out of the main text and enlarged), drop caps (large initial letters at the beginning of paragraphs), page borders, and other special formatting features that you don't frequently see in letters and other documents distinguish desktop-published documents.
- Graphics—Clip art, horizontal or vertical lines (called **rules**), text boxes, and photographs help illustrate a concept or product, draw a reader's attention to the document, and make the text visually appealing.
- Multiple fonts—Two or three fonts, font sizes, and font colors provide visual interest, guide the reader through the text, and convey the tone of the document.
- High-quality printing—A laser printer or high-resolution inkjet printer produces the final output.

Although professional desktop publishers use software specially designed for desktop publishing, you can use Word to create basic desktop-published documents. You already know how to format text in multiple fonts and font sizes, and you know how to create a graphic using SmartArt. In this tutorial, you'll incorporate more of the desktop publishing elements listed to produce the newsletter shown in Figure 4-1.

Figure 4-1 ▶ **Shepherd Bay Medical Center newsletter**

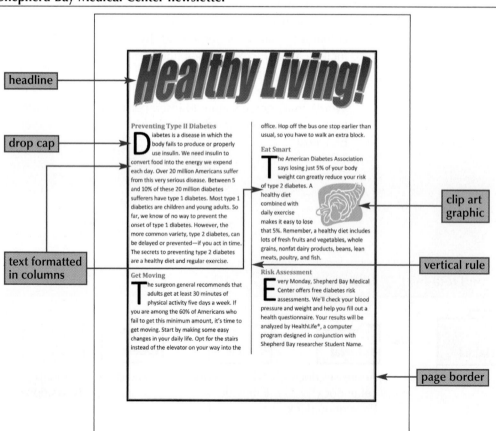

Before you can start creating the newsletter shown in Figure 4-1, you need to open Joel's document and review the text of the newsletter.

To open the newsletter document:

▶ **1.** Start Word and open the file **Prevention** from the Tutorial.04\Tutorial folder included with your Data Files.

▶ **2.** To avoid altering the original file, save the document as **Prevention Newsletter** in the same folder.

▶ **3.** Display nonprinting characters, switch to Print Layout view, display the rulers, and set the zoom so you can see the entire width of the newsletter. Throughout this tutorial, feel free to zoom in or zoom out if you prefer to see more or less of the newsletter.

▶ **4.** Read the document to familiarize yourself with its content.

▶ **5.** At the end of the document, replace "Shawn Kampa" with your first and last name. This will make it easier for you to find your copy of the newsletter when you print it.

Now that the newsletter contains all the necessary details, you can turn your attention to your first desktop publishing task—adding a headline.

Using WordArt to Create a Headline

Joel wants the title of the newsletter, "Healthy Living," to be eye-catching and dramatic. You can create such a headline using **WordArt**, a feature that allows you to create specially formatted text. You type the text for a piece of WordArt in the Edit WordArt Text dialog box and then insert it into the document. Unlike regular text, a WordArt headline is considered an **object**—that is, something that you can manipulate independently of the text. You can think of the WordArt object as a thing that lies on top of, or next to, the text in a document. This means that, for example, to alter its size you drag its handles, just as you would for a SmartArt graphic. A set of WordArt tools appears on the Ribbon when the WordArt is selected. You can use these tools to change its shape, size, and color and to add special effects such as 3-D and shadowing.

Creating WordArt	Reference Window

- Click the Insert tab, and then, in the Text group, click the WordArt button.
- In the WordArt gallery, click the style of text you want to insert.
- Type the text you want in the Edit WordArt Text dialog box.
- Click the Font and Size arrows to select the font and font size you want. If you want, click the Bold or Italic button, or both.
- Click the OK button.
- Use the tools on the WordArt Tools Format tab to format the WordArt.
- Drag any handle to resize and reshape the WordArt. To avoid altering the WordArt's proportions, press and hold down the Ctrl key while you drag a handle.

You're ready to use WordArt to create the newsletter title.

To create the title of the newsletter using WordArt:

▶ **1.** Press the **Ctrl+Home** keys to move the insertion point to the beginning of the document, and then click the **Insert** tab.

▶ **2.** In the Text group, click the **WordArt** button. The WordArt gallery opens. Joel wants to use the WordArt style in the middle row, second column from the left. See Figure 4-2.

Figure 4-2 WordArt gallery

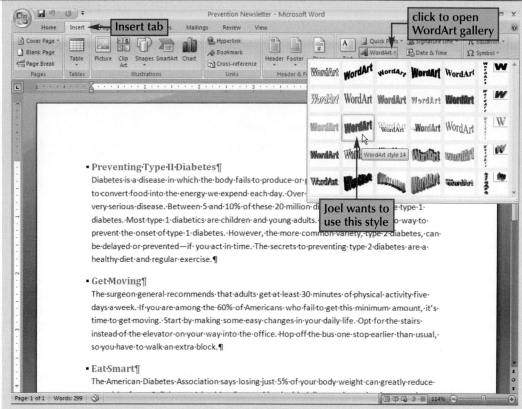

▶ **3.** Position the mouse pointer over the style Joel wants to use, as shown in Figure 4-2. A ScreenTip displays the name of this style: "WordArt style 14."

▶ **4.** Click **WordArt style 14**. The Edit WordArt Text dialog box opens, displaying the placeholder text "Your Text Here," which you will replace with the newsletter title. See Figure 4-3.

Edit WordArt Text dialog box ◄ **Figure 4-3**

5. Type **Healthy Living** to replace the placeholder text with the newsletter title, and then click the **OK** button. The Edit WordArt Text dialog box closes, and the Word-Art is inserted as a graphic at the beginning of the newsletter. The "Preventing Type II Diabetes" heading moves to the right to accommodate the new headline. The WordArt Tools Format tab appears on the Ribbon. The border around the Wor-dArt tells you that it is currently selected. The squares on the border are **sizing handles**, which you can drag to change the size of the WordArt. See Figure 4-4.

WordArt inserted into document ◄ **Figure 4-4**

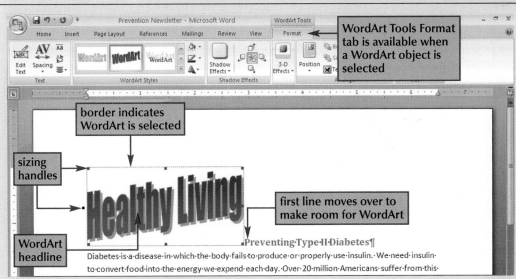

Eventually, you will position and resize the headline, so that it stretches from margin to margin. But for now, you can leave it in its current position.

Editing a WordArt Object

The WordArt object you have created is not regular text. You cannot edit it as you would other text. You can think of WordArt as an object that lies on top of or next to the text in a document. To edit WordArt, it must be selected. Then you can make changes using the tools on the WordArt Tools Format tab or by dragging its sizing handles.

The WordArt object you just created is already selected, so you can get to work modifying its appearance. First, Joel would like you to add an exclamation point at the end of the headline and format the headline in italic.

To edit the text and formatting of the WordArt object:

► **1.** Verify that the WordArt object is selected, as indicated by the border and the sizing handles. The WordArt Tools Format tab, which is visible only when a WordArt object is selected, contains tools for editing WordArt.

► **2.** In the Text group on the WordArt Tools Format tab, click the **Edit Text** button. The Edit WordArt Text dialog box opens. You used this dialog box earlier when you first created the WordArt object.

► **3.** Click at the end of the headline (to the right of the "g" in "Living"), and then type **!** (an exclamation point).

► **4.** Click the **Italic** button _I_ in the Edit WordArt Text dialog box. The headline in the text box is now formatted in italic.

► **5.** Click the **OK** button. The Edit WordArt Text dialog box closes, and you can see the edited headline in the document. See Figure 4-5.

Figure 4-5 ▶ **Edited WordArt headline**

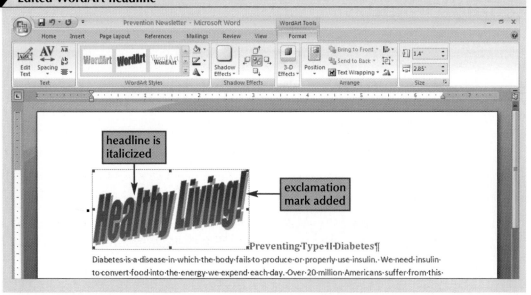

Changing the Shape of a WordArt Object

You can quickly change the shape of a WordArt graphic using the Change WordArt Shape button in the WordArt Styles group on the WordArt Tools Format tab. Right now, the WordArt headline has a straight shape, without any curve to it. Joel wants to use an arched shape.

To change the shape of the WordArt object:

▶ **1.** Verify that the WordArt object is selected, and then, in the WordArt Styles group, click the **Change WordArt Shape** button 🅰️. A palette of shape options opens.

▶ **2.** Move the mouse pointer over each option in the palette to display a ScreenTip with the name of each shape and to see the live preview of each shape in the document.

▶ **3.** Point to (but don't click) the **Can Up** shape (top row in the Warp section, third column from the left), as shown in Figure 4-6.

Selecting a new WordArt shape ◀ Figure 4-6

▶ **4.** Click the **Can Up** shape. The newsletter title is formatted in the new WordArt shape, which arches upward in the middle.

▶ **5.** Save your work.

The headline has the shape you want. Now you can position the WordArt object in relation to the text of the newsletter.

Wrapping Text Below a WordArt Object

At this point, the WordArt object is an **inline graphic**, which means it is located in a specific position in a specific line of the document (in this case, at the beginning of the first line). If you type text before an inline graphic, the graphic moves to accommodate the new text. You have more control over the position of a graphic, such as a WordArt object, if you change it to a floating graphic. A **floating graphic** is attached, or **anchored**, to a specific paragraph; however, you can drag a floating graphic to any location in the document. The text then flows, or **wraps**, around it. Adding or deleting text does not affect the position of a floating graphic.

To change an inline WordArt object to a floating graphic, you need to select a text wrapping style. You can wrap text around graphics many different ways. For example, you can have the text wrap above and below the graphic, or so the text follows the shape of the graphic, even if it has an irregular shape. The Arrange group on the WordArt Tools Format tab contains two useful tools for controlling the way text wraps around all graphics, including WordArt, pictures, and charts. First, there's the Position button, which allows you to position the WordArt or graphic in one of several locations on the page (top left, top middle, top right, and so on) and to wrap the document text around it. Second, there's the Text Wrapping button, which assumes the WordArt is already positioned where you want it and allows you to choose from a number of more refined wrapping options. Because the WordArt object is already located at the beginning of the document, where you want it, you'll use the Text Wrapping button in the Arrange group.

To wrap the newsletter text below the WordArt object:

▶ **1.** With the WordArt object selected, click the **Text Wrapping** button in the Arrange group. A menu of text wrapping options opens. See Figure 4-7.

Figure 4-7 ▶ **Text Wrapping menu**

▶ **2.** Click **Top and Bottom**. The heading text is moved below the WordArt object. The WordArt is still selected, although now you see only the sizing handles, without the box. Also, there are more handles, and not all the handles are squares. Like the blue squares, the blue circles are sizing handles. However, the circle-shaped handles indicate that the graphic is a floating graphic. A number of other items appear around the WordArt object, as shown in Figure 4-8. The anchor symbol to the left of the heading "Preventing Type II Diabetes" tells you that the WordArt is attached, or anchored, to that paragraph.

WordArt after wrapping text ◀ **Figure 4-8**

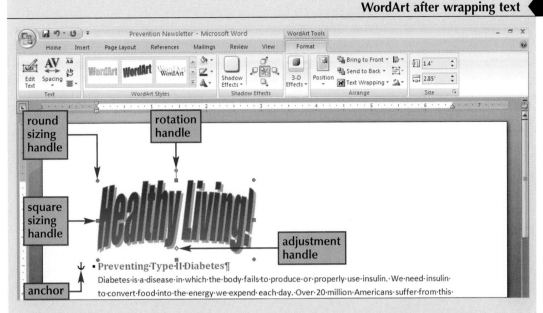

Trouble? If you can't see the anchor symbol, your Zoom setting is probably too high. Zoom out until you can see the full width of the page.

Positioning and Sizing the WordArt Object

After you choose a text wrapping style for a WordArt object, you can adjust its position in the document by dragging it with the mouse pointer. To change the size of a WordArt object, drag one of its sizing handles. To keep the headline the same proportion as the original, hold down the Ctrl key as you drag the sizing handle. This prevents "stretching" the headline more in one direction than the other.

Joel asks you to widen the headline so it stretches neatly across the margins. Before you enlarge the headline, you will drag it to a new position.

To position and enlarge the WordArt object:

▶ **1.** Move the mouse pointer over the headline.

▶ **2.** Use the ⬚ pointer to drag the WordArt object to the right until it is centered below the 3-inch mark on the horizontal ruler. Release the mouse button.

▶ **3.** With the WordArt object still selected, position the pointer over the lower-right sizing handle. The pointer changes to ⬚.

▶ **4.** Press and hold the **Ctrl** key while you drag the sizing handle almost to the right margin. Use the horizontal ruler as a guide. As you drag the handle, the pointer changes to ┼ and a dotted outline appears to show you how big the WordArt will be when you release the mouse button. Take care not to drag the handle down too far, or the WordArt object will be too tall. See Figure 4-9.

Figure 4-9 ▶ **Resizing the WordArt**

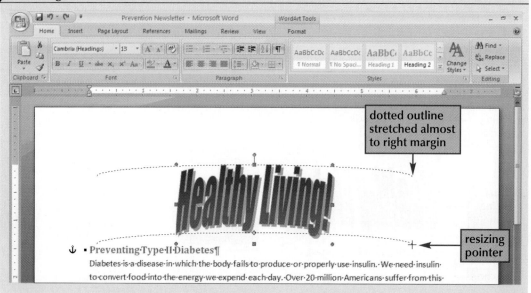

5. Release the mouse button when the dotted horizontal line stretches almost from the left to the right margin. The WordArt heading should be about 5.5 inches wide and a little less than 1.5 inches high at its tallest.

Trouble? If the WordArt heading spans the margins, but is not tall enough to read easily, you probably didn't hold down the Ctrl key when you dragged the mouse pointer. Undo the change and repeat Steps 4 and 5.

6. If necessary, drag the headline down slightly, so that the top of the headline does not extend into the top margin.

Trouble? If the headline jumps to the middle of the first paragraph of text, you dragged it too far. Undo the change, and then repeat Step 6.

Next, you need to turn your attention to the anchor symbol located by the lower-left corner of the WordArt headline.

Anchoring the WordArt Object to a Blank Paragraph

The text wrapping that you applied earlier changed the WordArt object into a floating graphic that is anchored to the paragraph containing the heading "Preventing Type II Diabetes." Later in this tutorial, you will format the newsletter text in narrow, newspaper-style columns. To prevent the column format from affecting the WordArt object, you need to anchor it to its own, blank paragraph. Then you can format that paragraph as a separate section.

At this point, the anchor symbol is probably located to the left of, and just above, the first paragraph (the heading "Preventing Type II Diabetes"). However, yours may be in a different position—for instance, it might be positioned above and to the left of the WordArt. In the next set of steps, you will move the anchor to a new, blank paragraph at the beginning of the document.

To anchor the WordArt object to a blank paragraph:

▶ **1.** Press the **Ctrl+Home** keys. The insertion point moves to the left of the "P" in the heading "Preventing Type II Diabetes," where you need to insert a blank paragraph. The WordArt object is no longer selected, so you cannot see the anchor at this point.

▶ **2.** Press the **Enter** key. A new paragraph symbol is inserted just above the Preventing Type II Diabetes heading.

▶ **3.** If the new paragraph symbol is inserted above the WordArt heading, drag the WordArt heading up slightly until the paragraph mark moves below the WordArt heading.

▶ **4.** Click the **WordArt** object. The selection handles and the anchor symbol appear. The anchor symbol is probably positioned to the left of, and just above, the new paragraph, although it might be positioned to the left of the "Preventing Type II Diabetes" paragraph instead.

▶ **5.** If necessary, click the anchor and drag it up to position it to the left of the new, blank paragraph, as shown in Figure 4-10, if it is not already positioned there.

Properly anchored WordArt ◀ Figure 4-10

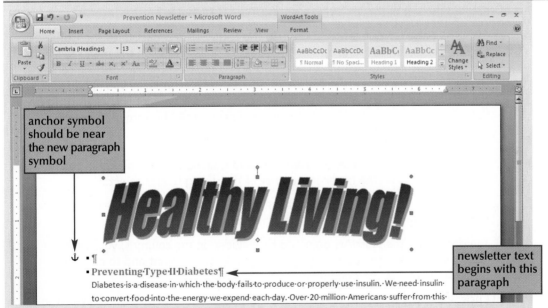

anchor symbol should be near the new paragraph symbol

newsletter text begins with this paragraph

Trouble? If you notice any other differences between your headline and the one shown in Figure 4-10, edit the headline to make it match the figure. For example, you may need to drag the WordArt left or right slightly, or you may need to adjust its size by dragging one of its sizing handles.

▶ **6.** Click anywhere in the newsletter to deselect the WordArt, and then save your work.

Your WordArt is finished. The headline draws attention to the newsletter and makes it visually appealing.

Formatting Text in Newspaper-Style Columns

Because newsletters are meant for quick reading, they are usually laid out in newspaper-style columns. In **newspaper-style columns**, a page is divided into two or more vertical blocks, or columns. Text flows down one column, continues at the top of the next column, flows down that column, and so forth. The columns allow the eye to take in a lot of text and to scan a newspaper quickly for interesting information.

To quickly format a document in columns, click the Columns button on the Page Layout tab, and then select the number of columns you want on the Columns menu. If your document is already divided into sections, the column format is applied only to the section that currently contains the insertion point. For more detailed options, use the More Columns command (at the bottom of the Columns menu), which opens the Columns dialog box. In the Columns dialog box, you can insert a vertical line between columns, select a specific column width, and insert a section break at the same time you apply the column formatting, so that only part of a document is formatted in columns.

Joel wants you to format the text below the WordArt object into two columns and add a vertical line between them. To accomplish this, you need to use the Columns dialog box.

To apply newspaper-style columns to the body of the newsletter:

1. Click to the left of the "P" in "Preventing Type II Diabetes."

2. Click the **Page Layout** tab, and then, in the Page Setup group, click the **Columns** button. The Columns menu opens. You could click an option on the menu to format the entire document, including the paragraph containing the WordArt, in columns. However, you don't want the WordArt to be part of a column, so you need to start the columns below the paragraph to which the WordArt object is anchored. To do this, you need to use the More Columns command at the bottom of the menu.

3. Click **More Columns**. The Columns dialog box opens.

4. In the Presets section, click the **Two** icon, and then verify that the Equal column width check box (in the lower-left corner of the dialog box) is selected.

5. Click the **Line between** check box to select it. The text in the Preview box changes to a two-column format with a vertical rule between the columns.

   You don't want the WordArt object to be included in the columns; you want the columns to start at the current location of the insertion point and to continue through the rest of the document.

6. Click the **Apply to** arrow, and then click **This point forward**. This tells Word to insert a section break at the insertion point and format the columns starting there. See Figure 4-11.

Correct settings in Columns dialog box | Figure 4-11

creates columns of the same width

adds a section break at the insertion point

places a line between columns

shows how columns will look with current settings

▶ **7.** Click the **OK** button to return to the document window. A continuous section break appears below the WordArt object; the first section contains the WordArt and the second section contains the rest of the document, which is now formatted in columns. The word "Continuous" indicates that the new section continues on the same page as the preceding text—in other words, the section break does not start a new page.

▶ **8.** Zoom out so you can see the entire page. The newsletter headline is centered over the two columns of text. The text fills the left column but not the right column. You'll fix this later, after you add a graphic and formatting to some of the text. See Figure 4-12.

Document formatted in two columns | Figure 4-12

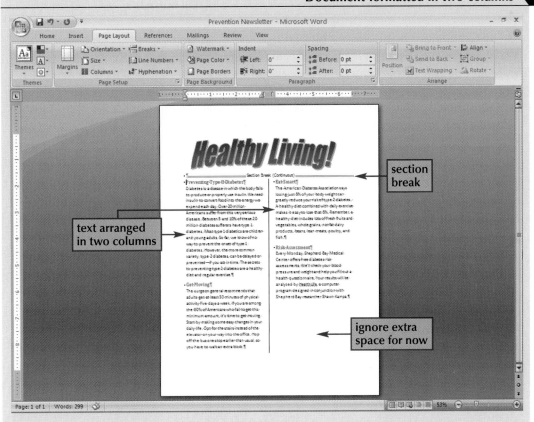

section break

text arranged in two columns

ignore extra space for now

> ▶ **9.** Save your work.
>
> **Trouble?** Your columns may break at a slightly different line of text from those shown in the figure. This is not a problem.

Keep in mind that you can modify columns as you work on a document; you can change the number of columns or return the document to its original format by formatting it as one column. You can also insert column breaks to control where text moves from one column to the next.

Inserting Graphics

Word makes it easy to insert graphics, or illustrations, in your documents. The term **graphic** can refer to a drawing, a photograph, clip art, a chart, and so on. The Illustrations group on the Insert tab contains five buttons, for five types of graphics, as described below:

- The Picture button opens a dialog box where you can locate and insert an image that already exists, such as a picture taken with a digital camera or a scan of a paper drawing.

- The Clip Art button opens the Clip Art task pane on the right side of the Word window, where you can select from premade images known as **clip art**. A collection of clip art images is installed with Word, and you are free to use them in your documents. You can also search the Web for free clip art, available from the Microsoft Web site and from other Web sites devoted to clip art.

- The Shapes button opens a gallery where you can select from over a hundred basic shapes, such as arrows, stars, and banners. You click the shape you want in the gallery, and then drag the mouse pointer in the document to draw the shape. When the shape is selected in the document, you can change its color, shape, text wrapping settings, and so on using the options on the Drawing Tools Format tab.

- The SmartArt button, as you already know, opens a dialog box where you can create diagrams.

- The Chart button opens the Insert Chart dialog box, where you can create a variety of charts similar to the charts you can create in a spreadsheet program such as Microsoft Excel. You can choose from bar charts, pie charts, and line charts, to name a few. After you select a chart type, a spreadsheet window opens where you can enter the chart data. When the chart is selected in the document, you can edit it using the three tabs that appear under the label "Chart Tools."

Tip

To search for clip art on the Microsoft Web site, click Clip art on Office Online at the bottom of the Clip Art task pane.

Working with Graphics Files | InSight

There are several types of graphics files, many of which were developed for use in Web pages. In desktop publishing, you will often work with **bitmaps**. The most common types of bitmaps are:

- BMP—Used by Microsoft Paint and other graphics programs to store graphics you create. These files, which have the .bmp file extension, tend to be very large.
- TIFF—Commonly used for photographs or scanned images. TIFF files are usually much larger than GIF or JPEG files, but smaller than BMP files. A TIFF file has the file extension .tif.
- GIF—Suitable for most types of simple art. A GIF file is compressed, so it doesn't take up much room on your computer. A GIF file has the file extension .gif.
- JPEG—Suitable for photographs and drawings. Files stored using the JPEG format are even more compressed than GIF files. A JPEG file has the file extension .jpg.

A document containing graphics can take up a lot of memory, making it difficult to work with. To save file space, use JPEG graphics as much as possible.

You'll have a chance to work with graphics files in the Case Problems at the end of this tutorial. You'll also have a chance to work with text boxes, which are similar to graphics. A **text box**, as its name implies, is a box in which you can type text. The box sets off the text and draws special attention to it. You can use a text box to create a **pull quote**—a brief quotation from the main document.

Joel wants you to insert a clip art image in the newsletter. He asks you to use one of the food-related images that are installed with Word.

To insert the clip art image into the newsletter:

▶ 1. With the document still zoomed out so you can see the whole page, and the insertion point located anywhere in the document, click the **Insert** tab, and then in the Illustrations group, click the **Clip Art** button. The Clip Art task pane opens, as shown in Figure 4-13. You use the top part of the Clip Art task pane to search for graphics related to a specific topic. The Search for text box on your computer may contain text left from a previous search. You can click the Organize clips option (near the bottom) to open the Microsoft Clip Organizer window, where you can browse among the various clip art images stored on your computer. You'll use the Microsoft Clip Organizer to insert an image into the newsletter.

Figure 4-13 ▶ Clip Art task pane

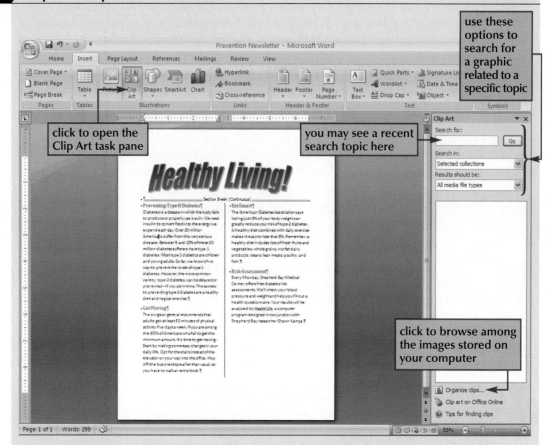

2. Click **Organize clips** near the bottom of the Clip Art task pane. The Favorites - Microsoft Clip Organizer window opens. This window is similar to Windows Explorer. For example, you click the plus sign next to a folder to display its subfolders. You select a subfolder to display its contents in the right pane. The default Microsoft Office clip art is stored in subfolders within the Office Collections folder. See Figure 4-14. You might see different folders from those shown in Figure 4-14, but you should see the Office Collections folder.

Microsoft Clip Organizer | **Figure 4-14**

> **3.** If necessary, scroll down to display the Office Collections folder in the left pane, and then click the **plus sign** next to the Office Collections folder. A list of subfolders within the Office Collections folder appears. This list of folders, which is created when you install Word, organizes clip art images into related categories. The folders with plus signs next to them contain subfolders and clip art images.

> **4.** Scroll down and examine the list of folders. Click any plus signs to open subfolders, and then click folders to display clip art images in the right pane.

> **5.** Click the **Food** folder to select it. Four images stored in the Food folder are displayed in the right pane.

> **6.** Move the pointer over the image of the cornucopia (the second image from the left). An arrow button appears on the right side of the image. You might also see a ScreenTip with information about the file.

> **7.** Click the **arrow button** that appears when your pointer is over the image. A menu of options opens, as shown in Figure 4-15.

Figure 4-15 ▶ **Selected image in Food folder**

▶ **8.** Click **Copy** in the menu. The image is copied to the Clipboard.

Now that you have copied the image to the Clipboard, you can paste it into the document at the insertion point. Joel asks you to insert the graphic in the paragraph below the heading "Eat Smart." Before you insert the image, you will close the Clip Art task pane.

To paste the clip art into the document:

▶ **1.** Click the **Close** button [X] in the Microsoft Clip Organizer title bar, and then click **Yes** when you see a dialog box asking if you want the item to remain on the Clipboard. You return to the document window.

▶ **2.** Click the **Close** button [X] on the Clip Art task pane.

▶ **3.** Zoom back in so you can read the document, and then position the insertion point to the left of the word "The" below the heading "Eat Smart." At this point, you could switch to the Home tab and click the Paste button, but it's faster to use a keyboard shortcut.

Tip

To delete a graphic (clip art, WordArt, etc.), click it to select it, and then press the Delete key.

▶ **4.** Press the **Ctrl+V** keys. The cornucopia clip art is inserted into the document at the insertion point. The text moves right to accommodate the image, which nearly fills the right column.

▶ **5.** Save the document.

▶ **6.** Click the **cornucopia** image. A border with sizing handles appears, indicating that the image is selected. The Picture Tools Format tab also appears, containing tools related to working with graphics. The Insert tab is still selected, however, so at this point you can't actually see the tools on the Picture Tools Format tab. See Figure 4-16.

Joel would like the image to be smaller so it is better balanced with the text. You'll make that change in the next section.

Resizing a Graphic

It's often necessary to change the size of a graphic to make it fit into a document. This is sometimes called **scaling** the image. You can resize a graphic either by dragging its sizing handles or, for more precise control, by specifying an exact height and width in the Size group on the Picture Tools Format tab. For Joel's newsletter, the dragging technique will work well. You can then use the height and width controls on the Picture Tools Format tab to check the exact size of the graphic.

To resize the clip art graphic:

▶ **1.** Make sure the clip art graphic is selected, click the **Picture Tools Format** tab, and then locate the Shape Height and Shape Width boxes in the Size group on the right edge of the Picture Tools Format tab. These boxes tell you that the cornucopia graphic is currently 1.98 inches high and 1.95 inches wide.

▶ **2.** Move the mouse pointer over the lower-right sizing handle of the clip art. The pointer changes to ⬉. When you drag the pointer in the next step, a faint copy of the cornucopia image will resize accordingly, allowing you to see how the image will alter when you release the mouse button.

▶ **3.** Drag the handle up and to the left until the faint copy of the cornucopia image is approximately 1.5 inches wide. Use the horizontal ruler as a guide. The measurements in the Shape Height and Shape Width boxes will not change until you release the mouse button, in the next step. See Figure 4-17.

Figure 4-17	Resizing the graphic

4. Release the mouse button. The cornucopia image is now about half as wide as the left column. According to the Shape Height and Shape Width boxes in the Size group, the graphic is approximately 1.5 inches wide.

   Trouble? If the measurement in your Shape Width box is greater than 1.53 inches, or less than 1.45 inches, resize the graphic until its width is closer to 1.5 inches.

Joel wonders if the graphic would take up less space if you deleted the tip of the cornucopia at the top of the image. You'll make that change in the next section.

Cropping a Graphic

You can **crop** a graphic—that is, cut off one or more of its edges—using the Crop button on the Picture Tools Format tab. Once you crop a graphic, the part you cropped is hidden from view. It remains a part of the graphic, which means you can change your mind and restore a cropped graphic to its original form.

To crop the graphic:

1. If necessary, click the clip art to select it. The sizing handles appear.

2. Click the **Crop** button in the Size group on the Picture Tools Format tab. The Crop button turns orange, indicating that it is currently selected; it stays selected until you click it again. The graphic is surrounded by a broken black box, and the pointer changes to 🔧 when you move it over the text.

3. Position the pointer directly over the middle sizing handle on the top of the picture. The pointer changes to ⊥.

4. Press and hold down the mouse button. The pointer changes to +.

5. Drag the handle down. As you drag, a solid outline appears to indicate the new shape of the graphic.

6. Position the top edge of the solid outline along the top of the cornucopia's orange background. See Figure 4-18.

Cropping the graphic | Figure 4-18

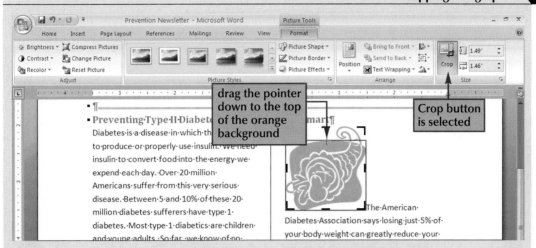

7. Release the mouse button. The tip of the cornucopia is cropped from the image. The Crop button is still selected. The cropping pointer and the broken black box around the graphic remain visible, in case you want to crop the graphic some more. You are finished cropping the graphic, so you can turn off the cropping feature.

8. Click the **Crop** button in the Size group to deselect it. The broken black box around the graphic is replaced with the solid box with the round and square selection handles (shown earlier in Figure 4-16).

In the next session you will wrap the newsletter text around the graphic and move the graphic to a new location. Then you'll finalize the newsletter and turn your attention to creating the cover letter with mail merge.

Session 4.1 Quick Check | Review

1. List four elements you might see in a desktop-published document.
2. Explain how to change the text of a WordArt object after you've already inserted it into the document.
3. True or False: To avoid altering the proportions of a WordArt object, you press and hold down the Alt key while you drag a handle.
4. What button should you use to change the way text flows around a WordArt object? Where is this button located?
5. Suppose you want to format only part of a document in columns, and you haven't inserted any section breaks. Should you use the Columns menu or the Columns dialog box?
6. Name four types of bitmap files.
7. On what tab are the buttons for inserting graphics located?

Session 4.2

Wrapping Text Around a Graphic

Earlier in this tutorial, you used Top and Bottom text wrapping with the WordArt object so the WordArt would appear above the columns of text. Now you'll apply Tight text wrapping to make the text follow the shape of the cornucopia.

To wrap text around the graphic:

▶ 1. If you took a break after the previous session, make sure Word is still running and that the Prevention Newsletter file is open with the document in Print Layout view and with the nonprinting characters and rulers displayed.

▶ 2. If necessary, click the cornucopia graphic to select it, and, if necessary, click the Picture Tools Format tab to display it.

▶ 3. In the Arrange group on the Picture Tools Format tab, click the **Text Wrapping** button. A menu of text wrapping options appears.

▶ 4. Click **Tight**. The text wraps to the right of the cornucopia, roughly following its shape. See Figure 4-19.

Figure 4-19 ▶ Text wrapped around the graphic

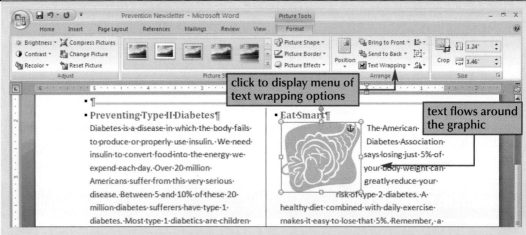

▶ 5. Click anywhere in the newsletter text to deselect the graphic, and then save the newsletter. Don't be concerned if the heading "Eat Smart" wraps to the right of the graphic. You will move the graphic away from the heading in the next section. If the heading does not wrap around the graphic, that's fine too.

Trouble? If the heading "Eat Smart" moves back down to the bottom of the left column, you probably didn't make the WordArt object tall enough. Undo the insertion of the graphic, increase the height of the WordArt object so that it is about 1.5 inches tall at its highest point, drag it down if necessary so it doesn't overlap the top margin, click at the beginning of the paragraph under the heading "Eat Smart," and begin again with Step 2.

You are almost finished with the graphic. You just need to move it to the middle of the paragraph, so that it is not so close to the heading.

Moving and Aligning a Graphic

You can move a graphic by dragging it, just as you dragged the WordArt object. Like WordArt, a clip art graphic is anchored to a specific paragraph in a document. When you drag a graphic to a new paragraph, the anchor symbol moves to the beginning of that paragraph. When you drag a graphic to a new position within the same paragraph, the anchor symbol remains in its original position and only the graphic moves. You'll see how this works when you move the cornucopia clip art to the middle of its current paragraph, next to the right margin.

When you move a graphic, it's a good idea to specify exactly where you want to align it. For example, you can choose to align a graphic along any one of the page margins, or you can choose to align it along the edge of the page. Specifying an alignment option prevents the graphic from moving if you make changes to the document later. The Align button in the Arrange group on the Picture Tools Format tab provides some preset alignment options that are appropriate for most documents. You'll see how this works in the following steps.

To move the graphic:

▶ **1.** Click the graphic to select it if necessary. You should see an anchor symbol either within the graphic or to the left of the heading "Eat Smart."

▶ **2.** Move the mouse pointer ⬚ over the graphic.

▶ **3.** Click and slowly drag the pointer down. As you move the mouse, a faint copy of the image moves too, so that you can see where you're moving the image.

▶ **4.** Position the image near the middle of the paragraph, next to the right margin, and then release the mouse button. The graphic moves to its new position, with the text wrapped to its left. The anchor is probably located to the left of the first line under the heading "Eat Smart," although it may have moved to somewhere else near the top of the newsletter. In the next few steps, you'll make some adjustments to make sure the position of your graphic and anchor matches Figure 4-20. First, you'll align the graphic along the right margin.

Trouble? If paragraph text wraps to the right of the graphic, you need to drag the graphic farther to the right.

Tip

To move a graphic to one of several preset positions on the page, click the Position button in the Arrange group on the Picture Tools Format tab.

Graphic in new position ◀ **Figure 4-20**

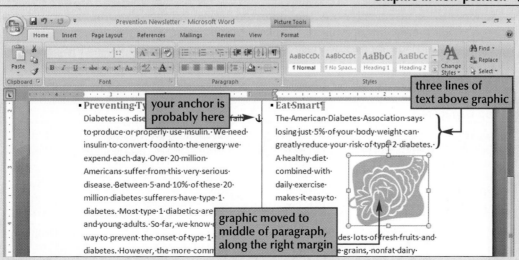

5. On the Picture Tools Format tab in the Arrange group, click the **Align** button. A menu of alignment options opens. You want to align the graphic along the right margin. It's possible to align the graphic along the edge of the page, so first you have to make sure the Align to Margin option is selected.

6. Verify that you see a check mark before "Align to Margin." Now you can specify what margin you want to align the graphic to.

7. Near the top of the Align menu, click **Align Right**.

8. If necessary, drag the anchor up or down slightly until it is positioned as in Figure 4-20, with three lines of text wrapped above it. If the anchor is not located next to the first line under the heading "Eat Smart," click it and drag it there now. When you are finished, your newsletter should match Figure 4-20.

   Trouble? If you can't get the text to wrap properly around the graphic (for example, if individual words wrap to the right of the graphic), try reducing the size of the graphic slightly by dragging the lower-right sizing handle.

9. Click anywhere outside the graphic to deselect it and save your work.

The graphic helps draw the reader's attention to the newsletter, but the rest of the text looks plain. Joel suggests adding a drop cap at the beginning of each section.

Inserting Drop Caps

A **drop cap** is a large, capital letter that begins the text of a paragraph, chapter, or some other document section. You can place a drop cap in the margin, next to the paragraph, or you can have the text of the paragraph wrap around the drop cap. In the following steps, you will create a drop cap for each of the four paragraphs that follow each heading in the newsletter. The drop cap will extend three lines into the paragraph, with the text wrapping around it.

To insert drop caps in the newsletter:

1. Click in the paragraph below the heading "Preventing Type II Diabetes."

2. Click the **Insert** tab, and then, in the Text group, click the **Drop Cap** button. The Drop Cap menu opens.

3. Move the mouse pointer over the In margin option and then the Dropped option, and observe the live preview of the two types of drop caps in the document. The default settings applied by these two options are fine for most documents. Clicking Drop Cap Options, at the bottom of the menu, opens the Drop Cap dialog box, where you can select more detailed settings. See Figure 4-21.

Figure 4-21 **Drop Cap menu**

▶ **4.** Click **Dropped** in the Drop Cap menu. The Drop Cap menu closes, and Word formats the first character of the paragraph as a drop cap, just as in the live preview in Figure 4-21. The blue box with square selection handles around the drop cap tells you the drop cap is selected.

▶ **5.** Click in the paragraph following the heading "Get Moving," and then repeat Steps 3 and 4 to insert a drop cap in that paragraph.

▶ **6.** Insert a drop cap in the paragraph following the heading "Eat Smart." Word adjusts the text wrapping around the graphic.

   Trouble? If a drop cap does not appear after you perform Step 6, there might be a blank space at the beginning of the paragraph that is left over from when you inserted the graphic. Delete the space and repeat Step 6.

▶ **7.** Insert a drop cap in the paragraph following the last heading, click anywhere in the text to deselect the drop cap, and scroll so you can see the drop caps.

Tip

To change the size of the drop cap, you can drag one of the sizing handles.

The drop caps are a nice, eye-catching detail. Next, you turn your attention to inserting a registered trademark symbol (®) next to a registered trademark name.

Inserting Symbols and Special Characters

In printed publications, it is customary to change some of the characters available on the standard keyboard into more polished-looking characters called **typographic characters**. Word's AutoCorrect feature automatically converts some standard characters into typographic characters as you type. For instance, as Joel typed the paragraph under the heading "Preventing Type II Diabetes," he typed two hyphens after the phrase "be delayed or prevented." As he began to type the rest of the sentence, "if you act in time," Word automatically converted the two hyphens into a single, longer character called an em dash.

Figure 4-22 lists some of the other character combinations that AutoCorrect automatically converts to typographic characters. In most cases you need to press the spacebar and type more characters before Word inserts the appropriate typographic character. If you don't like the typographic character inserted by Word, click the Undo button to revert to the characters you originally typed.

Common typographic characters ◀ **Figure 4-22**

To insert this symbol or character	Type	After you press the spacebar, Word converts to
Em dash	word--word	word—word
Smiley	:)	☺
Copyright symbol	(c)	©
Trademark symbol	(tm)	™
Ordinal numbers	1st, 2nd, 3rd, etc.	1st, 2nd, 3rd, etc.
Fractions	1/2, 1/4	½, ¼
Arrows	--> or <--	← or →

In addition to characters inserted by AutoCorrect, Word also has many typographic characters that you can insert into a document. You can access these with the Symbol button on the Insert tab.

Inserting Symbols and Special Characters

- Move the insertion point to the location where you want to insert a particular symbol or special character.
- Click the Insert tab, and then, in the Symbols group, click the Symbol button.
- If you see the symbol or character you want in the Symbol gallery, click it. For a more extensive set of choices, click More Symbols to open the Symbol dialog box.
- In the Symbol dialog box, locate the symbol or character you want on either the Symbols tab or the Special Characters tab.
- Click the symbol or special character you want, click the Insert button, and then click the Close button.

Joel needs to include a registered trademark symbol (®) after "HealthLife" in the last paragraph of the newsletter.

To insert the registered trademark symbol:

▶ **1.** Scroll down to display the paragraph below the heading "Risk Assessment" at the bottom of the right column, and then click to the right of the word "HealthLife." (Take care to click between the final "e" and the comma.)

▶ **2.** Click the **Insert** tab, if necessary, click the **Symbol** button in the Symbols group, and then click **More Symbols**. The Symbol dialog box opens.

▶ **3.** If necessary, click the **Special Characters** tab. See Figure 4-23.

Figure 4-23 | Symbol dialog box

▶ **4.** Click **Registered** to select it, and then click the **Insert** button.

▶ **5.** Close the Symbol dialog box. Word inserts an ® immediately after and slightly above the word "HealthLife."

Next, you need to adjust the columns of text, so they are approximately the same length.

Balancing the Columns

You can shift text from one column to another by adding blank paragraphs to move the text into the next column or by deleting blank paragraphs to shorten the text, so it will fit into one column. The problem with this approach is that any edits you make later could throw off the balance. Instead, you can insert a continuous section break at the end of the document. This tells Word to automatically **balance** the columns, or make them of equal length. You'll balance the columns in the newsletter next.

To balance the columns:

▶ 1. Press the **Ctrl+End** keys to move the insertion point to the end of the text in the right column, just after the period following your name.

▶ 2. Zoom out, so you can see the entire newsletter at once.

▶ 3. Click the **Page Layout** tab, and then, in the Page Setup group, click the **Breaks** button. The Breaks menu opens.

▶ 4. Below "Section Breaks," click **Continuous**. Word inserts a continuous section break at the end of the text. As shown in Figure 4-24, Word balances the text between the two columns, so they are approximately the same length.

Newsletter with balanced columns ◀ Figure 4-24

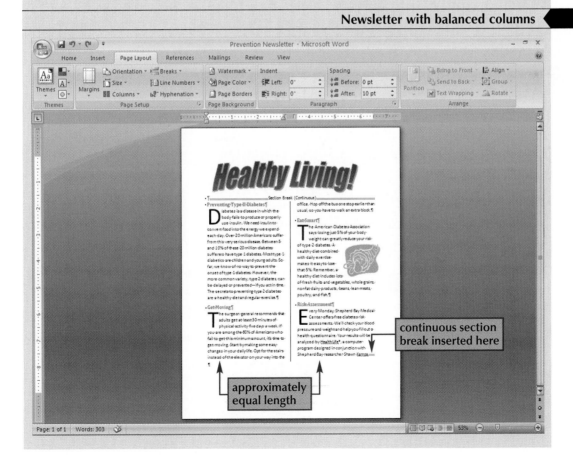

Inserting a Border Around a Page

You can add definition to a paragraph or an entire page by adding a border. Borders can be simple lines or they can be elaborate artwork. You can also emphasize pages and paragraphs by adding shading (a colored background). In both cases, you use the Page Borders button on the Page Layout tab, which opens the Borders and Shading dialog box. Right now, Joel wants to add a border around the entire newsletter page.

To insert a border around the newsletter:

1. Make sure the document is still zoomed out, so you can see the whole page and that the Page Layout tab is selected.

2. In the Page Background group, click the **Page Borders** button. The Borders and Shading dialog box opens.

3. If necessary, click the **Page Border** tab. (Take care not to click the Borders tab by mistake.) You use the Setting options on the left side of this tab to specify the type of border you want. In this case, you want a simple box.

4. In the Setting section, click the **Box** option. Now that you have selected the type of border you want, you can choose the style of line that will be used to create the border.

5. In the Style list box, scroll down and select the ninth style down from the top (the thick line with the thin line underneath), and then verify that the Apply to option is set to **Whole document**. See Figure 4-25. While the Borders and Shading dialog box is open, notice the Art arrow, which you can use to select a border consisting of graphical elements such as lightening bolts, boxes, or specially designed borders.

Figure 4-25   Adding a border to the newsletter

6. Click the **Options** button in the lower-right corner of the Borders and Shading dialog box. The Border and Shading Options dialog box opens. Here you can change settings that control where the border is positioned on the page. By default, the border is positioned 24 points from the edges of the page. To ensure that your printer will print the entire border, you need to change the Measure from setting so that it is positioned relative to the outside edge of the text rather than the edge of the page.

7. Click the **Measure from** arrow, and then click **Text**. The settings in the Top and Bottom boxes change to 1 pt, and the settings in the Left and Right boxes change to 4 pt, indicating the border's position relative to the edge of the text. You can leave the other settings as they are. See Figure 4-26.

 Border and Shading Options dialog box Figure 4-26

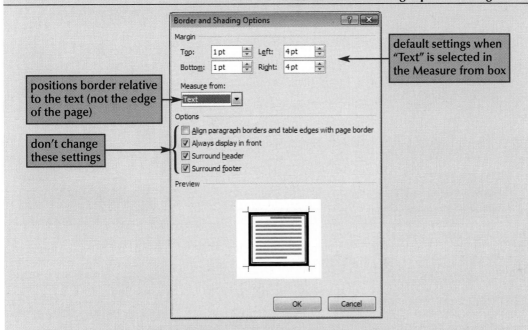

8. Click the **OK** button in the Border and Shading Options dialog box, click the **OK** button in the Borders and Shading dialog box, and then save your work. The newsletter now has an attractive border, although the cornucopia graphic may not be positioned neatly inside the border.

9. If necessary, drag the cornucopia graphic to position it inside the border, as shown in Figure 4-27. You may also need to drag the graphic up or down, so that the text wraps neatly around it. When you are finished, save the document.

Figure 4-27 ▷ **Newsletter with border**

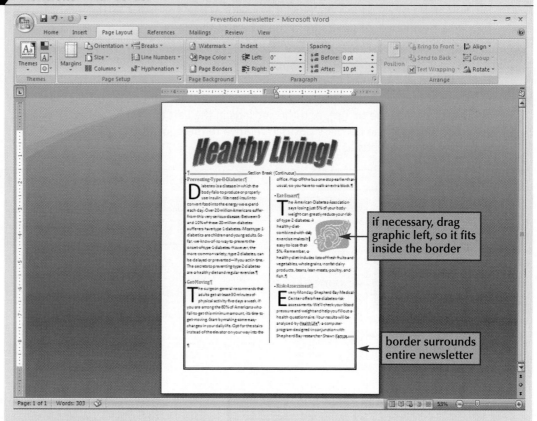

10. Print the newsletter, and then close the document, saving it if prompted to do so.

Joel will print the newsletter later on a high-quality color printer. But first, he asks you to use Word's mail merge feature to insert customer names and addresses into a cover letter he's written. He plans to send the cover letter with the newsletter.

Performing a Simple Mail Merge

The term **mail merge** refers to the process of combining information from two separate documents to create many final documents, each containing customized information. The two separate documents are called a main document and a data source. A **main document** is a document that contains text, such as a business letter, as well as place-holders called **merge fields**. The merge fields tell Word where to insert customized information such as a name or an address. You can distinguish merge fields from the text of the main document because each merge field name is enclosed by pairs of angled brackets like this: << >>.

Joel's main document is a letter that contains the text shown in Figure 4-28. You will replace the text in brackets with merge fields.

Joel's main document   **Figure 4-28**

June 26, 2010

[INSERT ADDRESS FIELDS]

Dear [INSERT FIRST NAME FIELD]:

Enclosed you will find an informational newsletter published by Shepherd Bay Medical Center. We
would like to make this a regular publication that focuses on health-related topics. To ensure that it is as
helpful as possible, we are soliciting feedback from potential readers. Would you have a moment to give
me your opinion regarding the newsletter's content and layout? My office is located at the South Clinic.
You can reach me everyday from noon to 5 P.M. at 555-5555.

Sincerely,

Joel Conchola

Public Outreach Specialist

A **data source** is a document that contains the data, such as clients' names and
addresses, that you can insert into the main document. Joel plans to send the newsletter
to a small test group of clients. His data source is a table in a Word document that contains the names and addresses of five Shepherd Bay Medical Center clients. This table is
shown in Figure 4-29. The header row in the table contains the names of the merge
fields. Each row in the table contains information about an individual client. In mail
merge terminology, all of the information about one person or one object is called a
record.

Joel's data source   **Figure 4-29**

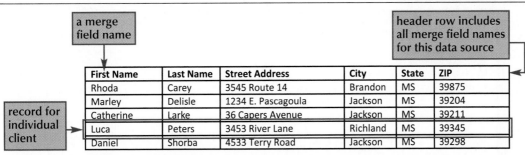

a merge
field name

header row includes
all merge field names
for this data source

First Name	Last Name	Street Address	City	State	ZIP
Rhoda	Carey	3545 Route 14	Brandon	MS	39875
Marley	Delisle	1234 E. Pascagoula	Jackson	MS	39204
Catherine	Larke	36 Capers Avenue	Jackson	MS	39211
Luca	Peters	3453 River Lane	Richland	MS	39345
Daniel	Shorba	4533 Terry Road	Jackson	MS	39298

record for
individual
client

During a mail merge, the merge fields in the main document instruct Word to retrieve
information from the data source. For example, one merge field in the main document
might retrieve a first name from the data source; another merge field might retrieve a
street address. For each record in the data source, Word will create a separate letter in
the final document, which is called the **merged document**. Thus, if the data source contains five sets of client names and addresses, the merged document will contain five
separate letters, each one containing a different client name and address in the appropriate places.

The Mailings tab contains all the options you need for performing a mail merge. However, when you're just getting started with mail merge, it's helpful to use the Mail Merge
task pane, which walks you through the process.

In the following steps, you'll open the Word document that you'll use as the data
source, so you can see how it's set up. Then you'll open the Mail Merge task pane and
start the mail merge.

To begin the mail merge process:

▶ 1. Open the document named **Addresses** from the Tutorial.04\Tutorial folder included with your Data Files. Review the table, which contains addresses for five clients of Shepherd Bay Medical Center.

▶ 2. Close the Addresses document without making any changes, and then open the document named **Letter** from the Tutorial.04\Tutorial folder included with your Data Files. When he typed this letter, Joel included text in brackets as placeholders to indicate where he wants to insert the merge fields.

▶ 3. Near the end of the letter, replace "Joel Conchola" with your first and last name, and then save the document as **Cover Letter** in the Tutorial.04\Tutorial folder included with your Data Files.

▶ 4. Click the **Mailings** tab, and then, in the Start Mail Merge group, click the **Start Mail Merge** button. The Start Mail Merge menu opens.

▶ 5. In the Start Mail Merge menu, click **Step by Step Mail Merge Wizard**. The Mail Merge task pane opens, displaying the first of six steps related to completing a mail merge. See Figure 4-30. Your first task is to specify the type of main document you want to use for the merge.

Figure 4-30	Mail Merge task pane

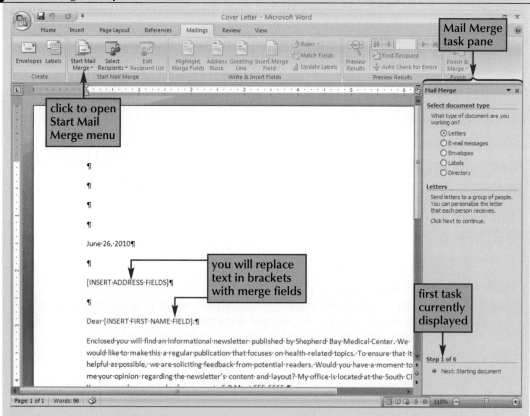

▶ 6. Verify that the **Letters** option button is selected in the Mail Merge task pane.

▶ 7. At the bottom of the Mail Merge task pane, click **Next: Starting document**. The Mail Merge task pane now displays information and options that you can use to select a starting document—that is, to select a main document. In this case, you want to use the current document, Cover Letter.

▶ **8.** Verify that the **Use the current document** option button is selected.

▶ **9.** At the bottom of the Mail Merge task pane, click **Next: Select recipients**. You'll continue working with the Mail Merge task pane in the next set of steps.

You've finished the first two tasks, which relate to selecting the main document. Now you are ready to tell Word where to find the list of recipients for Joel's letter.

Selecting a Data Source

You can use many kinds of files as data sources for a mail merge, including Word tables, Excel worksheets, Access databases, or Contacts lists from Microsoft Outlook. You can select a preexisting file or you can create a new data source. In this case, you will use the table in the Addresses document, which you examined earlier.

To select the data source:

▶ **1.** In the Mail Merge task pane, verify that the **Use an existing list** option button is selected.

▶ **2.** Click **Browse** in the Mail Merge task pane. The Select Data Source dialog box opens. This dialog box works similarly to Word's Open dialog box.

▶ **3.** Navigate to the Tutorial.04\Tutorial folder, select the **Addresses** document, and then click the **Open** button. The table from the Addresses document is displayed in the Mail Merge Recipients dialog box. See Figure 4-31.

Mail Merge Recipients dialog box ◀ Figure 4-31

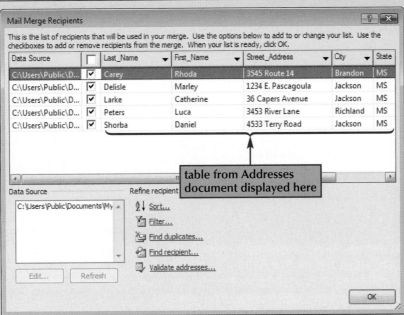

table from Addresses document displayed here

▶ **4.** Click the **OK** button. The Mail Merge Recipients dialog box closes, and you return to the Cover Letter document with the Mail Merge task pane open. Under "Use an existing list," you see the name of the file selected as the data source—or, depending on where you store your Data Files, you may see only the beginning of a directory path, which identifies the location where the data source file is stored.

▶ **5.** Click **Next: Write your letter** at the bottom of the Mail Merge task pane. The task pane displays options related to inserting merge fields in the main document, which you'll learn about next.

Inserting Merge Fields

Joel's letter is a standard business letter, so you'll place the recipient's name and address below the date. You could insert individual merge fields for the client's first name, last name, address, city, and ZIP code. But it's easier to use the **Address block** link in the Mail Merge task pane, which inserts a merge field for the entire address with one click.

To insert an Address Block merge field:

▶ **1.** Select the text **[INSERT ADDRESS FIELDS]**, and then delete it. Remember to delete the opening and closing brackets. Do not delete the paragraph mark following the text.

▶ **2.** Verify that there are three blank paragraphs between the date and the salutation and that the insertion point is positioned in the second blank paragraph below the date.

▶ **3.** Click **Address block** in the Mail Merge task pane. The Insert Address Block dialog box opens. See Figure 4-32. The options in this dialog box allow you to fine-tune the way the address will be inserted in the letter. The Preview box shows you how the address will look in the document after the merge is complete.

Figure 4-32 **Insert Address Block dialog box**

▶ **4.** Verify that the **Insert recipient's name in this format** check box is selected, and also verify that **Joshua Randall Jr.** is selected in the list box. This ensures that Word will insert each recipient's first and last name. (The other options in this list are useful with more complicated data sources.)

▶ **5.** Verify that the **Insert postal address** check box is selected. It doesn't matter whether the other check box and option buttons are selected; you only need to be concerned with them when working with more complicated data sources.

6. Click the **OK** button. An Address Block merge field is inserted in the letter. See Figure 4-33. Depending on how your computer is set up, you might see a gray background behind the merge field. Notice the angled brackets that surround the merge field. The angled brackets are automatically inserted when you insert a merge field. It is important to note that you cannot type the angled brackets and merge field information—you must enter it via a dialog box selection.

Tip

A selected merge field is highlighted with a gray background to distinguish it from regular text.

Address Block merge field in letter ◀ **Figure 4-33**

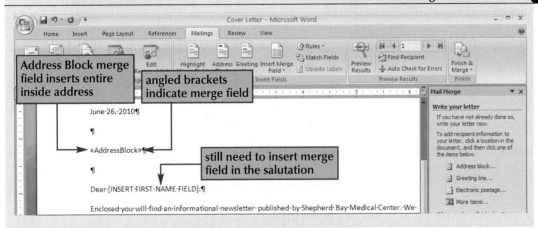

Later, when you merge the main document with the data source, Word will replace the Address Block merge field with the address information for each record in the data source. Your next job is to insert a merge field that will include each client's first name in the salutation. To insert an individual merge field (rather than a field for the entire address), you need to use the More items option in the Mail Merge task pane.

To insert the merge field for the salutation:

1. Select and delete **[INSERT FIRST NAME FIELD]** in the salutation. Remember to delete the opening and closing brackets. Do not delete the colon.

2. If necessary, insert a space to the left of the colon. When you finish, the insertion point should be positioned between the space and the colon.

3. In the Mail Merge task pane, click **More items**. The Insert Merge Field dialog box opens. The Fields list shows all the merge fields in the data source. See Figure 4-34. Note that merge fields cannot contain spaces, so Word replaces any spaces in the merge field names with underlines. You want to insert the client's first name into the main document, so you need to make sure the First_Name merge field is selected.

Figure 4-34 | **Insert Merge Field dialog box**

merge fields
in data source

space in merge
field name replaced
with underline

▶ **4.** Verify that **First_Name** is selected, click the **Insert** button, and then close the Insert Merge Field dialog box. The First_Name merge field is inserted in the document at the location of the insertion point. See Figure 4-35.

Figure 4-35 | **First_Name merge field inserted in document**

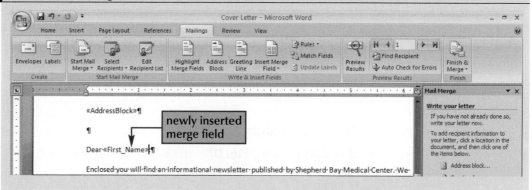

newly inserted
merge field

Trouble? If you make a mistake and insert the wrong merge field or insert the correct field in the wrong location, undo the insertion and then repeat Steps 1 through 4.

▶ **5.** Save your changes to the main document.

The main document now contains all the necessary merge fields, so you're ready to merge the main document with the data source. First, however, you should preview the merged document.

Previewing the Merged Document

When you preview the merged document, you see the main document with the customized information inserted in place of the merge fields. Previewing a merged document allows you to check for errors or formatting problems before you perform the merge.

To preview the merged document:

1. In the Mail Merge task pane, click **Next: Preview your letters**. The data for the first client in the data source (Rhoda Carey) replaces the merge fields in the cover letter. The top of the task pane indicates which record is currently displayed in the document. As shown in Figure 4-36, Word's default paragraph and line spacing results in too much space between the lines of the address. You can fix this by adjusting the spacing for the paragraph containing the Address Block merge field.

   Trouble? If the address is highlighted with a gray background, the merge field is selected. Click anywhere in the document outside the address to deselect the merge field.

Previewing the merge document | Figure 4-36

2. At the bottom of the Mail Merge task pane, click **Previous: Write your letter**. This moves you back one step in the Mail Merge task pane, to where the letter is displayed with the merge fields, rather than the recipient data, as shown earlier in Figure 4-35.

3. Click in the margin to the left of the **<<AddressBlock>>** merge field to select the merge field, as well as the paragraph mark to its right.

4. Click the **Home** tab, and in the Styles group, click the **No Spacing** Quick Style, and then, at the bottom of the Mail Merge task pane, click **Next: Preview your letters**. Now the address for Rhoda Carey is single spaced.

5. Carefully check the rest of the letter to make sure the text and formatting are correct. In particular, check to make sure that the spacing before and after the first name in the salutation is correct; it is easy to omit spaces or add extra spaces around merge fields.

Adjusting the Spacing in an Inside Address | InSight

In Tutorial 1, you used the Line spacing button to reduce the paragraph and line spacing in an inside address. Here, you used the No Spacing Quick Style. Which is better? The No Spacing Quick Style is faster, because it involves just one click. But keep in mind that it adjusts the line spacing and paragraph spacing at the same time. If you want more control over your spacing selections, use the Line spacing button instead.

You are ready for the final step—completing the merge.

Merging the Main Document and Data Source

Because your data source consists of five records, merging the main document with the data source will result in five copies of the letter to five different clients of Shepherd Bay Medical Center. Each letter will appear on its own page. Keep in mind that mail merges often involve hundreds or even thousands of records. As a result, the resulting document can be extremely long, with one page for every record in the data source.

To complete the mail merge:

1. In the Mail Merge task pane, click **Next: Complete the merge**. The task pane displays options related to merging the main document and the data source. You can use the Print option to have Word print the customized letters immediately, without displaying them on the screen. Instead, you'll use the Edit individual letters option to merge to a new document.

2. Click **Edit individual letters** in the Mail Merge task pane. The Merge to New Document dialog box opens. Here, you need to specify which records you want to include in the merge. You want to include all the records in the data source.

3. Verify that the **All** option button is selected, click the **OK** button, and then scroll as needed to display the entire first letter. Word creates a new document (the merged document) called Letters1, which contains five pages, one for each record in the data source. Each letter is separated from the one that follows it by a Next Page section break. See Figure 4-37. The main document with the merge fields (Cover Letter) remains open, as indicated by its button on the taskbar.

Figure 4-37 Newly merged document with customized letters

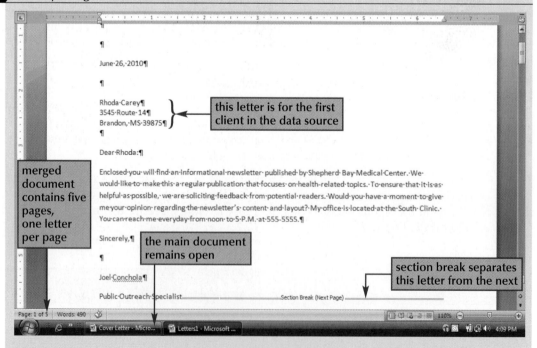

this letter is for the first client in the data source

merged document contains five pages, one letter per page

the main document remains open

section break separates this letter from the next

4. Save the merged document in the Tutorial.04\Tutorial folder, using the filename **Merged Cover Letters**.

5. Scroll down and review the five letters. Note the different address and salutation in each.

6. Close the Merged Cover Letters document. The document named Cover Letter reappears, along with the Mail Merge task pane.

7. Save the document and then close it.

Tip

There's usually no need to waste disk space by saving large merged documents. Typically, you would just print the merged document and close it without saving it.

You have completed a mail merge and generated a merged document. Joel will send the cover letters out with sample copies of his newsletter. Next, he wants to explore another means of communicating with the public—a blog.

Creating a Blog Post

A **blog** is an online journal that other people can read via the World Wide Web. The word "blog" is short for "Web log." Blogs typically include headings, paragraphs of text, pictures, and links to other blogs or Web sites. Although individuals often use blogs for personal reasons, in the business world a blog can serve the same function as a printed newsletter—providing news, product updates, and schedules of events. Because it can be updated instantly, and because the business doesn't incur printing costs, a blog is an effective way for a business or organization to communicate with the public.

A **blog post** is an addition to a blog, similar to an entry in a journal. When you create a blog post in Word, the file is a regular .docx file like an ordinary Word document, except that it doesn't have any of the formatting that controls the way a document looks on a printed page. It doesn't need that kind of formatting, because a blog is meant to be read on a computer screen. For example, the margins of a blog post are not fixed; instead, the margins change to accommodate the current zoom setting, with the text rewrapping as necessary. When it's finished, you can **post** it, or publish it—that is, add it to your online blog. At that point, the file is changed to an HTML file, so that it can easily be transferred over the Web.

Before you can post material to a blog, you need to create an account with a service that manages blogs and makes them available on the Web. Joel hasn't yet set up an account, but he wants to experiment with creating a blog post in Word. You can take an existing document and save it as a blog post, or you can start with a new, blank blog post. Joel wants to create a blog post from scratch. In the Case Problems at the end of this tutorial you'll save an existing document as a blog post.

To create a new blog post:

1. If necessary, start Word.

2. Click the **Office Button**, and then click **New**. The New Document dialog box opens. The middle pane contains an option for creating a new blog post. (Note that your New Document dialog box may not include the Recently Used Templates section.) See Figure 4-38.

Figure 4-38 Selecting a blog post in the New Document dialog box

▶ **3.** Click **New blog post**, and then click the **Create** button. The New Document dialog box closes and the Register a Blog Account dialog box opens. You don't need to create a blog account in order to create a blog post, so you'll skip this step. Later, if you decide to start an online blog, you could use this dialog box to register with a blog provider.

▶ **4.** Click **Register Later**. The Register a Blog Account dialog box closes. A blank blog post opens. It includes some placeholder text, which you can replace with a title for the new post. Notice that the Ribbon has only two tabs, both containing tools related to working with blog posts. See Figure 4-39.

Figure 4-39 Blank blog post

▶ **5.** Click the placeholder text **[Enter Post Title Here]** and type **Shepherd Bay Medical Center's New Blog**. The placeholder text is replaced with the new post title.

6. Click in the blank paragraph below the horizontal line and type **This is a sample blog post for Shepherd Bay Medical Center.** See Figure 4-40. A typical blog post is at least several lines long, and may contain graphics, tables, and links to other information on the Web. The Insert tab simplifies the process of adding this type of material. If you had registered with a blog provider, you could click the Publish button in the Blog group to post this to your online blog. Because you have not registered with a blog provider, you will simply save the blog post instead. Even if you publish a blog post, you should always save a copy on your computer, so you have a complete record of all your posts.

Sample blog post   Figure 4-40

if you had registered with a blog provider, you could click here to add this post to your online blog

7. Click the **Save** button on the Quick Access Toolbar, and then save the blog post as **Sample Blog Post** in the Tutorial.04\Tutorial folder included with your Data Files.

8. Print the blog post just as you would print an ordinary Word document, and then close the blog post.

Now that Joel understands how easy it is to create a blog post in Word, he will look into registering with a blog provider. A blog, along with the newsletter and the mass mailings he can create in Word, will help him communicate important information to the clients of Shepherd Bay Medical Center.

Session 4.2 Quick Check | Review

1. What type of text wrapping makes text follow the shape of the graphic?
2. True or False: When inserting a drop cap, you can specify the number of lines you want the drop cap to extend into the paragraph.
3. Explain how to open the Borders and Shading dialog box.
4. Name the two types of documents you need in a mail merge.
5. Define "record" as a mail merge term.
6. List the steps in performing a mail merge.
7. Explain how to open a new, blank blog post.

In this tutorial, you planned a newsletter and learned about the elements of desktop publishing. You created a headline using WordArt, anchored the WordArt object, and for-matted text in newspaper-style columns. You also inserted a graphic into a document, edited the graphic, inserted drop caps, and inserted symbols and special characters. Next, you balanced the newsletter columns, drew a border around the page, and used mail merge to create customized cover letters to accompany the newsletter. Finally, you created a blog post.

Key Terms

anchoring	floating graphic	pull quote
balance	graphic	record
bitmap	inline graphic	rules
blog	mail merge	scaling
blog post	main document	sizing handles
clip art	merge fields	template
crop	merged document	text box
data source	newspaper-style column	typographic symbols
desktop publishing	object	WordArt
drop cap	post	wrap

Apply the skills you learned in the tutorial using the same case scenario.

Data Files needed for the Review Assignments: Addresses.docx, Eating.docx, and Nutrition.docx

Joel's Healthy Living newsletter was well received. Now the Nutrition Department of the Shepherd Bay Medical Center has asked him to create a newsletter providing information and encouragement for Shepherd Bay clients to eat well. Joel has already written the text of the newsletter and asks you to transform it into a professional-looking newsletter. He asks you to create an accompanying cover letter using Word's mail merge feature, and then to create the first blog post for a new nutrition blog. (Note: Text you need to type is shown in bold for ease of reference only; do not bold the text unless otherwise instructed.) Complete the following:

1. Open the file **Eating** from the Tutorial.04\Review folder included with your Data Files, and then make sure your Word document is displayed in Print Layout view and that the nonprinting characters and rulers are displayed.
2. Save the document as **Eating Well** in the same folder.
3. In the last paragraph, replace "STUDENT NAME" with your first and last name.
4. At the top of the document, create the headline **Healthy Servings** using WordArt. In the WordArt Gallery, choose the fourth style from the left in the third row down from the top (the rainbow style with the shadow—WordArt style 16).
5. Change the shape of the WordArt object to Double Wave 2, and then italicize the WordArt text.
6. Apply the Top and Bottom text wrapping style to the WordArt object.
7. Drag the WordArt object to center it at the top of the page, then enlarge the WordArt object to span the width of the page. When you are finished, the WordArt object should be slightly less than one inch high and a little more than six inches wide.
8. Insert a blank paragraph at the beginning of the document, anchor the WordArt object to the new blank paragraph, and then save your work. If the WordArt moves below the new paragraph symbol, drag it up above the new paragraph. When you are finished, the anchor symbol should be positioned to the left of, and just above, the new paragraph symbol, with the WordArt object positioned above the new paragraph symbol.
9. Position the insertion point at the beginning of the newsletter text (to the left of the heading "Eat Light, Eat Right"), and then format the newsletter text in two columns. Insert a section break so that the two-column formatting is applied below the insertion point and insert a line between the two columns.
10. Click at the beginning of the paragraph below the heading "Eating Well in a Busy World."
11. At the insertion point, insert the clip art graphic of the running person with the cell phone from the Business folder in the Office Collections folder. (The image is black and blue.)
12. Close the Clip Art task pane, and then resize the graphic, so it is approximately 1.5 inches square.
13. Crop the image slightly on the top to remove most of the dotted blue line. Make sure not to crop any part of the satellite dish or the black and blue background behind the running figure.
14. Wrap text around the graphic using Tight text wrapping, and then drag the graphic down to position it near the middle of the paragraph, next to the left margin. Three lines of the paragraph text should wrap below the graphic. Use the Align button to align the graphic at the left margin. You may have to move the graphic around a bit until you find a location that allows the text to wrap neatly around it.

15. Create a drop cap in the first paragraph under each heading. When you are finished, adjust the position of the graphic if necessary, so the text wraps neatly around it, without excessive space between words.

16. In the paragraph below the heading "Eating Well in a Busy World," insert the trademark symbol after "20 Fast Food Friends."

17. Check to make sure the document is still only one page long. If the text has flowed to the second page, then you probably made the WordArt headline too tall. Resize the WordArt object (and the graphic, if necessary) until the document is only one page long.

18. If you think it's necessary, balance the columns by inserting a Continuous section break at the bottom of the document. If you do insert a Continuous section break, and a new page is added at the end of the document, delete the section break. You probably sized the WordArt object and the graphic in a way that makes the section break unnecessary.

19. Add a border around the page using the Box setting and the border style with three thin lines (eighth from the top). Remember to position the border relative to the text, and not the edge of the page. Adjust the position of the clip art graphic if necessary.

20. Preview, save, and print the newsletter. When you are finished, close the document.

21. Open the file **Nutrition** located in the Tutorial.04\Review folder, replace "Joel Conchola" at the end of the letter with your name, and then save the document as **Nutrition Letter** in the same folder.

22. Merge the Nutrition Cover Letter document with the Addresses file found in the Tutorial.04\Review folder. Use the Address Block merge field for the inside address. Next, include a merge field that will insert the customer's first name in the salutation. Preview the merged letters and make any necessary changes before completing the merge. Remember to adjust the spacing for the Address Block field, so the inside address is single spaced.

23. Save the merged document as **Merged Nutrition Letters** and close it. Save your changes to the main document and close it. Close the task pane if necessary.

24. Create a new blog post. Use "Eating Right for Life" as the post title. For the blog post, type two sentences introducing a health and nutrition blog sponsored by the Nutrition Department at Shepherd Bay Medical Center. Save the blog post as **Nutrition Blog** in the Tutorial.04\Review folder included with your Data Files, and then close it.

25. Submit the finished documents to your instructor, either in printed or electronic form, as requested.

Apply | **Case Problem 1**

Apply the skills you learned to create a newsletter and a blog post for a public library.

Data File needed for this Case Problem: Audio.docx

Florentina, Arizona, Public Library Michaela Novoa is the director of the Florentina, Arizona, Public Library. She and her staff have developed a new program that makes it possible for library patrons to download audio books over the Web as MP3 files. Michaela has written the text of a newsletter explaining the download system. She asks you to finalize the newsletter and then create a blog post from the formatted newsletter. (Note: Text you need to type is shown in bold for ease of reference only; do not bold the text unless otherwise instructed.) Complete the following:

1. Open the file **Audio** located in the Tutorial.04\Case1 folder included with your Data Files. Make sure your document is displayed in Print Layout view at Page width zoom and that the ruler and the nonprinting characters are displayed.

2. At the end of the document, replace "STUDENT NAME" with your first and last name. Save the document as **Audio Books** in the same folder.

3. At the top of the document, create the headline **Downloading Audio Books** using WordArt. In the WordArt Gallery, choose WordArt style 11, in the second column from the right, second row from the top (blue block letters).

4. Set the text wrapping style to Top and Bottom.

5. Drag the WordArt object to center it at the top of the page, and then enlarge the WordArt object to span the entire width of the page. When you are finished, the WordArt object should be a little less than 1 inch high and about 6.5 inches wide.

6. Edit the WordArt object to set the font to Arial and to apply bold to it. Then apply the Inflate Top shape to the headline and save your work.

7. Make sure the WordArt is anchored to the paragraph containing the subtitle of the newsletter, "Florentina, Arizona, Public Library." (The anchor should be located in the margin, on the same line as the subtitle.) In this newsletter, you don't need to insert a blank paragraph and anchor the WordArt to it, because the columns will begin below the subtitle, not directly below the WordArt.

✦ EXPLORE
8. Select the paragraph containing the subtitle and center and italicize it. Open the Borders and Shading dialog box, click the Borders tab, and apply a Box border with the default line style. Make sure the Apply to box shows Paragraph. Click the Shading tab, click the Fill arrow, and click the pink box in the second row from the top. Be sure Paragraph is still selected in the Apply to list box, and then click the OK button.

9. Format all the text below the subtitle in two newspaper style columns, without a line between them. The subtitle should be centered over the two columns.

10. Open the Clip Art task pane and use the Clip Organizer to locate the image of a man in a brown suit typing on a keyboard. The image is stored in the Business folder within the Office Collections folder. Paste the image at the beginning of the first paragraph under the heading "How do I Listen to a Downloaded Book?" Close the Clip Art task pane.

11. Resize the picture, so that it is 1.5 inches wide.

12. Apply the Square text wrapping option. Drag the graphic down to the middle of the paragraph, next to the right column border. Align the graphic using the Align Right option in the Align menu.

13. Balance the columns, then zoom out, so you can see the whole page and review your work. If the newsletter text flows to a second page, reduce the height of the WordArt object until the newsletter is again only one page long.

14. Save and print the newsletter.

✦ EXPLORE
15. Click anywhere in the document text to make sure the graphic and the WordArt object are not selected. Click the Office Button, point to Publish, and then click Blog. If you are asked to register a blog account, click Register Later. Save the new blog post as **Audio Books Blog** in the Tutorial.04\Case1 folder included with your Data Files. When saved as a blog post, the document loses the two-column formatting. You can format a blog in columns, but you need to do it through the blog provider, not when you create individual blog posts in Word.

16. Increase the zoom setting to at least 130%, so you can easily read the text. Notice how, in a blog post, the text wraps to fit the zoom size.

17. Click the WordArt title and delete it. Enter **Downloading Audio Books** as the post title. Select the subtitle in the pink box, and align it on the left margin. Delete the section break, as it is no longer necessary. If necessary, drag the clip art down to the paragraph below the heading "How do I download a book from ListenBooks?" Note that the final position of graphics in an online blog is often determined by the blog service provider.

18. Save your work, submit the finished documents to your instructor, either in printed or electronic form, as requested, and then close the files.

Apply | **Case Problem 2**

Apply the skills you learned to create an employee newsletter.

Data Files needed for this Case Problem: Island.jpg and News.docx

Flannery Investments   You work in the Personnel Department for Flannery Investments, a national investment company with headquarters in Minneapolis, Minnesota. You've been assigned the task of preparing the monthly newsletter *Flannery News*, which provides news about employees of Flannery Investments. You will use text written by other employees for the body of the newsletter. The newsletter will ultimately be three pages long, but at this point you have enough text to fill only one page and part of another. Complete the following:

1. Open the file **News** located in the Tutorial.04\Case2 folder included with your Data Files, and then save it as **Flannery Newsletter** in the same folder.

2. Use the Find and Replace command to replace all instances of the name "Daniela" with your first name. Then replace all instances of "Alford" with your last name.

3. At the top of the newsletter, create a **Flannery News** WordArt headline. Use the WordArt style in the second row down, third column from the left (WordArt style 9), select Arial as the font, and apply bold formatting. Set the wrapping style to Top and Bottom, and then anchor the WordArt to the blank paragraph at the top of the document, if it isn't already.

4. Center the WordArt if necessary, and resize the WordArt proportionally, so that it spans the width of the page and is about 1 inch high and 6 inches wide.

5. Make sure the WordArt object is positioned above the blank paragraph and anchored to the blank paragraph. Format the body of the newsletter into three newspaper-style columns. Place a vertical rule between the columns.

⊕ EXPLORE   6. Position the insertion point at the beginning of the paragraph below the heading "Win a Vacation Get-Away." Click the Insert tab, and then, in the Illustrations group, click the Picture button. In the Picture dialog box, navigate to the Tutorial.04\Case2 folder, select the **Island** file, and then click the Insert button.

7. Crop about a third of the photo from the left and right sides, so that you only see the pier stretching out into the water. When you are finished, the image should be about .5 inches wide.

⊕ EXPLORE   8. Make sure the photo is still selected and that the Picture Tools Format tab is displayed. In the Arrange group, click the Position button, and then, under With Text Wrapping, click the option in the left column, middle row. This aligns the photo on the left margin, halfway down the page, with the text wrapped around it. You don't need to select an alignment option on the Align menu when you use the Position button.

9. Click in the first paragraph under the heading "Win a Vacation Get-Away," and insert a drop cap that drops two lines into the paragraph. Insert a similar drop cap in the first paragraph after each of the other two headings in the newsletter.

10. Zoom out so you can see the whole page and review your work. Don't be concerned that the newsletter spans more than one page.

11. Add a page border to the newsletter. Select yellow stars as the art for the border. Apply the border to both pages of the newsletter (the entire document).

12. Save your work, submit the finished documents to your instructor, either in printed or electronic form, as requested, and then close any open files.

| Challenge | **Case Problem 3** |

Explore new techniques as you create the two-sided brochure shown in Figure 4-41.

Data File needed for this Case Problem: Hill.docx

Hill Star Dairy Cooperative   Haley Meskin is the publicity director for Hill Star Dairy Cooperative in Lawrence, Kansas. Local residents pay a membership fee to join the co-op and then receive a 10% discount on purchases of organic dairy products. Many members don't realize that they can take advantage of other benefits, such as free cooking classes and monthly mailings with recipe cards and coupons. To spread the word, Haley would like to create a brochure describing the benefits of joining the co-op. She has already written the text of the brochure. She would like the brochure to consist of one piece of paper folded in three parts, with text on both sides of the paper, as shown in Figure 4-41. (Note: Text you need to type is shown in bold for ease of reference only; do not bold the text unless otherwise instructed.)

Figure 4-41

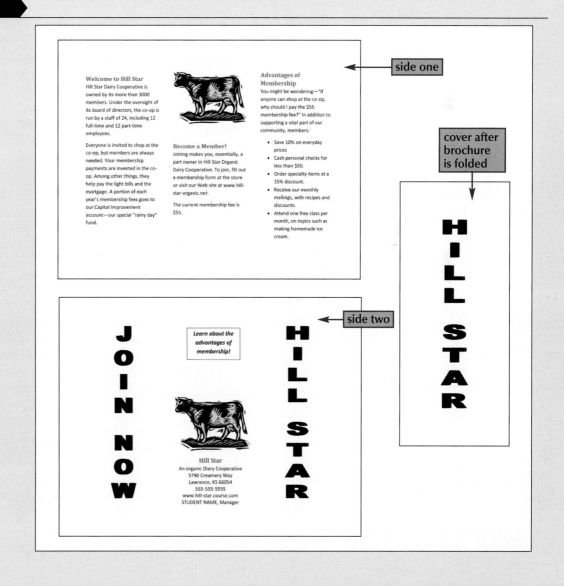

Complete the following:

1. Open the file **Hill** located in the Tutorial.04\Case3 folder included with your Data Files, and then save it as **Hill Star Brochure** in the same folder. This document contains a graphic of a cow. Because no text wrapping has been applied to it, it is an inline graphic. In this case, you want the graphic to remain an inline graphic, because you want it to move with the text as you edit the document.

2. On the second page, below the cow graphic, replace "STUDENT NAME" with your first and last name.

3. Format the entire document in three columns of equal width. Do not include a vertical line between columns. Ignore the page break at the bottom of page 1.

⊕ EXPLORE 4. You are already familiar with adding section breaks and page breaks to a document. You can also add a column break, which forces the text after the insertion point to move to the next column. Click at the beginning of the heading "Become a Member!" (just to the left of the "B"), click the Page Layout tab, and then, in the Page Setup group, click the Breaks button. In the Breaks menu, click Column. Insert another column break before the heading "Advantages of Membership." On the second page, click the second blank paragraph on the page, and then insert another column break. This column break moves the cow graphic and the text below it to the middle column. Press the Ctrl+End keys to move the insertion point to the blank paragraph at the end of the document, and insert another column break; this moves the blank paragraph to the third column on the second page.

5. Zoom out so you can see the whole page and review your work. The document should consist of two pages, with three columns each. The cow graphic and the co-op address should appear in the middle column on the second page.

⊕ EXPLORE 6. Click the cow graphic in the second page, copy the graphic to the Clipboard, click to the left of the heading "Become a Member!", and then insert two blank paragraphs. Click in the first new paragraph (at the top of the column), and then paste the graphic from the Clipboard. The middle column of the first page now contains the cow graphic, with the heading "Become a Member!" below, followed by two paragraphs of text.

7. On page 2, click in the blank paragraph at the top of the left column. Insert a WordArt object. In the WordArt Gallery, select the style in the left column, fourth row down. Use **JOIN NOW** (use uppercase letters) as the text. *Save your work.*

⊕ EXPLORE 8. Select the WordArt object if it is not already selected, and make sure the WordArt Tools Format tab is visible. In the Text group, click the WordArt Vertical Text button. This arranges the letters vertically down the column.

9. Adjust the size of the WordArt object (by dragging a sizing handle), so that it spans the height of the column—do *not* press the Shift key as you drag the handle. When you are finished, the WordArt object should be approximately 6 inches high and 1 inch wide. If you make it too wide, the WordArt will be hard to read. If you increase the height too much, the WordArt will disturb the column breaks, possibly resulting in a third page being added to the document. If that happens, click the Undo button and try again.

⊕ EXPLORE 10. In the WordArt Styles group on the WordArt Tools Format tab, click the Shape Fill button arrow. Click the black square in the top row of the palette. The WordArt changes from a marbleized brown to all black. Save your work.

11. Copy the WordArt object to the Clipboard. Paste a copy of the WordArt in the right column of page 2, select the newly pasted copy, click the Edit Text button in the Text group on the Format tab, and then change the text to **HILL STAR**. When you are finished, page 2 should consist of the JOIN NOW WordArt in the left column, the graphic and address information in the middle column, and the HILL STAR WordArt in the right column. Zoom out so you can see the whole page and examine your work.

12. Use the Center button on the Home tab to center both WordArt objects in their respective columns.

⊕ **EXPLORE** 13. Click the Page Layout tab, and then, in the Page Setup group, click the Dialog Box Launcher. In the Page Setup dialog box, click the Layout tab, click the Vertical alignment arrow, click Center, and then click the OK button. This centers the text vertically on the page (between the top and bottom margins) and ensures that the brochure will look right when folded. Save your work.

⊕ **EXPLORE** 14. Change the Zoom setting to 100% and scroll to display the top of the middle column on the second page. Click the top of the middle column, insert five blank paragraphs, click the Insert tab, and then, in the Text group, click the Text Box button. In the Text Box gallery, click Simple Text Box, and then, in the text box inserted in the document, type **Learn about the advantages of membership!**. Select the text in the text box and, using the appropriate tools on the Home tab, format the text in 16-point Calibri, italic, and bold. Center the text in the text box. Place the mouse pointer on the border of the text box, and drag the text box up to position it at the top of the middle column, above the cow. Drag the border of the text box to make the text box narrower than the column, and only as tall as necessary to display all of the text. Zoom out, so you can see the whole page, and adjust the text box size and the position of the graphic as needed, so that the content of the middle column fits nicely on the page. Save your work.

15. To print the brochure, you need to print the first page and then print the second page on the reverse side. Ask your instructor if you should print the brochure before doing so. To print the brochure, click the Office button, click Print, click the Pages option button, type **1**, and then click the OK button. Retrieve the printed page, and then insert it into your printer's paper tray, so that "JOIN NOW" prints on the reverse side of the list of member benefits; likewise, "HILL STAR" should print on the reverse side of the "Welcome to Hill Star" text. Whether you should place the printed page upside down or right-side up depends on your printer. You may have to print a few test pages until you get it right. When you finish, you should be able to turn page 1 (the page with the heading "Welcome to Hill Star") face up, and then fold it inward in thirds, along the two column borders. Fold the brochure, so that the "HILL STAR" column lies on top.

16. Save your work, submit the finished documents to your instructor, either in printed or electronic form, as requested, and then close any open files.

Create | **Case Problem 4**

Create the table shown in Figure 4-42, and then use it as the data source for a mail merge resulting in cover letters and envelopes for your own internship search.

There are no Data Files needed for this Case Problem.

Internship Search Cover Letters   You're ready to start looking for an internship, and you plan to use Word to create customized cover letters to accompany your resume. You've decided to use mail merge to customize the letters. You'll start by creating the table shown in Figure 4-42 and filling it with address information for potential internship sponsors. Then you'll create a cover letter to use as a main document, and customize it by inserting the appropriate mail merge fields. (Note: Text you need to type is shown in bold for ease of reference only; do not bold the text unless otherwise instructed.) Complete the following:

1. Open a new, blank document, and then save it as **Intern Data** in the Tutorial.04\ Case4 folder included with your Data Files.
2. Create the table shown in Figure 4-42, and then enter information for three potential internship sponsors. The information can be real or fictitious. For the First Name and Last Name columns, use a fictitious name for an appropriate contact at each company. Use Ms. or Mr. for the Title field. Note that the Title field has to be the column on the far right, or the Address Block merge field won't work correctly. (The Address Block merge field assumes the first seven columns on the left are the fields you want to include in the address.) Save your work and close the document.

Figure 4-42

First Name	Last Name	Company Name	Street Address	City	State	ZIP	Title

3. Open a new, blank document and save it as **Intern Letter** in the Tutorial.04\Case4 folder.
4. Create a cover letter that introduces yourself and describes your experience and education. Instead of an inside address, include the placeholder text **[INSIDE ADDRESS]**. For the salutation, use **Dear [TITLE] [LAST NAME]**. Refer the reader to your resume (even if you don't have one) for more information. Use a proper business letter style for your cover letter. Include a sentence in the cover letter that mentions the company name. Use the placeholder **[COMPANY NAME]** to remind you to insert the appropriate merge field later. Save your work.
5. Save the letter, and open the Mail Merge task pane and follow the steps outlined in it. Use the Intern Letter document as the main document, and select the Intern Data file as the data source.
6. Use the Address block merge field for the inside address (in the "Joshua Randall Jr." format), and verify that the Insert company name check box is selected in the Insert Address Block dialog box. Adjust the paragraph and line spacing for the paragraph containing the Address Block merge field, so the inside address is single spaced.
7. Add a merge field for the title and the last name in the salutation of the letter, and add a merge field to replace the company name placeholder text in the body of the letter. Save your changes to the main document before completing the merge.
8. Preview your letters, and then complete the merge (choosing the Edit individual letters option). Save the merged document as **Merged Intern Letters** in the Tutorial.04\ Case4 folder, close it, and close the Mail Merge task pane.
9. Print your main document, and then close it.

⊕ EXPLORE

10. Open a new, blank document, and then save it as **Intern Envelopes** in the Tutorial.04\Case4 folder.

11. Open the Mail Merge task pane, click the Envelopes option button under Select document type, and then click Next: Starting document. Click Envelope options, and then click the OK button in the Envelope Options dialog box to select the default settings. The document layout changes to resemble a business size envelope.

12. Continue with the steps in the Mail Merge task pane, selecting the Intern Data file as the data source.

13. Click Next: Arrange your envelope, and notice that the insertion point is positioned in the return address, ready for you to begin typing. Type your name and address as the return address. (Change the Zoom setting if necessary to make the text easier to read.) Click the paragraph mark in the center of the document and insert an Address block merge field in the "Joshua Randall Jr." format. You do not have to adjust the paragraph or line spacing for the Address block field for an envelope. Save your work.

14. Preview the envelopes, and complete the merge (choosing the Edit individual envelopes option). Don't worry about the section break that appears after the return address; the envelopes will print correctly. Save the merged document as **Merged Intern Envelopes** in the Tutorial.04\Case4 folder. If your computer is connected to a printer that is stocked with envelopes, print the main document. Close the Mail Merge task pane and save your changes to the main document.

15. Submit the finished documents to your instructor, either in printed or electronic form, as requested, and then close any open files.

| Research | **Internet Assignments** |

Go to the Web to find information you can use to create documents.

The purpose of the Internet Assignments is to challenge you to find information on the Internet that you can use to work effectively with this software. The actual assignments are updated and maintained on the Course Technology Web site. Log on to the Internet and use your Web browser to go to the Student Online Companion for New Perspectives Office 2007 at **www.course.com/np/office2007**. Then navigate to the Internet Assignments for this tutorial.

| Assess | **SAM Assessment and Training** |

If you have a SAM user profile, you may have access to hands-on instruction, practice, and assessment of the skills covered in this tutorial. Log in to your SAM account (**http://sam2007.course.com**) to launch any assigned training activities or exams that relate to the skills covered in this tutorial.

Session 4.1

1. The document uses multiple fonts; the document incorporates graphics; the document uses typographic symbols; the document uses columns and other special formatting features; the printing is of high quality.
2. Click the WordArt object to select it, click the Edit Text button in the Text group on the WordArt Tools Format tab, edit the text in the Edit WordArt Text dialog box, and then click the OK button.
3. False
4. Text Wrapping button; located in the Arrange group on the WordArt Tools Format tab
5. Columns dialog box
6. BMP, GIF, JPEG, and TIFF
7. Insert tab

Session 4.2

1. Tight
2. True
3. Click the Page Layout tab, and then, in the Page Background group, click the Page Borders button
4. Main document and data source
5. A single row in a data source
6. Select or create a main document. Select or create a data source. Use the Mail Merge task pane to insert merge fields into the main document. Preview the merged document. Merge the data source and the main document.
7. Click the Office button, click New, click New blog post, click the Create button.

Ending Data Files

Tutorial.04 →

Tutorial
Addresses.docx
Cover Letter.docx
Merged Cover Letters.docx
Prevention Newsletter.docx
Sample Blog Post.docx

Review
Addresses.docx
Eating Well.docx
Merged Nutrition Letters.docx
Nutrition Blog.docx
Nutrition Letter.docx

Case1
Audio Books.docx
Audio Books Blog.docx

Case2
Flannery Newsletter.docx

Case3
Hill Star Brochure.docx

Case4
Intern Data.docx
Intern Envelopes.docx
Intern Letter.docx
Merged Intern Envelopes.docx
Merged Intern Letters.docx

Reality Check

You've seen how Microsoft Word 2007 allows you to create polished, professional-looking documents in a variety of business settings. The word-processing skills you've learned will be useful to you in many areas of your life. For example, you could create a Word table to keep track of a guest list for a wedding, or you could use Word's desktop publishing features to create a flyer promoting a garage sale or a concert for a friend's band. In the following exercise, you'll create a number of useful documents of your choosing using the Word skills and features presented in Tutorials 1 through 4.

Using Templates

You can create the documents in this exercise from scratch, or you can use the templates that are available in the New documents dialog box. A **template** is a special Word document that comes with predefined headings, formatting, document controls, and graphical elements. In the New Document dialog box, click Installed Templates, and then click the template you want. To use a template after you've opened it, save it like an ordinary document, and then replace the placeholder text with your own information. If a template includes a sample picture, you can replace the picture with your own JPEG photo file or a clip art image.

Note: Please be sure *not* to include any personal information of a sensitive nature in the documents you create to be submitted to your instructor for this exercise. Later on, you can update the documents with such information for your own personal use.

1. Create a resume that you could use to apply for your ideal job.
2. Create a cover letter to accompany your resume and portfolio. Where appropriate, insert placeholders for merge fields.
3. Create a data source that includes one record for each company or organization you plan to send your resume to.
4. Perform a mail merge, using your cover letter and your data source. Save the merged document.
5. Perform a second mail merge to create the envelopes for your cover letter and resume. In the first step of the Mail Merge task pane, click the Envelopes option button. In the second step, click Envelope options, and then click the OK button to accept the default envelope settings. Continue following the steps in the Mail Merge task pane. Save the merged document.
6. Create a multiple-page report. For the text of the report, you can use a report you have already written for another class or any text of your choosing. Choose an appropriate theme. Include a cover page, header, and footer. Include at least two footnotes or endnotes, and format the headings with appropriate Quick Styles.
7. Use a Word table to design a one-page flyer for an upcoming event. Remember that you can insert graphics into a table cell and that you can format the text in each cell differently. Also, keep in mind that the buttons in the Merge group on the Table Tools Layout tab allow you to combine and divide table cells.
8. Create a newsletter containing information you want to share with friends, family, or colleagues. Include graphics, newspaper-style columns, and other desktop publishing elements, as appropriate, to enhance your newsletter.
9. Save the newsletter as a blog post. Make any changes necessary to make the blog post attractive and easy to read.
10. Review all your documents carefully in Print Preview, and then submit the finished documents to your instructor, either in printed or electronic form, as requested.

Working with Templates and Outlines

Creating a Site Selection Report

Case | Department of City Planning

Clarenbach, Tennessee is a rapidly growing suburb of Nashville. Clarenbach's Department of City Planning prepares reports on many public projects that contribute to this growing community. Sam Hooper, a senior member of the department, has asked you to help prepare a report on possible sites for a new public swimming pool. He'd like you to use one of Word's templates as the basis for the new report. He'd also like you to create a template that can be used for all the reports the department creates.

Starting Data Files

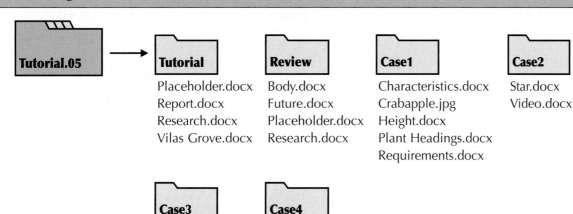

Tutorial.05 → **Tutorial**
Placeholder.docx
Report.docx
Research.docx
Vilas Grove.docx

Review
Body.docx
Future.docx
Placeholder.docx
Research.docx

Case1
Characteristics.docx
Crabapple.jpg
Height.docx
Plant Headings.docx
Requirements.docx

Case2
Star.docx
Video.docx

Case3
Text.docx

Case4
(none)

Session 5.1

Creating a New Document from an Installed Template

A **template** is a file that you use as a starting point to create other files so that you don't have to re-create formatting and text for each new file. You can think of a template as a pattern for a series of similar documents. A template can contain customized Quick Styles (often referred to simply as styles), text, graphics, or any other element that you want to repeat from one document to another. Word provides numerous types of templates that you can use to create reports, fax cover sheets, letters, and other types of documents. For an even wider selection of templates, you can look online, where you'll find templates for certificates, contracts, brochures, and greeting cards, just to name a few. As you'll learn in this tutorial, you can also create your own templates to suit your specific needs.

Although you might not realize it, you already have experience working with templates. Every new, blank document that you open in Word is a copy of the Normal template. Unlike all other templates, the **Normal template** does not have any text, formatting, or graphics, but it does include all the default settings that you are accustomed to in Word. For example, the default theme in the Normal template is the Office theme. The Office theme, in turn, supplies the default body font (Calibri) and the default heading font (Cambria). The default 1.5 line spacing and the extra space after paragraphs are also specified in the Normal template.

InSight	Changing the Normal Template

If the settings in the Normal template don't suit your needs or tastes, you can change them. For example, you could change the default theme for the Normal template from Office to Oriel; or, instead of changing the entire theme, you could change just the default body font from Calibri to Verdana or another font. You could also change the default line spacing or the space that is supplied after each paragraph by default. It's important to remember, though, that when you change the default settings for the Normal template, the new settings will be apparent in all the new documents that you open in Word.

Tip

Templates have the file extension .dotx to differentiate them from regular Word documents, which have the extension .docx.

Sam would like to base his report on the Equity Report template, which is one of the templates installed along with Word. You open a template from the New Document dialog box. By default, when you open a new template, Word actually opens a document that is an exact copy of the template. The template itself remains untouched, so that you can continue to use it as the basis of future documents.

To open a new document based on the Equity Report template:

▶ **1.** Start Word, click the **Office Button** , and then click **New**. The New Document dialog box opens. You've used the Blank document option in this dialog box before to open a new, blank document. The Templates panel on the left side of this dialog box gives you access to templates that are stored on your computer and to templates available online. In this case, you want to open a template that was installed with Word.

2. Click **Installed Templates**. The middle pane of the New Documents dialog box displays thumbnail images of the templates that were installed with Word. Scroll down, if necessary, and then click **Equity Report**. See Figure 5-1. In the lower-right corner of the New Document dialog box, the Document option button is selected by default. This indicates that Word will open a new document that is a copy of the template, not the template itself.

Selecting the Equity Report template Figure 5-1

3. Click **Create**. The New Document dialog box closes, and a new document, named Document2, opens.

4. Switch to Print Layout if necessary, change the Zoom setting to Page width, display nonprinting characters if necessary, and then scroll down and review the parts of the document. The first page is a cover page with five controls: the document title, the subtitle, the company name, the date, and the author. The second page contains controls for the title and subtitle. It also contains heading and body text and a sample photograph. To the right of the photograph is a vertically formatted figure caption, which also contains a control. The lower-left corner of the second page contains a page number in an orange circle and a footer that is formatted vertically so that it runs up the left side of the page. The footer consists of two controls—one for the document title and one for the date. Each page is surrounded by a border with rounded corners. Figure 5-2 shows all the elements of the Equity Report template. The colors, the fonts, and the other elements you see in the document are specified by the Equity theme, which is the default theme for the Equity Report template.

Figure 5-2 ▶ **Equity Report template**

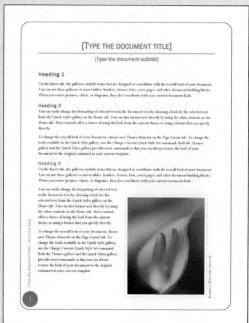

▶ **5.** Save the document as **Pool Sites** in the Tutorial.05\Tutorial folder included with your Data Files.

InSight | **Using Template Elements**

When you create a document from a template, you don't have to use all the elements the template provides. For example, you could replace the default cover page with a different one by using the Cover Page button on the Insert tab, or you could delete the cover page entirely. Likewise, the sample photograph in the Equity Report template is just a suggestion; it shows how to format a photograph so that it blends harmoniously with the other elements of the Equity Report template. The same is true of the page number inside the orange circle. If you don't like it, you can switch to Header and Footer view, click the orange circle, and delete it. The secret to getting the most out of templates is to use only the elements that suit your needs.

After you open a new document based on a template, you can type the appropriate text in the controls and then replace the sample body text with text that is specific to your document. As you learned in Tutorial 3, a document control (also known as a **content control**, or just a control) serves as a repository of information; Word reuses the information from a document control in various places within the same document. For example, if you enter the title in a title document control, it will appear in all the title document controls in that document. You'll gain more practice with document controls in the following steps as you begin work on the pools report.

To enter text into the document controls:

▶ **1.** In the orange bar on the cover page, click the **[Type the document title]** place-holder text. The text is selected within the document control, ready for you to replace it. Sam wants to use the department name as the document title.

▶ **2.** Type **Department of City Planning**. The new title replaces the placeholder text. The document control is still visible around the new title, because it contains the insertion point. Next, you need to enter the subtitle.

▶ **3.** Click the **[Type the document subtitle]** placeholder text and type **Sites for New Swimming Pool**. The new subtitle appears in the control.

▶ **4.** Scroll down, if necessary, and click the **[TYPE THE COMPANY NAME]** placeholder text. The placeholder text is selected inside the company name control. A blue dot-ted rectangle with selection handles appears, enclosing the bottom of the cover page, including the company name, date, and author controls. This rectangle is part of the formatting that governs the placement of the controls on the page. You can ignore it. Sam does not want to include anything in the company name control, so you will delete it.

▶ **5.** Right-click the selected text. A shortcut menu appears. The Mini toolbar also appears, but you can ignore it. See Figure 5-3. Note that the Zoom in Figure 5-3 is set to 80% so you can see all the parts of the cover page in one figure. On your computer, the Zoom should be set to Page width.

Shortcut menu for the company name control ◀ **Figure 5-3**

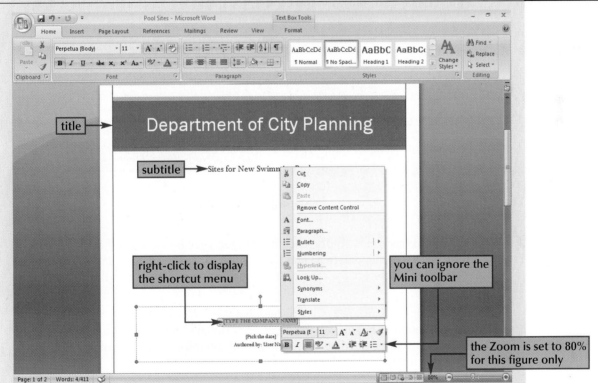

▶ **6.** Click **Remove Content Control**. The company name control is deleted.

Next, you turn your attention to inserting the date and your name as the author.

To insert the date and your name:

▶ **1.** Click the **[Pick the date]** placeholder text. A document control with an arrow button appears, surrounding the placeholder text.

▶ **2.** Click the arrow button next to the date control. A calendar appears, with a rectangle around the current date. See Figure 5-4.

Figure 5-4 ▶ Cover page with calendar displayed

▶ **3.** Click the current date. The calendar closes and the current date is displayed in the Date control.

▶ **4.** Click to the right of the text "Authored by" to display a control where you can insert the name of the author of the report. Depending on how your computer is set up, you might see a name displayed in this control, you might see the placeholder text "[Type the author name]," or the control might be empty. See Figure 5-5.

Figure 5-5 ▶ Author control

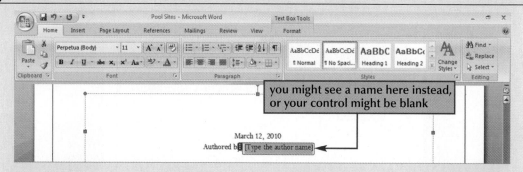

▶ **5.** If the Author control is empty, click it and type your first and last name. If the control contains a name, delete it, and then type your first and last name. Press the **Escape** key to deselect the control. Your name is now displayed in the control.

The cover page for Sam's report is finished. Now you can work on the second page. Sam wants the report to begin with the heading "Contents" followed by a table of contents. You'll insert the heading now; you'll work on inserting a table of contents in Session 3 of this tutorial.

To enter the "Contents" heading on page 2:

▶ **1.** Scroll down to display page 2. Notice that the title and subtitle controls at the top of page 2 now display the title and subtitles you typed on the cover page. Likewise, the controls in the vertical footer (in the lower-left corner of the page) display the document title and the current date.

2. Move the mouse pointer over the text in the body of the report, which begins "Heading 1." The text area is highlighted in blue.

3. Click anywhere in the body of the report. The blue highlight darkens and now covers only the text itself. A blue tag above the highlighted text indicates that the body of the report is actually a content control. See Figure 5-6. This control is included in the document only so you can see a sample of the heading and body fonts and a suggestion for how to format a photograph, should you decide to include one in the report. Before you can create the body of the report, you need to delete this control.

Document with sample text highlighted ◄ **Figure 5-6**

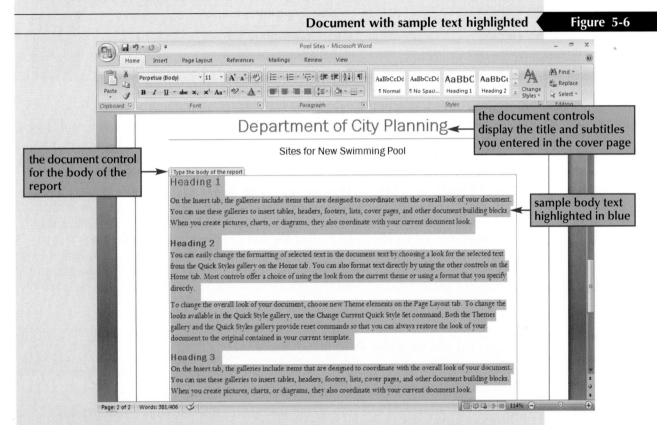

the document controls display the title and subtitles you entered in the cover page

the document control for the body of the report

sample body text highlighted in blue

4. Right-click the **body control** to display a shortcut menu, and then click **Remove Content Control**. The control is deleted. You are ready to start typing the body of the report.

5. Verify that the insertion point is located in the blank paragraph on the left margin below the subtitle, and then type **Contents**. The text is formatted in the Perpetua font, which is the default body font for the Equity Report template. In the next step, you'll format the text using a heading style.

6. In the Styles group, click the **Heading 1** Quick Style. The Contents heading is formatted in 14-point Franklin Gothic Book font with a dark orange color.

7. Press the **Enter** key to start a new paragraph, type **[Insert a table of contents.]**, and then press the **Enter** key. This placeholder text will remind Sam to insert a table of contents later. Notice that the new text is formatted in the Normal style, not in the Heading 1 style. A new paragraph after a heading is formatted in the Normal style by default. See Figure 5-7.

| Figure 5-7 | Page 2 of Sam's report |

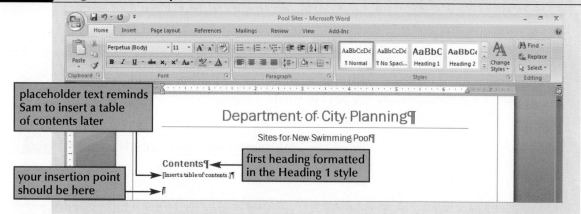

placeholder text reminds Sam to insert a table of contents later

your insertion point should be here

Department of City Planning¶

Sites for New Swimming Pool¶

Contents¶

[Insert a table of contents.]¶

first heading formatted in the Heading 1 style

Sam has already typed the remainder of his report and saved it in a separate Word document. In the next section, you'll learn how to insert this Word file into the Pool Sites document.

Inserting a File into a Word Document

To insert a file into a document, you start by clicking the Object button in the Text group on the Insert tab. When you insert a Word file into an open Word document, the text of the inserted file is inserted at the location of the insertion point, so you need to make sure the insertion point is at the correct location. Word always inserts a blank paragraph at the end of text inserted from another file. If you don't want to include this extra paragraph, you can delete it.

To insert a file into the Pool Sites document:

1. Verify that the insertion point is located in the blank paragraph below the placeholder text, as shown earlier in Figure 5-7.

2. Click the **Insert** tab, and then, in the Text group, click the **Object** button arrow. (Take care to click the Object button arrow, and not the Object button itself.) A menu appears with two options.

   Trouble? If the Object dialog box opens, you clicked the Object button instead of the Object button arrow. Close the dialog box, and then click the Object button arrow instead.

3. In the Object menu, click **Text from File**. The Insert File dialog box opens. This looks like the Open dialog box, which you've used many times before.

4. If necessary, navigate to the Tutorial.05\Tutorial folder included with your Data Files, click the **Report** document, and then click the **Insert** button. The text of the Report document is inserted in the Pool Sites document. Sam formatted the headings of the Report document with Quick Styles when he first typed the document, so you don't need to format the headings now. Note that Word inserted a blank paragraph after the report text. You can leave that extra paragraph there for now. See Figure 5-8.

Trouble? If a menu appears below the Insert button in the Insert File dialog box, you clicked the Insert button arrow, rather than the Insert button itself. Press the Escape key to close the menu, and then click the Insert button.

Report document inserted into the Pool Sites document ◀ Figure 5-8

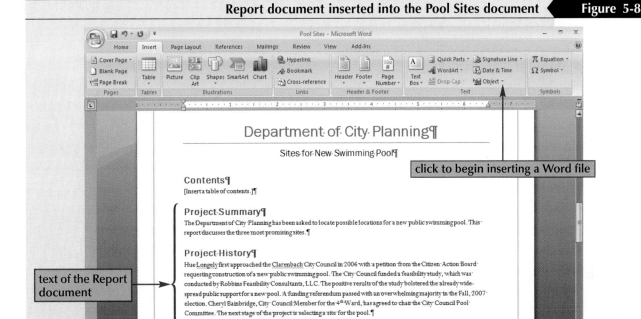

Review the document and notice that it now includes five main headings formatted with the Heading 1 style: Contents (which you typed earlier), Project Summary, Project History, Project Personnel, and Project Description. Below the Project Description heading are three subheadings: Breese Terrace Park, Langbrook Farm, and Flora Park. The subheadings Breese Terrace Park and Flora Park are formatted with the Heading 2 style. Sam mistakenly formatted the Langbrook Farm heading in the Heading 3 style. Later in this tutorial, when you learn about outlines, you will fix this problem.

5. Save your work.

Now that the document contains the report text, you can turn your attention to customizing its formatting. You'll start with the document theme.

Customizing the Document Theme

A document theme consists of three main components: colors, fonts, and effects. The **theme colors** control the colors used for every element in a document, including text, shading, hyperlinks, and so on. The **theme fonts** control the document's heading and body fonts. Remember that each theme specifies one font to be used for headings and one font to be used for body text. These two fonts appear at the top of the Font list on the Home tab. The **theme effects** control the look of a document's graphics. A specific set of colors, fonts, and effects is associated with each theme, but you can mix and match them to create a customized theme for your document. You change the theme colors, fonts, and effects for a document using the options in the Themes group on the Page Layout tab. When you change the theme colors, fonts, and effects for a document, the new elements affect only that document.

Customizing the Document Theme

- To select a different set of theme colors, click the Theme Colors button in the Themes group on the Page Layout tab, and then click the color palette you want.
- To select a different combination of heading and body fonts, click the Theme Fonts button in the Themes group on the Page Layout tab, and then click the font combination you want.
- To select a different set of theme effects, click the Theme Effects button in the Themes group on the Page Layout tab, and then click the icon for the effects you want.

The Pool Sites document, which was based on the Equity Report template, is formatted with the Equity theme. That means it draws its colors, fonts, and effects from the default settings of the Equity theme. Although Sam likes the overall layout of the document, which was provided by the Equity Report template, he doesn't like the colors or the fonts supplied by the Equity theme. He decides to select different theme colors and theme fonts for the Pool Sites document. He doesn't plan to include any graphics, so he will not take the time to customize the theme effects. He'll start with the theme colors.

Changing the Theme Colors

To get a better understanding of what happens when you change a document's theme colors, suppose you are working on a new document with the Office theme selected. The colors associated with the Office theme format headings in blue. If you prefer headings formatted in pink instead, you could select the colors of the Verve theme, which formats headings in pink.

Sam doesn't like the orange and red colors used in the Equity theme and asks you to change it to something more neutral. Before you begin customizing the theme, you will take a moment to verify that the Equity theme is in fact the current theme.

To change the theme colors in the Pool Sites document:

1. Verify that the second page of the document is displayed, so that you can see the document headings.

2. Click the **Page Layout** tab, and then position the mouse pointer over the **Themes** button. A ScreenTip appears indicating that the current theme is Equity. Next, you begin customizing the Equity theme's colors.

3. In the Themes group, click the **Theme Colors** button. A gallery of color sets appears, with one color set for each theme. A pale orange outline indicates that the Equity color set is the current color set. You see eight colors in each color set. The third color from the left in each set is the color used for headings. For example, the third color from the left in the Equity color set is dark orange, which is the color currently applied to the headings in the document. The remaining colors are used for other types of elements, such as hyperlinks, shading on cover pages, and so on. See Figure 5-9.

Tip

To see a ScreenTip that tells you the current theme colors, move the mouse pointer over the Theme Colors button in the Themes group on the Page Layout tab.

Theme Colors gallery ◀ Figure 5-9

Trouble? If you see additional color sets at the top of the menu under the heading Custom, someone else created custom color sets on your computer. You can ignore them.

▶ **4.** Move the mouse pointer over the options in the gallery and observe the live preview of the colors in the document.

▶ **5.** Scroll down if necessary, and then click the **Urban** color set, which is the second from the bottom. The document headings are now formatted in dark blue. The page number circle in the document footing changes from orange to blue.

▶ **6.** Scroll up and review the new colors applied to the cover page. The colored bar is dark blue with a brown bottom border, instead of dark orange with a light orange bottom border.

▶ **7.** Save your work.

Keep in mind that the new colors you just selected affect only the Pool Sites document. Your changes do not affect the Equity theme that was installed with Word and that is available to all new documents. In the next section, you will finish customizing the document's theme by changing the theme fonts.

Customizing the Theme Fonts

Before you get to work changing the theme fonts for the Pool Sites document, you need to take a moment to learn some general principles that are useful when deciding which fonts to use in your documents:

- Fonts are divided into two types: serif and sans serif fonts. A **serif** is a small embellishment at the tips of the lines of a character, as shown in Figure 5-10. "Sans" is French for "without," thus, a **sans serif font** is a font without embellishments.

Figure 5-10 ▶ **Elements of fonts**

- One of the most popular serif fonts is Times New Roman. Cambria, the default Headings font in the Office theme, is a new serif font created specifically by Microsoft for Office 2007. Perpetua, the default Body font for the Equity theme, is also a serif font.
- Arial is a popular sans serif font. Calibri, the default body font in the Office theme, is a new sans serif font created specifically by Microsoft for Office 2007. Franklin Gothic Book, the default Headings font for the Equity theme, is also a sans serif font.
- As a rule, you should avoid unusual fonts, or fonts that look like handwriting, except in certificates, invitations, advertisements, and other specialty documents.
- You can add special effects to most fonts by adjusting the settings in the Font dialog box, which you open by clicking the Dialog Box Launcher in the Font group on the Home tab. For example, you can format a font as small caps (a reduced version of regular capital letters), superscript (slightly above the main line), subscript (slightly below the main line), outline (only the outline of the letters), or with shadows (light shading in the shape of the letter).

With these guidelines in mind, you are ready to select a new set of fonts for the Pool Sites document. As with theme colors, when changing the theme fonts, you can select from all the font combinations available in any of the themes installed with Word.

To select a different set of theme fonts for the Pool Sites document:

▶ **1.** Scroll down so you can see page 2 of the document.

2. In the Themes group, move the mouse pointer over the **Theme Fonts** button [A⁻]. A ScreenTip appears, indicating that the current fonts are Franklin Gothic book for headings and Perpetua for body text.

3. Click [A⁻]. The Theme Fonts gallery opens, displaying the heading and body font combinations for each theme.

4. Scroll down until you see the heading and body fonts for the Equity theme. The orange highlighting indicates that these are the current fonts for the Pool Sites document. Sam prefers the Lucida Sans Unicode font, which has a bolder, more modern look than the default fonts for the Equity theme. The Concourse theme uses the Lucida Sans Unicode font for both headings and body text, so you will select the Concourse font set in the next step. (Although the Concourse font set consists of the same font for headings and body text, it's still called a "set.") See Figure 5-11.

Theme Fonts gallery ◄ **Figure 5-11**

5. Click the **Concourse** font set. The Theme Fonts gallery closes, and the Lucida Sans Unicode Font is applied to the headings and body text in the Pool Sites document. See Figure 5-12.

Figure 5-12 ▶ **Pool Sites document with new theme fonts and colors**

6. Save your work.

Remember that the new font set you just selected affects only the Pool Sites document. The new fonts do not affect the original Equity theme that was installed with Word and that is available to all new documents.

Creating Custom Theme Colors and Theme Fonts

It is possible to create customized sets of theme fonts and theme colors. Customized sets of theme colors and theme fonts include combinations that are not included in any of the themes installed with Word. (It is not possible to create customized theme effects in Word.) When you create a customized set of theme fonts or theme colors, they are saved as part of Word, so that you can use them in other documents.

Creating Custom Theme Colors and Theme Fonts | Reference Window

- To create a custom set of theme colors, click the Theme Colors button in the Themes group on the Page Layout tab, click Create New Theme Colors to open the Create New Theme Colors dialog box, click the arrow for the color you want to change, click a color, repeat for additional colors as necessary, type a descriptive name for the new color scheme in the Name text box, and then click the Save button. The custom set of theme colors appears as an option in the Themes Color menu.
- To delete a custom set of theme colors, click the Theme Colors button in the Themes group on the Page Layout tab, right-click the custom set of colors you want to delete, click Delete, and then click Yes.
- To create a custom set of heading and body fonts, click the Theme Fonts button in the Themes group on the Page Layout tab, click Create New Theme Fonts to open the Create New Theme Fonts dialog box, use the list boxes to select the Heading and Body fonts you want, type a descriptive name for the new set of fonts in the Name text box, and then click the Save button. The custom set of theme fonts appears as an option in the Theme Fonts menu.
- To delete a new set of theme colors or fonts, click the Theme Colors or Theme Fonts button in the Themes group on the Page Layout tab, right-click the custom set of colors or fonts you want to delete, click Delete, and then click Yes.

The sets of theme colors and theme fonts installed with Word were created by Microsoft designers who are experts in creating harmonious-looking documents. As a rule, it's best to stick with these predesigned options, rather than trying to create your own.

Creating a Custom Theme

Keep in mind that the new theme colors and theme fonts you selected for the Pool Sites document affect only that document. To make your new choices available to other documents, you would need to create a custom theme. When you create a custom theme, it is saved as part of Word and appears as an option in the Themes gallery so that you can apply it to any document.

Creating a Custom Theme | Reference Window

- Modify the document theme as much as you want by selecting new theme colors, theme fonts, and theme effects.
- In the Themes group on the Page Layout tab, click the Themes button.
- Click Save Current Theme to open the Save Current Theme dialog box, type a name for the theme in the File name text box, and then click the Save button. The new theme appears at the top of the Themes menu, under the "Custom" heading.
- To delete a custom theme, click the Themes button in the Themes group on the Page Layout tab, right-click the theme you want to delete, click Delete, and then click Yes.

Sam is happy with the new look of the Pool Sites document. He doesn't need to save his changes to the fonts and colors as a custom theme, though. In the next session, you will focus on modifying the Quick Styles used in Sam's report.

1. Which template includes all the default settings that you are accustomed to in Word?
2. How do you delete a content control?
3. What tab should you click if you want to insert a Word file into a document?
4. What are the three main components of a document theme?
5. List the two types of fonts.
6. True or False. It is not possible to create a new theme.

Session 5.2

Understanding Themes, Styles, and Style Sets

Before you begin working more extensively with styles, you need to make sure you understand the relationship between styles and themes. The elements of a theme (colors, fonts, and effects) are like the building materials for a house. Styles, on the other hand, are like blueprints for the many types of houses that you can create with those building materials.

For example, by default, the Heading 1 style applies the heading font specified in the document theme. However, it doesn't just apply to the heading font. That would be like a blueprint that said only that a house should be made out of brick, but failed to specify the number of rooms, the style of windows, and so on. The Heading 1 style, for example, includes numerous additional details that, taken together, format text with a particular look—its style. Among other things, the Heading 1 style applies a particular font size and adds boldface. It also adds color—whatever color specified by the current Accent 1 color for the current theme.

As you know, you select a style from the Quick Styles gallery on the Home tab. By default, the Quick Styles gallery displays 20 different styles. Additional sets of styles are also available via the Change Styles button in the Styles group on the Home tab.

You can modify an existing style, or you can create a new style by modifying an existing one and saving it with a new name. By default, a new or modified style is saved only in the current document. If you prefer, you can save a new or modified style as part of the current template, so that it is available in all new documents based on that template.

InSight | **Saving Styles to the Current Document**

Keep in mind that all new, blank documents are based on the Normal template. So if you open a blank document, modify or create a style, and then save the style to the current template (rather than to the current document), the style will be available in all new blank documents that you open in Word in the future. Continually modifying or creating styles in the Normal template can result in a Quick Styles gallery that is disorganized, making it hard to find the styles you want. To avoid this problem, consider saving specialized styles to the current document (rather than to the current template), and then saving the current document as a template. All future documents based on that new template will contain your new styles. Meanwhile, the Normal template will remain unaffected by the new styles.

Sam wants to select a different style set for the Pool Sites document. Then he would like to modify the Heading 1 style, and finally, create a new style for the Project Summary heading.

Selecting a Style Set

Every built-in theme comes with 11 sets of styles, with names such as Elegant, Modern, and Manuscript. Each style set is, in turn, made up of 31 styles. So far, you've worked with only the sixteen styles, such as Heading 1 and Heading 2, that are available from the Quick Styles gallery on the Home tab. You can access additional styles via the Styles window, by clicking the More button in the Styles group on the Home tab.

The **style sets** have the same names in each theme, but they look different from one theme to the next. Likewise, the styles that make up the style sets have the same name in each style set, but they look different from one style set to the next. The default style set for built-in themes is the Office 2007 style set. This is the style set you are used to seeing in the Quick Styles gallery whenever you open a new, blank document.

Each set of styles includes a Normal style for formatting body text, several heading styles, and styles for titles, captions, and other special types of text. To select a different style set, you use the Change Styles button in the Styles group on the Home tab. The Style Sets menu allows you to preview the various style sets in your document before actually selecting one.

In the following steps, you select a new style set for the Pool Sites document.

To select a new style set for the Pool Sites document:

▶ 1. Verify that the Pool Sites document is open, in Print Layout view, the Zoom set at Page width, and nonprinting characters displayed. If necessary, scroll down so the second page of the document is visible. This will allow you to see how changing the style set affects the document headings. Recall that some headings are formatted with various heading styles. The body text below each of the headings is formatted in the Normal style.

▶ 2. Click the **Home** tab if necessary, and then in the Styles group, click the **Change Styles** button. The Change Styles menu opens. To select a new style set, you use the Style Set option.

▶ 3. Point to **Style Set**. The Style Set menu opens, displaying a list of style sets.

▶ 4. Drag the mouse pointer down and point to **Modern**. In the document, you see a preview of some of the styles that make up the Modern style set. In the Modern style set, the Heading 1 style applies a blue box that spans the left and right margins, with the heading text in white. The font for the document is still Lucida Sans Unicode for both headings and the body text, as you specified in Session 1 when you changed the theme fonts. The colors are still the colors you picked when you changed the theme colors in Session 1. See Figure 5-13.

Tip

To restore the default style set specified by the document's template, click Reset to Quick Styles from *Name* Template (where *Name* stands for the template's name) at the bottom of the Style Set menu.

Figure 5-13 | Live Preview of the Modern style set

preview of the Heading 1 style in the Modern style set

preview of body text in the Modern style set

document currently shows a preview of the Modern style set

> 5. Move the mouse pointer over other options in the Style Set menu and observe the live preview in the document.

> 6. Click **Modern** in the Style Set menu. The styles in the document change to reflect the styles in the Modern style set, and the Quick Styles gallery in the Styles group displays the first four styles in the Modern Style set.

> 7. In the Styles group, click the **More** button ☰ to review the set of styles available in the Quick Styles gallery, and then click anywhere in the document to close the Quick Styles gallery.

Tip

If you forget which style set is currently applied to a document, you can always check the Style Set menu to see which style has a check mark next to it.

Now that you've selected the Modern style set for Sam's document, you can customize the styles in the Modern style set. You'll start by modifying the Heading 1 style.

Modifying Styles

To modify a style, you select text formatted with the style you want to modify, apply new formatting, and then save your changes to the style. You'll start modifying the Heading 1 style by selecting some text formatted in that style and then applying the new formatting. Specifically, you will expand its character spacing, paragraph spacing, and apply italics. After you finish applying this new formatting, you will modify the Heading 1 style to match the newly formatted heading. To apply this formatting, you need to turn your attention briefly away from styles to focus on character spacing and paragraph spacing.

Changing Character Spacing

Word offers a number of ways to adjust the spacing between characters—that is, to adjust **character spacing**. In some situations, you might want to use **kerning**, the process of adjusting the spacing between characters to make them look like they are spaced evenly. Kerning is helpful because in text formatted in large font sizes, characters sometimes look unevenly spaced, even though they are in fact spaced evenly. Turning on Word's automatic kerning feature ensures that the spacing is adjusted automatically so that letters appear evenly spaced. In most documents, however, it's easiest to select a group of characters and then uniformly expand or condense the spacing between them. Notice that space between characters is measured in points, with one point equal to 1/72 of an inch.

Adjusting Character Spacing | Reference Window

- Select the text whose character spacing you want to adjust.
- In the Font group on the Home tab, click the Dialog Box Launcher to open the Font dialog box, and then click the Character Spacing tab.
- Click the Spacing arrow, and then click Expanded or Condensed. If you like, you can specify the amount of spacing to apply to each character by adjusting the setting in the By text box.
- To switch from Expanded or Condensed spacing back to regular spacing, click the Spacing arrow, and then click Normal.
- To turn on automatic kerning, click the Kerning for fonts check box to insert a check, and then select a point size in the Points and above check box.

You are ready to modify the character spacing of the Contents heading. While you have the Font dialog box open, you will also add italics.

To modify the character spacing of the Contents heading:

▶ **1.** Click in the left margin to select the heading **Contents**. Note that the blue selection highlighting might be hard to see in the blue box surrounding the "Contents" heading.

▶ **2.** In the Font group on the Home tab, click the Dialog Box Launcher. The Font dialog box opens.

▶ **3.** Click the **Character Spacing** tab. This tab includes several options for changing the space between characters. Currently, the setting in the Spacing list box is Expanded. The setting you see here depends on the style applied to the text that is selected in the document. If you wanted to move the selected character closer together, you could click the Spacing arrow and then click Condensed. In this case, you will keep the Expanded setting but increase the space between the characters by changing the setting in the By box next to the Spacing list box.

▶ **4.** Next to the Spacing list box, delete the contents of the By text box, type **2** (you don't have to type "pt"), and then press the **Tab** key. The Preview section shows a sample of the expanded character spacing. See Figure 5-14.

Figure 5-14 Changing character spacing in the Font dialog box

Expanded spacing is selected by default

change this setting to 2

preview of expanded characters appears after you press the Tab key

Next, you need to apply italics. It's normally easiest to use the buttons on the Home tab to perform this task. However, since the Font dialog box is open, it makes sense to make these changes there.

▶ **5.** In the Font dialog box, click the **Font** tab. Here you can make numerous changes affecting the appearance of the selected text, including adding special effects such as shadows or outlines. The "Contents" heading is already formatted in all capital letters, so the All caps check box is selected. This setting was specified by the Heading 1 style. In the Font style list box, Bold is also selected, indicating that the Heading 1 style also applied bold formatting to the "Contents" heading. (In the case of the white font color applied to the "Contents" heading, bold makes the white characters thicker rather than darker.) You want to keep the bold formatting and also add italics.

▶ **6.** In the Font style list box, click **Bold Italic**. The Preview section of the Font tab shows a preview of the new formatting. See Figure 5-15.

Applying italics in the Font dialog box | Figure 5-15

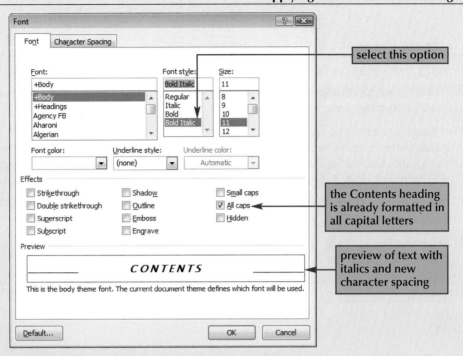

7. Click the **OK** button to close the Font dialog box. The selected heading is now italicized, with the individual characters spread slightly farther apart.

8. Save your work.

Next, you need to change the Heading 1 style so there is some extra spacing below each heading formatted with this style. Increasing the paragraph spacing is the last change Sam wants for the headings. After you're done formatting the Contents heading, you will tell Word that you want to modify the Heading 1 style to match the formatting of the Contents heading. This will affect all the headings that are currently formatted with the Heading 1 style.

Changing Paragraph Spacing

You already know how to add or delete a default amount of space before or after a paragraph using the Line spacing button in the Paragraph group on the Home tab. To specify an exact amount of space, you use the Paragraph dialog box.

Adjusting Spacing Between Paragraphs | Reference Window

- Select the paragraph whose spacing you want to adjust.
- To add or delete Word's default amount of space, click the Line spacing button in the Paragraph group on the Home tab, and then click Add Space Before Paragraph or Remove Space After Paragraph.
- To add or delete a specific amount of space, in the Paragraph group on the Home tab, click the Dialog Box Launcher to open the Paragraph dialog box, click the Indents and Spacing tab, and then use the Before box to specify the amount of space you want to insert above the selected paragraph. Use the After box to specify the amount of space you want to insert below the selected paragraph.

Sam wants 6 points of space after the Contents heading. The extra space will help draw attention to the heading.

To increase the space after the Contents heading:

▶ **1.** Verify that the Contents heading is still selected.

▶ **2.** In the Paragraph group on the Home tab, click the Dialog Box Launcher. The Paragraph dialog box opens.

▶ **3.** If necessary, click the **Indents and Spacing** tab. You use the Before and After boxes in the Spacing section of this tab to add space before or after the selected paragraph. Currently, there are 10 points of space before the selected paragraph and no points after it. Sam wants to change the After setting to 15.

▶ **4.** In the Spacing section, select the contents of the After box, and then type **15**. (You don't have to type "pt.")

▶ **5.** Press the **Tab** key to enter the new setting. The Preview section of the dialog box shows a sample of the increased paragraph spacing. See Figure 5-16.

Figure 5-16 ▷ **Changing paragraph spacing**

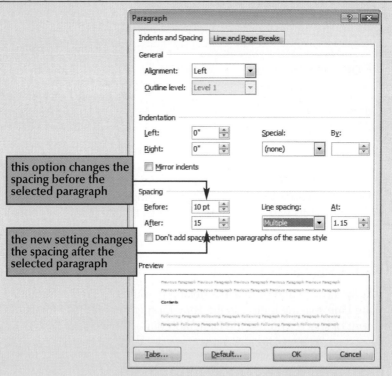

this option changes the spacing before the selected paragraph

the new setting changes the spacing after the selected paragraph

▶ **6.** Click the **OK** button. The Paragraph dialog box closes. Notice that there is now a little extra space below the Contents heading and above the paragraph of body text that says "[Insert a table of contents.]."

Adding Space Before or After a Paragraph | InSight

You might be tempted to increase the space before or after a paragraph by pressing the Enter key to insert a blank paragraph. However, inserting blank paragraphs in a document is rarely a good idea. For one thing, inserting a blank paragraph after a heading prevents Word from keeping a heading and its body text together when they span page or column breaks. Also, if you insert a blank paragraph, and then later increase the paragraph spacing in the entire document, you may end up with more blank space in the document than you really want. As a rule, using the Line spacing button in the Paragraph group on the Home tab or using the Paragraph dialog box gives you much more control over spacing before and after paragraphs. Make it a habit to use these options rather than inserting blank paragraphs.

Updating a Style to Match Selected Text

Now that the selected text is formatted the way you want, you can modify the Heading 1 style to match the selected text. As mentioned earlier, to modify a style, you select text formatted with the style you want to modify, apply new formatting, and then save your changes to the style. When saving the style, you need to decide whether you want to save the style to the current document or to the current template. If Sam modified the Heading 1 style and saved it to the current template, the modified version of the Heading 1 style would appear in all new documents based on the Equity Report template (the template his document is based on). However, Sam doesn't want to alter the Equity Report template. So in this case, it makes sense to save the modified version of the Heading 1 style just to the current document. You'll start by opening the Styles window.

Modifying Styles | Reference Window

- In the Styles group on the Home tab, click the Dialog Box Launcher to open the Styles window.
- In the document, select text formatted with the style you want to modify.
- Format the selected text with the font, paragraph, and other formatting you want.
- With the text still selected in the document, move the mouse pointer over the style you want to modify in the Styles window. A down arrow appears next to the style's name in the Styles window.
- Click the down arrow next to the style's name.
- To save the modified style to the current document, click Update *Style Name* to Match Selection (where *Style Name* is the name of the style you want to modify).
- To save the modified style to the current template, click Modify to open the Modify Style dialog box, click the New documents based on this template option button, and then click the OK button.

The **Styles window** displays a complete list of all the document's styles and provides easy access to the relevant commands. If you're doing a lot of work with styles in a document, it's often easier to use the Styles window rather than the Quick Styles gallery. You open the Styles window with the Dialog Box Launcher in the Styles group on the Home tab. You can click a style in the Styles window to apply it to selected text, just as you would click a style in the Quick Styles gallery.

To open the Styles window and modify the Heading 1 style:

▶ **1.** In the Styles group on the Home tab, click the Dialog Box Launcher. The Styles window opens. It might be located on the right or left side of the document window, floating over the document text, or it might be locked on the right side, in which case the document window has been resized to accommodate it. In the following step, you will lock the Styles window on the right side of the document window, if it isn't there already.

▶ **2.** Click the title bar of the Styles window, and then drag the Styles window to the right as far as you can, almost as if you are going to drag it off the screen. The Styles window snaps in place on the right side of the screen, and the document window resizes accordingly. The blue outline around the Heading 1 style in the Styles window tells you that the text currently selected in your document, the Contents heading, is formatted with the Heading 1 style—even though you've made several changes to that heading. See Figure 5-17.

Figure 5-17 | Styles window

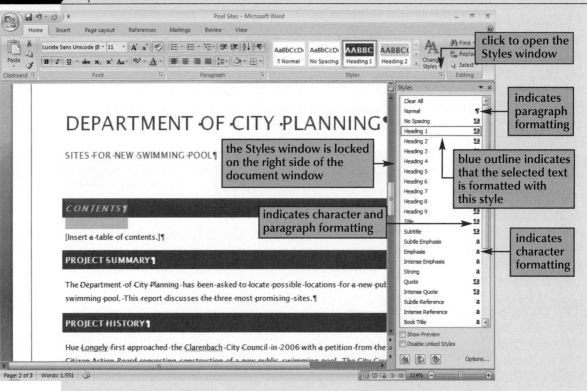

The Styles window contains a complete list of all the styles available in the document, along with some helpful commands and buttons. You can apply styles from the Styles window, just as you would from the Quick Styles gallery; just select the text you want to format and click a style in the Styles window.

Using the Styles Window | InSight

There are a lot of advantages to using the Styles window instead of the Quick Styles gallery. First, the Styles window includes styles that are not displayed in the Quick Styles gallery. Also, in the Styles window, styles are listed alphabetically, making it easier to locate a specific style in a document that contains lots of styles. So if you are looking for a style and can't find it in the Quick Styles gallery, check the Styles window. Another advantage of the Styles window is that it remains open until you close it. This makes the Styles window easier to use than the Quick Styles gallery when you need to apply a lot of styles. Finally, the symbols next to each style in the Styles window allow you to see quickly if a style is considered a paragraph style, a character style, or both.

Note that a paragraph symbol to the right of a style name in the Styles window indicates that the style applies paragraph formatting—such as line spacing, indentation, a border, and so on. A lowercase letter "a" to the right of a style name indicates the style applies character formatting—such as bold, italics, or a particular font size. Styles with both symbols next to their names apply both character and paragraph formatting. As you'll see in the following steps, you can display even more information about a style by moving the mouse pointer over the style's name in the Styles window.

To use the Styles Window to modify the Heading 1 style:

▶ **1.** In the Styles window, move the mouse pointer over **Heading 1**. A blue box with detailed information about the Heading 1 style appears, and a down arrow appears next to the style. Note that this information makes no mention of italics because, although you added italics to the "Contents" heading, you haven't yet altered the Heading 1 style itself. The information in this box relates only to the Heading 1 style.

▶ **2.** Click the **Heading 1** down arrow. A menu opens with options related to working with the Heading 1 style. The first option on the menu modifies the Heading 1 style to match the selected text and saves the newly modified style to the current document. To open a dialog box where you can save the modified style to the current template instead, you click the Modify option. Sam wants to save the newly modified Heading 1 style to the current document, so you'll use the first option. See Figure 5-18.

Figure 5-18 | Modifying the Heading 1 style

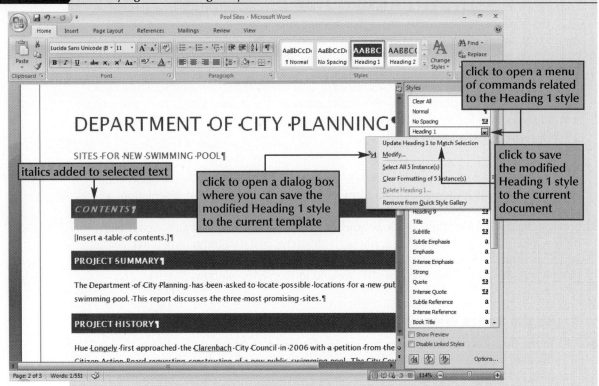

> **3.** Click **Update Heading 1 to Match Selection**. The Heading 1 style changes to include expanded character spacing, italics, and additional paragraph spacing— all the changes Sam asked you to make to the Contents heading. All the headings in the document formatted in the Heading 1 style are now formatted this way as well, and any other text you format with the Heading 1 style in this document will also have the italics, expanded character spacing, and additional paragraph spacing.

> **4.** Save your work. The modified version of the Heading 1 style is saved along with the document. No other documents are affected by this change to the Heading 1 style.

You've successfully modified the Heading 1 style by adding italics and by expanding its character and paragraph spacing. Next, you will create a new style to be used for the Project Summary heading, because it's helpful to set off a summary and its heading from the rest of a report.

Creating a New Style

When creating a new style, you have two important choices. First, as when modifying styles, you need to decide whether to save the style to the current document or to the current template. Second, you need to decide whether you want to base your new style on an existing style or create a new style from scratch.

When you base a new style on an existing style, you modify a style, as explained in the preceding section, and then, instead of updating the style to match your changes, you save the style with a new name. For example, suppose you modify the Heading 1 style by removing the bold formatting, and then save the modified style with the name "Budget," so that you can use it exclusively for formatting a "Budget" heading. A new style created in this way is called a **linked style**, because it remains linked to the style on which it is based; changes to the original style also affect the new style. This means that if you change the font for the Heading 1 style to Algerian, the font for the new Budget style would also change to Algerian. Note that the opposite is not true: changes to the new style do *not* affect the style on which it is based.

If you instead choose to create a new style from scratch—that is, if you create a style that is not based on any existing styles—the new style has no connection to any other styles. This usually isn't a good idea, because it prevents Word from enforcing the kind of formatting consistency that is possible with linked styles. As you'll see later in this tutorial, creating a style from scratch is especially troublesome in long documents, where you might want to work in Outline view.

Creating a New Style | Reference Window

- In the Styles group on the Home tab, click the Dialog Box Launcher to open the Styles window.
- Select text formatted with the style that most closely resembles the new style you want to create.
- Format the selected text with the font and paragraph formatting you want.
- In the lower-left corner of the Styles window, click the New Style button to open the Create New Style from Formatting dialog box.
- Type a name for the new style in the Name text box.
- The Style based on list box tells you which existing style the new style will be based on. If you don't want to base the new style on an existing style, click the Style based on arrow, and then click (no style).
- To save the new style to the current document, verify that the Only in this document option button is selected, and then click the OK button.
- To save the style to the current template, click the New documents based on this template option button, and then click the OK button.
- To delete a style you have created, point to the style's name in the Styles window, click the down arrow next to the style's name, click Revert to *Style Name*, (where *Style Name* is the style it was based on), and then click Yes.

Sam is ready to create a new style for the Project Summary heading. The new style will be based on the Heading 1 style. It will look just like the Heading 1 style, except that it will be not be in all uppercase (capital) letters, and it will include an underline. You'll start by selecting the text you want to format.

To format the Project Summary heading in uppercase and lowercase, with an underline:

▶ 1. Select the **Project Summary** heading. A quick way to change uppercase letters to lowercase, or vice versa, is to use the Change Case button in the Font group on the Home tab. However, in the next step you'll use the Font dialog box instead, because there you can apply a shadow effect at the same time.

▶ 2. In the Font group on the Home tab, click the Dialog Box Launcher, and then, in the Font dialog box, click the **Font** tab if necessary.

▶ 3. In the Effects section, click the **All caps** check box to remove the checkmark, click the **Underline style** arrow, scroll to the bottom of the list, and select the double-wavy underline style. The Preview section of the Font dialog box displays a preview of the new formatting. See Figure 5-19.

Figure 5-19　　　▶　**Formatting the Project Summary heading**

4. Click the **OK** button. The Font dialog box closes.

5. Click anywhere in the document to deselect the "Project Summary" heading so you can clearly see its new formatting.

Now that the text is formatted the way you want, you can create the new style.

To create a new style for the Project Summary heading:

1. Select the **Project Summary** heading, and then verify that the Styles window is still open.

2. In the lower-left corner of the Styles window, click the **New Style** button 🔳. The Create New Style from Formatting dialog box opens. A default name for the new style, "Style1," appears in the Name text box. In the next step, you will change the default name to something more meaningful.

3. In the **Name** text box, select the default name, if necessary, and then type **Summary**. The default style name is replaced with the new one. The Style based on list box tells you that the new Summary style is based on the Heading 1 style, which is what you want. See Figure 5-20.

Naming a new style   Figure 5-20

If you wanted to make the new style available to all future documents based on the current template, you would click the New documents based on this template option button. However, you want to save the new Summary style only to the current document, so you will accept the default setting, with the Only in this document option button selected. Note that, by default, the Automatically update check box is *not* selected. As a general rule, you should never select this check box. If you do select it, subsequent changes to the Summary style in future documents will be automatically updated in all documents based on the same template. This can produce unpredictable results and introduce problems that you might have difficulty resolving.

▶ **4.** Click the **OK** button. The Create New Style from Formatting dialog box closes. The new Summary style is added to the Quick Styles gallery and to the Styles window. If Sam needs to format additional headings with this new style, he can access it in either location. See Figure 5-21.

Summary style added to Quick Styles gallery and Styles window   Figure 5-21

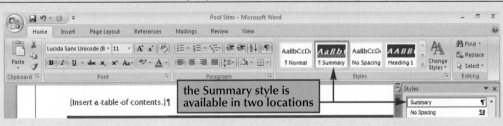

▶ **5.** Save the document.

| InSight | | **Basing New Styles on Existing Styles** |

Although it's possible create a new style that is not based on any other style, it's rarely a good idea. The link between a new style and the style it is based on ensures that changes affecting the overall look of a document are made consistently throughout the document. For example, suppose that, after creating his new Summary style, Sam decides to add extra paragraph spacing above and below the headings in the Pool Sites document. He can do that by modifying the Heading 1 style. Because his new Summary style is based on the Heading 1 style, the new paragraph spacing will automatically apply to the Summary style, thus enforcing a consistent appearance among all headings in the document. Another advantage to basing a new style on an existing style has to do with using Outline view. As you will see later in this tutorial, basing a new style on an existing style ensures that all the headings appear in the proper level in the document's outline.

Comparing Styles with the Reveal Formatting Window

If you create a document with many new or modified styles, it's easy to lose track of the formatting associated with each style. To see a quick comparison of two styles, you can use the **Reveal Formatting window**. In the following steps, you'll use the Reveal Formatting window to compare the Normal style to the Subtitle style in the document.

To compare the Heading 1 style to the Subtitle style using the Reveal Formatting window:

▶ **1.** Click in the left margin to select the **[Insert a table of contents.]** paragraph.

▶ **2.** At the bottom of the Styles window, click the **Style Inspector** button. The Style Inspector window opens, displaying options that allow you to quickly inspect the formatting associated with a particular style. In most situations, you'll find the Reveal Formatting window more useful, so you'll open that next.

▶ **3.** At the bottom of the Style Inspector window, click the **Reveal Formatting** button. The Reveal Formatting window opens, displaying information about the style applied to the text that is currently selected in the document. Your Reveal Formatting window and Style Inspector windows might be positioned as in Figure 5-22, or they might be located elsewhere in the document window. Their position is unimportant.

Reveal Formatting window ◄ Figure 5-22

▶ **4.** In the Reveal Formatting window, click the **Compare to another selection** check box to select it. The options in the Reveal Formatting window change to allow you to compare one style to another. Under Selected text, both text boxes display copies of the text that is currently selected in the document, "[Insert a table of contents.]" This tells you that, currently the Normal style, the style applied to the text "[Insert a table of contents.]," is being compared to itself. In the next step, you'll compare the Normal style to the Subtitle style.

▶ **5.** In the document, click in the left margin to select the text **SITES FOR NEW SWIMMING POOL**, which is formatted with the Subtitle style. The text "SITES FOR NEW SWIMMING POOL" appears in the Reveal Formatting window, in the text box below "[Insert a table of contents.]" The Formatting differences section displays information about the styles to the two different text samples. This information is divided into two sections, Font and Paragraph. The information in the Reveal Formatting can sometimes be hard to interpret. But generally, if you see two settings separated by a hyphen and a greater than sign (->),the setting on the left relates to the top text box, and the item on the right relates to the bottom text box. For example, in the Font section, you see "10pt -> 12 pt." This tells you that the item in the top text box, "[Insert a table of contents.]," is formatted in a 10-point font, whereas the item in the bottom text box, "SAMPLE TEXT," is formatted in a 12-point font. See Figure 5-23.

Tip

Text formatted in a white font, such as the Contents heading, is not visible in the text boxes at the top of the Reveal Formatting window. To use the Reveal Formatting window with white text, temporarily format it in black.

Figure 5-23   Comparing two styles

> **6.** Click the **Close** button ⊠ in the title bars of the Style Inspector window, the Reveal Formatting window, and the Styles window to close them. The document window readjusts, displaying the document at Page width zoom.

You are finished formatting the Pool Sites document. Sam likes its appearance so much that he would like to be able to reuse its formatting in the future reports issued by his department. To do that, you need to save the Pool Sites document as a template.

Saving a Document as a Template

If you know you'll often need to create a particular type of document, it's a good idea to create your own template for that type of document. In this case, Sam wants to create a template that will be used for all reports issued by the Department of City Planning. When creating a template, you can save it to any folder on the computer. However, if you save it to the Templates folder that is installed with Word, you can easily open the template later by clicking My templates in the New Document dialog box.

Saving a Document as a Template | Reference Window

- Click the Office Button, point to Save As, and then click Word Template.
- Navigate to the folder in which you want to save the template. To save the template to the Templates folder that is installed as part of Word, click the Templates folder under "Favorite Links."
- In the File name text box, type a name for the template.
- Click the Save button.

In the following steps, you will save the new template in the Tutorial folder for Tutorial 5, so that you can easily submit the completed tutorial files to your instructor. You'll start by saving the Pool Sites document again, just in case you didn't earlier.

To save the Pool Sites document as a new template:

▶ **1.** Save the Pool Sites document.

▶ **2.** Click the **Office Button** , point to **Save As**, and then click **Word Template**. The Save As dialog box opens, with Word Template selected in the Save as type list box.

▶ **3.** If necessary, navigate to the Tutorial.05\Tutorial included with your Data Files. You'll type the new filename next using "DCP," the acronym for "Department of City Planning," in the filename.

▶ **4.** Delete the default filename in the File name text box, and then type **DCP Report**. See Figure 5-24.

Saving a document as a template ◀ Figure 5-24

▶ **5.** Click the **Save** button. The Save As dialog box closes, and the document, which is now a template with the .dotx file extension, remains open.

To make the new DCP Report template really useful, you need to delete the specific information related to the Pool Sites report and replace it with placeholder text explaining what type of information is required in each section. You'll start by editing the document controls on page 1. Then you will delete the body of the report and replace it with some placeholder text that Sam has already typed and saved as a separate Word document.

To replace the Pool Sites report information with placeholder text:

▶ **1.** Scroll up to page 1. Sam wants to use the current title, "Department of City Planning," as the title in all department reports, so there's no need to change it. However, the subtitle will vary from one report to the next, so you need to replace it with a suitable placeholder.

▶ **2.** Delete the subtitle "Sites for New Swimming Pool," and then type **[Insert subtitle here.]** as a replacement. Be sure to include the brackets, so Sam's co-workers will quickly see that this is placeholder text.

▶ **3.** Scroll down, if necessary, so you can see the date, select the date in the date control, delete it, and then type **[Select current date.]** as a replacement. You'll leave your name in the Author control, so you can find the template later when you print it.

▶ **4.** Scroll down to page 2 and notice that the new subtitle placeholder has been inserted in the subtitle control at the top of page 2. Also, the placeholder for the date has been inserted in the vertical footer on the lower-left side of the page.

▶ **5.** Click in the left margin to select the **Project Summary** heading, drag down to select the remainder of the document, and press the **Delete** key. Deleting the text deleted some of the formatting codes that are included as hidden text in a Word document. (You can't see these codes, but they control the way the document is formatted.) As a result, the text "[Insert a table of contents.]" is now formatted in the Heading 1 style. You need to change it back to the Normal style.

▶ **6.** Verify that the insertion point is located within the paragraph containing the text "[Insert a table of contents.]," and then in the Quick Styles gallery in the Styles group, click the **Normal** style. The text returns to its original formatting.

▶ **7.** Press the **Enter** key to start a new paragraph. Now you are ready to insert a file containing placeholder text for the body of the report template.

▶ **8.** Click the **Insert** tab, in the Text group click the **Object** arrow, click **Text from File**, use the options in the Insert File dialog box to select the file **Placeholder** from the Tutorial.05\Tutorial folder included with your Data Files, and then click the **Insert** button. The placeholder text is inserted in the document. Scroll down to review the document and notice that the headings are all correctly formatted with the Heading 1 style. When Sam created the Placeholder document, he formatted the text in the default Heading 1 style provided by the Office theme. But when you inserted the file into the Pool Sites document, Word automatically reformatted the headings with your modified Heading 1 style. The only remaining issue is the "Project Summary" heading, which you need to format with the Summary style you created earlier.

▶ **9.** Click in the left margin to select the **Project Summary** heading, click the **Home** tab, and then in the Quick Styles gallery, click the **Summary** style. The heading is formatted with the wavy underline.

▶ **10.** Save your work and close the template.

The template you just created will simplify the process of creating new reports in Sam's department. In the next section, you'll have a chance to use the template as the basis of a new document.

Working Around Hidden Formatting Codes		InSight

When you are working with a highly formatted document, you may sometimes encounter unexpected issues, such as in Step 5 in the preceding set of steps, when the Heading 1 style was applied to the text "[Insert a table of contents.]." Such problems are related to formatting codes that are included in a Word document, but which you can't normally see. Sometimes when you delete or insert a large amount of text, these hidden formatting codes are disrupted, causing unexpected results. Keep in mind that many hidden formatting codes are attached to the last paragraph symbol in a Word document. You can avoid formatting problems in a document by inserting a blank paragraph at the end of the document, and then taking care never to delete that last paragraph. Alternatively, if you encounter a formatting problem that you can't resolve, insert a blank paragraph at the end of the document, copy everything in the document except the last paragraph to a new document, and work with that new document instead.

Opening a New Document Based on Your Template

At this point, the new template is ready to be used by the Department of City Planning for all new reports. In fact, Sam would like to use it now to begin a report on possible sites for a new public library.

To begin a new document based on the DCP Report template:

▶ 1. Start Word, if necessary, click the **Office Button** 🖫 , and then click **New**. The New Document dialog box opens.

▶ 2. In the Templates section on the left, click **My templates**. The New dialog box opens. If you had saved the DCP Report template to Word's Template folder, you would see an icon for it here. To open a new document based on the template, you could click the template's icon and then click the OK button. However, because you saved the DCP Reports template with your Data Files, you need to open it using a different method. See Figure 5-25.

Figure 5-25   New dialog box

if you had saved the DCP Reports template to Word's Templates folder, you would see an icon for it here

> **3.** Click the **Cancel** button. The New dialog box closes, and you return to the New Document dialog box.

> **4.** On the left side of the New Document dialog box, under Templates, click **New from existing**. The New from Existing Document dialog box opens. This dialog box looks like the Open dialog box, which you have used many times before.

> **5.** If necessary, select the Tutorial.05\Tutorial folder included with your Data Files, click **DCP Report**, and then click the **Create New** button. A new document opens containing the text and formatting from the DCP Report template. The document is named "Document2" (or possibly "Document3" or "Document4," depending on whether Word was closed earlier in this tutorial). Changes you make to this new document will not affect the DCP Report template file, which remains untouched in the Tutorial.05\Tutorial folder.

> **6.** Delete the placeholder **[Insert subtitle here.]** on the cover page and type **Possible Sites for New Public Library**, and then click anywhere outside the Subtitle control to deselect it. That's all the work you need to do on the library report for now. Sam will finish it later. You can save the document with a new name and close it.

> **7.** Save the document as **Library Sites** in the Tutorial.05\Tutorial folder included with your Data Files.
>
> **Trouble?** If the Subtitle control displays the placeholder text "[Insert subtitle here.]" after you save the document, you didn't deselect the control before saving the document. Retype the subtitle, deselect the control, and save your changes to the document.

> **8.** Preview the document, print it, and then close it.

1. True or False. By default, a new or modified style is saved only in the current document.
2. Explain the relationship between the themes installed with Word, style sets, and styles.
3. If you can't see the style you want in the Quick Styles gallery, where should you look?
4. Explain how to open a dialog box tab where you can adjust the character spacing for selected text.
5. Explain how to open a dialog box tab where you can add a specific amount of space below a selected paragraph.
6. Where can you see a quick comparison of two styles?
7. True or False. If you save a template to the Templates folder that is installed with Word, you can easily open the template later by clicking My templates in the New Document dialog box.

Session 5.3

Using Outline View

An **outline** is a list of the basic points of a document, usually organized into main topics and subtopics. Once you have formatted a document with heading styles, you can use these headings and Word's **Outline view** to display the various levels of headings as an outline. For instance, you can display only the Heading 1 headings, or the Heading 1 and Heading 2 headings, or all the text in the document, including text formatted with the Normal style. In fact, you can display and work with as many as nine levels of headings in Outline view. The top level heading (the Heading 1 style) is Level 1, with subheadings (Heading 2, Heading 3, etc.) labeled as Level 2, Level 3, and so on.

If your document contains a heading style that you created, that heading style is assigned to the same outline level as the style on which your heading style is based. For example, the "Project Summary" heading in the Pool Sites document is formatted in the Summary style you created, which is based on the Heading 1 style. That means the "Project Summary" heading appears as Level 1 in the outline, just like the other main headings in the document. A new heading style that is not based on any other heading style is assigned an outline level that is one level lower than the lowest heading style in the document. This is why it's much wiser to base a new heading style on an existing style, rather than creating new styles from scratch.

The purpose of Outline view is to simplify the process of reorganizing a document. Imagine a long document with many Level 1 headings, several Level 2 headings for each Level 1 heading, and body text below each heading. With Outline view, you can click a heading and move it below or above other headings; the subheadings and body text associated with the heading you are moving get moved along with the heading. This is a powerful tool when you are reorganizing a large document.

Outline view has several symbols and buttons that you use in viewing and reorganizing your document. An **outline symbol** is displayed to the left of each paragraph. An outline symbol in the shape of a plus sign indicates a heading with subordinate text below it, a minus sign indicates a heading without subordinate text, and an empty gray circle indicates body text (that is, text that is not formatted with a heading style). To select an entire section, you click the outline symbol next to that section's heading. To move a section after you select it, you click the Move Up or Move Down button on the Outlining tab, which is visible only in Outline view. You can also use buttons on the Outlining tab to change the precedence of headings. For instance, you might want to change a Level 1 heading to a Level 2 heading, or to change a Level 3 heading to a Level 1 heading.

Reference Window | **Creating and Editing Outlines**

- Format a document with heading styles, such as Heading 1, Heading 2, and so on.
- Click the Outline view button in the lower-right corner of the Word window.
- If necessary, select the Show Text Formatting check box in the Outline Tools group on the Outlining tab. This ensures that you can see the document formatting.
- Use the Show Level arrow in the Outline Tools group to display the desired number of headings. For example, to see only text formatted with heading styles 1 through 3, click Level 3. To see all the document text, including the body text, click All Levels.
- To select a section, click the Outline symbol next to the section's heading.
- To move a section, select the section, and then in the Outline Tools group, click the Move Up button or the Move Down button until the section is at the desired location.
- Use the Promote button or the Demote button in the Outline Tools group to increase or decrease the levels of headings.
- Click the Page Layout button to return to Page Layout view.

Sam wants to do some more work on the Pool Sites document. Specifically, he wants to reorganize some of the sections. Outline view is the perfect tool for this task. You'll start by reopening the Pool Sites document and reviewing its organization.

To open the Pool Sites document and review its organization:

▶ 1. Open the **Pool Sites** document from the Tutorial.05\Tutorial folder included with your Data Files.

▶ 2. If necessary, switch to Print Layout view, set the Zoom to Page width, and display nonprinting characters.

▶ 3. Review pages 2 and 3 so you are familiar with the report's structure. Notice that the headings "Breese Terrace Park," "Langbrook Farm," and "Flora Park," are formatted as subheadings below the "Project Description" heading.

Sam decides that the Flora Park section should appear before the Breese Terrace Park section. First you need to switch to Outline view and display the appropriate heading levels.

To switch to Outline view and view the outline levels:

▶ 1. Scroll up, if necessary, to display the first page of the document.

▶ 2. Click the **Outline** button ▤ in the lower-right corner of the Word window. The document is displayed in Outline view, and the Outlining tab appears on the Ribbon. At this point, you may see all of the document, just some of the headings, or all of the document except for some of the headings. In the next two steps, you will check to make sure you can see the entire document.

▶ **3.** If necessary, in the Outline Tools group on the Outlining tab, click the **Show Text Formatting** check box to remove the checkmark. When this check box is selected, Word displays the document headings in the same font, font color, and font size that you see in Page Layout view. Because the major headings in the Pool Sites document are formatted in a white font, you don't want to show the document formatting in Outline view, because you wouldn't be able to see the white text on the white background. With the Show Text Formatting check box deselected, all the text in Outline view is displayed in the body text font.

▶ **4.** If necessary, in the Outlining tools group on the Outlining tab, click the **Show Level** arrow, and then click **All Levels**. This tells Word to display the entire document, including the headings and the body text. At this point, your document should look like the one in Figure 5-26.

Pool Sites document in Outline view ◀ Figure 5-26

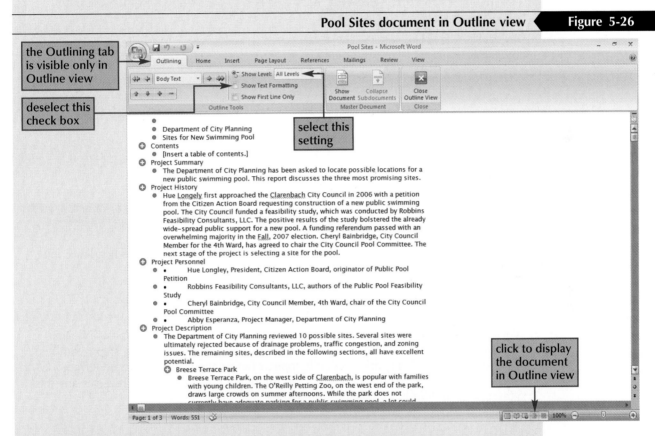

You can use the Show Level list box to display only the document headings. This is especially useful in long documents, because it allows you to see all the document headings at a glance, without having to scroll through several pages of body text. In the next step, you will display only the document headings.

▶ **5.** In the Outline Tools group, click the **Show Level** arrow, and then click **Level 3**. You see only Level 1, Level 2, and Level 3 headings. In other words, you see only the text formatted with the Heading 1, Heading 2, and Heading 3 styles. Sam was concerned that he might have mistakenly applied the Heading 3 style to a heading that actually required the Heading 2 style. As you can see in Figure 5-27, he did make this mistake. You'll fix this problem later. Notice the plus sign next to each heading, indicating that the text is a heading with subordinate text. The gray lines represent text that is not currently visible.

Figure 5-27 ▶ Levels 1 through 3 displayed in Outline view

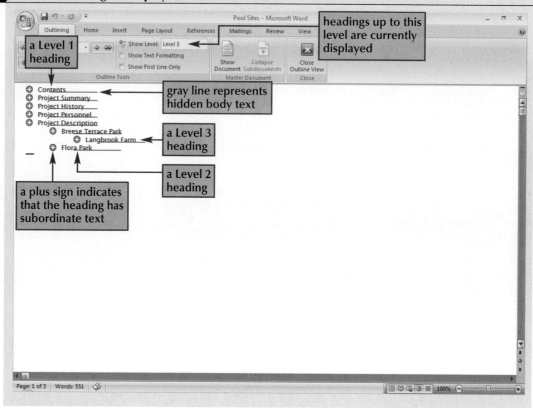

Now that you see only the document headings, you can reorder some headings and change the level of another.

Working with Headings in Outline View

When you move a heading in Outline view, any subordinate headings and all the text associated with those headings moves with the heading. In the following steps, you'll move the heading "Flora Park" so that it appears before the heading "Breese Terrace Park." As you work in Outline view, keep in mind that the Undo button reverses any mistakes, just as in Print Layout view.

To move the "Flora Park" heading and its subordinate text:

▶ 1. Double-click the **plus sign** ➕ next to the heading "Flora Park." The subordinate text below the heading is now visible.

▶ 2. Double-click the **plus sign** ➕ next to the heading "Flora Park" again. The subordinate text is again hidden.

▶ 3. Verify that the "Flora Park" heading and the paragraph mark following it are selected, and then click the **Move Up** button ⬆ in the Outline Tools group. The heading moves up above the heading "Langbrook Farm." Its subordinate text moved along with the heading, even though you can't see it.

▶ 4. Click the **Move Up** button ⬆ again. The "Flora Park" heading (and its subordinate text) move up above the heading "Breese Terrace Park." See Figure 5-28.

5. Double-click the **plus symbol** ⊕ next to the heading "Flora Park," verify that the subordinate text did indeed move along with the heading, and then double-click ⊕ next to the heading "Flora Park" again to hide the subordinate text. Note that each time you click the Move Up button, the selected section moves up above the preceding section. To move a section down, you would use the Move Down button. Note that to select a section before moving it, you need to click the Outline symbol only once. You double-clicked it in these steps to display and then hide the subtext.

Now that the topics of the outline are in the desired order, you need to change the level of the Langbrook Farm heading, so it matches the level of the other two headings under "Project Description."

Promoting and Demoting Headings in an Outline

To **promote** a heading means to increase the level of a heading—for example, to change a Level 3 heading to a Level 2 heading. To **demote** a heading means to decrease the level—for example, to change a Level 1 heading to a Level 2 heading. When you promote or demote a heading in Outline view, the heading style applied to the heading changes accordingly. For example, if you promote a Level 3 heading to a Level 2 heading, the style applied to the heading changes from Heading 3 to Heading 2.

Sam wants to correct the error he made earlier by promoting the "Langbrook Farm" heading to a Level 2 heading.

To promote the Langbrook Farm heading:

1. Click anywhere in the heading **Langbrook Farm**, and then in the Outline Tools group on the Outlining tab, click the **Promote** button ⬅ . (Take care not to click the Promote to Heading 1 button by mistake.) The heading moves left and becomes a Level 2 heading, formatted with the Heading 2 style. Note that demoting a heading in Outline view is similar to promoting a heading. You place the insertion point in the heading and click the Demote button. See Figure 5-29.

Figure 5-29 | **Heading promoted in Outline view**

click to promote
selected headings

click to demote
selected headings

you promoted this heading
from Level 3 to Level 2

Contents
Project Summary
Project History
Project Personnel
Project Description
 Flora Park
 Breese Terrace Park
 Langbrook Farm

Trouble? If the "Langbrook Farm" heading moved all the way to the left margin, you clicked the Promote to Heading 1 button by mistake. Undo the change, and then repeat Step 1.

2. Print the outline as you would print any other Word document.

3. Return to Print Layout view, and then review the Project Description section and its subheadings. Note that the "Langbrook Farm" heading is formatted in the Heading 2 style, and that the Flora Park section now appears before the Breese Terrace Park section. However, the blank paragraph that was originally at the end of the document, after the Flora Park section, moved up along with the Flora Park section. You need to delete it.

4. Click at the end of the Flora Park Section, press the **Delete** key to delete the blank paragraph, and then save your work.

Next, Sam would like to create a table of contents for his report.

Creating a Table of Contents

You can use Word to create a **table of contents** with page numbers for any paragraphs to which you have applied heading styles. The page numbers and headings in a table of contents in Word are actually hyperlinks that you can click to jump to a particular part of the document. If you add or delete text in the document later, and one or more headings move to a new page, you can quickly update the table of contents by clicking the Update Table button in the Table of Contents group on the References tab. After you create a table of contents, you can select additional text in the document and add it to the table of contents.

When inserting a table of contents, you can insert one of the predesigned formats available via the Table of Contents button in the Table of Contents group on the References tab. If you prefer to select from more options, you can open the Table of Contents dialog box.

Working with a Table of Contents | Reference Window

- Make sure you have applied heading styles such as Heading 1, Heading 2, and Heading 3 to the appropriate headings in your document.
- Move the insertion point to the location in the document where you want to insert the table of contents.
- Click the References tab, and then in the Table of Contents group, click the Table of Contents button. This opens the Table of contents menu.
- To insert a predesigned table of contents, click one of the Automatic table of contents styles in the Table of Contents menu.
- To open a dialog box where you can choose from an array of table of contents settings, click Insert Table of Contents in the Table of Contents menu, and then in the Table of Contents dialog box, click the Table of Contents tab if necessary. Click the Formats arrow and select a style, change the Show levels setting to the number of heading levels you want to include in the table of contents, verify that the Show page numbers check box is selected, and then click the OK button.
- To update a table of contents, click the Update Table button in the Table of Contents group on the References tab.
- To add text to a table of contents, select the text in the document, then in the Table of Contents group on the References tab, click the Add Text button. In the Add Text menu, click the level at which you want to insert the selected text, and then update the table of contents.
- To delete a table of contents, click the Table of Contents button, and then click Remove Table of Contents.

The current draft of Sam's report is fairly short, but the final document will be much longer. He asks you to create a table of contents for the report now, just after the "Contents" heading. Then, as Sam adds sections to the report, he can update the table of contents.

To insert the table of contents into the Pool Sites document:

1. Below the heading "Contents," select and delete the placeholder text **[Insert a table of contents.]**. Do not delete the paragraph mark after the placeholder text. When you are finished, your insertion point should be in the blank paragraph between the "Contents" heading and the "Project Summary" heading.

2. Click the **References** tab, and then in the Table of Contents group, click the **Table of Contents** button. The Table of Contents menu opens, displaying two Automatic table of contents formats, one Manual Table option, and two commands to insert and delete a table of contents. The Automatic options insert a table of contents made up of the first three levels of document headings, in a predefined format. Each of the Automatic options also includes a heading for the Table of Contents. Because Sam's document already contains the heading "Contents," you do not want to use either of the Automatic options. The Manual option is useful only if you need to type the table of contents yourself. In this case, you want to take advantage of the document headings and allow Word to build the table of contents for you, so you will use the Insert Table of Contents command at the bottom of the menu. See Figure 5-30.

Figure 5-30 Table of Contents menu

click either one to insert a table of contents made up of the document headings with the default settings

click to insert a table of contents with placeholder text that you can replace

click to open a dialog box where you can select from numerous table of contents settings

3. At the bottom of the Table of Contents menu, click **Insert Table of Contents**. The Table of Contents dialog box opens, with the Table of Contents tab displayed. The Formats list box allows you to select a format for your table of contents. The default option, From template, uses the styles provided by the document's template. In this case, you'll accept that default setting. Note that the Show page numbers check box is selected by default, so the table of contents will include a page number for each heading. Also by default, the "Use hyperlinks instead of page numbers" check box is selected. This setting means that Word will make each entry in the table of contents a hyperlink that links to the relevant section in the document. You can accept this default setting. Finally, you need to consider the Show levels headings. The document contains two levels of headings (Heading 1 and Heading 2). However, Sam might add some headings formatted in the Heading 3 style later, so you will leave the Show levels setting at 3. See Figure 5-31.

Sam knows that Word will compile the table of contents based on the heading styles in the document. But what about the Summary style, which you created earlier? Remember that the Summary style is based on the Heading 1 style, so Word will treat it as a heading of the same level as the Heading 1 style, just like in Outline view. To verify that this is true, you can check the heading levels by clicking the Options button.

4. Click the **Options** button in the lower-right corner of the Table of Contents dialog box. The Table of Contents Options dialog box opens. The Styles check box is selected, indicating that Word will compile the table of contents based on the styles applied to the document headings.

5. Use the vertical scroll in the TOC level list to see how the various styles in the document are assigned levels in the table of contents. (Note that "TOC" is short for "Table of Contents.") You can see that Heading 1 is assigned to Level 1, and Heading 2 is assigned to Level 2. Like Heading 1, the Summary style is also assigned to Level 1. If you wanted to change the level of a heading style, you could type a different number for it in the style's TOC level text box. To add a style to the table of contents, you could type a level number in the style's TOC level text box. See Figure 5-32.

Figure 5-32 | **Checking the styles used in the table of contents**

The settings in the Table of Contents Options dialog box are all correct, so you can close it.

▶ **6.** Click the **Cancel** button to close the Table of Contents Options dialog box without making any changes.

▶ **7.** Click the **OK** button to accept the default settings in the Table of Contents dialog box. Word searches for text formatted with styles Heading 1, Heading 2, and Heading 3, and then places those headings and their corresponding page numbers in a table of contents. The table of contents is inserted below the "Contents" heading, where you placed the insertion point in Step 1. Depending on how your computer is set up, the table of contents might appear on a light gray background. See Figure 5-33.

Figure 5-33 | **Table of contents inserted into document**

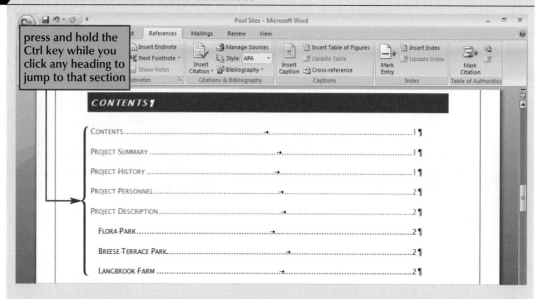

In the following step, you'll check the hyperlink formatting to make sure the headings really do function as links.

8. Press and hold down the **Ctrl** key while you click **LANGBROOK FARM** in the table of contents. The Langbrook Farm section is displayed.

9. Save the report.

Sam remembers that he needs to add a new section to the document describing another potential pool site. He's already typed the new section and saved it as a Word file. He asks you to insert it at the end of the Pool Sites document and then add the new heading to the table of contents. You can do this using the Add Text button in the Table of Contents group in the References tab. You start by selecting the text you want to add to the table of contents. Then you use the Add Text button in the Table of Contents group on the References tab to format the text in the appropriate heading level. Finally, you update the table of contents.

To add a section to the Pool Sites document, add the heading text to the table of contents, and update the table of contents:

1. Press the **Ctrl+End** keys to move the insertion point to the end of the document, insert a new blank paragraph, and then insert the file **Vilas Grove** from the Tutorial.05\Tutorial folder included with your Data Files.

2. Select the heading **Vilas Grove**.

3. Click the **References** tab, and then, in the Table of Contents group on the References tab, click the **Add Text** button. The Add Text menu opens. See Figure 5-34.

Add Text menu ◄ | **Figure 5-34**

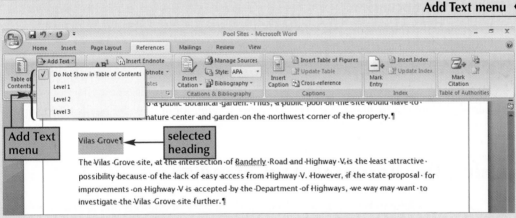

In the Add Text menu, you need to indicate at what level you want to insert the selected text in the table of contents.

4. Click **Level 2**. The text is formatted with the Heading 2 style, to match the headings for the sections about the other possible pool sites. Now that the text is formatted with a heading style, you can update the table of contents.

5. Scroll up so you can see the table of contents, and then in the Table of Contents group in the References tab, click the **Update Table** button. The Update Table of Contents dialog box opens. You can use the Update page numbers only option button if you don't want to update the headings in the table of contents. However, it's usually best to use the Update entire table option because it ensures that the table of contents is completely up to date.

6. Click the **Update entire table** option button to select it, and then click the **OK** button. The table of contents is updated to include the Vilas Grove heading. See Figure 5-35.

Tip

You can also format new text with a heading style in the Quick Styles gallery, and then update the table of contents.

Figure 5-35 ▶ **Updated table of contents**

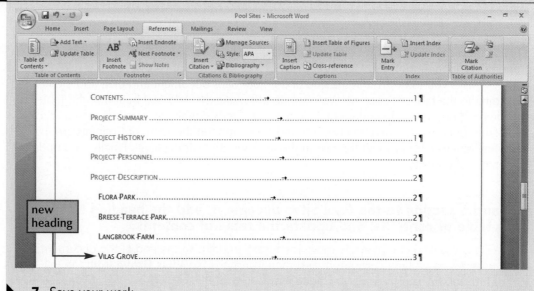

▶ **7.** Save your work.

Sam is finished with the Pool Sites report for now, so you can print it and close it.

To print the document:

▶ **1.** Preview the document, and then print it. If you see a dialog box asking about updating the table of contents, update the entire table.

▶ **2.** Close the document.

Sam will continue work on the Pool Sites report later. Right now, he needs to do some research for another city project: an open-air theater.

Using the Research Task Pane

You can use the **Research task pane** to look up dictionary definitions and to search for synonyms in Word's thesaurus. In addition, you can search for information in online general interest encyclopedias and in sources devoted to particular topics, such as business and finance. If you prefer, you can use the MSN search engine to search the entire Web from the Research task pane. You can even use the Research task pane to translate a word or phrase into the language of your choice.

The Department of City Planning has been asked to evaluate a proposed open-air theater, which will be funded by a grant from a state arts organization. The proposal includes a number of theater-related terms. Sam wants to make sure he understands the term *proscenium* and decides to use Word's Research task pane to look it up in Encarta, the dictionary installed with Word. He also wants to experiment with looking up synonyms in Word's thesaurus.

To look up a definition in the Research task pane:

▶ **1.** Open the document named **Research** from the Tutorial.05\Tutorial folder and save it as **Theater Research** in the same folder. This document contains the terms you will look up, along with space to insert the results of your research.

▶ **2.** If necessary, set the Zoom to Page width and display nonprinting characters. To open the Research task pane, you need to switch to the Review tab.

▶ **3.** Click the **Review** tab, and then locate the Proofing group on the left side of the Review tab. The Research, Thesaurus, and Translate buttons in the Proofing group all open the Research task pane, although each with different options displayed. Once the Research task pane is open, you can easily switch among the various options, depending on whether you want to research a topic, look up a word in the thesaurus, or translate some text.

▶ **4.** In the Proofing group, click the **Research** button. The Research task pane opens on the right side of the document window. For starters, Sam wants to look up the word *proscenium*, one of the terms in the theater proposal.

▶ **5.** Delete any text in the Search for text box, and then type **proscenium**. Next, you need to specify where you want to search for information.

▶ **6.** In the list box that currently contains the text "All Reference Books," click the arrow to open a drop-down menu, and then click **Encarta Dictionary: English (North America)**. Two definitions of the term *proscenium* are displayed in the Research task pane. See Figure 5-36.

Tip

If you select a new reference source and don't see the information you expect in the Research task pane, click the green Start searching arrow at the top of the task pane to start the search.

Definitions displayed in the Research task pane ◀ **Figure 5-36**

▶ **7.** Drag the mouse pointer to select the first definition, which reads **the part of a theater stage that is in front of the curtain**, right-click the selected text, click **Copy**, click in the blank paragraph below the text "Definition of *proscenium*" in the document, and press the **Ctrl+V** keys to paste the definition into the document.

Next, Sam wants to look up a synonym for *playwright*. If he didn't have the Research task pane open already, he would begin his search by clicking the Thesaurus button in the Proofing group. But because the Research task pane is already open, he can simply select a new reference work.

To look up a synonym in the thesaurus:

▶ **1.** In the document, click in the blank paragraph below the text "Synonym for *playwright*."

▶ **2.** In the Research task pane, delete the word **proscenium** from the Search for text box, and then type **playwright**.

▶ **3.** Click the arrow button below the Search for text box, and then click **Thesaurus: English (United States)**. Synonyms for *playwright* are displayed in the Research task pane, where the definitions for *proscenium* appeared earlier.

▶ **4.** Move the mouse pointer over **writer**, the second synonym in the list. A list box appears around the word.

▶ **5.** Click the down arrow next to the word "writer." A menu of options appears. See Figure 5-37.

Tip

To move back to previous search items, click the Previous Search button in the Research task pane. To return to later search items, click the Next Search button.

Figure 5-37 | **Synonyms displayed in the Research task pane**

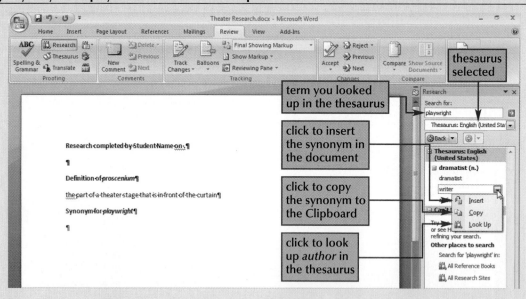

You can click Insert to insert the synonym in the document at the insertion point, or you can click Copy to copy the synonym to the Clipboard, so that you can paste it into other locations in the document or in other documents. To look up synonyms of *writer*, you could click Look Up. Right now, Sam simply wants to insert the word *writer* into the document.

▶ **6.** Click **Insert**. The term *writer* is inserted into the document, below "Synonym for *playwright*."

▶ **7.** Save the document, and then click the **Close** button in the title bar of the Research task pane to close it.

If your computer is connected to the Internet, you can type a word or phrase in the Search for box, click the down arrow and select Translation, and then use the options that appear in the Research task pane to retrieve a translation of your word or phrase over the Internet. The translations provided by the Research task pane are performed by computers, and therefore are useful only when you need a quick idea of what a term or phrase refers to.

You are finished with your research. All that remains is to insert your name and the current date at the top of the document.

Inserting the Current Date

You could begin typing the current date and have Word finish it for you using AutoComplete. But by using the Date and Time button in the Text group on the Insert tab, you can take advantage of several formatting options. These formats allow you to include the time or the day of the week. You can also choose to have Word update the date every time you open the document. Sam wants to use one of the date formats available via the Date and Time dialog box.

To insert your name and the current date into the Theater Research document:

▶ **1.** In the first line of the document, replace **Student Name** with your first and last name.

▶ **2.** Click at the end of the first line, just to the left of the period. This is where you want to insert the current date.

▶ **3.** Click the **Insert** tab, and then, in the Text group, click the **Date & Time** button. The Date and Time dialog box opens. The Available formats list shows the different ways you can insert the current date.

▶ **4.** In the Available formats list box, click the format that provides the day of the week and the date—for example, Monday, March 8, 2010. This is probably the second item in the Available formats list. See Figure 5-38.

Date and Time dialog box ◀ **Figure 5-38**

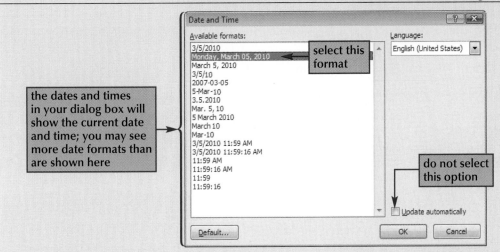

Note that your Date & Time dialog box will show the current date, and not the date shown in Figure 5-38. Notice the Update automatically check box, which you could click if you wanted Word to update the date and time each time you open the document. In this case, you want to insert today's date without Word updating it when you reopen the document.

▶ **5.** Verify that the Update automatically check box is *not* selected.

▶ **6.** Click the **OK** button. Word inserts the date into the document.

▶ **7.** Save the document, print it, and then close it.

Review | **Session 5.3 Quick Check**

1. What type of outline symbol indicates a heading with subordinate text under it?
2. Define *promote* as it relates to Outline view.
3. What do you have to do before you can create a table of contents?
4. What button can you click to revise a table of contents, and where is the button located?
5. True or False. You can use the Research task pane to look up definitions, but not synonyms.
6. What's the advantage of using the Date & Time button in the Text group on the Insert tab to insert a date?

Review | **Tutorial Summary**

In this tutorial, you learned how to create a new document from a template, insert a Word file into a document, and customize the document theme. You also learned how to select a style set, modify a style, create a new style, and compare styles with the Reveal Formatting window. Finally, you learned how to create a new template, use Outline view, create a table of contents, use the Research task pane, and insert the current date into the document.

Key Terms

character spacing	outline symbol	style sets
content control	Outline view	Styles window
demote	promote	table of contents
kerning	Research task pane	template
linked style	Reveal Formatting window	theme colors
Normal template	sans serif font	theme fonts
outline	serif	theme effects

Practice	**Review Assignments**

Apply the skills you learned in the tutorial using the same case scenario.

Data Files needed for the Review Assignments: Body.docx, Placeholder.docx, Future.docx, Research.docx

Sam's DCP Report template is now used for all reports created by employees of Clarenbach Department of City Planning. Inspired by Sam's success with the template, the director of the Department of Water Safety (DWS), Heather Sheehan, wants you to help with a report on improving the city's water testing system. After you format the report, she'd like you to save the document as a new template. Finally, she'd like you to look up some terms using the Research task pane. (*Note:* Text you need to type is shown in bold for ease of reference only; do not bold the text unless otherwise instructed.)

Complete the following:

1. Start Word if necessary, open a new document based on the **Oriel Report** template, and then save the document as **Water Testing** in the Tutorial.05\Review folder included with your Data Files.
2. Make sure that nonprinting characters are displayed, and if necessary, switch to Print Layout view.
3. Replace the placeholder text in the Title control with **Department of Water Safety**. Replace the subtitle placeholder text with **Plans for Improving City Water Testing**.
4. Replace the placeholder text in the Abstract control with **This report analyzes possibilities for improving the city's water testing system.** Type your name in the Author control and select the current date in the Date control.
5. Delete the placeholder text in the Body control on page 2, and then insert the file named **Body** from the Tutorial.05\Review folder included with your Data Files. This is just a skeletal draft of the report, but it includes the necessary headings.
6. Format the five headings (Table of Contents, Project History, Improved Bacterial Testing, Protecting the Municipal Reservoir, and Installing New Pumping Stations) with the Heading 1 style.
7. Change the theme colors to Concourse, and then change the theme's fonts to the Apex fonts.
8. Select the Formal style set, and then open the Styles window.
9. Select the Project History heading and modify it by changing its character spacing to condensed, changing the paragraph spacing after the heading to 20 points, and adding italics.
10. Update the Heading 1 style to match the newly formatted Project History heading.
11. Create a new style for the Table of Contents heading that is based on the Heading 1 style. The style should be identical to the Heading 1 style, except that it should format text in 18-point font, in bold. Name the new style **Contents** and save it to the current document.
12. Open the Reveal Formatting window and compare the Contents style with the Heading 1 style.
13. Save your changes to the Water Testing document.
14. Save the Water Testing document as a template named **DWS Template** in the Tutorial.05\Review folder included with your Data Files.
15. On page 1, replace the subtitle with the placeholder **[Insert subtitle here.]**. Replace the abstract with the placeholder **[Insert report abstract here.]**.
16. Delete the body of the report, beginning with the Table of Contents heading to the end of the report (Tip: To maintain the formatting of the subtitle at the top of page 2, do not delete the last paragraph of the document.)

17. In the blank paragraph below the subtitle on page 2, insert the Word file **Placeholder** from the Tutorial.05\Review folder included with your Data Files.

18. Format the Table of Contents heading with the Contents style.

19. Save the template, preview it, print it, and close it.

20. Open a new document based on the DWS Template, enter **Estimate for New Wells** as the document subtitle, save the new document as **New Wells** in the Tutorial.05\Review folder included with your Data Files, preview it, print it, and close it.

21. Open the **Water Testing** document from the Tutorial.05\Review folder included with your Data Files.

22. In Outline view, demote the last three headings in the document to Level 2, and then move the heading Protecting the Municipal Reservoir up so it comes before the heading Improved Bacterial Testing.

23. Save your work and print the outline.

24. Insert a table of contents below the Table of Contents heading. Use the default settings in the Table of Contents dialog box.

25. At the end of the document, insert the Word file **Future** from the Tutorial.05\Review folder included with your Data Files, and then add the heading Future Plans to the table contents as a Level 1 heading.

26. Save, preview, print, and close the Water Testing document.

27. Open the document named **Research** from the Tutorial.05\Review folder included with your Data Files, and then save it as **Water Research** in the same folder.

28. Open the Research task pane, look up the definition of *aquifer*, and then insert the definition into the document in the appropriate place. Look up synonyms for *reservoir*, and insert the third synonym in the list into the appropriate place in the document.

29. At the top of the document, replace STUDENT NAME with your first and last name, replace DATE with the current date and time in the format 3/04/10 10:25 AM, and then save, preview, print, and close the document.

30. Submit the finished documents to your instructor, either in printed or electronic form, as requested.

Apply	**Case Problem 1**

Apply the skills you learned to create a template for a plant information handout.

Data Files needed for this Case Problem: Characteristics.docx, Crabapple.jpg, Height.docx, Plant Headings.docx, Requirements.docx.

Bluestem Landscape Design   Carla Niedenthal is the manager of the retail store owned by Bluestem Landscape Design. Customers often ask her for information about particular plants. Over the years, she has created fact sheets for some of the most popular plants, but now Carla would like to create a set of one-page plant descriptions. Her first step is to create a template that will serve as the basis of the handouts. As you'll see in the following steps, you can use templates intended for one purpose, such as a letter, for another purpose, such as a handout. (*Note:* Text you need to type is shown in bold for ease of reference only; do not bold the text unless otherwise instructed.)

Complete the following:

1. Open a new document based on the **Median Letter** template, and then save the document as **Plant** in the Tutorial.05\Case1 folder included with your Data Files.

2. Make sure that nonprinting characters are displayed and that Print Layout view is selected.

3. Replace the placeholder text in the Company Name control with **Bluestem Landscape Design**. Replace the company address placeholder text with **Plant-at-a-Glance**.

4. Delete the date control, and then type **[Insert common plant name]** in the brown box that used to contain the date control. Click the blue bar next to the brown box and type **[Insert Latin plant name.]**.

5. Below the blue bar, delete the sender company address control, the recipient title control, the recipient address control, and the salutation control. Delete the body text control, the closing control, and the name control. If a name remains visible in the document after you delete the name control, delete the name as well.

6. Delete all the blank paragraphs in the document below the brown and blue boxes except one. Make sure the remaining blank paragraph below the brown box is formatted with the Normal style, and that it is positioned at the left margin.

7. With the insertion point located in the blank paragraph below the brown box, insert the file Plant Headings from the Tutorial.05\Case1 folder included with your Data Files.

8. Format the three headings with the Heading 1 style. Remember that if you can't find a style in the Quick Styles gallery, you can look in the Styles window.

9. Change the theme colors to Foundry.

10. Change the theme's fonts to Verve.

11. Modify the Heading 1 style for the current document by changing its character spacing to Expanded, changing the paragraph spacing after the heading to 12 points, and adding italics.

12. At the bottom of the document, replace "STUDENT NAME" with your first and last name. Save and print the Plant document.

13. Save the Plant document as a template named **Plant Template** in the Tutorial. 05\Case1 folder included with your Data Files, and then close the template.

14. Open a document based on your template. Save the new document as **Crabapple** in the Tutorial.05\Case1 folder included with your Data Files.

15. For the common plant name, enter **Crabapple**. For the Latin plant name, enter **Malus**.

16. Under the Characteristics heading, delete the placeholder text but not the paragraph mark at the end of the paragraph, verify that the blank paragraph is formatted in the Normal style, and insert the Word file **Characteristics** from the Tutorial.05\Case1 folder included with your Data Files. Delete the extra paragraph mark at the end of the new text. Replace the placeholder text below the Mature Height heading and the Requirements heading with the files **Height** and **Requirements** from the Tutorial.05\Case1 folder included with your Data Files. Delete any extra new paragraphs.

17. At the bottom of the document, read the placeholder text about inserting a photograph. Select the placeholder text (but not the paragraph mark at the end of it), and delete it so you can insert a photo in its place.

⊕ EXPLORE

18. Verify that the insertion point is positioned in the blank paragraph just above the line that begins "Created by..." and then insert the photo named **Crabapple.jpg** from the Tutorial.05\Case1 folder included with your Data Files. (*Hint*: Use the Picture button in the Illustrations group on the Insert tab.) With the photograph selected, click the Drop Shadow Rectangle style in the Picture Styles group on the Picture Tools Format tab.

19. At the bottom of the document, replace DATE with the current date, including the day of the week.

20. Save, print, and close the Crabapple document.

21. Submit the finished documents to your instructor, either in printed or electronic form, as requested.

Apply | **Case Problem 2**

Apply the skills you learned to create a template for a consultant's report.

Data Files needed for this Case Problem: Star.docx, Video.docx

Star Avenue Consulting Steven Yang is a consultant for Star Avenue Consulting, a firm that helps retail chains evaluate and improve the organization of their retail floor space. Steven and his colleagues often have to produce reports that summarize their recommendations. Your job is to create a template they can use to generate these reports. (*Note:* Text you need to type is shown in bold for ease of reference only; do not bold the text unless otherwise instructed.)

Complete the following:

1. Open the document **Star** from the Tutorial.05\Case2 folder included with your Data Files, and then save it as **Star Report** in the same folder.
2. Make sure that nonprinting characters are displayed. If necessary, switch to Print Layout view. This document is based on the Normal template, and was created using all the default settings.
3. Format the five headings (starting with Recommendation and ending with Advantages of Current Layout) with the Heading 1 style.
4. Select the Opulent theme, and change the theme colors to Flow. Change the style set to Traditional.
5. Format the "Recommendation" heading by changing its character spacing to Expanded, changing the font size to 16 points, and changing the paragraph spacing after the paragraph to 12 points. Update the Heading 1 style for the current document to match the "Recommendation" heading.
6. Create a new style for the company name at the top of the document that is based on the Title style. The style should be identical to the Title style, except that it should format text in 20-point font, with bold and italic formatting, and should include 6 points of space after the paragraph. Name the new style **Company**, and save it to the current document.
7. Open the Reveal Formatting window and compare the Company style to the Title style.
8. In Outline view, move the Recommendation section down so it is the last section in the document. Demote the headings "Variations by Location," "Disadvantages of Current Layout," and "Advantages of Current Layout" to Level 2 headings.
9. In the blank paragraph above the heading "Assessment of Current Store Layout," insert a table of contents using the Automatic Table 2 format. Delete any extra blank paragraphs after the table of contents. The table of contents might seem unnecessary in such a short document, but as consultants create their multipage reports, they will need a table of contents.
10. Save your changes to the Star Report document, and then save the Star Report document as a template named **Star Report Template** in the Tutorial.05\Case2 folder included with your Data Files. Close the template.
11. Open a document based on your new template. You will use this document as the basis of a new report for HomeFlix Video Outlets. You will not complete the entire report; instead you'll leave the placeholder text in the body of the report for another consultant to replace.
12. Save the new document as **HomeFlix** in the Tutorial.05\Case2 folder included with your Data Files.
13. For the client name, insert **HomeFlix Video Outlets**. Replace CONSULTANT NAME with your first and last name.

⊕ EXPLORE   14. Replace DATE with the current date and time in the format 3/4/2010 3:25:25 PM. Select the Update automatically check box. Note the exact time inserted into the document, save the document, close it, pause briefly, and reopen the document. Note the updated time. Click the date, and then click Update. Note the updated time.

15. Save, print, and close the HomeFlix document.

16. Open the document named **Video** from the Tutorial.05\Case2 folder included with your Data Files, and then save it as **Video Research**. Open the Research task pane, look up the definition of *video*, and insert the third definition into the document in the appropriate place. Look up synonyms for *video* and insert the last synonym under "videotape" into the appropriate place in the document.

17. Save, print, and close the document.

18. Submit the finished documents to your instructor, either in printed or electronic form, as requested.

Challenge | Case Problem 3

Go beyond what you've learned to edit a business plan for a new Internet company named AllSecure, Incorporated.

Data File needed for this Case Problem: Text.docx

AllSecure, Inc.   Camden Lui has written a business plan for his new Internet business, AllSecure, Incorporated. On its Web site, the company will publish security information on data storage and transmission services. Camden has written part of the report and needs help formatting it. (*Note:* Text you need to type is shown in bold for ease of reference only; do not bold the text unless otherwise instructed.)

Complete the following:

1. Open a new document based on the Origin Report template and save it as **AllSecure Plan** in the Tutorial.05\Case3 folder included with your Data Files.

2. Remove the cover page at the beginning of the document. (*Hint:* Use the Cover Page button on the Insert tab.)

3. Use **AllSecure, Inc.** for the document title and **Business Plan** for the subtitle.

4. Delete the body control, and insert the file named **Text** from the Tutorial.05\Case3 folder included with your Data Files.

5. Format the four headings in the left column with the Heading 1 style. In the right column, format the first three headings in the Heading 1 style. Format the last three headings in the right column in the Heading 2 style.

⊕ EXPLORE   6. Create a new character style for the company name where it is used in the body of the report. Base the style on the Intense Reference style. It should be identical to the Intense Reference style, but without underline formatting. In the Create New Style from Formatting dialog box, select Character in the Style type list box. If necessary, select Intense Reference in the Style based on list box and deselect the Underline button. Name the style **Company Name** and save it to the current document.

⊕ EXPLORE   7. Open the Find and Replace dialog box, find all instances of "AllSecure" in the body of the document, and format them with the new Company Name style. After you find the first instance using the Find and Replace dialog box, close the dialog box, and click the button with the double blue down arrows at the bottom of the vertical scroll bar to find additional instances without using the Find and Replace dialog box. Use the button with the double blue up arrows at the bottom of the vertical scroll bar to move back to preceding instances.

⊕EXPLORE

8. Use Word Help to look up information on Find and Replace. Click the "Find and replace text or other items" topic, and then read about how to find and highlight text on the screen. Use this feature to highlight all instances of "AllSecure" in the document. Turn off the highlighting and close the Find and Replace dialog box.

9. Insert a new paragraph before the Executive Summary heading, format the new paragraph with the Normal style, type **Contents**, and insert a new paragraph. Format the paragraph containing the heading Contents in the Heading 1 style.

10. Use the Table of Contents dialog box to insert a table of contents in the blank paragraph below the Contents heading. Use the Distinctive format. Deselect the Right align page numbers check box so the entire table of contents is aligned in the left column.

11. At the end of the document, change the heading Audience Needs to **Audience Requirements**, and then update the table of contents.

⊕EXPLORE

12. Click the Select Browse Object button (the circle near the bottom of the vertical scroll bar). Move the pointer over the buttons in the palette and review the name of each option. Click the Go To button in the palette, and then use the Go To tab of the Find and Replace dialog box to move the insertion point to the top of page 2. Close the Find and Replace dialog box. Click the Select Browse Object button again, click the Browse by Heading button, and then click the button with the double blue down arrows (at the bottom of the vertical scroll bar) to move from one heading to the next. Use the double blue up arrow button to browse up through the document by heading.

13. Save, print, and close the document.

14. Submit the finished documents to your instructor, either in printed or electronic form, as requested.

Create	**Case Problem 4**

Create the outline shown in Figure 5-39 by using the Numbering button in the Paragraph group on the Home tab.

There are no Data Files needed for this Case Problem.

Public Health Report Outline   Shakira Ankor is a communications specialist at the Municipal Association for Public Health (MAPH). Each year she begins her work on the association's annual report by creating an outline using Word's multilevel list feature. She has asked you to help. (*Note:* Text you need to type is shown in bold for ease of reference only; do not bold the text unless otherwise instructed.)

1. Open a new Word document, and save it as **MAPH Report** in the Tutorial.05\Case4 folder included with your Data Files.

2. Switch to Print Layout view, if necessary, and make sure nonprinting characters are displayed.

3. To begin creating the report outline, insert a new paragraph, click the Numbering button in the Paragraph group on the Home tab, and type **A Message from the Director**. Press the Enter key, and then type **Report Highlights**. Press the Enter key, and then type **Summaries from Regional Committees**.

⊕EXPLORE

4. To demote a heading to a lower level, you can press the Tab key or click the Increase Indent button in the Paragraph group on the Home tab. Press the Enter key, press the Tab key, and then type **Northeast Region**. Continue typing the names of the following regions on separate lines: **Southeast Region**, **Midwest Region**, **West Region**. Insert another paragraph, click the Decrease Indent button, and then type **National Health Information Campaigns**.

5. Continue using the techniques described in Step 4 to complete the outline shown in Figure 5-39.

Figure 5-39

1. A Message from the Director
2. Report Highlights
3. Summaries from Regional Committees
   a. Northeast Region
   b. Southeast Region
   c. Midwest Region
   d. West Region
4. National Health Information Campaigns
   a. Vaccinations for Adolescents and Young Adults
      i. Special Needs of High School Students
      ii. Considerations for the College-Bound
   b. Lupus Signs and Symptoms
   c. Childhood Obesity
   d. Geriatric Nutrition Needs
      i. Calcium Intake
      ii. Protein Requirements

⊕ EXPLORE

6. Select the outline, click the Multilevel List button in the Paragraph group on the Home tab, and then select the style that uses Roman numerals and capital letters (in the lower-left corner of the Multilevel List gallery).

7. In Outline view, move the Southeast Region heading up before the Northeast Region heading.

8. Switch to Print Layout view, click at the beginning of the document, and then add **Municipal Association for Public Health** and the subtitle **Annual Report Outline**. Below the subtitle, insert **Created by Student Name**. (Replace "Student Name" with your first and last name.) On a line below your name, insert the current date in the March 7, 2010, format.

9. Format the title in the Title style, and then reduce the title's font size to 18 point. (Do not modify the Title style.) Format the subtitle in the Subtitle style.

10. Save your work, preview the document, and print it.

11. Submit the finished documents to your instructor, either in printed or electronic form, as requested.

Research | **Internet Assignments**

Go to the Web to find information you can use to create documents.

The purpose of the Internet Assignments is to challenge you to find information on the Internet that you can use to work effectively with this software. The actual assignments are updated and maintained on the Course Technology Web site. Log on to the Internet and use your Web browser to go to the Student Online Companion for New Perspectives Office 2007 at **www.course.com/np/office2007**. Then navigate to the Internet Assignments for this tutorial.

Assess | **SAM Assessment and Training**

If you have a SAM user profile, you may have access to hands-on instruction, practice, and assessment of the skills covered in this tutorial. Log in to your SAM account (**http://sam2007.course.com**) to launch any assigned training activities or exams that relate to the skills covered in this tutorial.

Review | **Quick Check Answers**

Session 5.1

1. Normal template
2. Right-click the content control, and then click Remove Content Control.
3. Insert tab
4. Colors, fonts, effects
5. Serif and sans serif
6. False

Session 5.2

1. True
2. Every built-in theme comes with 11 sets of styles. Each style set is, in turn, made up of 31 styles.
3. Styles window
4. In the Font group on the Home tab, click the Dialog Box Launcher to open the Font dialog box, and then click the Character Spacing tab.
5. Click the Dialog Box Launcher in the Paragraph group on the Home tab to open the Paragraph dialog box, and then click the Indents and Spacing tab.
6. Reveal Formatting window
7. True

Session 5.3

1. Plus sign
2. To increase the level of a heading
3. Format the document headings with heading styles.
4. Update Table button in the Table of Contents group in the References tab
5. False
6. It allows you to choose from a variety of date and time formats.

Ending Data Files

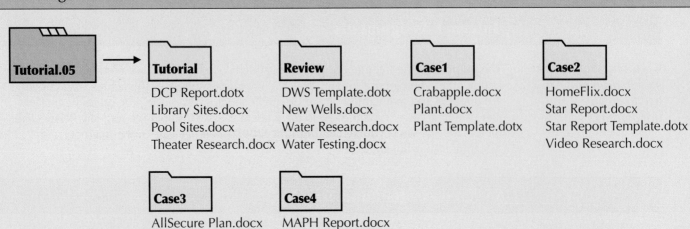

Tutorial.05 →

Tutorial
DCP Report.dotx
Library Sites.docx
Pool Sites.docx
Theater Research.docx

Review
DWS Template.dotx
New Wells.docx
Water Research.docx
Water Testing.docx

Case1
Crabapple.docx
Plant.docx
Plant Template.dotx

Case2
HomeFlix.docx
Star Report.docx
Star Report Template.dotx
Video Research.docx

Case3
AllSecure Plan.docx

Case4
MAPH Report.docx

Using Mail Merge

Creating a Form Letter, Mailing Labels, and a List

Case | Lily Road Yoga Studio

Nina Ranabhat is the owner and chief instructor at Lily Road Yoga Studio in Boise, Idaho. The studio has just moved to a new, expanded location. Nina wants to invite clients to try out the new facility during free, open-studio days in the month of June. She plans to send a letter to each client announcing the new location and the open-studio days.

Nina doesn't have time to type a personal letter to each of the studio's many clients. Instead, she plans to create a **form letter** that contains the information she wants to send to all clients. The form letter will also contain specific details for individual clients, such as name, address, and each client's favorite class and instructor. Nina has already written the text of the form letter. She plans to use the mail merge process to add the personal information for each client. She asks you to create the form letter using Word's Mail Merge feature. She also needs a set of letters that will go just to the clients who take power yoga classes. After you create the merged letters, she'd like you to create the mailing labels for the envelopes and a telephone directory that lists a phone number for each teacher. Next, you will create an additional document with name and address information by converting text to a table. Finally, you will create and format a list of names by converting a table to text.

Starting Data Files

Tutorial.06 →	Tutorial	Review	Case1	Case2
	Client.docx	Bonus.docx	Gallery.docx	Mortgage.docx
	Phone.docx	Contacts.docx		Mortgage Data.xlsx
	Yoga.docx	More.docx		

Case3	Case4
Letter.docx	(none)
Pasta.txt	

Session 6.1

Understanding the Mail Merge Process

To insert individualized information into a form letter, you combine, or **merge**, a form letter with a separate file containing specific information, whether that information is names and addresses, product information, or another type of data. The form letter is called a **main document**, and the file containing the specific information is called the **data source**.

A main document can be a letter or any other kind of document. It contains codes called **fields** that tell Word where to insert names, addresses, and other variable information. A field can be a data field, such as date and time fields, or **merge fields**, such as First Name and Last Name fields. As you will see in this tutorial, one of the steps you must complete before merging the main document with the data source is inserting the merge fields into the main document. Nina's main document is the letter shown in Figure 6-1. As you complete the steps in this tutorial, you will replace the red text with merge fields.

Figure 6-1 ▶ **Nina's main document**

[Date]

[First Name] [Last Name]
[Street Address]
[City], ID [ZIP Code]

Dear [First Name]:

I am happy to announce that Lily Road Yoga Studio has moved to an expanded location at 4722 Lily Road. This is just two blocks south of our original location, but it feels like a whole new world. Our sunny new studio offers off-street parking, private changing rooms, and a much larger studio space. We also have a separate, smaller space for individual instruction.

To welcome you to our new home, we are hosting open studio hours every Thursday through the month of June. Classes on open studio days are free. Of course, we will continue to offer a full range of yoga instruction, including group classes and private practice.

Please check out our schedule online at *www.lilyroad.course.com*. You'll be glad to know that we now offer two additional [Favorite Type] classes. Also, keep in mind that [Favorite Teacher] is available for individual instruction.

We hope to see you soon at one of our open-studio Thursdays. Come soon, and bring a friend!

Sincerely yours,

Nina Ranabhat

Owner and Certified Ashtanga Instructor

Nina's data source will include the name and address of each client, as well as information about each client's preferred type of class and favorite teacher.

Inserting information from a data source into a main document produces a final document called a **merged document**. Figure 6-2 illustrates how the data source and main document combine to form a merged document.

Merging a main document with a data source to create a merged document ◀ Figure 6-2

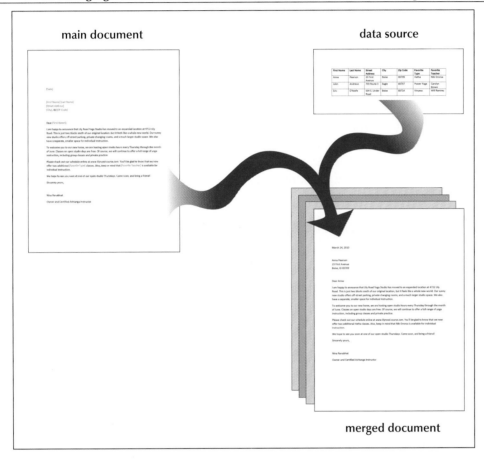

Merge Fields and Records

Merge fields appear in the main document and tell Word which pieces of information to retrieve from the data source. One merge field might retrieve an address from the data source; another merge field might retrieve a telephone number. Merge fields are easy to spot in the main document because each merge field name is enclosed by pairs of angled brackets, which look like this: << >>. You can insert merge fields into a main document only by using the Mail Merge task pane or the tools in the Mailings tab. You cannot simply type merge fields into the main document—even if you type the brackets.

A data source is a table of information similar to the one shown in Figure 6-3. The header row, the first row of the table, contains the name of each merge field. The cells below the header row contain the specific information that replaces the merge fields in the main document. This information is called **data**. Each row of data in the table makes up a complete **record**. You can also think of a record as the information about one individual or object.

Figure 6-3 ▷ **Sample data source**

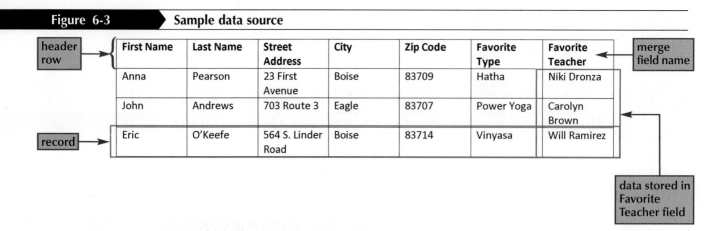

header row →

First Name	Last Name	Street Address	City	Zip Code	Favorite Type	Favorite Teacher
Anna	Pearson	23 First Avenue	Boise	83709	Hatha	Niki Dronza
John	Andrews	703 Route 3	Eagle	83707	Power Yoga	Carolyn Brown
Eric	O'Keefe	564 S. Linder Road	Boise	83714	Vinyasa	Will Ramirez

record →

merge field name ←

data stored in Favorite Teacher field

Data sources are commonly used to store names and addresses. However, you can also create data sources with inventory records, records of suppliers, or records of equipment. After you understand how to manage and manipulate the records in a data source, you'll be able to use them for many different types of information.

Using the Mail Merge Task Pane

The **Mail Merge task pane** walks you through the following six steps for merging documents:

1. Select the type of document you want to use as the main document. Possible types of main documents include letters, envelopes, e-mails, labels, and directories.
2. Select the document you want to use as the main document. You can create a new document or edit an existing one.
3. Select the list of recipients (that is, the data source) you want to use for the merge or create a new list of recipients.
4. Complete the main document by adding merge fields.
5. Preview the merged document.
6. Complete the mail merge.

To ensure that you see the same thing in the Mail Merge task pane each time you open it, start with a new, blank document before you open the Mail Merge task pane. Once you are familiar with merging documents, you can also use the options on the Mailings tab to perform the same tasks described in the Mail Merge task pane.

Nina is ready for you to start the mail merge process for her form letter.

To start Word and open the Mail Merge task pane:

▶ **1.** Start Word and make sure a new, blank document is displayed. Note that this new document is named "Document1."

▶ **2.** Switch to Print Layout view, and then display nonprinting characters, if necessary. Use any Zoom setting you want for now. You won't need the rulers in this tutorial, so close them if they are displayed.

▶ **3.** Click the **Mailings** tab, then in the Start Mail Merge group, click the **Start Mail Merge** button, and then click **Step by Step Mail Merge Wizard**. The Mail Merge task pane opens, displaying information and options related to the first step in merging documents. See Figure 6-4.

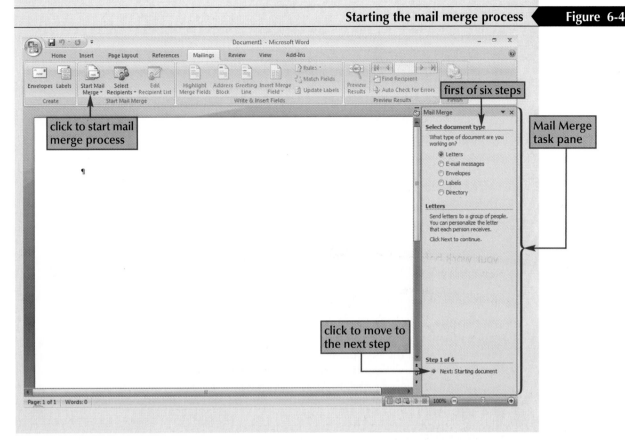

With the Mail Merge task pane open, you are ready to perform the first two steps in merging a document.

Selecting a Main Document

According to the Mail Merge task pane, your first task is to specify the type of main document you want to use for the merge. The Mail Merge task pane provides a number of options, including e-mail messages and labels. In this case, you want to create a letter.

To specify the type of merged document to create:

▶ **1.** Verify that the **Letters** option button is selected in the Mail Merge task pane.

▶ **2.** At the bottom of the task pane, click **Next: Starting document**. The Mail Merge task pane displays information and options that you can use to select a starting document—that is, to select a main document.

Now that you've selected letters as the type of document you'll use for your main document, you need to specify which document you'll use for Nina's form letter. When selecting a main document, you have three choices: use the document currently displayed in the document window; start a new document from a pre-installed mail merge template; or open an existing document. Nina has already written the letter she wants to send to all of her yoga clients, so you don't need to create a new document. Instead, you'll use her existing document, which she saved in a file named Yoga.

When you open an existing document from the Mail Merge task pane, Word actually opens a *copy* of the document you select so that any changes you make to the file will not affect the original file. You'll see how this works in the following steps.

To select a main document for the form letter:

▶ **1.** In the Mail Merge task pane, click the **Start from existing document** option button (just below the "Select starting document" heading). A list box appears, with an Open button below it. The list box contains names of files that have been used for a mail merge on your computer in the past. (If this is the first time anyone has performed a mail merge on your computer, the list box will be blank except for a More Files link.) If you perform mail merges regularly with the same group of files, you can click the name of the file you want in this list box. For now, however, you will use the Open button below the list box.

▶ **2.** In the Start from existing section of the Mail Merge task pane, click the **Open** button. The Open dialog box is displayed. You'll use this dialog box to select Nina's document.

▶ **3.** Navigate to the **Tutorial.06\Tutorial** folder included with your Data Files.

▶ **4.** Click **Yoga**, and then click the **Open** button. A copy of the file named Yoga is opened and is named Document1. The Use the current document option button is now selected in the task pane because you are now ready to use the current document as the main document. Because Nina had set the top margin of the Yoga document at 2 inches, the top margin of the Document1 document changes to 2 inches as well. This will leave enough room for Nina's letterhead.

▶ **5.** Make sure nonprinting characters are displayed.

▶ **6.** Change the zoom so you can see the entire width of the text, but not the left or right margins. On most monitors, **120%** is a good zoom setting. At the bottom of the task pane, you see the next step in the mail merge process. See Figure 6-5.

Main document Normal view ◀ Figure 6-5

7. Scroll down to display the letter's closing, change "Nina Ranabhat" to your name, and then scroll back up to the beginning of the letter.

8. Save the file as **Yoga Letter with Merge Fields** in the Tutorial.06\Tutorial folder.

Next, you need to specify your data source—the list of recipients for Nina's letter.

Creating a Data Source

As you learned earlier, a data source is a file with information organized into fields and records. Typically, the data source for a mail merge contains a list of names and addresses, but it can also contain e-mail addresses, telephone numbers, and other data. Various kinds of files can be used as the data source, including a simple text file, a Word table, an Excel worksheet, an Access database, or a Microsoft Office Address Lists file, which stores addresses for Microsoft Outlook and other Microsoft Office applications. (In Word Help, this type of file is sometimes called a Microsoft Office Contacts Lists file.) In this tutorial, you will create a Microsoft Office Address Lists file to use as your data source. Word's Mail Merge task pane walks you through the steps required to create the data source.

When performing a mail merge, you can select a data source file that already contains names and addresses, or you can create a new data source and enter names and addresses into it. When you create a new data source, the file is saved by default as a Microsoft Office Address Lists file. In this section, you will create a data source using the tools provided by the Mail Merge task pane. This involves two steps: deciding which fields to include in the data source and entering address information.

You need to create a data source that contains information on Nina's clients, including the name, address, preferred type of class, and favorite teacher. Nina collected all the necessary information by asking clients to fill out a form when they registered for their first yoga class. Figure 6-6 shows one of these forms.

Figure 6-6 **Client information form**

The information on each form will make up one record in the data source. Your job is to create a data source for three of Nina's clients, which means you'll have just three records. A real yoga studio would of course have tens or hundreds of records, one for each client. When you create your data source, you must include the field names shown in Figure 6-7.

Figure 6-7 **Field names to include in data source**

Field Names	Description
First Name	Client's first name
Last Name	Client's last name
Address	Client's street address
City	City in Idaho
ZIP Code	ZIP code in Idaho
Favorite Type of Yoga	Client's preferred type of yoga
Favorite Teacher	Client's preferred yoga teacher

When you create a new data source from within the Mail Merge task pane, Word provides a number of default fields, such as First Name, Last Name, and Company. You can customize the data source by adding new fields and removing the default fields that you don't plan to use. As you create a data source, keep in mind that each field name must be unique; you can't have two fields with the same name.

Creating a Data Source for a Mail Merge | Reference Window

- In Step 3 of the Mail Merge task pane, select the Type a new list option button, and then click Create; or, in the Start Mail Merge group on the Mailings tab, click the Select Recipients button, and then click Type New List.
- In the New Address List dialog box, click the Customize Columns button.
- To delete unnecessary fields, in the Customize Address List dialog box, click a field you want to delete, click the Delete button, and then click the Yes button. Continue to delete any other unnecessary fields.
- To add a new field, click the Add button, type the name of the field in the Add Field dialog box, and then click the OK button.
- To rearrange the order of the field names, click a field name, and then click the Move Up or Move Down button.
- Click the OK button to close the Customize Address List dialog box.
- In the New Address List dialog box, enter information for the first record, click the New Entry button, and type another record. Continue until you are finished entering information into the data source, and then click the OK button to open the Save Address List dialog box.
- Type a name for the data source in the File name text box, and then click the Save button. The file is saved with the .mdb file extension.

You're ready to begin creating the data source for Nina's form letter.

To begin creating the data source:

▶ 1. In the bottom of the Mail Merge task pane, click **Next: Select recipients**, and then click the **Type a new list** option button.

▶ 2. Below the heading "Type a new list," click **Create**. The New Address List dialog box opens, as shown in Figure 6-8.

Creating a data source ◀ Figure 6-8

these fields are included in the new data source by default

You will use the New Address List dialog box to enter a complete set of information for one person—that is, you will enter one record into the data source. However, before you begin entering information, you need to customize the list of fields to match the fields shown earlier in Figure 6-7.

To customize the list of fields:

1. Click the **Customize Columns** button. The Customize Address List dialog box opens. Here you can delete the fields you don't need, add new ones, and arrange the fields in the order you want. You'll start by deleting fields.

2. In the Field Names list box, verify that **Title** is selected, and then click the **Delete** button. A message appears asking you to confirm the deletion.

3. Click the **Yes** button. The Title field is deleted from the list of field names.

4. Continue using the Delete button to delete the following fields: **Company Name**, **Address Line 2**, **State**, **Country or Region**, **Home Phone**, **Work Phone**, and **E-mail Address**. Next, you need to add some new fields. When you add a new field, it is inserted below the selected field, so you will start by selecting the last field in the list if it is not already selected.

5. In the Field Names list box, verify that **ZIP Code** is selected, and then click the **Add** button. The Add Field dialog box opens, instructing you to type a name for your field.

6. Type **Favorite Type**, and then click the **OK** button. The field "Favorite Type" is added.

7. Use the Add button to add a **Favorite Teacher** field below the Favorite Type field. When you are finished, your Customize Address List dialog box should look like the one shown in Figure 6-9. You could use the Move Up and Move Down buttons to rearrange the field names (for instance, to move the Favorite Teacher field above the Favorite Type field), but in this case the order is fine. You are finished customizing the list of field names.

Figure 6-9   **Customized list of field names**

new merge fields

moves the selected field up one place in the list

moves the selected field down one place in the list

▶ **8.** Click the **OK** button in the Customize Address List dialog box. The Customize Address List dialog box closes, and you return to the New Address List dialog box. This dialog box reflects the changes you just made. For instance, it no longer includes the Title field. The fields are listed in the same order they appeared in the Customize Address List dialog box. In the next step, you'll scroll right so you can see the fields you just added.

▶ **9.** Use the horizontal scroll bar near the bottom of the New Address List dialog box to display the Favorite Type and Favorite Teacher fields. Although part of "Favorite Teacher" is cut off in the dialog box, the entire field name is stored as part of the data source. See Figure 6-10.

Changes made to New Address List dialog box   ◀   **Figure 6-10**

new fields

use the scroll bar to display the new fields

Organizing Field Names | InSight

Although the order of field names in the data source doesn't affect their placement in the main document, it's a good idea to arrange field names logically in the data source so you can enter information quickly and efficiently. For example, you'll probably want the First Name field next to the Last Name field. Also, note that if you include spaces in your field names, Word will replace the spaces with underscores when you insert the fields into the main document. For example, Word transforms the field name First Name into First_Name.

Now that you have specified the fields you want to use, you are ready to enter the client information into the data source.

Entering Data into a Data Source

You are now ready to begin entering information about each client into the data source. Nina gives you three copies of the form shown earlier in Figure 6-6, with information entered in each form. She asks you to transfer the information from the paper forms into the data source. Each paper form will be used to create one new record in the data source. You'll use the New Address List dialog box to enter the information.

To enter data into a record using the New Address List dialog box:

▶ 1. Scroll left to display the First Name field, click in the **First Name** text box, if necessary, and then type **Anna** to enter the first name of the first client. Make sure you do not press the spacebar after you finish typing an entry in the New Address List dialog box. You should add spaces only in the text of the main document, not in the data source, to prevent too many or too few spaces between words.

▶ 2. Press the **Tab** key to move the insertion point to the Last Name field.

▶ 3. Type **Pearson**, and then press the **Tab** key to move the insertion point to the Address Line 1 field.

▶ 4. Type **23 First Avenue**, and then press the **Tab** key to move the insertion point to the City field.

▶ 5. Type **Boise**, and then press the **Tab** key to move the insertion point to the ZIP Code field.

▶ 6. Type **83709**, and then press the **Tab** key to move to the Favorite Type field. The Favorite Type field scrolls into view on the right side of the dialog box.

▶ 7. Type **Hatha**, and then press the **Tab** key. The insertion point is now in the Favorite Teacher field, which has scrolled into view on the right side of the dialog box.

▶ 8. Type **Niki Dronza**, but do *not* press the Tab key. See Figure 6-11.

| Figure 6-11 | Completed record 1 |

You have completed the information for the first record of the data source document. Now you're ready to enter the information for the next two records. You can create a new record by clicking the New Entry button. When the insertion point is in the far-right text box in the New Address List dialog box, you can also create a new record by pressing the Tab key. In the steps that follow, you use both methods.

To add additional records to the data source:

▶ 1. In the New Address List dialog box, click the **New Entry** button. This creates a new, blank record.

▶ 2. Enter the information shown in Figure 6-12 into the new record.

Information for record 2 | **Figure 6-12**

First Name	Last Name	Street Address	City	Zip Code	Favorite Type	Favorite Teacher
John	Andrews	703 Route 3	Eagle	83707	Power Yoga	Carolyn Brown

▶ **3.** After entering data into the last field, press the **Tab** key.

▶ **4.** Enter the information for the third record, as shown in Figure 6-13. After entering the information for the third record, do not create a fourth record.

Information for record 3 | **Figure 6-13**

First Name	Last Name	Street Address	City	Zip Code	Favorite Type	Favorite Teacher
Eric	O'Keefe	564 S. Linder Road	Boise	83714	Vinyasa	Will Ramirez

Trouble? If you create a fourth record by mistake, click the Delete Entry button to remove the blank fourth record.

You have entered the records for three clients. Next, you need to proofread each record to make sure you typed the information correctly.

To proof the records in the data source:

▶ **1.** Review the information about Anna Pearson in the first record. Compare the record to Figure 6-11, which shows all the data for Anna Pearson except for her name. Make any necessary corrections by selecting the text and retyping it.

▶ **2.** Proofread record 2 by comparing your information with Figure 6-12. Make any necessary corrections.

▶ **3.** Proofread record 3 by comparing your information with Figure 6-13. Make any necessary corrections.

Nina's data source eventually will contain hundreds of records for Lily Road Yoga Studio clients. The current data source, however, contains only the records Nina wants to work with now. Next, you need to save the data source.

Saving a Data Source

You have finished entering data, so you are ready to close the New Address List dialog box. When you close this dialog box, a new dialog box opens, where you can save the data source as a Microsoft Office Address Lists file.

To save the data source:

▶ 1. In the New Address List dialog box, click the **OK** button. The New Address List dialog box closes, and the Save Address List dialog box opens, as shown in Figure 6-14. By default, Word offers to save the file to the My Data Sources folder, which is a subfolder of the Documents folder. In this case, however, you will save the data source in the Tutorial.06\Tutorial folder. Notice that the Save as type box indicates that the data source will be saved as a Microsoft Office Address Lists file.

| Figure 6-14 | Saving the data source |

▶ 2. Navigate to the **Tutorial.06\Tutorial** folder.

▶ 3. Click the **File name** text box, type **Yoga Data**, and then click the **Save** button. The Mail Merge Recipients dialog box opens, as shown in Figure 6-15. As in the New Address List dialog box, the header row in this dialog box contains the names of the fields. You need to scroll right to see all the fields. You can use the Mail Merge Recipients dialog box to rearrange the records in the list and to choose which clients you want to include in the mail merge. You'll use this dialog box later in this tutorial.

Mail Merge Recipients dialog box ◀ Figure 6-15

4. Click the **OK** button. The Mail Merge Recipients dialog box closes and you return to the document window. The Mail Merge task pane indicates that you have selected an Office Address List file named "Yoga Data.mdb" as your data source. The task pane also indicates that the next step in the mail merge process is writing (in this case, editing) the main document. See Figure 6-16.

Tip

You can also open the Mail Recipients dialog box by clicking the Edit Recipient List button in the Start Mail Merge group on the Mailings tab.

Selected data source ◀ Figure 6-16

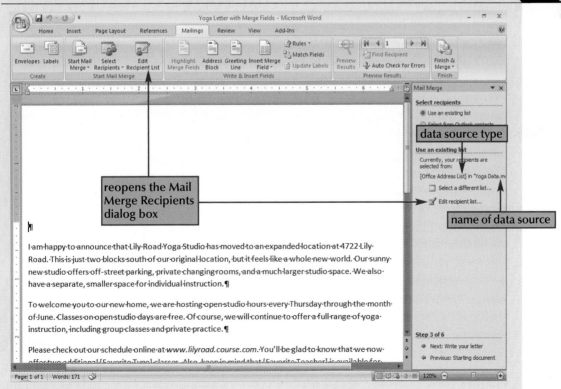

Editing a Main Document

In the first two steps of the mail merge process, you selected Nina's letter as your main document. A copy of this letter is open on your screen, next to the Mail Merge task pane. In the third step, you created and saved the data source. Now you will turn your attention back to the main document. You'll edit Nina's letter to add the current date and the merge fields.

Adding a Date Field

Tip

You can also update a date field by selecting it, and then pressing the [F9] key.

As you've learned, merge fields tell Word where to insert information from the data source. You can also insert other kinds of fields in a document, including a **date field**, which inserts the current date. You can set up a date field up so Word updates the field each time the document is opened.

You insert a date field via the Insert Date and Time dialog box. You already know how to use this dialog box to add the current date as text. To insert a date field that Word updates automatically, you select the Update automatically check box.

Nina wants the date to appear at the top of the document, just below where the yoga studio logo appears on the printed stationery.

To insert the date field:

▶ 1. In the Mail Merge task pane, click **Next: Write your letter**. The Mail Merge task pane displays information and options related to working with the main document. If you had originally selected a new, blank document as your main document, you would need to write the text of the form letter now. In this case, you will edit the existing letter.

▶ 2. Make sure the insertion point is at the beginning of the form letter on the first blank line. You will insert the date on the first line of the document.

▶ 3. Click the **Insert** tab, and then, in the Text group, click the **Date & Time** button. The Date and Time dialog box opens.

▶ 4. Click the second format in the Available formats list, which includes the month, the day, and the year, as in March 24, 2010.

▶ 5. If it's not selected, click the **Update automatically** check box to select it. See Figure 6-17.

Figure 6-17 ▶ **Inserting a date field**

6. Click the **OK** button. The current date appears in the document.

Trouble? If you see {DATE \@ "MMMM d, yyyy"} instead of the current date, your system is set to display field codes. To view the date instead of the field code, click the Office Button, click Word Options, click Advanced, scroll down to display the Show document content section, deselect the "Show field codes instead of their values" check box, and then click the OK button.

Now, whenever you print the merged document, the current date will appear in the document. Next, you will insert the merge fields for the letter's inside address.

Inserting Merge Fields

Nina's letter is a standard business letter, so you'll place the client's name and address below the date. You'll use merge fields for the client's first name, last name, address, city, and zip code. You must enter proper spacing and punctuation around the fields so that the information in the merged document will be formatted correctly.

The Mail Merge task pane includes links, such as the Address block link, which you can use to insert a standard set of fields. The More items link offers more flexibility because it allows you to insert fields one at a time, rather than in predefined groups. In the following steps you will use the More link in the Mail Merge task pane to begin inserting merge fields in the main document. But first, you will re-display the Mailings tab, so that you can see the options on the Mailings tab that correspond to the options in the Mail merge task pane.

To insert a merge field:

1. Click the **Mailings** tab.

2. Verify that the insertion point is positioned in the first line immediately to the right of the date field, and then press the **Enter** key two times to leave space between the date and the first line of the inside address.

3. In the Mail Merge task pane, click **More items**. The Insert Merge Field dialog box opens. As shown in Figure 6-18, the Database Fields option button is selected, indicating that the dialog box displays all the fields in the data source.

Inserting merge fields into the main document ◄ **Figure 6-18**

Trouble? If you see a different list than the one shown in Figure 6-18, the Address Fields option button might be selected rather than the Database Fields option button. Click the Database Fields option button to select it, and then continue with Step 4.

> **4.** In the Fields list, click **First Name** if necessary to select it, click the **Insert** button, and then click the **Close** button. The Insert Merge Field dialog box closes, and the merge field is inserted into the document. The merge field consists of the field name surrounded by double angled brackets << >>, also called **chevrons**. Note that Word replaces spaces in field names with underscores, so the field name "First Name" is displayed as "First_Name." Also note that the Highlight Merge Fields button is now available, which means you can use it to display the merge field on a gray background.
>
> **Trouble?** If you make a mistake and insert the wrong merge field, click to the left of the merge field, press the Delete key to select the field, and then press the Delete key again to delete it.
>
> **5.** In the Write & Insert Fields group, click the **Highlight Merge Fields** button. The First Name merge field is displayed on a gray background, making it easier to see in the document.

Later, when you merge the main document with the data source, Word will replace this merge field with information from the First Name field in the data source. Now, you're ready to insert the merge fields for the rest of the inside address. You'll add the necessary spacing and punctuation to the main document as well.

To insert the remaining merge fields for the inside address:

> **1.** Press the **spacebar** to insert a space after the First Name field, and then on the Mailings tab, click the **Insert Merge Field** button arrow. A menu appears displaying a list of the fields in the data source.
>
> **Trouble?** If the Insert Merge Field dialog box opens, you clicked the Insert Merge Field button instead of the Insert Merge Field button arrow. Close the dialog box, and then click the Insert Merge Field button arrow.
>
> **2.** Click **Last_Name**. The Last_Name merge field is inserted in the document. As you continue entering the remaining merge fields in the inside address, you will use manual line breaks to avoid inserting paragraph spacing after each line. Remember that a manual line break moves the insertion point to the next line without actually starting a new paragraph, so no extra space is inserted.
>
> **3.** Press the **Shift+Enter** keys to create a manual line break, click the **Insert Merge Field** button arrow, and then click **Address Line 1**. Word inserts the Address Line 1 merge field into the form letter.
>
> **4.** Press the **Shift+Enter** keys to create another manual line break, and then, using either the Insert Merge Field button arrow on the Mailings tab or the More items link in the task pane, insert the **City** merge field. Word inserts the City merge field into the form letter.
>
> **5.** Type **,** (a comma), press the **spacebar** to insert a space after the comma, and then type **ID** to insert the abbreviation for the state of Idaho.
>
> **6.** Press the **spacebar** to insert a space after ID, and then insert the **ZIP Code** merge field. See Figure 6-19.

Form letter with merge fields | Figure 6-19

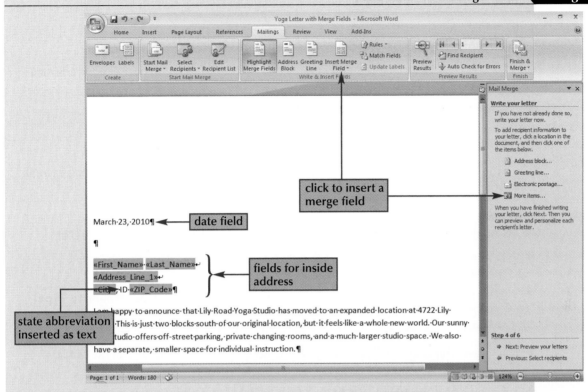

Planning Your Data Source | InSight

It's important to take some time to think about the structure of your data source before you create it. As you plan a data source, try to break information down into as many fields as seems reasonable. For example, it's always better to include a First Name field and a Last Name field, rather than simply a Name field, because including two separate fields makes it possible, later, to alphabetize the information in the data source by last name. If you entered first and last names in a single Name field, you could only alphabetize by first name, because the first name would appear first in the Name field.

If you're working with a very small data source, breaking information down into as many fields as possible is less important. However, it's very common to start with a small data source, and then, as time goes on, find that you need to keep adding information to the data source, until you have a large file. If you failed to plan the data source adequately at the beginning, the expanded data source could be hard to work with.

In this tutorial, you are working with a data source that does not include a State field because all of the yoga studio's clients live in the state of Idaho. This allows you to get some practice building an inside address out of merge fields and text. As a general rule, however, it's smart to include a State field in every address data source you create. That way, if your pool of addresses should expand in the future to include residents of other states, you won't have to make major changes to your data source to accommodate the new records. Also, if your data source includes a State field, you can use the Address Block merge field to insert an entire address at once, as you did in Tutorial 4. Finally, as you'll see later in this tutorial, including a State field in your data source simplifies the process of creating mailing labels.

The inside address is set up to match the form for a standard business letter. You can now add the salutation of the letter, which will contain each client's first name.

To insert the merge field for the salutation:

▶ **1.** Press the **Enter** key twice to insert a line between the inside address and the salutation, type **Dear**, and then press the **spacebar**.

▶ **2.** Insert the **First Name** field into the document.

▶ **3.** Type **:** (a colon), and then save your work. This completes the salutation.

You'll personalize the letter even more by including references to each client's favorite type of class and teacher.

To add each client's favorite type of class and teacher to the letter:

▶ **1.** Scroll down to display the third main paragraph of the letter, which begins "Please check out our schedule...."

▶ **2.** In the third main paragraph of the letter, select the placeholder **[Favorite Type]** (including the brackets). You'll replace this phrase with a merge field. (Don't be concerned if you also select the space following the closing bracket.)

▶ **3.** Insert the **Favorite Type** merge field. Word replaces the selected text with the Favorite Type merge field.

▶ **4.** Verify that the field has a single space before it and after it. Add a space on either side if necessary.

▶ **5.** Replace **[Favorite Teacher]** in the third main paragraph of the form letter with the **Favorite Teacher** field, and adjust the spacing as necessary.

▶ **6.** Carefully check your document to make sure the field names and spacing are correct. Your document should look like Figure 6-20.

Form letter after inserting merge fields | **Figure 6-20**

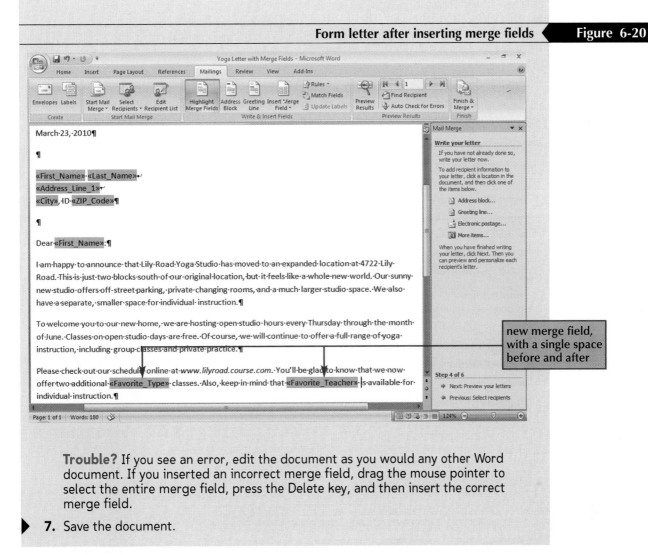

Trouble? If you see an error, edit the document as you would any other Word document. If you inserted an incorrect merge field, drag the mouse pointer to select the entire merge field, press the Delete key, and then insert the correct merge field.

▶ **7.** Save the document.

The main document now contains all the necessary merge fields. The next step is to merge the main document and the data source. Word allows you to preview the merged document before you complete the merge.

Previewing the Merged Document

Referring again to the Mail Merge task pane, your next step is to preview the merged document to see how the letter will look after Word inserts the information for each client. When you preview the merged document, you can check one last time for any missing spaces between the merge fields and the surrounding text. You can also look for any other formatting problems, and, if necessary, make final changes to the data source.

To preview the merged document:

▶ 1. In the Mail Merge task pane, click **Next: Preview your letters**. The Mail Merge task pane displays information and options related to previewing the merged document. The data for the first record (Anna Pearson) replaces the merge fields in the form letter. See Figure 6-21. Carefully check the letter to make sure the text and formatting are correct. In particular, check to make sure that the spaces before and after the merged data are correct; it is easy to accidentally omit spaces or add extra spaces around merge fields. Finally, notice that both the task pane and the Go to Record box in the Preview Results group show which record is currently displayed in the document.

Figure 6-21 | **First letter with merged data**

▶ 2. If you need to make any changes to the form letter, click **Previous: Write your letter** in the Mail Merge task pane, edit the document, save your changes, and then click **Next: Preview your letters** in the task pane. When you are finished, your screen should look like Figure 6-21. Before you complete the merge, you should review the data for the other two records.

▶ 3. In the Preview Results group on the Mailings tab, click the **Next Record** button ▶. The data for John Andrews is displayed in the letter.

▶ 4. Click the **Next Record** button ▶ to display the data for Eric O'Keefe in the letter.

▶ 5. Click the **First Record** button ◀ in the Preview Results group to redisplay the first record in the letter (with data for Anna Pearson).

Tip

You can also use the right-facing double-arrow button in the Mail Merge task pane to display the next record and the left-facing double-arrow button to display the previous record.

The main document of the mail merge is completed. At this stage, you could also use the Mail Merge task pane to make changes to the data source, but Nina says the data source is fine for now. You are ready for the final step, completing the merge.

Merging the Main Document and Data Source

Now that you've created the form letter (main document) and the list of client information (data source), you're ready to merge the two files and create personalized letters to send to Nina's clients. Because the data source consists of three records, your merged document will contain three letters; each will be one page long.

When you complete a merge, you can choose to merge directly to the printer. In other words, you can choose to have Word print the merged document immediately without saving it as a separate file. However, Nina wants to keep a copy of the merged document on disk for her records. So you'll merge the data source and main document to a new document first, and then print it.

> ### Tip
> You can use the Finish & Merge button in the Finish group on the Mailings tab to merge to a new document, merge to the printer, or send out the merged documents as e-mails.

To complete the mail merge:

▶ 1. In the Mail Merge task pane, click **Next: Complete the merge**. As shown in Figure 6-22, the task pane displays options related to merging the main document and the data source. You can use the Print option to merge directly to the printer. Alternatively, you can use the Edit individual letters option to merge to a new document.

Last step in Mail Merge task pane ◀ **Figure 6-22**

▶ 2. In the Mail Merge task pane, click **Edit individual letters**. The Merge to New Document dialog box opens. Here, you need to specify which records to include in the merge. You want to include all three records from the data source.

▶ 3. Verify that the **All** option button is selected, and then click the **OK** button. Word creates a new document called Letters1, which contains three pages, one for each record in the data source. In this new document, the merge fields have been replaced by the specific names, addresses, and so on, from the data source. See Figure 6-23. The date field, however, has not been replaced. Instead, a date field appears at the top of every page, highlighted in gray. The gray highlighting will not print.

Figure 6-23   **Merged document**

4. Save the merged document in the Tutorial.06\Tutorial folder, using the filename **Yoga Merged Letters 1**.

5. Zoom out so the text is large enough to read. Next, you will use the Select Browse Object button at the bottom of the vertical scroll bar to move from one page to the next.

6. Click the **Select Browse Object** button ⊙ near the bottom of the vertical scroll bar, click the **Browse by Page** button ☐ on the palette, and then click the **Previous Page** button ± or **Next Page** button ∓ to move among the letters. Note that each letter is addressed to a different client and that the favorite type and teacher vary from one letter to the next. A page break separates each letter from the one that follows. Nina will print the letters later. For now, you will close the file.

7. Close the **Yoga Merged Letters 1** document. The document named "Yoga Letter with Merge Fields" is now the active document. You see the Mail Merge task pane again, displaying the last step of the mail merge process. Note that if you need to take a break while working on a mail merge, you can save the main document and close it. The data source and field information are saved along with the document. When you're ready to work on the merge again, you can open the main document again and update the connection to the data source. You'll see how this works at the beginning of the next session. For now, you will close the main document.

8. Save and close the **Yoga Letter with Merge Fields** document.

You have completed the six steps of the Mail Merge task pane and generated a merged document. In the next session, you will learn how to use additional Mail Merge features.

1. Define the following in your own words:
   a. date field
   b. main document
   c. merge field
   d. record
2. A _____ is a file with information organized into fields and records.
3. True or False. In the Mail Merge task pane, you can select a data source file that already contains names and addresses, or you can create a new data source and enter names and addresses into it.
4. True or False. You cannot use an Excel worksheet as a data source.
5. Explain how to insert a merge field into a main document.
6. Explain how to add a date field to a document.

Session 6.2

Editing a Data Source

After you complete a mail merge, you might find that you need to make some changes to the data source and redo the merge. You can edit a data source in two ways—from within the program used to create the data source in the first place, or via the Mail Merge Recipients dialog box in Word. If you are familiar with the program used to create the data source, it's often simplest to edit the file from within that program. For example, if you were using an Excel worksheet as your data source, you could open the file in Excel, edit it (perhaps by adding new records), save it, and then reselect the file as your data source. To edit a Microsoft Office Address Lists file from within Word, you can use the Mail Merge Recipients dialog box.

Editing a Data Source in Word | Reference Window

- Open the main document for the data source you want to edit.
- In the Start Mail Merge group on the Mailings tab, click the Edit Recipient List button.
- In the Data Source list box in the Mail Merge Recipients dialog box, select the data source you want to edit, and then click the Edit button.
- To add a record, click the New Entry button, and then type a new record.
- To delete a record, click any field in the record, and then click the Delete Entry button.
- To add or remove fields from the data source, click the Customize Columns button, make any changes, and then click the OK button. Remember that if you remove a field, you will delete any data entered into that field.

In the following steps, you will reopen the main document, which you closed at the end of the last session.

After you complete a mail merge, a connection exists between the main document file and the data source file, even after you close the main document and exit Word. You can be certain the connection is maintained as long as you keep both files in their original locations. The two files don't have to be in the same folder; each file just has to remain in the folder it was in when you first created the connection between the two files.

What happens if you move one of the files to a different folder? That depends on how your computer is set up and where you move the files. On most Windows Vista computers, you can't move the *data source* file on its own, but if you move the *main document* file to another location on the same computer, the connection is usually maintained. However, if you move the document to another computer on a network, or to a different storage media (say from the hard drive to a memory stick), the connection might be broken. In that case, when you open the main document, you'll see a series of message boxes informing you that the connection to the data source has been broken. Eventually, you will see a Microsoft Word dialog box with a button labeled Find Data Source, which you can click, and then use the Select Data Source dialog box to select your data source.

To avoid difficulties with locating a data source, it's a good idea to either store the data source in the default My Data Sources folder and keep it there, or store the data source and the main document in the same folder (a folder other than the My Data Sources folder) and keep them there. The latter option is best if you think you might need to move the files to a different computer. That way, if you do need to move them, you can move the entire folder.

To add records to Nina's data source:

1. Open the document named **Yoga Letter with Merge Fields** from the Tutorial.06\Tutorial folder. You see a warning message indicating that opening the document will run an SQL command. SQL is the database programming language that controls the connection between the main document and the data source.

2. Click **Yes** to continue, and then click the **Mailings** tab. The main document still displays the data for the last record you displayed in the document when you previewed the merged document (probably Anna Pearson). As you'll see in the next step, you can alternate between displaying the merge fields and the client data by toggling the Preview Results button on the Mailings tab.

   Trouble? If you see data for a client other than Anna Pearson, don't be concerned. Simply proceed to Step 3.

   Trouble? If you see the merge fields instead of the data for one of the yoga clients, read but do not perform Step 3, and then proceed to Step 4.

3. In the Preview Results group, click the **Preview Results** button to deselect it. The merge fields are displayed in the main document.

   Trouble? If you see the data for one of the clients instead of the merge fields, click the Preview Results button again to deselect it.

4. If necessary, highlight the merge fields by clicking the **Highlight Merge Fields** button in the Write & Insert Fields group.

5. In the Start Mail Merge group, click the **Edit Recipient List** button. The Mail Merge Recipients dialog box opens. You saw this dialog box earlier, when you first selected the data source to use for the mail merge. The Data Source list box in the lower-left corner allows you to select a data source to edit. If you had multiple data sources stored in the Tutorial.06\Tutorial folder, you would see them all in this list box.

▶ **6.** In the Data Source list box, in the lower-left corner of the Mail Merge Recipients dialog box, click **Yoga Data.mdb**. The filename is selected.

▶ **7.** Click the **Edit** button. The Edit Data Source dialog box opens. Note that this dialog box looks similar to the New Address List dialog box, which you used earlier when you first entered information into the data source.

▶ **8.** Use the New Entry button to enter the information shown in Figure 6-24 into the data source. When you are finished, you should have added three new records, for a total of six.

New data ◄ Figure 6-24

First Name	Last Name	Street Address	City	Zip Code	Favorite Type	Favorite Teacher
Hannah	Blackmore	2054 First Avenue	Boise	83709	Hatha	Niki Dronza
Antonio	Morelos	55 Moraine Road	Eagle	83707	Hatha	Niki Dronza
Clara	Beck	34 Vilas Street	Boise	83710	Power Yoga	Carolyn Brown

After you finish entering the data for Clara Beck, review your work and make any necessary corrections.

▶ **9.** Click the **OK** button. When you are asked if you want to update the Yoga Data.mdb file, click the **Yes** button. You return to the Mail Merge Recipients dialog box, as shown in Figure 6-25. If your records look different from those in Figure 6-25, select the data source, click the Edit button, edit the data source, and then click the OK button.

New records added to data source ◄ Figure 6-25

You'll leave the Mail Merge Recipients dialog box open so you can use it to make other changes to the data source.

Sorting Records

As Nina looks through the letters to her clients in the merged document, she notices one problem—the letters are not grouped by zip codes. Currently, the letters are in the order in which clients were added to the data source file. She plans to use bulk mailing rates to send her letters, and the U.S. Postal Service requires bulk mailings to be separated into groups according to zip code. She asks you to sort the data file by zip code and perform another merge, this time merging the main document with the sorted data source.

You can sort information in a data source table just as you sort information in any other table. Recall that to **sort** means to rearrange a list or a document in alphabetical, numerical, or chronological order. You can sort information in ascending order (A to Z, lowest to highest, or earliest to latest) or in descending order (Z to A, highest to lowest, or latest to earliest) by clicking a column heading in the Mail Merge Recipients dialog box. The first time you click the heading, the records are sorted in ascending order. If you click it twice, the records are sorted in descending order.

Reference Window | **Sorting a Data Source**

- In the Start Mail Merge group on the Mailings tab, click the Edit Recipient List button to display the Mail Merge Recipients dialog box.
- To sort data in ascending order, click the heading for the column you want to sort. For example, if you want to arrange the records alphabetically according to the contents of the First Name column, click the First Name column heading.
- To sort data in descending order, click the column heading a second time.

Currently, the records in the data source are listed in the order you entered them, with the information for Anna Pearson at the top. You'll sort the records in ascending order, based on the contents of the ZIP Code column.

To sort the data source by zip code:

▶ **1.** Verify that the Mail Merge Recipients dialog box is still open.

▶ **2.** Scroll right, if necessary, to display the entire ZIP code column.

▶ **3.** Click the **ZIP Code** column heading. Word sorts the rows of the data table from lowest zip code number to highest. The information for Antonio Morelos is now at the top of the list. See Figure 6-26. When you merge the data source with the form letter, the letters will appear in the merged document in this order.

Records sorted in ascending order by ZIP code ◄ **Figure 6-26**

4. Click the **OK** button. The Mail Merge Recipients dialog box closes.

5. In the Finish group, click the **Finish & Merge** button, click **Edit Individual Documents**, verify that the **All** option button is selected in the Merge to New Document dialog box, and then click the **OK** button. Word generates the new merged document with six letters, one letter per page as before—but this time the first letter is to Antonio Morelos, who has the lowest zip code (83707).

6. Use the Select Browse Object button 🔘 to browse by page and verify that the letters in the newly merged document are arranged in ascending order by zip code. Nina will print the letters later. For now, you will close the document.

7. Save the new merged document in the Tutorial.06\Tutorial folder, using the filename **Yoga Merged Letters 2**, and then close it. You return to the main document.

As Nina requested, you've created a merged document with the letters to her clients sorted by zip code. Now she would like you to create a set of letters to just those clients who attend power yoga classes.

Selecting Records to Merge

Nina wants to inform students of Carolyn Brown that she is available for individual instruction only on Tuesdays and Thursdays. She asks you to modify the form letter slightly and then merge it with only those records of clients who have indicated that Carolyn is their favorite teacher. To select specific records in a data source, you use the Mail Merge Recipients dialog box.

To select specific records for a merge:

1. Make sure the document named Yoga Letter with Merge Fields is displayed in the document window.

▶ **2.** Click at the end of the third main paragraph, which begins "Please check out our schedule online...."

▶ **3.** Press the ← key to move the insertion point to the left of the period, insert a space, and type **on Tuesdays and Thursdays** and then verify that the sentence reads "...is available for individual instruction on Tuesdays and Thursdays."

▶ **4.** Save the document as **Carolyn Letter with Merge Fields** in the Tutorial.06\Tutorial folder.

▶ **5.** Click the **Edit Recipient List** button in the Start Mail Merge group. The Mail Merge Recipients dialog box opens. To remove an individual record from a merge, you can deselect its check box. You want to include only the records for John Andrews and Clara Beck in this merge, because they are the only clients who listed Carolyn Brown as their favorite teacher.

▶ **6.** Click the **check box** next to the first record (for Antonio Morelos). The check mark is removed.

▶ **7.** Remove the check marks for all the records *except* for the John Andrews and Clara Beck records. See Figure 6-27. Now that you have selected only the records you want, you can complete the merge.

Figure 6-27 ▶ **Specific records selected in data source**

▶ **8.** Click the **OK** button. The Mail Merge Recipients dialog box closes.

▶ **9.** In the Finish group, click the **Finish & Merge** button, click **Edit Individual Documents**, in the Merge to New Document dialog box verify that the **All** option button is selected, and then click the **OK** button. Word generates the new merged document with two letters, one letter per page. This time the first letter is to John Andrews.

▶ **10.** Scroll through the letters in the new merged document to see that they are both addressed to clients who listed Carolyn Brown as their favorite teacher.

▶ **11.** Save the new merged document in the Tutorial.06\Tutorial folder using the file-name **Yoga Merged Letters 3**, close it, save your changes to the document named **Carolyn Letter with Merge Fields**, and then close it.

Next, you'll create and print mailing labels for the form letter so Nina doesn't have to address the letters by hand.

Creating Mailing Labels

Now that you've created and printed the personalized letters, Nina is ready to prepare envelopes in which to mail the letters. She could print the names and addresses directly on envelopes, or she could create mailing labels to stick on the envelopes. The latter method is easier because she can print 14 labels at once, rather than printing one envelope at a time.

Nina has purchased Avery® Laser Printer labels, which are available in most office-supply stores. Word supports most of the Avery label formats, allowing you to choose the layout that works best for you. The labels Nina has come in 8½ × 11-inch sheets designed to feed through a laser printer. Each label measures 4 × 1.33 inches. There are seven rows of labels per sheet, with two labels in each row, for a total of 14 labels. See Figure 6-28.

Layout of a sheet of Avery® labels ◀ **Figure 6-28**

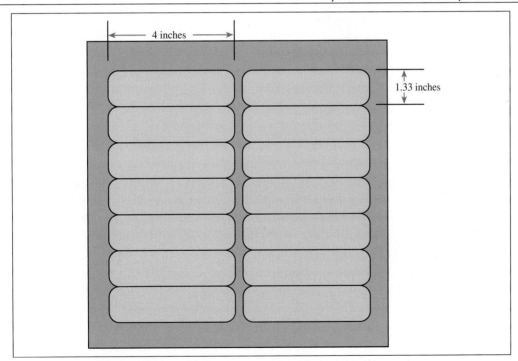

Creating mailing labels is similar to creating form letters, and the Mail Merge task pane walks you through all six steps. You'll begin creating the mailing labels by opening a blank document and the Mail Merge task pane. You can use the same data source file (Yoga Data.mdb) that you used earlier.

To specify the main document for creating mailing labels:

▶ **1.** Open a new, blank document, make sure nonprinting characters are displayed, and zoom out so you can see the whole page.

▶ **2.** Click the **Mailings** tab, and then open the Mail Merge task pane.

▶ **3.** In the Mail Merge task pane, click the **Labels** option button, and then click **Next: Starting document**. The Mail Merge task pane displays information and options for setting up the document layout for labels. (*Note:* If Nina wanted you to print envelopes instead of mailing labels, you would have selected Envelopes as the type of main document.)

▶ **4.** Under "Select starting document," verify that the **Change document layout** option button is selected, and then, under "Change document layout," click **Label options**. The Label Options dialog box opens.

▶ **5.** Click the **Label vendors** arrow, and then click **Avery US Letter**.

▶ **6.** Scroll down the Product number list box, and then click **5162**. This number is found on the packages of most labels that you buy at office supply stores. Your Label Options dialog box should look like Figure 6-29.

Figure 6-29	Label Options dialog box

▶ **7.** Click the **OK** button. The Label Options dialog box closes. Word inserts a table structure into the document, with one cell for each of the 14 labels on the page. You might not be able to see the table structure if the table gridlines are not displayed.

▶ **8.** If you don't see the table structure, click the **Table Tools Layout** tab, and then, in the Table group, click the **View Gridlines** button to select it. You can now see that the document is divided into label-sized rectangles, as shown in Figure 6-30. The gridlines are visible only on the screen; they will not be visible on the printed labels.

Document ready for labels ◀ **Figure 6-30**

You are finished setting up the document. Next, you need to save the main document and select the data source you created earlier.

To continue the mail merge for the labels:

▶ 1. Save the main document to the Tutorial.06\Tutorial folder using the filename **Yoga Labels with Merge Fields**.

▶ 2. Click **Next: Select recipients**. Under "Select recipients," verify that the **Use an existing list** option button is selected, and then, under "Use an existing list," click **Browse**. The Select Data Source dialog box opens.

▶ 3. Navigate to and select the file named **Yoga Data** in the Tutorial.06\Tutorial folder, and then click the **Open** button. The Mail Merge Recipients dialog box opens.

▶ 4. Verify that all the records are displayed with all check boxes selected, and then click the **OK** button. The Mail Merge Recipients dialog box closes. A special code (<<Next Record>>) is inserted into all the labels except the one in the upper-left corner. To see the <<Next Record>> code, you need to adjust the Zoom setting.

▶ 5. Zoom in so you can read the document. The <<Next Record>> code is a special code that tells Word how to insert data into the document. You can ignore it.

▶ 6. Click **Next: Arrange your labels**. The Mail Merge task pane displays options for inserting merge fields into the document. Note that if the data source included a State field, you could use the Address block option to insert a complete set of fields for a single address. However, because the data source does not include a State field, you need to insert the fields individually, as you did when creating the form letter.

> **7.** Verify that the insertion point is located in the upper-left label, and then, in the Write & Insert Fields group on the Mailings tab, click the **Insert Merge Field** button arrow.

> **8.** Click **First_Name**, and then in the Write & Insert Fields group, click the **Highlight Merge Fields** button. The First_Name merge field is inserted in the document and displayed on a gray background.

> **9.** Press the **spacebar** to add a space after the First Name field, insert the **Last_Name** field, press the **Enter** key, insert the **Address_Line_1** field, press the **Enter** key, insert the **City** field, type **,** (a comma), press the **spacebar** to insert a space, type **ID**, press the **spacebar**, and then insert the **ZIP_Code** field. You are finished inserting the fields for the first label. Now you will update your labels so the merge fields appear on all the labels.

> **10.** Near the bottom of the Mail Merge task pane, click the **Update all labels** button. (You might have to scroll down to see it; use the scroll button at the bottom of the task pane.) The address fields are inserted into all the labels in the document, as shown in Figure 6-31. In all except the upper-left label, the Next Record code appears to the left of the First Name merge field.

Figure 6-31	Field codes inserted into document

You are ready to preview the labels and complete the merge.

To preview the labels and complete the merge:

> **1.** Click **Next: Preview your labels** in the Mail Merge task pane. (You might have to scroll down to display this option, again using the scroll button at the bottom of the task pane.) The data for the clients is displayed in the labels. For now, ignore the extra ", ID" in labels that would otherwise be blank. You are ready to merge to a new document.

▶ **2.** Click **Next: Complete the merge** in the task pane, click **Edit individual labels** in the task pane, verify that the **All** option button is selected in the Merge to New Document dialog box, and then click the **OK** button. The finished labels are displayed in a new document.

The labels are almost finished. All you need to do is edit the document to remove the "ID" text from the unused labels, save the document, and print the labels. For now, you'll just print the labels on an 8½ × 11-inch sheet of paper so you can see what they look like. Later, Nina will print them on the sheet of labels.

To edit, save, and print the labels:

▶ **1.** Scroll through the document. The document contains space for 14 labels, but the data source contained only six records. However, when you clicked the Update Labels button in the task pane earlier, the comma and the state abbreviation (ID) were copied to all the labels, including those that don't contain any address information. See Figure 6-32, where the document is zoomed to show the whole page, so you can see all the labels. You can solve this problem with the extra text by deleting the extra text in the bottom four rows of labels.

Extra text in labels document | **Figure 6-32**

labels that would otherwise be blank have a comma and state abbreviation

▶ **2.** Change the Zoom setting to **Whole Page**, drag the mouse pointer to select the bottom four rows of labels, and then press the **Delete** key. The extra text is deleted.

▶ **3.** In the upper-left label, change "Anna Pearson" to your name, and then save the merged document in the Tutorial.06\Tutorial folder using the filename **Yoga Merged Labels**.

▶ **4.** Print the labels on a sheet of paper, just as you would print any other document.

   Trouble? If you want to print on a sheet of labels, ask your instructor or technical support person how to feed the label sheet into the printer. If you're using a shared printer, you might need to make special arrangements so other users' documents aren't accidentally printed on your label sheet.

▶ **5.** Close the merged document, and then close the task pane if necessary.

▶ **6.** Save changes to the main document, and then close it.

| InSight | | **Printing Labels** |

Labels are expensive, so it's extra important to take care in completing the merge to avoid wasting label sheets. When you create labels, keep these tips in mind:

- It's a good idea to print one page of a label document on regular paper so you can check your work before printing on the more expensive sheets of adhesive labels.
- Always check the few rows of a labels document for extra text, just as you did with the Yoga studio labels.
- If you include a State field in your data source, you can avoid the problem with extra text in unused labels by inserting an Address Block merge field instead of individual merge fields mixed with regular text.

Creating a Telephone Directory

Next, Nina wants you to create a list of telephone numbers for all the teachers at Lily Road Yoga Studio. Nina has already created a Word document containing the phone numbers; you will use that document as the data source for the merge. You'll set up a mail merge as before, except this time you'll select Directory as the main document type. You'll start by examining the Word document that Nina wants you to use as the data source.

To begin creating the telephone list:

▶ **1.** Open the document named **Phone** from the Tutorial.06\Tutorial folder, and then save it as **Phone Data** in the same folder.

▶ **2.** Review the document. Note that the information is arranged in a table with three column headings: "First Name," "Last Name," and "Phone." The information in the table has already been sorted in alphabetical order by last name.

▶ **3.** In the bottom row, replace "Nina Ranabhat" with your name.

▶ **4.** Save and close the Phone Data document, open a new, blank document, display nonprinting characters, if necessary, and display the rulers.

▶ **5.** Open the Mail Merge task pane, and then zoom out if necessary so you can see the 6-inch mark on the ruler.

▶ **6.** In the Mail Merge task pane under "Select document type," click the **Directory** option button, click **Next: Starting document**, verify that the **Use the current document** option button is selected, click **Next: Select recipients**, verify that the **Use an existing list** option button is selected, and then click **Browse**. The Select Data Source dialog box opens.

7. Navigate to and select the file named **Phone Data** in the Tutorial.06\Tutorial folder as the data source, click the **Open** button, review the records in the Mail Merge Recipients dialog box, and then click the **OK** button.

8. In the task pane, click **Next: Arrange your directory**. The document is still blank; you'll insert the merge fields next.

You're ready to insert the fields in the main document. Nina wants the telephone list to include the names at the left margin of the page and the phone number at the right margin. You'll set up the main document so that the phone number is preceded by a dot leader. A **dot leader** is a dotted line that extends from the last letter of text on the left margin to the beginning of the nearest text aligned at a tab stop.

To create the main document with dot leaders:

1. With the insertion point at the top of the blank document, insert the **First_Name** merge field, insert a space, insert the **Last_Name** merge field, and then in the Write & Insert Fields group, click the **Highlight Merge Fields** button. The First Name and Last Name merge fields are displayed on a gray background. Now you'll set a tab stop at the right margin (at the 6-inch mark on the ruler) with a dot leader.

2. Click the **Page Layout** tab, then in the Paragraph group, click the **Dialog Box Launcher** to open the Paragraph dialog box, and then in the lower-left corner of the Paragraph dialog box, click the **Tabs** button. The Tabs dialog box opens.

3. Type **6** in the Tab stop position text box, then in the Alignment section, click the **Right** option button, and then in the Leader section, click the **2 ....** option button. See Figure 6-33. While the Tabs dialog box is open, notice the Clear All button, which you could click to delete all the current tab stops.

| | Creating a tab with a dot leader | Figure 6-33 |

set tab stop at 6-inch mark on ruler

set alignment to Right

select this type of leader

4. Click the **OK** button. Word clears the current tab stops and inserts a right-aligned tab stop at the 6-inch mark on the horizontal ruler.

5. Press the **Tab** key to move the insertion point to the new tab stop. A dotted line stretches across the page, from the Last Name field to the right margin.

6. Switch back to the Mailings tab, and then insert the **Phone** merge field at the location of the insertion point.

▶ **7.** Press the **Enter** key. You must insert a hard return here so that each name and telephone number will appear on a separate line. Notice that the dot leader shortened to accommodate the inserted field. The completed main document should look like Figure 6-34.

Figure 6-34 ▶ Completed main document for telephone directory

▶ **8.** Save the main document in the Tutorial.06\Tutorial folder using the filename **Phone Directory with Merge Fields**.

You are now ready to merge this file with Nina's data source.

To merge the files for the phone list:

▶ **1.** In the Mail Merge task pane, click **Next: Preview your directory**, and then review the data for the first record in the document.

▶ **2.** Click **Next: Complete the merge** in the task pane, click **To New Document** in the task pane, verify that the **All** option button is selected in the Merge to New Document dialog box, and then click the **OK** button. Word creates a new document that contains the completed telephone list. See Figure 6-35.

Figure 6-35 ▶ Completed telephone directory

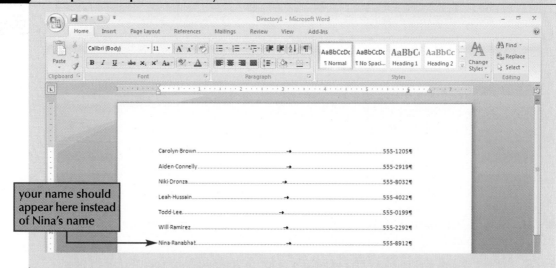

▶ **3.** Save the document as **Phone Directory** in the Tutorial.06\Tutorial folder, and then close it.

▶ **4.** Save and close the **Phone Directory with Merge Fields** document.

You have created the telephone list. Nina will print it and distribute it to each of the teachers. Now that you are familiar with the many types of documents you can create using Word's Mail Merge feature, you can use mail merge whenever you need to distribute customized information to a group of people.

Converting Text to Tables and Tables to Text

Nina needs your help with a few other tasks related to managing information about the teachers and clients at Lily Road Yoga Studio. First, she needs to convert names and addresses of new clients, which her assistant typed for her, into a table. She will then use the table later as the data source in a mail merge.

Before you can convert text into a table, you need to verify that the information in the document is set up properly. That is, you need to make sure that **separator characters**—typically commas or tabs—are used consistently to divide the text into individual pieces of data. Upon conversion, each data item is formatted as a separate cell in a column, and each paragraph mark starts a new row.

To convert text into a table:

▶ **1.** Open the document named **Client** from the Tutorial.06\Tutorial folder, and then save it as **Client Table** in the same folder. Display nonprinting characters, if necessary.

▶ **2.** Review the document. Notice that it consists of three paragraphs. Each paragraph contains seven separate pieces of information (first name, last name, address, city, zip code, favorite type of yoga, and favorite teacher) separated by commas.

▶ **3.** Drag the mouse to select the three paragraphs, click the **Insert** tab, click the **Table** button, and then, at the bottom of the Table menu, click **Convert Text to Table**. The Convert Text to Table dialog box opens. See Figure 6-36. Because the information in each paragraph is separated by commas, the Commas option button at the bottom of the dialog box is selected. Note that the Number of columns setting is 7. This corresponds to the seven pieces of information in each paragraph.

Converting text to a table ◀ **Figure 6-36**

► **4.** Click the **OK** button. The Convert Text to Table dialog box closes, and the text in the document is converted into a table consisting of seven columns and three rows. Next, you need to add the column headings.

► **5.** Click in the left margin to select the top row of the table, click the **Table Tools Layout** tab, and then in the Rows & Columns group, click the **Insert Above** button. A blank row is added at the top of the table.

► **6.** Enter the following column headings: **First Name**, **Last Name**, **Street Address**, **City**, **ZIP Code**, **Favorite Type**, and **Favorite Teacher**. Format the column headings in bold. When you are finished, your table should look like the one in Figure 6-37.

Figure 6-37 ▶ Text changed to table

► **7.** Save the document, and then close it. Nina will use the Client Table in another mail merge she has planned for next month, and eventually she'll combine it with her current list of clients.

You have finished converting text into a table. Now, Nina needs your help doing the opposite—that is, converting a table into text. After the conversion, she will use the text to create a list of yoga teachers for the studio.

To convert a table into text:

► **1.** Open the document named **Phone Data** from the Tutorial.06\Tutorial folder, and then save it as **Teacher List** in the same folder. Display nonprinting characters, if necessary. You want to include only the names of Nina's teachers, so you will start by deleting the header row and the Phone column.

▶ **2.** Click in the left margin to select the header row, click the **Table Tools Layout** tab, then in the Rows & Columns group, click the **Delete** button, and then click **Delete Rows**.

▶ **3.** Select the column containing the phone numbers, and then use the Delete button in the Rows & Columns group to delete the column. The table now contains only the first and last name of each yoga teacher. You are ready to convert this table into text.

▶ **4.** Select the entire table, verify that the Table Tools Layout tab is displayed, and then in the Data group, click **Convert to Text**. The Convert to Text dialog box opens.

▶ **5.** Click the **Other** option button. In the text box next to this option button, you can specify how you want to divide the information in each row. In this case, you want to separate the first and last names by a space.

▶ **6.** In the text box next to the Other option button, delete the hyphen, verify that the insertion point is at the far-left edge of the text box, and then press the **spacebar** to insert a space. See Figure 6-38.

Converting a table to text ◀ Figure 6-38

▶ **7.** Click the **OK** button. The Convert Table to Text dialog box closes. The contents of the table are now formatted as seven separate paragraphs, one for each row in the table. Each first name is separated from its corresponding last name by a space.

You now have seven paragraphs, each containing the name of a teacher at Lily Road Yoga studio. In the next section, you will use Word's list features to manipulate these paragraphs, creating a useful list for Nina.

Working with Lists

Nina often has to respond to calls from potential clients asking about teachers at the yoga studio. To make her job easier, Nina wants to create a quick reference list with information about each teacher, such as what they teach and how strenuous their classes are. She wants you to format the names of the yoga teachers as a list, alphabetize it, and then add more information.

To convert the text to a list and sort it:

▶ **1.** If necessary, select the seven paragraphs containing the names of the yoga teachers, and then format the selected text as a bulleted list using the default bullet style.

▶ **2.** Select the bulleted list, and then, in the Paragraph group, click the **Sort** button ![Sort icon]. The Sort Text dialog box opens. This is similar to the dialog box you've already used several times before to sort tables. You want to sort the paragraphs in the list in ascending alphabetical order.

▶ **3.** Verify that **Paragraphs** appears in the Sort by text box and that the **Ascending** option button is selected, and then click the **OK** button. The Sort Text dialog box closes, and the bulleted paragraphs are arranged alphabetically. The list begins with Aiden Connelly, unless your name comes alphabetically before "Aiden," in which case your name appears at the top of the list.

▶ **4.** Save the document.

Now that the list is sorted, you need to add some more information about each teacher. When working with a bulleted or numbered list, you can indent items in the list. When you do, Word automatically applies a different bullet or numbering style to the indented item, to help create a visual distinction between the various levels of the list. Indenting an item in a numbered or bulleted list is known as **demoting** the item. Moving an item in a list back to the left is known as **promoting** the item. You'll see how this works in the following steps.

To add information to the list:

▶ **1.** Click to the right of Aiden Connelly's name, and then press the **Enter** key to insert a new bulleted paragraph. The round, black bullet looks just like the other bullets in the list.

▶ **2.** In the Paragraph group on the Home tab, click the **Increase Indent** button 𝄖. The bulleted paragraph is indented, and the bullet changes to a white bullet with a black outline.

▶ **3.** Type **Specialties include Flow Yoga and Pilates**, and then press the **Enter** key to insert another bulleted paragraph. The new paragraph is indented at the same level as the previous paragraph, with the same style of bullet.

▶ **4.** Click 𝄖. The bulleted paragraph is indented even more. The bullet changes to a black square.

▶ **5.** Type **Flow Yoga is not recommended for beginners**, press the **Enter** key, and then type **Pilates requires four hours of individual instruction**.

▶ **6.** Press the **Enter** key to insert a new bulleted paragraph, click the **Decrease Indent** button 𝄖 in the Paragraph group to promote the new bulleted paragraph, and then type **His classes are generally considered very challenging**. When you are finished, your bulleted list should look like the list in Figure 6-39. Nina's assistant will finish adding information to the bulleted list later. For now, you can save and close it.

Figure 6-39 ▶ **Bulleted list with multiple levels**

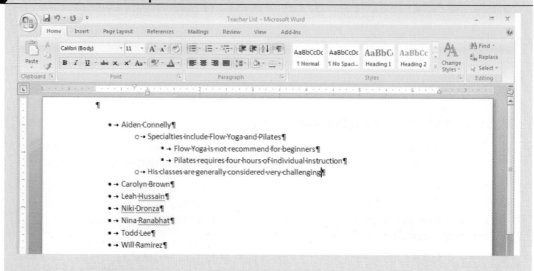

▶ **7.** Save the document and close it.

Session 6.2 Quick Check | Review

1. True or False: After you complete a mail merge and close the main document, the connection between the main document file and the data source file is broken.
2. Explain how to edit a data source for a main document that is already open.
3. Explain how to select records to merge.
4. When you create a directory with a dot leader, what do you have to do after you insert the merge field on the right side of the page?
5. True or False. You can convert data in a document to a table only if the individual pieces of data are separated by tabs.

Tutorial Summary | Review

In this tutorial, you opened the Mail Merge task pane and then completed a mail merge by selecting a main document, creating a data source, inserting merge fields into the main document, and merging the form letter with the data source. You then used the Mail Merge feature to create mailing labels and a telephone directory. In the process, you edited a data source and sorted records in a data source. Finally, you converted text to a table to create a new data source, and you converted a table to text, which you then formatted as a bulleted list with multiple levels.

Key Terms

chevrons	fields	merged document
data	form letter	promote
data source	Mail Merge task pane	record
date field	main document	sort
demote	merge	separator character
dot leader	merge fields	

Practice	**Review Assignments**

Apply the skills you learned in the tutorial using the same case scenario.

Data Files needed for the Review Assignments: Bonus.docx, Contacts.docx, More.docx

Nina's clients are happy with the new facility, and the open-studio days she offered in June were a big success. Nina was pleased with how convenient it was to send out form letters with the Word Mail Merge feature. Now she wants to send a letter inviting clients who have purchased an annual membership to sign up for their membership bonus—either a massage or a meditation session, depending on which option they selected when they purchased their membership. (*Note:* As you complete the following steps, print only those documents your instructor asks you to print.)

1. Start Word if necessary with a new, blank document, and then open the Mail Merge task pane.
2. Verify that Letters is selected as the type of main document, then in Step 2 of the Mail Merge Task pane, select the file **Bonus** in the Tutorial.06\Review folder included with your Data Files as the main document, and then save the current document as **Bonus Letter with Merge Fields** in the Tutorial.06\Review folder. In the letter's closing, replace Nina's name with yours.
3. In Step 3 of the Mail Merge task pane, create a new data source with the following fields: First Name, Last Name, Address Line 1, City, State, ZIP Code, and Bonus. Remove any extra fields so that the data source contains only seven fields.
4. Create four records using the following information (don't include the commas in the records; they are inserted here to help you see which text belongs in which fields):
   - Jane Cussler, 299 Hollister Street, Boise, ID, 83710, massage
   - May Simon, 922 Flambeau Road, Cloverdale, ID, 83712, meditation session
   - Carl Hesse, 933 Wildway Avenue, Beatty, ID, 83722, massage
   - William Greely, 52 Eton Way # 3, Boise, ID, 83714, meditation session
5. Save the data source as **Bonus Data** in the Tutorial.06\Review folder.
6. Edit the data source to replace "William Greely" with your first and last name.
7. Sort the data source by zip code from the lowest to the highest.
8. In Step 4 of the Mail Merge task pane, insert a date field in the format "March 7, 2010" at the top of the letter. Create an inside address consisting of the necessary merge fields; don't forget to use the Shift+Enter keys to prevent extra paragraph spacing. Add a salutation that includes the First Name merge field. Insert the Bonus field into the body of the letter where indicated. Add the appropriate number of blank paragraphs so the letter is formatted like a standard business letter. Insert blank paragraphs as necessary to center the letter vertically on the page.
9. Save your changes to the main document, and then preview the merged document. Correct any formatting or spacing problems.

10. In Step 6 of the Mail Merge task pane, merge to a new document and view all the letters. Save the merged document as **Merged Bonus Letters**, scroll to view the letters, and then close the file.

11. Return to Step 5 in the Mail Merge task pane, edit the data source to select only records for clients interested in a meditation session, and then complete a second merge. Save the new merged document as **Merged Meditation Letters**. Close all documents, saving all changes.

12. Open a new, blank document, open the Mail Merge task pane, and create a set of mailing labels using the vendor Avery US Letters and product number 5162. Save the main document as **Labels with Merge Fields** in the Tutorial.06\Review folder.

13. In Step 3 of the Mail Merge task pane, select the Bonus Data file you created earlier as the data source.

14. In Step 4 of the Mail Merge task pane, insert the necessary merge fields.

15. Update all the labels, preview the merged labels, merge all the records to a new document, and then save the new document as **Merged Labels** in the Tutorial.06\Review folder and close it. Save and close all open documents.

16. Create a telephone directory using the same format as the telephone directory you created in the tutorial. Use the file named **Contacts** from the Tutorial.06\Review folder as the data source. Set a right tab at six inches and use a dot leader. Save the main document as **Directory with Merge Fields** in the Tutorial.06\Review folder and the merged document as **Merged Directory** in the same folder. Close the files.

17. Open the document named **More** from the Tutorial.06\Review folder and save it as **More Bonus Data**. Convert the data in the document to a table. Insert a header row with the following column headers: First Name, Last Name, Street Address, City, State, ZIP Code, and Bonus. Replace "Sandy Martinez" with your name. Save and close the document.

18. Open the document named **Contacts** from the Tutorial.06\Review folder and save it as **Contacts Info** in the same folder. Delete the header row and the phone number column, and then convert the table to four paragraphs of text.

19. Format the company names as a bulleted list, and then add the extra information shown in Figure 6-40. Be sure to demote the subordinate bullets, as shown in Figure 6-40.

Figure 6-40

- Bright Day Window Cleaning
    - o Scheduled for the first Monday of every month
        - ▪ In summer, may have to switch to the first Tuesday of every month
        - ▪ Move the table away from the front window before cleaners arrive
    - o Paid by direct deposit
- Franklin Security
    - o Tom Smith manages our security
    - o Notify Tom if orange light blinks on alarm box
- Boise Federal Savings
    - o Deposits must be in by 5 P.M.
    - o Include a yellow deposit slip with every deposit
- Regent Property Management
    - o Sally Thomson manages our account
    - o Rent paid by direct deposit
        - ▪ Verify deposit on the 15th of every month
        - ▪ Call Sally to confirm if necessary

20. In the bullet under "Regent Property Management," change "Sally Thomson" to your name. Save and close the document.

21. Submit the documents to your instructor, either in printed or electronic form, as requested.

Apply | Case Problem 1

Apply the skills you learned to create a letter to customers of an art gallery.

Data File needed for this Case Problem: Gallery.docx

Nightingale Gallery Nell Williams owns Nightingale Gallery, a purveyor of fine art photography in Saginaw, Michigan. She wants to send out a letter to past customers informing them of an upcoming show by a local photographer. (*Note:* As you complete the following, print only those documents your instructor asks you to print.)

1. Open a new, blank document, and then begin a mail merge using Letters as the document type. For the starting document, select the document named **Gallery** from the Tutorial.06\Case1 folder, and then save it in the same folder as **Gallery Letter**. In the closing, replace "Student Name" with your name.

2. Create a data source with the following field names: Title, First Name, Last Name, Address Line1, ZIP Code, and E-mail Address.

3. Enter the following four records into the data source (don't include the commas in the records; they are inserted here to help you see what text belongs in what fields):
   - Mr., David, Joliet, 1577 Cooperville Drive, 48601, joliet@world.net
   - Mr., Paul, Robertson, 633 Wentworth, 48603, d_roberts@pmc.org
   - Ms., Maya, Suyemoto, 4424 Bedford, 48602, m_suyemoto@TaylorCulkins.com
   - Ms., Kira, Gascoyne, 844 Winter Way, 48601, gascoyne@saginaw.school.edu

4. Save the data source as **Gallery Data** in the Tutorial.06\Case1 folder, and then sort the records alphabetically by last name.

5. Edit the data source to replace "Kira Gascoyne" with your name. Change the title to "Mr." if necessary. Replace the e-mail address for that record with your e-mail address.

6. Add an inside address (use the Shift+Enter keys after each line) and a salutation to the document, using merge fields where necessary. Use "Saginaw, MI" as the city and state. Use the Title merge field and the Last Name merge field in the salutation.

7. Save your changes to the main document. Preview the merged document, and then merge to a new document. If you don't see the row of photographs at the top of the first letter, don't be concerned. You may not have a fast enough video card or enough memory to display them properly. After you close the document in the next step, and then re-open it, you will see the photographs on the first page.

8. Save the merged letters document as **Merged Gallery Letters** in the Tutorial.06\Case1 folder and then close it. If you did not see the photographs on the first page of the document in Step 7, re-open the document, verify that the photographs are properly displayed, and then close the document again.

9. Close the **Gallery Letter** document, saving any changes.

10. Open a new blank document, save it as **Gallery Envelopes** in the Tutorial.06\Case1 folder, and then open the Mail Merge task pane.

✪ EXPLORE
11. Use the Mail Merge task pane to create envelopes, as follows:
    - In Step 1 of the Mail Merge task pane, select Envelopes as the type of main document.
    - In Step 2 of the Mail Merge task pane, verify that the Change document layout option button is selected, and then click Envelope options. In the Envelope Options dialog box, verify that Envelope size 10 (4$\frac{1}{8}$ × 9$\frac{1}{2}$ in) is selected in the Envelope size box, and then click the OK button.
    - In Step 3 of the Mail Merge task pane, select the **Gallery Data** file you created earlier as the data source.
    - In Step 4 of the Mail Merge task pane, click the recipient address area of the envelope, and then insert the necessary merge fields to print a title, first name, last name, and street address and zip code on each envelope. For the city and state, use "Saginaw, MI."
    - In Step 5, preview the merged envelopes.
    - In Step 6, merge to a new document, and then save the document as **Merged Gallery Envelopes**.

12. Close all open documents, saving changes as necessary.

13. Create a customer e-mail directory that includes first and last names but not titles. Use the file named **Gallery Data** (which you created earlier) as the data source. Do not include the record for David Joliet in the merge. Use a dot leader, with the right tab stop set at the 6-inch mark, to separate the name on the left from the e-mail address on the right.

14. Save the main document for the e-mail directory as **E-mail Directory** in the Tutorial.06\Case1 folder.

15. Save the merged document as **Merged E-mail Directory** in the Tutorial.06\Case1 folder.

16. Save and close all open documents. Submit the documents to your instructor, in either printed or electronic form, as requested.

| Apply | **Case Problem 2** |

Apply the skills you learned to create a form letter for a mortgage company using an Excel file as a data source.

Data File needed for this Case Problem: Mortgage.docx, Mortgage Data.xlsx

Lensville Mortgage Corporation   As an account manager at Lensville Mortgage Corporation, you need to send out letters to past customers asking them to consider refinancing with a new loan. Your data source for this case problem is in an Excel file. (*Note:* As you work on this Case Problem, print only those documents your instructor asks you to print.)

1. Open a new, blank document, and begin a mail merge using Letters as the document type. For the starting document, select the document named **Mortgage** from the Tutorial.06\Case2 folder, and then save it in the same folder as **Mortgage Letter**. In the closing, replace "Student Name" with your name.

⊕ **EXPLORE**   2. For the data source, select the Excel file **Mortgage Data** from the Tutorial.06\Case2 folder.

3. Edit the data source to replace "Barb Russ" with your name.

4. At the beginning of the main document, insert a date field.

5. Insert an Address Block merge field for the inside address in the form "Joshua Randall Jr.," and format the Address block merge field using the No Spacing Quick Style. Insert a salutation using the First Name merge field. Use a proper business-letter format throughout.

6. In the body of the letter, replace the placeholders [NUMBER OF YEARS], [CURRENT LOAN TERM], and [NEW LOAN TERM] with the appropriate merge fields.

7. Open the Mail Merge Recipients dialog box, and then sort the records in ascending order by Current Loan Term.

8. Preview the merged document, and then merge to a new document. Save the merged document as **Merged Mortgage Letters** in the Tutorial.06\Case2 folder.

9. Close all open documents, saving all changes.

10. Create a main document for generating mailing labels on sheets of Avery US Letter Address labels, product number 5162, using the **Mortgage Data** file as your data source. Use the same Address Block merge field code that you used for the inside address of the Mortgage Letter file. Save the main document as **Mortgage Labels** in the Tutorial.06\Case2 folder.

11. Preview the merged document, merge to a new document, and then save the merged document as **Merged Mortgage Labels** in the Tutorial.06\Case2 folder. Close all open documents, saving any changes.

⊕ **EXPLORE**   12. Use Word Help to look up the topic "Use mail merge to create and print letters and other documents" and learn how to filter records in a data source. Open your **Mortgage Letter** file from the Tutorial.06\Case2 folder (click Yes if you are asked to run an SQL command), and save it as **Mortgage Letter Filtered**. Start a mail merge, and then select the **Mortgage Data** file as the data source. Use what you learned from Help to filter out all records except records for customers in Fort Myers. You should end up with two records displayed in the Mail Merge Recipients dialog box.

13. Preview the merged document, and then complete the merge to a new document. Save the merged document as **Merged Fort Myers** in the Tutorial.06\Case2 folder.

14. Close all open documents, saving any changes. Submit the documents to your instructor, in either printed or electronic form, as requested.

| Challenge | **Case Problem 3** |

Perform a mail merge using the Mailings tab instead of the Mail Merge task pane.

Data Files needed for this Case Problem: Letter.docx, Pasta.txt

Fierenze Pasta Kayla Souza is manager of Fierenze, a manufacturer of fresh pasta in Racine, Wisconsin. Fierenze has just bought out a competitor, JD Pasta. Now Kayla wants to send a letter to JD Pasta's longtime customers, who she hopes will become Fierenze customers. She wants to use Word's mail merge feature to create a letter that informs each customer of the price of his or her favorite type of pasta. Kayla retrieved the customer data from the JD Pasta's computer system in the form of a text file, with the data fields separated by commas. Kayla needs your help to convert the text file to a Word table, which she can then use as the data source for a mail merge. (*Note:* As you complete the following steps, print only those documents your instructor asks you to print.)

⊕ **EXPLORE**

1. In Word, open the text file named **Pasta.txt** from the Tutorial.06\Case3 folder. To find the text file in the Open dialog box, click the arrow next to the Files of type list box, and then click All Files. Once the file is open, save it as a Word document (in the Save As dialog box, click Word document in the Files of type list box) in the same folder using the filename **Pasta Data**.

2. Format the data in the Normal style, and then convert it to a table. Insert your first and last name where indicated. Insert a header row with the following column headers: First Name, Last Name, Street Address, City, State, ZIP Code, Type, and Price. Save the document and close it.

3. Open the file **Letter** from the Tutorial.06\Case3 folder, and then save it as **Pasta Letter** in the same folder. In the closing, replace "Student Name" with your first and last name.

⊕ **EXPLORE**

4. Begin a mail merge using the buttons on the Mailings tab instead of the Mail Merge task pane. Start by using the Start Mail Merge button to create a letter main document using the current document. As you perform the remaining steps in this case problem, continue to use the options on the Mailings tab rather than the Mail Merge task pane.

5. Use the Select Recipients button to select the **Pasta Data** document as the data source, and then use the Edit Recipient List button to sort the records in ascending alphabetical order by type of pasta.

6. Insert a date field where indicated by the brackets at the top of the document, and then use the Insert Merge Field button to replace the placeholder text that appears in brackets with an inside address.

⊕ **EXPLORE**

7. For the salutation, experiment with the Greeting Line button on the Mailings tab. Use the Greeting Line dialog box to insert a salutation that includes "Dear" and the customer's first name, followed by a colon.

8. Edit the body of the form letter to replace the placeholder text with the corresponding merge field names.

9. Save the document. Use the Preview Results button to view the merged document, and then use the Finish & Merge button to merge all the records to a new document. Save the merged document as **Merged Pasta Letters** in the Tutorial.06\Case3 folder.

10. Close all open documents, saving changes as necessary. Submit the documents to your instructor, in either printed or electronic form, as requested.

| Create | **Case Problem 4** |

Use the skills you learned in the tutorial to create the list shown in Figure 6-41.

There are no Data Files needed for this Case Problem.

Chronos Steel Corporation As a public relations specialist at Chronos Steel Corporation, you are often asked to explain the process of making steel to a general audience. To save time, you have decided to create a handout that summarizes the process. (*Note:* As you complete the following steps, print only those documents your instructor asks you to print.)

Figure 6-41

Steel Production

➢ Raw materials
   ○ Usually three components
      ▪ Iron ore
      ▪ Limestone
      ▪ Coke
         • Coke is a byproduct of coal
         • Created when coal is baked at a high temperature to purify it
   ○ Raw materials can vary by manufacturer
➢ Raw materials are heated in a blast furnace
➢ Slag floats to top and is drained, leaving molten iron suitable for steel
➢ Molten iron is transformed into steel
   ○ Molten iron is mixed with scrap metals
   ○ The iron and scrap metals are heated in an oxygen furnace
   ○ The resulting liquid steel is formed into slabs
➢ Slabs are milled to desired thickness and treated with acid

1. Open a new, blank document, save it as **Steel Handout** in the Tutorial.06\Case4 folder, and then change the document theme to Verve.
2. Type the multilevel bulleted list shown in Figure 6-41; don't specify the bullet type yet. Format the title, "Steel Production," in the Heading 1 style and center it.

⊕ EXPLORE
3. Click in the "Raw Materials" bulleted paragraph, and then select the arrow bullet style to change all the top-level bullets to the arrow style.

⊕ **EXPLORE** 4. In Word Help, look up *bullets* and then read the topic that explains how to add picture bullets or symbols to a list. Use what you learned to change the second-level bullets (the first of which is "Usually three components") from a white circle to an orange square. Then change the third-level bullets (the first of which is "Iron ore") to green squares and the lowest level bullets to brown squares.

5. Save your changes to the document, and then save it as **Numbered Handout** in the same folder so that you can change the bullets to numbering in the next step.

6. Select the bulleted list and use the Numbering button to format it as a numbered list instead. The multiple levels of the new numbered list are numbered in outline form.

7. Delete items 1.a and 1.b, but not the items under 1.a.

⊕ **EXPLORE** 8. Using the same technique you used to promote items in a bulleted list, promote the three paragraphs containing the three raw materials so they are lettered a, b, and c. Promote the two items about coke so they are numbered i and ii.

9. Save the document and close it. Submit the documents to your instructor, in either printed or electronic form, as requested.

Research | **Internet Assignments**

Go to the Web to find information you can use to create documents.

The purpose of the Internet Assignments is to challenge you to find information on the Internet that you can use to work effectively with this software. The actual assignments are updated and maintained on the Course Technology Web site. Log on to the Internet and use your Web browser to go to the Student Online Companion for New Perspectives Office 2007 at **www.course.com/np/office2007**. Then navigate to the Internet Assignments for this tutorial.

Assess | **SAM Assessment and Training**

If you have a SAM user profile, you may have access to hands-on instruction, practice, and assessment of the skills covered in this tutorial. Log in to your SAM account (**http://sam2007.course.com**) to launch any assigned training activities or exams that relate to the skills covered in this tutorial.

Session 6.1

1. a. A date field is an instruction that tells Word to insert the current date.
   b. A main document is a document (such as a letter) that, in addition to text, contains merge fields to mark where variable information (such as a name or an address) from the data source will be inserted.
   c. A merge field is a code in a main document that tells Word where to insert specific information from the data source.
   d. A record is a collection of information about one individual or object in a data source. For example, a record might include the first name, last name, address, and phone number for a client.
2. data source
3. True
4. False
5. Position the insertion point in the main document where you want to insert the merge field. Click More Items in the Mail Merge task pane, click the field you want to insert in the Insert Merge Field dialog box, click Insert, and then click Close. Alternately, in the Write & Insert Fields group on the Mailings tab, click the Insert Merge Field button, and then click the field you want to insert. Adjust the spacing or formatting around the merge field as necessary.
6. Click the Insert tab, and then, in the Text group, click the Date and Time button. In the Date and Time dialog box, click the date format you want, select the Update automatically check box, and then click the OK button.

Session 6.2

1. False
2. In the Start Mail Merge group on the Mailings tab, click the Edit Recipient List button. In the Data Source list box in the Mail Merge Recipients dialog box, select the data source you want to edit, and then click the Edit button. To add a record, click the New Entry button, and then type a new record. To delete a record, click any field in the record, and then click the Delete Entry button. To add or remove fields from the data source, click the Customize Columns button, and make any changes.
3. Click the Edit Recipients button in the Start Mail Merge group on the Mailings tab and then deselect the check boxes for the records you do not want to include in the merge.
4. Press the Enter key to insert a blank paragraph below the directory merge fields.
5. False

Ending Data Files

Tutorial.06 →

Tutorial
Carolyn Letter with
    Merge Fields.docx
Client Table.docx
Phone Data.docx
Phone Directory.docx
Phone Directory with
    Merge Fields.docx
Teacher List.docx
Yoga Data.mdb
Yoga Labels with
    Merge Fields.docx
Yoga Letter with
    Merge Fields.docx
Yoga Merged Labels.docx
Yoga Merged Letters 1.docx
Yoga Merged Letters 2.docx
Yoga Merged Letters 3.docx

Review
Bonus Data.mdb
Bonus Letter with
    Merge Fields.docx
Contacts.docx
Contacts Info.docx
Directory with
    Merge Fields.docx
Labels with
    Merge Fields.docx
Merged Bonus Letters.docx
Merged Directory.docx
Merged Labels.docx
Merged Meditation
    Letters.docx
More Bonus Data.docx

Case1
E-mail Directory.docx
Gallery Data.mdb
Gallery Envelopes.docx
Gallery Letter.docx
Merged E-mail Directory.docx
Merged Gallery Envelopes.docx
Merged Gallery Letters.docx

Case2
Merged Fort Myers.docx
Merged Mortgage Labels.docx
Merged Mortgage Letters.docx
Mortgage Data.xlsx
Mortgage Labels.docx
Mortgage Letter.docx
Mortgage Letter Filtered.docx

Case3
Merged Pasta Letters.docx
Pasta Data.docx
Pasta Letter.docx

Case4
Numbered Handout.docx
Steel Handout.docx

Objectives

Session 7.1
- Track changes in a document
- Insert and delete comments
- Accept and reject changes
- Compare and combine documents
- Embed and modify an Excel worksheet
- Link an Excel chart
- Modify and update a linked chart

Session 7.2
- Modify a document for online distribution
- Insert and edit hyperlinks
- Use Web Layout view
- Save a Word document as a Web page
- Format a Web document
- View a Web document in a Web browser

Collaborating with Others and Creating Web Pages

Writing a Program Description

Case | Green Fields Fresh Lunch Program

Zoe Rios is the owner and president of Rios Communications in Dubuque, Iowa, a public relations company that specializes in developing publicity documents and Web sites. She is currently working on a program description for Green Fields, an organization that is devoted to improving the quality of meals served in area schools.

As a professional writer, Zoe knows the importance of writing and revising several drafts of a document, and she knows it's vital to ask her clients and colleagues to review her documents and make suggestions. As a first step, she asked Henry Davis, a writer at Rios Communications, to review a draft of the program description. He will read the document in Word, make some corrections, and insert some comments. While Henry is revising the program description, Zoe has asked you to work on it, making additional changes. When you are finished, Zoe wants you to merge Henry's edited version of the document with your most recent draft.

After you create a new version of the document for Zoe, she wants you to add some budget figures compiled by Alison Jorgenson, the Program Director for the Green Fields organization. She also needs you to add a pie chart created by Henry. When you are finished, she wants you to e-mail the program description to Alison. Finally, to make the program description available to the organization's members, she asks for your help to distribute it in printed form and publish it on her company's Web site.

Starting Data Files

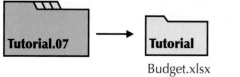

Tutorial.07 →	Tutorial	Review	Case1	Case2	Case3	Case4
	Budget.xlsx	Expenses.xlsx	Cook.docx	Kreelie.docx	Survey.xlsx	FAQ.docx
	Chart.xlsx	Menu.docx	Statement.xlsx	Sun.docx		
	Green.docx	Progress.docx				
	Green Fields HD.docx	Progress HD.docx				
	Resume.docx	Rates.xlsx				

Session 7.1

Tracking Changes and Making Comments in a Document

When you edit a printed copy of a document, it's common to use a brightly colored pen to draw lines through words or phrases you want to delete. You might write new text in the margin and then draw a line to the place in the document where you want to insert the text. You might also write notes to yourself or the writer in the margin, reminding you about facts you need to check or suggesting new sections for the writer to add. The problem with this revision method is that after you finish marking up the printed copy, you or the writer must go back to the computer and enter your changes into the document. In a long document, this can be very time-consuming. Instead of writing marks on a printed copy, it's more efficient to use Microsoft Word's Track Changes feature and the Comments feature.

Tracking Changes

When you turn on **Track Changes**, Word uses a variety of ways to mark the changes you make to the document. Any text that you insert appears in a contrasting color, with an underline. Text that you delete appears with a strikeout line, just as if you'd drawn a line through it on the printed page. If you make formatting changes, they are listed in the margin in oblong boxes known as **balloons**. In addition, a vertical line appears in the left margin next to text that has been changed in any way. Collectively, the colored text, the strikeout lines, the margin balloons, and the vertical margin lines are known as **revision marks**.

You can use the mouse to point to any marked revision in a document; this displays a ScreenTip that indicates who made the change and the date and time the change was made. By default, the name assigned to each change is taken from the User name text box on the Popular tab of the Word Options dialog box. This indication of who made a particular edit is especially useful when you are sharing revisions among a group of reviewers.

When you feel confident about the changes you or someone else has made to your document, you can accept the changes, at which point Word removes the revision marks from your document. You can accept all the changes at once, or you can go through them one by one, accepting or rejecting each one individually. When you reject a change, depending on what change you are rejecting, Word removes the text you inserted, or undoes the formatting you applied, or restores the text you deleted.

The Review tab contains all the options you need for working with track changes. Among other things, you can use the options on the Review tab to move from one change to another, to accept or reject changes, and to hide revision marks. When you hide revision marks, Word continues to track changes, but doesn't display them on the screen.

Reference Window	**Tracking Changes in a Document**

- Verify that the document is displayed in Print Layout view, click the Review tab, and then in the Tracking group, click the Track Changes button.
- Verify that Final Showing Markup is displayed in the Display for Review list box in the Tracking group.
- Edit the document as you ordinarily would. Adjust the document zoom as necessary, so you can easily see tracked changes in the document and in the margin.

Working with Comments

In addition to making changes to a document, you can also insert margin notes known as **comments**. You can attach a comment to a selected word, phrase, or paragraph. Text to which a comment has been attached is highlighted in a contrasting color so that you can easily see what the comment refers to. You type the text of your comment in a balloon that appears in the right margin. In addition to the text of your comment, the comment balloon displays the name of the person who made the comment, as well as the date and time it was made. As with tracked changes, the name assigned to each comment is taken from the User name text box on the Popular tab of the Word Options dialog box.

Although comments are often used in conjunction with the tracked changes, you don't have to turn on Track Changes in order to insert comments in a document. They are separate features. The Review tab contains all the options you need for working with Comments.

Inserting Comments | Reference Window

- Select the text to which you want to attach a comment.
- Click the Review tab, and then in the Comments group, click the New Comment button.
- Type the text of your comment in the balloon that appears in the margin.
- Adjust the document zoom as necessary so you can read the document text as well as the comment balloons in the margin.

Revising a Document with Tracked Changes and Comments

Zoe has already e-mailed a copy of her document to Henry. He will review it for her while she makes some additional changes. She decides to turn on Track Changes before she begins making these additional changes so she will have a record of the changes she makes after sending the file to Henry.

To edit Zoe's document with Track Changes turned on:

▶ **1.** Open the document named **Green** from the Tutorial.07\Tutorial folder included with your Data Files, and then save it as **Green Fields** in the same folder.

▶ **2.** Switch to Print Layout view if necessary, display nonprinting characters, and change the document zoom to Page width. There's no need to display the ruler.

▶ **3.** Review the document, and notice that it includes three headings formatted with the Heading 1 style for the Office theme. The first heading in the document is not formatted in a heading style; instead it is simply formatted in the heading font (Cambria) and in blue. Page 1 includes two placeholders in brackets, which you will eventually replace with an Excel chart and an Excel worksheet. Also notice the photograph on page 2.

▶ **4.** Click the **Review** tab, and then in the Tracking group, click the **Track Changes** button. (Do not click the Track Changes button arrow.) The Track Changes button is highlighted in orange, indicating that the Track Changes feature is turned on. You won't see any revision marks until you begin editing the document.

Trouble? If a menu appears below the Track Changes button, you clicked the Track Changes button arrow by mistake. Press the Escape key to close the menu, and then click the Track Changes button.

▶ **5.** In the Tracking group, verify that Final Showing Markup appears in the Display for Review list box. This is a default setting which tells Word to display the revision marks on the screen. See Figure 7-1.

Figure 7-1 ▶ Track Changes turned on

You'll start by making a change in the first main paragraph.

▶ **6.** In the paragraph below the first heading, select the number **50** in the last sentence, and then type **100**. A strikeout line appears through the number 50, and the new number, 100, appears in color. In Figure 7-2, the number 100 is red, but depending on how your computer is set up, it might be a different color. The new number is also underlined, and a vertical line appears in the left margin, drawing attention to the change.

Figure 7-2 ▶ Edit with revision marks turned on

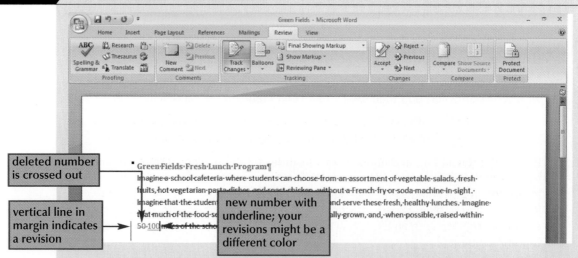

Next, you need to move a sentence. Zoe wants the second to last sentence in this paragraph to be the last sentence in the paragraph.

▶ **7.** Select the sentence **Imagine that the students themselves helped to prepare and serve these fresh, healthy lunches.** Take care to select the space after the sentence as well.

▶ **8.** Drag the sentence down to insert it at the end of the paragraph, and then click anywhere in the document to deselect it. The sentence is inserted with a double underline, in color. This time the color is different from the one used for the number "100" earlier, because Word uses a separate color to denote moved text. In Figure 7-3, the sentence appears in green, but it might be a different color on your computer. The sentence is still visible in its original location, but now it is also displayed in color, with a double strikeout line through it. A vertical line appears in the left margin, next to the sentence in its original location, and also next to the sentence in its new location. When you inserted the sentence, Word automatically deleted the space after it and added a space before it, to the left of the "I" in "Imagine."

Tracked changes showing text moved to a new location ◀ **Figure 7-3**

After reviewing the sentence in its new location at the end of the paragraph, Zoe decides she wants to shorten it slightly by deleting the word "healthy."

▶ **9.** Click to the left of the comma after "fresh," and then press the **Delete** key repeatedly to delete the comma, the space after it, and the word **healthy**. The deleted text ", healthy" appears with a strikeout line through it, so that the sentence reads "…serve these fresh lunches."

Finally, you need to format the first heading in the document with the Heading 1 style.

▶ **10.** Click in the left margin to select the heading **Green Fields Fresh Lunch Program**, click the **Home** tab, and then click the **Heading 1** style in the Quick Styles gallery. The heading is formatted with the larger font size of the Heading 1 style, a vertical line appears in the left margin next to the heading, and a balloon appears in the right margin containing the text "Formatted: Heading 1," indicating that you formatted the paragraph with the Heading 1 style. Because you selected Page width zoom earlier, the document zoom automatically adjusts to allow you to see the document text as well as the balloon in the right margin. See Figure 7-4.

Figure 7-4 ▸ **Tracked changes showing formatted text**

You are finished editing the document for now. For each edit, Word noted the current user name for the copy of Word on your computer, as well as the current date and time. You can display this information by moving the mouse pointer over one of your edits.

To display a ScreenTip that indicates the user name, date, and time for an edit:

▸ **1.** Move the mouse pointer over the newly inserted number **100**. A ScreenTip appears displaying the type of edit (an insertion), the user name for the copy of Word in which the edit was made, and the date and time the edit was made. In Figure 7-5, the user name is Zoe Rios, but you should see either your name or another name. See Figure 7-5. Later in this tutorial you will learn how to change the user name.

ScreenTip with user name and date ◄ **Figure 7-5**

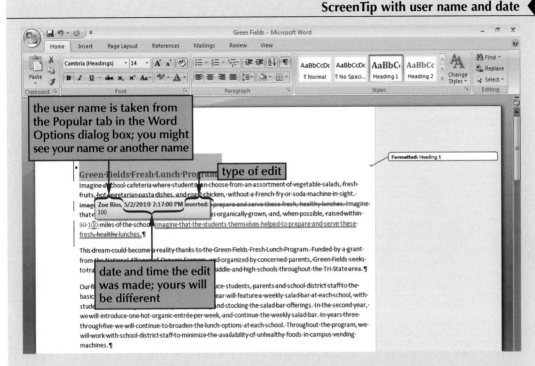

the user name is taken from the Popular tab in the Word Options dialog box; you might see your name or another name

type of edit

date and time the edit was made; yours will be different

2. Move the mouse pointer over the moved sentence, the deleted sentence, and the newly formatted heading, and review the ScreenTip that appears over each edit.

Zoe would like you to add a comment in the Budget section on page 2.

To add a comment to page 2:

1. Scroll down until you can see the Budget section on the top of page 2. The second sentence says that a complete budget will be available soon. Zoe wants to include a reminder to be more precise, if possible, about exactly when the full budget will be ready. She wants to attach the comment to the word "soon," so you start by selecting that word.

2. At the end of the Budget section, select the word **soon**.

3. Click the **Review** tab, and then in the Comments group click the **New Comment** button. The word "soon" is highlighted in color, a balloon is inserted in the right margin, and the insertion point moves to the balloon, ready for you to begin typing the comment. In Figure 7-6, the highlighting and the balloon are red, but they might be a different color on your computer. Also, in Figure 7-6, you see "Comment [ZR1]." The letters "ZR" are Zoe's initials; the number 1 after the initials tells you that this is the first comment inserted by Zoe Rios. On your computer, you see your initials or some other set of initials, depending on the settings on the Popular tab of the Word Options dialog box.

| Figure 7-6 | Inserting a comment |

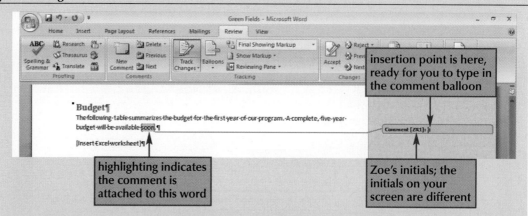

4. With the insertion point in the comment balloon, as shown in Figure 7-6, type **Can we give a precise date for the new budget?** The comment is displayed in the balloon in the right margin. The insertion point remains in the comment balloon until you click in the document.

5. Click anywhere in the document text, and then save your work.

Adjusting Track Changes Options

The default settings for Track Changes worked well as you edited Zoe's document. Note, however, that you can change these settings if you prefer. For instance, you could select a larger balloon for comments or a different color for inserted text. You could also change the user name that appears in the ScreenTip for each edit. You don't need to change any options now, but you will take a moment to learn how to change them, in case you want to later.

To learn how to change the Track Changes options:

1. Click the **Track Changes** button arrow. A menu appears below the Track Changes button.

   Trouble? If you don't see a menu and if the Track Changes button is now deselected, you clicked the Track Changes button rather than the arrow below it. Click the Track Changes button again to select it, and then click the Track Changes button arrow to open the menu.

2. Click **Change User Name**. The Popular tab of the Word Options dialog box opens. You've seen this tab before, when you used the Word Options dialog box to adjust Word settings. The User name text box on the Popular tab contains the current user name for the copy of Word installed on your computer. This is the name that appears in the ScreenTip associated with each edit when Track Changes is turned on. The letters in the Initials text box are the initials that appear in comment balloons. Do not change the user name or initials now. Simply note their location, and keep in mind that when you are working on your own computer, you should make sure the User name text box contains your full name, and that the Initials text box contains your initials.

3. Click the **Cancel** button to close the Word Options dialog box. You return to the Green Fields document.

4. Click the **Track Changes** arrow to display the menu again, and then click **Change Tracking Options**. The Track Changes Options dialog box opens. As shown in Figure 7-7, you can use the options in the Balloons section to control the size and location of the balloons in the margins. Other options in this dialog box allow you to select the colors you want to use for various types of edits. For example, you can use the Color list box next to the Insertions list box to select a color to use for inserted text. Note that the default setting for Insertions, Deletions, Comments, and Formatting is By author. This means that Word assigns one color to each person who edits the document. You'll see the significance of that later in this tutorial, when you merge your copy of the document with Henry's. Finally, note that you can deselect the Track moves check box or the Track formatting check box if you don't want to track those types of changes. Right now there's no need to change any of the settings in the Track Changes Options dialog box, so you can close it.

Examining the Track Changes Options dialog box ◄ **Figure 7-7**

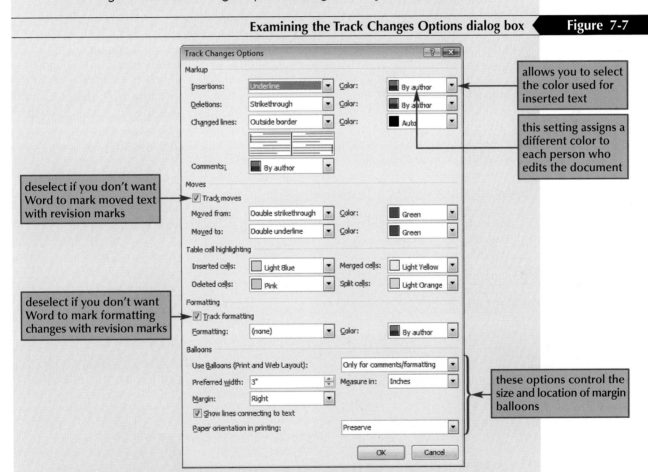

5. Click the **Cancel** button to close the Track Changes Options dialog box, and then click the **Balloons** button in the Tracking group. A menu opens, displaying options related to the way tracked changes are displayed in margin balloons. Currently, "Show Only Comments and Formatting in Balloons" is selected. To hide the margin balloons, you could click Show All Revisions Inline. To display a margin balloon for every edit (including insertions, moves, and deletions), you could click Show Revisions in Balloons. Right now, there's no need to change the default setting.

6. Press the **Escape** key to close the Balloons menu.

You are finished making Zoe's additional changes in the document. She has received Henry's edited copy via e-mail, and now she'd like your help in combining her copy of the Green Fields document with Henry's.

Comparing and Combining Documents

When you work in a collaborative environment, where multiple people work on the same document, Word's Compare and Combine features are essential tools. They allow you to compare documents, with revision marks highlighting the differences. The Compare and Combine features are similar, but they have different purposes.

Use the **Compare** feature when you have two different versions of a document that do not contain revision marks and you want to see the differences between the two. Use the **Combine** feature when you have two or more versions of a document that contain revision marks, which you want to combine into a single document. Note that it's also common to use the term **merge** rather than "combine" when talking about combining documents. However, keep in mind that merging, when used in this context, is different from the mail merge operation you learned about earlier.

When you compare two documents, you select one document as the original document and one as the revised document. Word then creates a new, third document, which consists of the original document with revision marks added to show how the revised document differs from the original document. The original document and the revised document are left unchanged.

For example, suppose the original document contains the sentence "The sky is blue." Also, suppose that in the revised document, the sentence reads "The sky is dark blue." When you compare these two documents, you create a third document where the sentence looks like you took the original document, turned on revision marks, and inserted the word "dark." See Figure 7-8.

Figure 7-8 ▶ **Comparing two documents**

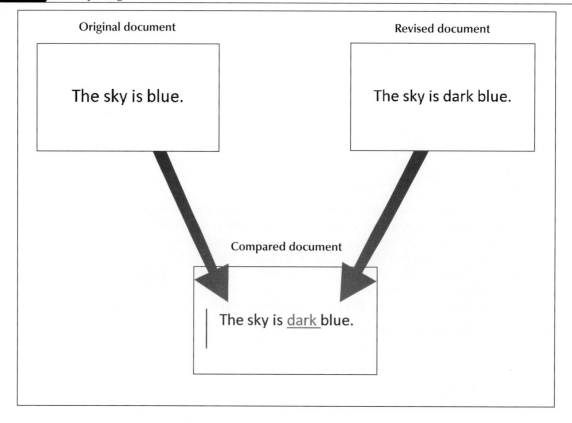

As when comparing documents, when you combine documents, you start by selecting one document as the original document and the other document as the revised document. Word then creates a new document that contains the revision marks from both the original document and the revised document. If you want, you can then take this new document and combine it with a third. In this way, you can continue, incorporating changes from as many authors as you want.

Comparing and Combining Documents | Reference Window

- With any document open in Word, click the Compare button in the Compare group on the Review tab.
- Click either Compare (to open the Compare Documents dialog box) or Combine (to open the Combine Documents dialog box). Except for their names, the two dialog boxes are identical.
- Next to the Original document list box, click the Browse for Original button, navigate to the location of the document, select the document, and then click the Open button.
- Next to the Revised document list box, click the Browse for Revised button, navigate to the location of the document, select the document, and then click the Open button.
- Click the More button, if necessary, to display options that allow you to select which items you want marked with revision marks. If the Less button is visible, these options are already displayed.
- Select or deselect any options as necessary. Verify that the New document option button is selected in the Show changes in list.
- Click the OK button, and then review the revision marks in the new document. Most likely you will want to save the combined or compared document.

You are ready to combine your document with Henry's. When you start combining or comparing documents, it doesn't matter what document is currently open in Word. It's not even necessary to have either the original document or the revised document open. In this case, the Green Fields document, which you will use as the original document, is currently open.

To combine your document with Henry's document:

▶ 1. Verify that you have saved your changes to the **Green Fields** document.

▶ 2. In the Compare group, click the **Compare** button. A menu opens. Here, you could click Compare if you wanted to compare two documents. However, you want to combine two documents, not compare them.

▶ 3. Click **Combine**. The Combine Documents dialog box opens. If you see a Less button, you also see a number of check boxes in the lower part of the document, which you can use to specify which items you want marked with revision marks. If you see a More button, you need to display these options.

▶ 4. If it is visible, click the **More** button. If the Less button is showing, skip this step. If you didn't see the check boxes earlier, you see them now. See Figure 7-9.

Figure 7-9   **Combine Documents dialog box**

Browse for
Original button

options in bottom
half of dialog box
control which items
will be marked by
revision marks

Browse for
Revised button

this default option tells
Word to create a new,
combined document

Note especially the New document option button, in the lower-right corner of the dialog box, which is selected by default. This tells Word to create a new, combined document, rather than importing the revision marks from the original document into the revised document, or vice versa. There's no reason to change any of the default options, so you can proceed with selecting the document you want to use as the original document. In this case, you want to use the Green Fields document as the original document. Even though this document is currently displayed on the screen, you need to select it.

▶ 5. Next to the Original document list box, click the **Browse for Original** button. This opens an Open dialog box that is identical to the Open dialog box you have used many times before.

▶ 6. Use the options in the Open dialog box to select the **Green Fields** document from the Tutorial.07\Tutorial folder included with your Data Files, and then click the **Open** button. You return to the Combine Documents dialog box, where the filename "Green Fields" now appears in the Original document list box. In the "Label unmarked changes with" text box, you see the user name from the Popular tab of the Word options dialog box. When you combine the documents, the edits you made earlier will be marked with this user name. Next, you need to select the document you want to use as the revised document. Henry took the file named "Green Fields" that Zoe sent to him earlier, and added his initials to the file name, to create the filename "Green Fields HD." This file is included with your Data Files.

▶ 7. Next to the Revised document list box, click the **Browse for Revised** button, use the options in the Open dialog box to navigate to and select the file named **Green Fields HD** in the Tutorial.07\Tutorial folder included with your Data Files, and then click the **Open** button. The filename "Green Fields HD" appears in the Revised document list box, and Henry's first and last name appear in the "Label unmarked changes with" text box. See Figure 7-10.

Tip

You can also use the Original document list arrow or the Revised document list arrow to select files that you have previously opened on your computer, but using the Browse for Original and Browse for Revised buttons ensures that you select the correct file from the correct folder.

the user name from the Popular tab in the Word Options dialog box is displayed here; yours will be different

8. Click the **OK** button. A new document opens and is named "Document1," "Document2," "Combine Result 1," or something similar. It contains the revision marks from both the original document and revised document. At this point, you might see only the new, combined document, or you might also see the original and revised documents open in separate windows. You might also see the Reviewing Pane, which lists each change in the new, combined document. In the next two steps, you will make sure your screen is set up to show the original and revised documents and the Reviewing Pane.

9. In the Compare group, click the **Show Source Documents** button, and, if you do not see a check mark next to Show Both, click **Show Both**. If you do see a check mark next to Show Both, press the **Escape** key to close the menu.

10. In the Tracking group, locate the Reviewing Pane button. If it is orange, then the Reviewing Pane is currently displayed. If it is not orange, click the **Reviewing Pane** button to display the Reviewing Pane. At this point, the Reviewing Pane might be displayed in a horizontal window at the bottom of the screen or vertically on the left side of the screen. In Figure 7-11, it is displayed vertically.

Figure 7-11 ▷ **Combining two documents**

▶ **11.** If your Reviewing Pane is displayed horizontally, in the Tracking group click the **Reviewing Pane** button arrow, and then click **Reviewing Pane Vertical**.

It's helpful to know how to display the original and revised documents, but if you have a small screen, having them displayed makes it harder to read the new document. You will close them in the next set of steps, and then you will take a moment to explore some options for displaying the edits made by multiple reviewers. Finally, you will save the new document with a new name.

To hide the source documents and change the reviewer options:

▶ **1.** In the Compare group, click the **Show Source Documents** button, and then click **Hide Source Documents**. The panes displaying the original and revised documents close.

▶ **2.** Use the vertical scroll bar in the Reviewing Pane to scroll down and review the list of edits. Notice that the document contains the edits you made earlier, as well as edits made by Henry Davis. By default, Word displays all the edits by all reviewers, but you can choose to display only the edits made by a specific reviewer or reviewers. You'll see how this works in the following step.

▶ **3.** In the Tracking group, click the **Show Markup** button, and then point to **Reviewers**. A menu opens with check marks next to Henry's name and the user name for your computer. Also, you see a check mark next to "All Reviewers." This tells you that currently the document displays all the edits of all the reviewers. To hide Henry's edits, you need to deselect his name.

▶ **4.** Click **Henry Davis**. The menu closes, and the Reviewing Pane and document show only the edits you made earlier.

▶ **5.** Scroll down, if necessary, so you can see that the edits for Henry Davis are no longer displayed.

▶ **6.** Click the **Show Markup** button again, point to **Reviewers**, and then click **Henry Davis**. Henry's edits are again displayed in the Reviewing Pane and in the document. At this point, you are finished with the Reviewing Pane, so you can close it.

▶ **7.** In the Tracking group, click the **Reviewing Pane** button. (Do not click the arrow next to the Reviewing Pane button.) The Reviewing Pane closes, and the document window adjusts to show the new document in Page width zoom.

▶ **8.** Save the document as **Green Fields Rev** in the Tutorial.07\Tutorial folder included with your Data Files.

▶ **9.** Scroll down to review the document. Notice that Henry's changes, at the bottom of page 1, appear in a different color than the changes you made earlier at the top of page 1. On some computers, the word "soon" at the end of the Budget section (where you inserted a comment) might be marked as a deletion, with another instance of the word "soon" also marked as an insertion. Combining documents that contain revision marks can sometimes produce unexpected results like this. You will fix this problem later, when you accept and reject the changes in the document.

As you have seen, the document you just created contains Zoe's edits, your edits, and Henry's edits. In the following section, you will review the edits, accepting most of the changes and rejecting one.

Accepting and Rejecting Changes

When you go through revision marks in a document, it's important to be systematic, so you don't accidentally miss a change. The best approach is to move the insertion point to the beginning of the document, and then go through the document one change at a time using the Next and Previous buttons. When you click the Next button, Word moves to and selects the first change after the insertion point. Likewise, when you click the Previous button, Word moves to and selects the first change before the insertion point.

Accepting and Rejecting Changes and Deleting Comments | Reference Window

- Move the insertion point to the beginning of the document.
- To move the insertion point from one edit or comment to another, in the Changes group on the Review tab click the Next button. To move the insertion point from one comment to another, in the Comments group on the Review tab click the Next button.
- To accept a change that currently contains the insertion point, in the Changes group on the Review tab click the Accept button. To accept all the changes in the document, click the Accept button arrow, and then click Accept All Changes in Document.
- To reject the change that currently contains the insertion point, click the Reject button in the Changes group on the Review tab. To reject all the changes in the document, click the Reject button arrow, and then click Reject All Changes in Document.
- To delete a comment, click in the comment balloon, and then click the Delete button in the Comment group. To delete all the comments in a document, click the Delete button arrow, and then click Delete All Comments in Document.

You are ready to review the changes in the Green Fields Rev document, so Zoe can decide which to accept and which to reject.

To accept and reject changes in the Green Fields Rev document:

▶ **1.** Press the **Ctrl+Home** keys to move the insertion point to the beginning of the document.

▶ **2.** In the Changes group on the Review tab, click the **Next** button.

▶ **3.** The heading "Green Fields Fresh Lunch Program" is highlighted. As you saw earlier, the margin bubble tells you that you formatted this paragraph with the Heading 1 style. This is one of your changes, and you need to accept it.

▶ **4.** In the Changes group, click the **Accept** button. The heading remains formatted with the Heading 1 style, and the margin bubble disappears, indicating that the change has been accepted. The highlighting moves to the next change, which is the deleted sentence, currently displayed in green (or another color) and with a strikeout line through it. You also need to accept this change.

   Trouble? If you see a menu below the Accept button, you clicked the Accept button arrow by mistake. Press the Escape key to close the menu, and then click the Accept button.

▶ **5.** Click the **Accept** button. The sentence with the strikeout line through it is removed from the document, and the highlighting moves to the deleted number 50.

▶ **6.** Accept the deletion of the number 50, the insertion of the number 100, the insertion of the space before the word "Imagine," and the deletion of word "healthy." After you accept the deletion of "healthy," the word "and," near the bottom of page 1, is highlighted. This is one of Henry's changes to the document. In this same paragraph, he also added a comment and deleted the word "coronary." See Figure 7-12.

Figure 7-12 ▶ **Reviewing Henry's changes**

▶ **7.** Click the **Accept** button to accept the insertion of the word "and." The insertion point moves to Henry's comment, which reads "This is not a complete sentence."

Henry is correct; something is missing from the sentence to which the comment is attached. You need to edit the sentence to correct it. Before you edit the sentence that Henry was concerned about, you need to turn off Track Changes if it was turned on by default when you created the combined document.

To continue accepting and rejecting changes:

▸ **1.** In the Tracking group, if the Track Changes button is highlighted, click the **Track Changes** button to deselect it.

▸ **2.** Click to the left of the word "The," press the **Delete** key to delete the "T" in "The" and then type **According to t** so that the sentence reads "According to the Center for Disease Control...". Because you turned off tracked changes, the new text looks like ordinary text. It is not displayed in revision marks. The last two letters in "The" are highlighted, indicating that the comment is still attached to them. You will delete the comment later in this set of steps.

▸ **3.** In the Changes group, click the **Next** button. The insertion point moves to the first change or comment after the insertion point, which is Henry's comment.

Trouble? If the insertion point moves to the deleted word "coronary" instead of to Henry's comment, then the insertion point was located somewhere after the comment. In that case, skip the following step.

▸ **4.** In the Changes group, click the **Next** button again. The deleted word "coronary," which appears with a strikeout line through it, is highlighted. Both "coronary" and "heart" are unnecessary; Zoe prefers to keep "coronary" and delete "heart." That means you need to reject Henry's deletion of "coronary." You don't want to move on to the next change in the document, because you need to remain at this location and edit this sentence. So instead of using the Reject button (which would reject the change and move the insertion point to the next change in the document), you will use the Reject arrow button.

▸ **5.** In the Changes group, click the **Reject** button arrow, and then click **Reject Change**. The word "coronary" appears as ordinary text and is selected. It is no longer marked as a deletion. See Figure 7-13. Next, you will delete the word "heart," which is next to the word "coronary" and is unnecessary.

Rejected change ◂ Figure 7-13

you accepted Henry's insertion of "and"

you added this phrase to complete the sentence

you rejected Henry's deletion of "coronary"

you still need to delete the word "heart"

▸ **6.** Double-click the word **heart** to select it, and then delete it, so the sentence reads "...and coronary disease." Next, as she reviews the edited sentence, Zoe notices that a comma is missing after the word "diabetes." You'll add the comma in the next step.

▸ **7.** Click to the right of the "s" in "diabetes," and then insert a comma. Finally, Zoe asks you to remove her comment, which she decides is no longer necessary. At the same time, you will delete Henry's comment. First, you need to move the insertion point to one of the comments.

▸ **8.** Click anywhere in the margin bubble for Henry's comment.

▶ **9.** In the Comments group, click the **Delete** button arrow, and then click **Delete All Comments in Document**. The comments are removed from the document.

Trouble? If only Henry's comment is deleted, and you do not see a menu with the command Delete All Comments in Document, you clicked the Delete button rather than the Delete button arrow. Undo the change, and then repeat Step 9.

If the word "soon" is marked as a deletion in your document and also marked as an insertion, then you need to complete Step 10. If the word "soon" appears in ordinary text, skip to Step 11.

▶ **10.** In the Changes group, click the **Next** button to select the deleted word "soon," accept the deletion of the word "soon," accept the insertion of the word "soon," and then click the **OK** button in the dialog box informing you that the document now contains no comments or tracked changes.

▶ **11.** Save your work on the Green Fields Rev document, click the button for the **Green Fields** document in the taskbar to display the document, and then close the **Green Fields** document. If you are asked if you want to save changes, click **Yes**. You return to the Green Fields Rev document.

InSight | **Understanding Tracked Changes**

Tracked changes allow you to see the evolution of a document from draft form to the finished product. They can be extremely useful during the revision process. However, you do not want the final readers of your document to encounter any tracked changes. Inadvertently including tracked changes in a final document can be embarrassing; in other situations, it could result in serious consequences. For example, suppose you sent out a letter offering a job and specifying a salary, but you accidentally left in tracked changes that showed that you originally contemplated offering a higher salary. Such a mistake would greatly complicate the salary negotiations with a potential employee.

The problem is, you can't always tell if a document contains comments or tracked changes, because the comments or changes for some or all of the reviewers might be hidden. Also, the Display for Review list box in the Tracking group on the Review tab might be set to something other than Final Showing Markup. To determine whether or not a document contains any tracked changes or comments:

- In the Tracking group on the Review tab, verify that the Display for Review list box is set to Final Showing Markup.
- In the Tracking group on the Review tab, click the Show Markup button, point to Reviewers, and make sure you see a check mark next to All Reviewers.
- Press the Ctrl+Home keys to move the insertion point to the beginning of the document, and then in the Changes group on the Review tab, click the Next button. This will either display a dialog box informing you that the document contains no comments or tracked changes, or the insertion point will move to the next comment or tracked changes.

Now that you have incorporated Henry's suggestions, you are ready to add Alison's budget and Henry's pie chart to the document.

Embedding and Linking Objects from Other Programs

Every software program is designed to accomplish a set of specific tasks. As you've seen with Word, you can use a word-processing program to create, edit, and format documents such as letters, reports, newsletters, and proposals. A **spreadsheet program**, on the other hand, allows you to organize, calculate, and analyze numerical data. A spreadsheet created in Microsoft Excel is known as a **worksheet**. Alison created the budget for the Green Fields Fresh Lunch Program in an Excel worksheet. Henry also used Excel to create his chart.

Both the worksheet and the chart are objects. An **object** is an item such as a graphic, WordArt, chart, or paragraph of text that you can modify and move from one document to another. Zoe asks you to place the worksheet and chart objects into her document, but she also wants to be able to modify the Excel objects after they are inserted into the document. A technology called **object linking and embedding**, or **OLE**, allows you to integrate information created in one program (such as Excel) into a document created in another program (such as Word), and then modify that information using the tools originally used to create it.

The program used to create the original version of the object is called the **source program** (in this case, Excel). The program into which the object is integrated is called the **destination program** (in this case, Word). Similarly, the original file that contains the object you are inserting is called the **source file**, and the file into which you insert the object is called the **destination file**.

The next two sections describe two options for transferring data between source files and destination files: embedding and linking.

Embedding is a technique that allows you to insert a copy of an existing object into a destination document. In the destination document, you can double-click an embedded object to access the tools of the source program. This allows you to edit the object within the destination document using the tools of the source program. Because the embedded object is a copy, any changes you make to it are not reflected in the original source file, and vice versa. For instance, you could embed a worksheet named Itemized Expenses into a Word document named Travel Report. Later, if you change the Itemized Expenses file, those revisions would not appear in the Travel Report document. The opposite is also true. If you edit the embedded object from within the Travel Report file, those changes will not be reflected in the source file Itemized Expenses. The embedded object retains a connection to the source program, Excel, but not to the source file.

Figure 7-14 illustrates the relationship between an embedded Excel object in Zoe's Word document and the source file.

| **Figure 7-14** | **Embedding an Excel worksheet in a Word document** |

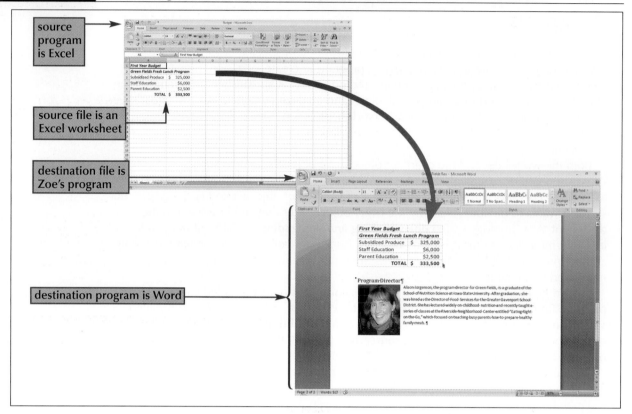

Linking is similar to embedding, except that the object inserted into the destination file maintains a connection to the source file—not just the source program. Just as with an embedded object, you can double-click a linked object to access the tools of the source program. However, unlike with an embedded object, if you edit the source file in the source program, those changes appear in the linked object; likewise, if you change the object from the destination program, the changes will also appear in the file in the source program. The linked object in the destination document is not a copy; it is a shortcut to the original object in the source file. As a result, a document that contains a linked object usually takes up less space on a disk than does a document containing an embedded version of the same object.

Figure 7-15 illustrates the relationship between the data in Henry's Excel chart and the linked object in Zoe's Word document.

Linking an Excel chart to a Word document | **Figure 7-15**

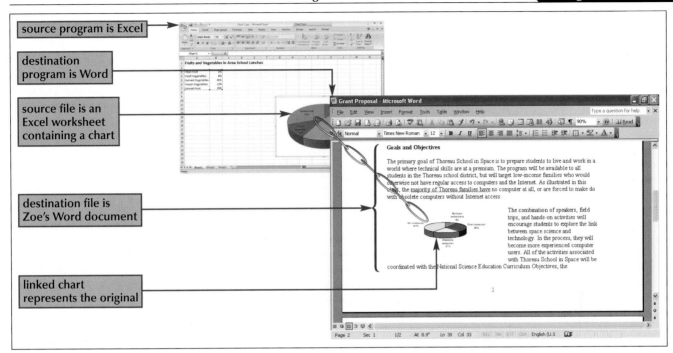

One drawback to linking is that by moving files or folders, you can accidentally disrupt the connection between the source file and the document containing the linked object. For example, suppose you insert a linked Excel file into a Word document, close the Word document and the Excel file, and then go home. Suppose then that later a colleague moves the source file (the Excel file) to a different folder or even deletes it. The next time you open the Word document containing the linked object, you will get an error message, or you won't be able to update the linked object.

Embedding and linking are both useful when you know you'll want to edit an object after inserting it into Word. Before you can use either embedding or linking, you must verify that you have the source program installed on your computer. Then you can decide if you want to embed or link the object.

How do you decide whether to embed or link? Create an embedded object if you won't have access to the original source file in the future, or if you don't need to maintain the connection between the source file and the document containing the linked object. The source file is unaffected by any editing in the destination document. You could even delete the source file from your disk without affecting the copy embedded in your Word document.

Create a linked object whenever you have data that is likely to change over time and when you want your document to be updated with those changes. For example, suppose you created a Word document called Refinancing Options into which you want to insert an Excel file containing the latest interest rates for home mortgages. Suppose also that your assistant updates the Excel file daily to make sure it reflects current rates. By linking the Excel file to the Refinancing Options Word document, you can be certain that the mortgage rates are updated every time your assistant updates the Excel file. The advantage to linking is that the data in both the source file (the Excel file) and destination file (the Word document) can reflect recent revisions. A disadvantage to linking is that you have to keep track of two files (the Excel file and the Word file) rather than just one.

If you won't need to edit the object, you can also simply paste a copy of the object into a Word document, using the regular Paste button, similar to the way you paste a selection of copied text.

Keep in mind that you must have Excel installed on your computer to perform the steps in the rest of this session. If Excel is not installed on your computer, read the remainder of this session, but you won't be able to perform the steps.

Embedding an Excel Worksheet

Embedding all or part of an Excel worksheet in a Word document is really a special form of pasting. You start by opening the Excel file and selecting the worksheet or part of a worksheet that you want to embed in the Word document. Then you copy the selection to the Office Clipboard. When you return to Word, you click the Paste button arrow in the Clipboard group on the Home tab and select the Paste Special command to open the Paste Special dialog box. In this dialog box, you can choose to paste the copied worksheet data in a number of different forms. To embed the worksheet data, you select Microsoft Office Excel Worksheet Object.

Zoe asks you to embed the budget from Alison's Excel file into the Green Fields Rev document. In OLE terminology, the budget is the object, the Excel file is the source file, and the Green Fields Rev document is the destination file. In the following steps, you will embed the Excel object in the Word document, replacing the "[Insert Excel worksheet]" placeholder at the top of page 2. (It was originally on page 1, but it moved to page 2 after you formatted the first heading with the Heading 1 style.) Then you can use Excel commands to modify the embedded object from within Word.

To embed the Excel worksheet:

▶ 1. Press the **Ctrl+Home** keys to move the insertion point to the beginning of the document, click the **Home** tab, in the Editing group click the **Find** button, find the placeholder **[Insert Excel worksheet]**, click **Cancel** to close the Find and Replace dialog box, and then press the **Delete** key. Take care to delete only the placeholder text and not the paragraph mark after it. When you are finished, the insertion point should be located in a blank paragraph above the heading Program Director. This is where you will embed the Excel worksheet. Now you are ready to open Alison's Excel file and copy the budget.

▶ 2. Click the **Start** button, point to **All Programs**, click **Microsoft Office**, and then click **Microsoft Office Excel 2007**. The Excel window opens, displaying a blank worksheet named Book1.

   Trouble? If you don't see Microsoft Office Excel 2007 as an option in the Start menu, or if a message indicates that Word can't find the source program, Excel might not be installed on your computer. Ask your instructor or technical support person for assistance.

▶ 3. In Excel, click the **Office Button** 🔘, click **Open**, navigate to the Tutorial.07\Tutorial folder included with your Data Files, click the file named **Budget,** and then click the **Open** button. The Budget worksheet opens, as shown in Figure 7-16.

Budget file open in Excel ◀ Figure 7-16

Notice that an Excel worksheet is arranged in rows and columns, just like a Word table. The intersection between a row and column is called a **cell**; an individual cell takes its name from its column letter and row number. For example, the intersection of column B and row 2 is "cell B2." Currently cell A1, in the upper-left corner of the worksheet, is selected, as indicated by its dark outline. To copy the budget data to the Office Clipboard, you need to select the entire block of cells containing the budget.

4. Click cell **A1** (the cell containing the text "First Year Budget"), drag the mouse down to select cells A1 through A6 (that is, down to the cell containing "TOTAL"), and then drag the mouse right to select the data in column B. See Figure 7-17.

Figure 7-17 **Budget data selected in the worksheet**

Now that the data is selected, you can copy it to the Office Clipboard and return to Word.

5. Press the **Ctrl+C** keys. The border around the selected cells is animated, indicating that you have copied the data in these cells to the Office Clipboard.

6. Click the **Green Fields Rev** button in the taskbar. You return to the Word window.

7. Verify that the insertion point is located at the top of page 2, in the blank paragraph above the heading "Program Director." You are ready to embed the copied budget into the Word document. As mentioned earlier, you need to use the Paste button arrow to do this, and not the Paste button. If you click the Paste button instead, the budget won't be embedded. Instead, Word will insert the Excel data as a Word table, which would prevent you from editing it using the Excel tabs and tools.

8. Click the **Home** tab if necessary, in the Clipboard group click the **Paste** button arrow, and then click **Paste Special**. The Paste Special dialog box opens.

Trouble? If the budget is inserted in the document, you clicked the Paste button rather than the Paste button arrow. Undo the change, and then repeat Step 8.

Here you can choose to embed the Excel object or link it, depending on whether you select the Paste option button or the Paste link option button. The Paste option button, which tells Word you want to embed the object, is selected by default. In the As list box, you can select the format in which you want to paste the Excel data. For example, you could click Picture (Enhanced Metafile) to insert a picture of the data, which you could not edit. In this case, you want to paste the data as a Microsoft Office Excel Worksheet Object, so you can edit it later.

9. In the As list, click **Microsoft Office Excel Worksheet Object**. See Figure 7-18.

Embedding an Excel object ◀ **Figure 7-18**

select this option to embed the object, not link it

select this option to embed the item as an Excel object

10. Click the **OK** button. The Excel object is inserted in the Word document, as shown in Figure 7-19.

Excel object embedded in Word document ◀ **Figure 7-19**

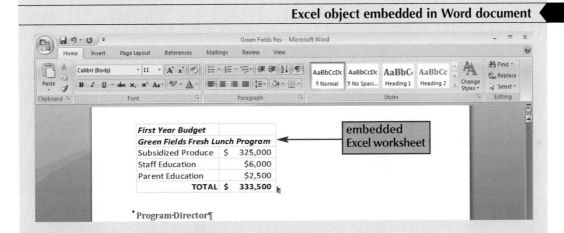

embedded Excel worksheet

Because the object is embedded, you can make changes to the object from within Word, which you'll do in the next section.

Modifying the Embedded Worksheet

After you embed an object in Word, you can modify it two different ways. First, you can click it to select it, and then move it or resize it, just as you would a picture or a piece of clip art. You can think of this as modifying the object's container—the box in which it is displayed. Second, you can double-click the object to display the tools of the source program, and then edit the contents of the object. After you modify the embedded object using the tools of the source program, you can click anywhere else in the Word document to deselect the embedded object and redisplay the usual Word tools.

Zoe would like to center the Excel object on the page. Also, Alison just e-mailed Zoe to tell her that she used an incorrect value for Staff Education, so Zoe needs to revise the worksheet data.

To modify the Excel object:

▶ **1.** Click anywhere inside the borders of the budget data. A dotted blue outline and selection handles appear around the Excel object, indicating that it is selected. With the object selected, you can center it as you would center any other selected item in a Word document. Notice that merely selecting the Excel object does not display the Excel tabs and buttons. That will happen later when you double-click the object.

▶ **2.** In the Paragraph group, click the **Center** button 🗐. The Excel object moves to the center of the page. See Figure 7-20.

Figure 7-20 > **Excel object centered on the page**

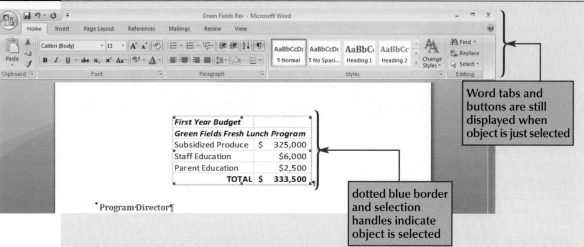

Word tabs and buttons are still displayed when object is just selected

First Year Budget
Green Fields Fresh Lunch Program
Subsidized Produce $ 325,000
Staff Education $6,000
Parent Education $2,500
TOTAL $ 333,500

Program·Director¶

dotted blue border and selection handles indicate object is selected

▶ **3.** Double-click the Excel object. The object's border changes to resemble the borders of an Excel worksheet, with horizontal and vertical scroll bars, row numbers, and column letters. The Word tabs at the top of the screen are replaced with Excel tabs. You need to change the value for Staff Education from $6,000 to $5,000. Decreasing the Staff Education value by $1,000 should also decrease the budget total by $1,000 because of the formula Alison entered in the worksheet.

▶ **4.** Click cell **B4**, which contains the number $6,000, type **5000** (you don't have to type a dollar sign or a comma), and then press the **Enter** key. The new value of "$5,000" replaces the old value of "$6,000." The budget total, in cell B6, decreases from $333,500 to $332,500. See Figure 7-21.

Revised data in Excel object ◄ **Figure 7-21**

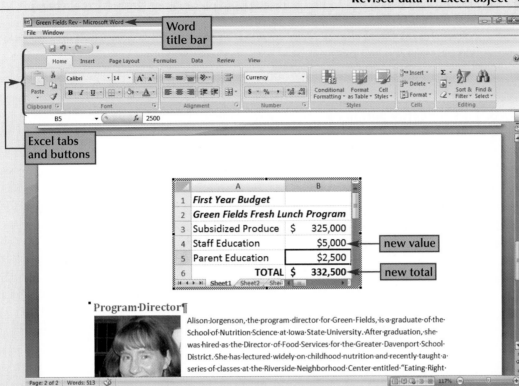

▶ **5.** Click in the blank area to the left or right of the Excel object (outside its borders) to deselect it.

The source file, Budget.xlsx, remains in its original form in your Data Files, with the $6,000 as the Staff Education value. You have modified only the object in Zoe's document because it is embedded, not linked. You'll see how linking works in the next section.

Linking an Excel Chart

Next, Zoe wants you to incorporate the chart that illustrates the percentage of fresh fruits and vegetables served in school lunches in her area. Because Henry plans to revise the data soon, Zoe decides to link the chart in the Excel file rather than embed it. That way, once Henry updates the chart in the source file, the update will appear in Zoe's program description as well.

You'll use the Chart file Henry created in Excel to create the linked object in the program description document. This file is located in the Tutorial.07\Tutorial folder included with your Data Files. Because you'll make changes to the chart after you link it, you should make a copy of the Chart file before you link it. This leaves the original file in the Tutorial folder unchanged in case you want to repeat the tutorial steps later. Normally you don't need to copy a file before you link it to a Word document.

To link an Excel chart to the program description document:

▶ **1.** Use the Find dialog box to find and select the placeholder **[Insert Excel chart]**, click **Cancel** to close the Find and Replace dialog box, and then delete the placeholder **[Insert Excel chart]**. Make sure the insertion point is positioned on a blank line between the two paragraphs of text.

▶ **2.** Click the **Microsoft Excel** button in the taskbar to display the Excel window. Next, you will close the Budget file before you open the Chart file.

▶ **3.** Click the **Office Button** 🔘, and then click **Close**. The Budget worksheet closes.

▶ **4.** Click the **Office Button** 🔘, click **Open**, and then open the file named **Chart** from the Tutorial.07\Tutorial folder included with your Data Files. The worksheet includes some data in the upper-left corner and the pie chart created from the data in the lower-right corner.

▶ **5.** Click the **Office Button** 🔘, click **Save As**, and then save the Excel file with the name **Chart Copy** in the Tutorial.07\Tutorial folder included with your Data Files.

As with embedding, to link an Excel object, you start by selecting the object and copying it to the Office Clipboard. You want to copy the chart, not the data.

▶ **6.** Click the chart border. Do not click any part of the chart itself. A selection border appears around the chart. The worksheet data is also outlined in color, indicating that this is the data used to create the chart. Note that the colored outlines do not indicate that the data itself is selected. See Figure 7-22.

Figure 7-22 ▶ **Pie chart selected in worksheet**

Trouble? If you see borders or handles around parts of the pie chart, click in the worksheet outside the chart border, and then repeat Step 6.

7. Press the **Ctrl+C** keys to copy the pie chart to the Office Clipboard, and then click the **Green Fields Rev** button in the taskbar. The Green Fields Rev document is displayed in the Word window. You'll leave the Excel window open, so you can return to it in a moment.

8. Verify that the insertion point is located in the blank paragraph between the two paragraphs of text, click the **Paste** button arrow, and then click **Paste Special**. The Paste Special dialog box opens. To link the worksheet chart to Zoe's Word document, you need to click the Paste link option button. You also need to specify that the chart is an object.

9. Click the **Paste link** option button to select it, and then click **Microsoft Office Excel Chart Object** in the As list box. See Figure 7-23.

Inserting a linked object ◀ Figure 7-23

10. Click the **OK** button. The Paste Special dialog box closes, and the Excel chart is inserted in the Word document. See Figure 7-24. It is too large to fit on page 1, so Word moved it to the top of page 2.

Figure 7-24 | **Linked chart inserted in Word document**

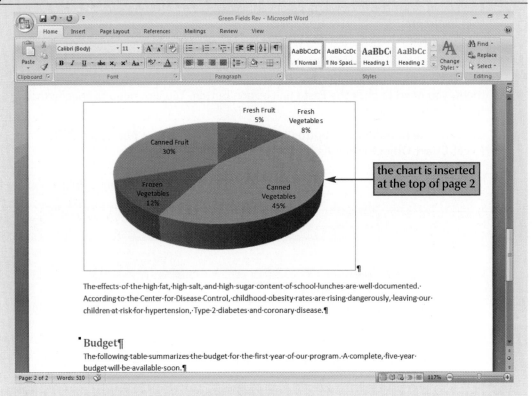

You can resize and move a linked object just as you would an embedded object. Later on, after Zoe incorporates suggestions and comments from other readers, she will resize the chart and wrap text around it. For now, she'll leave it as it is.

Modifying the Linked Chart

The advantage of linking a file over embedding it is that you can update the destination file to reflect modifications to the source file. If the destination file is closed while the source file is being modified, the linked object in the destination file will be updated automatically the next time you open the destination file. If the destination file is open while the source file is being modified, you need to right-click the linked object and then click Update Link.

In the following steps, you'll return to the Chart Copy file in Excel, change some values, and then view the updated information in the Word document.

To modify the chart in the source program:

1. Click the **Microsoft Excel** button in the taskbar. The Chart Copy workbook is displayed in the Excel window, with the chart still selected.

2. Click anywhere outside the chart to deselect it. To modify the chart, you need to edit the data in the upper-left corner of the worksheet. Currently the percentage for Fresh Fruit is 5%, and the percentage for Fresh Vegetables is 8%. In the next step, you will edit these values.

3. Click cell **B3**, which contains the percentage for Fresh Fruit, type **9** (you don't have to type the percentage sign), and then press the **Enter** key. The new percentage is entered in cell B3, and the label in the Fresh Fruit section of the pie chart changes from 5% to 9%. Cell B4, which contains the percentage for Fresh Vegetables, is now selected, ready for you to enter a new value.

4. Type **4**, and then press the **Enter** key. The new percentage is entered in cell B4, and the label in the Fresh Vegetables section of the pie chart changes from 8% to 4%. See Figure 7-25.

Modifying the chart in Excel ◄ **Figure 7-25**

5. On the Quick Access Toolbar, click the **Save** button 🖫, and then close the Chart Copy file and Excel. You return to the Word window, with the pie chart displayed. Because the destination file, Green Fields Rev, was open when you edited the source file, you need to update the chart before it will show the new percentages. If the Word file had been closed, the chart would be updated when you reopened the file in Word.

6. Right-click the chart in the Word window, and then in the shortcut menu click **Update Link**. After a pause, the chart is updated and shows a percentage of 9% for Fresh Fruit and 4% for Fresh Vegetables, just like the chart shown in Figure 7-25.

7. Click anywhere outside the chart to deselect it, and then save your work.

Zoe's program description is finished for now. Later, after she receives everyone's comments, she will further revise it. At that time, she will add additional text, adjust the size of the pie chart, and wrap text around it.

You are ready to print the program description for distribution to the parent volunteers at Green Fields who ask for printed copies.

To print and then close the document:

▶ **1.** Preview the document. Don't be concerned if the page breaks seem awkward. Zoe will add additional text to the document after her colleagues review it, so at this point she isn't concerned about adjusting page breaks in the document.

▶ **2.** Print the document, click the **Office Button** 🔘, and then click **Close**. You closed the document so you can see what happens later when you open a document that contains a linked object.

Next, Zoe wants to focus on the task of distributing the document electronically, which you'll do in the next session.

Review | **Session 7.1 Quick Check**

1. Explain how to use Track Changes to edit a document.
2. What button do you use to insert a comment and on what tab is it located?
3. Suppose you want to merge two documents, each containing revision marks. Should you combine them or compare them?
4. Explain the difference between a linked object and an embedded object.
5. What term refers to an item such as a graphic, WordArt, or chart that you can modify and move from one document to another?
6. What button do you use to begin embedding or linking an object that you've copied to the Clipboard? On what tab is the button located?
7. True or False. When you modify a linked object in the destination file, your changes are also made to the source file.

Session 7.2

Distributing Word Documents Online

Tip

You can save a document as a PDF file, which can be opened on any computer running Adobe Acrobat Reader. To learn how, search for "Enable support for other file formats, such as PDF and XPS" in Word Help.

In addition to printing the document for Green Fields members, Zoe wants to make the program description available to the organization's members **online**, which means they can read it on a computer screen rather than on a printed page. You can make a document available online in one of two ways—you can either e-mail the document to specific people, or you can make it available as a Web page.

Whichever online option you choose, keep in mind that reading a document online is different from reading it in printed form. If you are certain a document will be read only online, and therefore don't have to worry about how the document will look when printed on a black and white printer, you can sometimes use more interesting formatting options, such as a fancy background. Because it is difficult to "flip through pages" online, you might also need to organize online information for easy access, or provide hyperlinks for opening related files. (You'll learn more about hyperlinks later in this tutorial.) Finally, remember that when distributing documents online, large document files can be problematic.

To e-mail a Word document, you need to use an e-mail program such as Microsoft Outlook or a Web mail service such as Yahoo. First, you create an e-mail message, type the recipient's e-mail address, and then type the text of the e-mail. Finally, you need to attach the Word document to the e-mail message. The exact steps for attaching a document to an e-mail message vary from one e-mail program to another, but in all of them, you need to find and then select the file you want to attach.

When you e-mail documents, you should keep in mind a few basic rules:

- Many e-mail programs have difficulty handling large attachments. Consider storing large files in a compressed (or zipped) folder to reduce their size before e-mailing. Alternately, you could convert the Word document to a Web page as described later in this tutorial. A Web page is usually much smaller than a Word document containing the same amount of text.
- Other word-processing programs and early versions of Word are unable to open files created in Word 2007. Before e-mailing a file, ask the recipient what word processor he or she is using. To avoid problems with conflicting versions, save the Word document as a rich text file (using the Rich Text File document, type in the Save As dialog box) before e-mailing it. All versions of Word can open rich text files.
- If you plan to e-mail a document that contains links to other files, remember to e-mail all the linked files.
- Attachments, including Word documents, are sometimes used maliciously to spread computer viruses. Remember to include an explanatory note with any e-mail attachment so that the recipient can be certain the attachment is legitimate. Also, while every computer should have a reliable virus checker program installed, this is even more important if you plan to send and receive e-mail attachments.

E-mailing Word documents is especially useful when you are collaborating with a group. You can exchange documents with colleagues in the office or around the world with just a click of the mouse. To make a document available to a larger audience, however, it's easier to publish it as a Web page, because then you don't have to take time to read and manage numerous e-mail messages. You'll learn more about working with Web pages in the next section.

Publishing Word Documents as Web Pages

Web pages are special documents designed to be viewed in a program called a **browser**. The two most popular browsers are **Microsoft Internet Explorer** and **Mozilla Firefox**. You can create a Web page on just about any kind of computer, but if you want other people to be able to view your Web page, you must store it on a computer called a **Web server**. The Web server communicates with a computer user's browser in order to display the Web page in the browser window. The process of making a Web page available to others via a Web server is called **publishing** the Web page.

Web servers are found on two different types of networks—intranets and the Internet. An **intranet** is a self-contained network belonging to a single organization. For example, the computers at Zoe's company, Rios Communications, are connected via an intranet. Zoe could publish a document as a Web page on her company's intranet Web site, so that her coworkers could view it—but it would not be available to the general public.

At the same time, Zoe's computer is also connected to the largest, most widely used computer network in the world, the **Internet**. The part of the Internet that transfers and displays Web pages is called the **World Wide Web**, or simply, the **Web**. Each Web page has its own **Web address** (or **URL**), such as *www.course.com* or *www.microsoft.com*. A group of related Web pages is called a **Web site**. The main Web page within a Web site (the one that is usually displayed first) is called a **home page**.

You probably have experience using a browser to view Web pages. If so, you know that Web pages usually contain both text and graphics, and also can contain audio and video. Web pages also include **hyperlinks**, which you can click to open or "jump to" other Web pages. A hyperlink can be a word, a phrase, or a graphic. Text hyperlinks are usually underlined and appear in a different color from the rest of the document. Hyperlinks are usually referred to as **links**, but take care not to confuse them with the OLE links you worked with earlier in this tutorial.

While hyperlinks are widely used in Web pages, you can also use them in ordinary Word documents that are intended for online reading. In the next section, you will learn more about using hyperlinks in online Word documents and Web pages.

Using Hyperlinks in Word

Hyperlinks in Word documents can link to a Web page, to a separate Word document, or to another part of the same document as the one containing the link. You can also include e-mail links, which you can click to create an e-mail message from a document. Finally, if you have many Office 2007 documents that are related to each other, you can create a useful hyperlink system that allows users to retrieve and view related material. For example, a business proposal might include links to a budget stored in an Excel file and to product photographs stored in a PowerPoint presentation. In fact, instead of inserting Henry's chart as a linked object, you could have inserted a hyperlink that users could click to open the chart in Excel. You used a linked object instead, because you wanted the chart to appear in the printed version of the program description.

Zoe wants you to add two hyperlinks to the program description—one hyperlink that jumps to a location within the program description and one that will open a different document.

Inserting a Hyperlink to a Bookmark in the Same Document

Creating a hyperlink within a document is actually a two-part process. First, you need to mark the text you want the link to jump to—either by formatting the text with a heading style or by inserting a bookmark. A **bookmark** is an electronic marker that refers to a specific point in a document. Second, you need to select the text that you want users to click, format it as a hyperlink, and specify the bookmark or heading as the target of the hyperlink. The **target** is the place in the document to which the link connects.

In this case, Zoe wants to create a hyperlink that targets Alison's name, near the end of the document. Figure 7-26 illustrates this process.

Hyperlink that targets a bookmark ◄ Figure 7-26

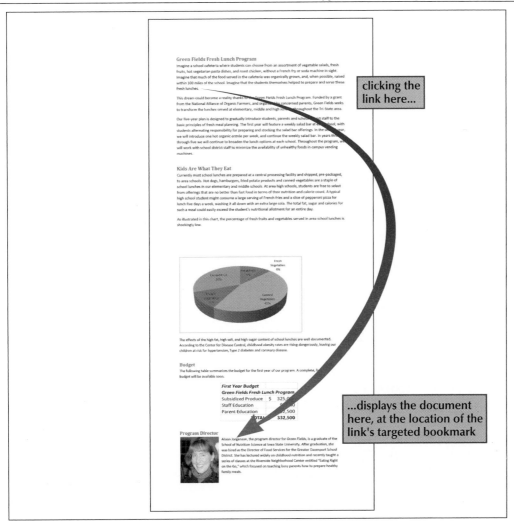

Linking to a Location in the Same Document | Reference Window

- Insert a bookmark at the target location or format text at the target location with a heading style. To insert a bookmark, select the text you want to mark as a bookmark, click the Insert tab, in the Links group click Bookmark, type a name for the bookmark, and then click the Add button.
- Select the text or graphic you want to use as the hyperlink.
- On the Insert tab in the Links group, click Hyperlink.
- Under Link to, click the Place in This Document option.
- Click the bookmark you want to link to, and then click the OK button.

To create a hyperlink in the Green Fields Rev document, you'll need to insert a bookmark in the Program Director section. But first, you need to reopen the Green Fields Rev document and update the linked object.

To reopen the document and insert a bookmark:

▶ **1.** Open the **Green Fields Rev** document from the Tutorial.07\Tutorial folder included with your Data Files. A dialog box opens, explaining that the document contains links (in this case, just one link) and asking if you want to update the data from the linked file. It's usually a good idea to click Yes in this dialog box, so you can be sure your document contains the latest version of all linked objects.

▶ **2.** Click **Yes** to update the links and close the dialog box, and then switch to Print Layout view and display nonprinting characters, if necessary.

▶ **3.** Use the Find dialog box to find and select the name **Alison Jorgenson** at the beginning of the Program Director section.

▶ **4.** Click the **Insert** tab, and then click the **Bookmark** button in the Links group. The Bookmark dialog box opens. You can now type the bookmark name, which must be one word, without spaces.

▶ **5.** Type **Director**. See Figure 7-27.

Figure 7-27 ▶ **Creating a bookmark**

▶ **6.** Click the **Add** button. The Bookmark dialog box closes. Although you can't see it, a bookmark has been inserted before Alison's name.

This bookmark you just created will be the target of the hyperlink. When you click the hyperlink, which you will create in the next set of steps, the insertion point will jump to this bookmark.

To create a hyperlink to the bookmark:

▶ **1.** Press the **Ctrl+Home** keys to move the insertion point to the beginning of the document, and then click at the end of the second paragraph under the heading Green Fields Fresh Lunch Program. The insertion point should be positioned immediately following the phrase "…throughout the Tri-State area."

▶ **2.** Insert a space, and then type **The program director is Alison Jorgenson, an expert in childhood nutrition.** (Include the period.) Next, you'll format part of this sentence as a hyperlink.

▶ **3.** Select the name **Alison Jorgenson** in the sentence you just typed, and then in the Links group on the Insert tab, click the **Hyperlink** button. The Insert Hyperlink dialog box opens.

4. Under Link to (on the left side of the dialog box), click **Place in This Document**. See Figure 7-28. The right side of the dialog box now lists the headings and bookmarks in the document. Here you can click the bookmark or heading you want the hyperlink to jump to.

Inserting a hyperlink   **Figure 7-28**

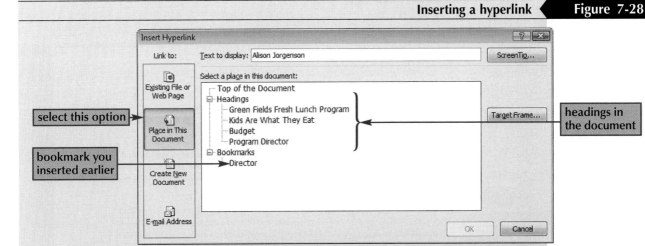

Trouble? If you don't see the document headings or the bookmark in the dialog box, click the plus signs next to Headings and Bookmarks.

5. Under Bookmarks, click **Director**, and then click the **OK** button. The name "Alison Jorgenson" appears in underlined blue text. The hyperlink now targets the Director bookmark that you created in the last set of steps.

Trouble? If you formatted the wrong text as a hyperlink, click the Undo button and begin again with Step 3.

After inserting a hyperlink into a document, you should test it.

To test the hyperlink in your document:

1. Without clicking, move the mouse pointer over the blue underlined hyperlink, **Alison Jorgenson**. After a moment, a ScreenTip appears with the name of the bookmark (Director) and instructions for following the link. See Figure 7-29.

Tip

To edit the text that appears in a ScreenTip when you place the mouse pointer over the hyperlink in the document, in the Insert Hyperlink dialog box click the ScreenTip button, type the text you want for a ScreenTip, and then click the OK button.

| **Figure 7-29** | Displaying the hyperlink ScreenTip |

2. Press and hold the **Ctrl** key, and then click the **Alison Jorgenson** hyperlink. The insertion point jumps to the beginning of Alison's name in the Program Director section, where you inserted the bookmark.

3. Press the **Ctrl+Home** keys to move the insertion point back to the beginning of the document. The hyperlink has changed color, indicating that it has been used. If you were to close and then reopen the document, the hyperlink would again be blue until you clicked it.

4. Save your work.

You have finished creating a hyperlink that jumps to a location in the same document. Next, you will create a hyperlink that jumps to a location in a different document.

Creating Hyperlinks to Other Documents

The greatest power of hyperlinks lies not in jumping to another location within the same document, but in jumping to other documents. These documents can be located on the World Wide Web, on your computer's hard drive, or on your company's network server. When you create a hyperlink to another document, you can target the URL of a document stored on the Web or the path and filename of a file on your computer or network. When you click a hyperlink to another document, the document opens on your computer, with the beginning of the document displayed. If you want, you can also specify a particular bookmark within the other document. In that case, when you click the link, the document opens, with the bookmarked location in the document displayed.

Creating a Hyperlink to Another Document

- Select the text you want to format as a hyperlink.
- In the Links group on the Insert tab, click the Hyperlink button.
- Under Link to, click Existing File or Web Page.
- To target a specific file on your computer or network, use the Look in list arrow to open the folder containing the file, and then click the file in the file list.
- To target a Web page, type the URL in the Address text box.

Zoe wants to insert a hyperlink that will open a Word document containing Alison's resume. Because she wants the hyperlink to take users to the beginning of the resume, you don't need to insert a bookmark. Instead, you can use just the name of the target document.

To create a hyperlink to another document:

1. Use the hyperlink again to jump to the bookmark in the Program Director section.

2. Click at the end of the Program Director section. The insertion point should be located immediately to the right of the period that concludes the phrase "healthy family meals." This is where you'll insert text, some of which will become the hyperlink.

3. Press the **spacebar**, and type **(See her resume.)**, making sure to include the parentheses.

4. Select the word **resume** in the text you just typed.

5. In the Links group on the Insert tab, click the **Hyperlink** button. The Insert Hyperlink dialog box opens.

6. Under Link to, click **Existing File or Web Page**. The right side of the dialog box displays options related to selecting a file or a Web page.

7. If necessary, use the **Look in** list arrow to open the Tutorial.07\Tutorial folder.

8. Click **Resume** in the file list. See Figure 7-30.

Inserting a hyperlink to a different document ◄ **Figure 7-30**

9. Click the **OK** button. The word "resume" is now formatted as a hyperlink, in blue with an underline.

InSight | **Keeping Track of Documents Containing Hyperlinks**

When your documents include hyperlinks to other documents, you must keep track of where you store the target documents. If you move a target document to a different location, hyperlinks to it might not function properly. In this case, you created a hyperlink in the Green Fields Rev document that links to the Resume document. Both documents are stored in the Tutorial.07\Tutorial folder, which is most likely located on your computer's hard disk. To ensure that the hyperlink in the program description document will continue to function, you must keep the two documents in the same folder as when you created the link. If you have to move a target document, then be sure to edit the hyperlink to select the target document in its new location. You'll learn how to edit hyperlinks later in this tutorial.

Now you're ready to test the hyperlink you just created.

To test the resume hyperlink:

1. Press and hold the **Ctrl** key and click the **resume** hyperlink. The Resume document opens. See Figure 7-31.

Figure 7-31 | **Resume document**

2. Read through the Resume document, and then close it. You return to the Green Fields Rev document. Notice that the hyperlink color has changed, indicating that you have used the hyperlink.

3. Save your work.

As you can see, hyperlinks allow you to display information instantaneously. When used thoughtfully, hyperlinks make it possible to navigate a complicated document or a set of files quickly and easily.

Viewing a Document in Web Layout View

Because the version of the program description you are now working on is intended for an online audience, Zoe suggests that you switch to Web Layout view. **Web Layout view** offers several advantages for online viewers:

- Text automatically wraps to suit the size of your screen, not the printed page.
- Documents can be displayed with a variety of background effects.
- Page setup elements, such as footers, headers, and breaks, are not displayed. Because users don't view the document as printed pages, these elements aren't necessary.

Web Layout view is useful when you need to format a document for online viewing. Text wrapping doesn't always survive the conversion from a Word document to a Web page, and graphics often shift position when you save a document as a Web page. Web Layout view prepares you for this by showing you what the graphics look like in their new positions.

Keep in mind that, despite its name, Web Layout view does not show you exactly how a document will look when saved as a Web page. Some features you see in Web Layout view, such as the embedded chart, might look different when you save the document as a Web page. (You will learn more about saving a document as a Web page later in this tutorial.)

If you switch to Web Layout view and then save the document in that view, the next time you open it, it will by default open in Web Layout view. Zoe asks you to display the program description document in Web Layout view, and then save it. Then when she e-mails the file to Alison, it will open for her in Web Layout view.

To display a document in Web Layout view:

▶ **1.** Scroll to the beginning of the document, and then click the **Web Layout** button 🖺 . This button is located in the status bar in the lower-right corner of the document window. Notice that paragraphs now span the width of the document window. The line widths are no longer constrained by the margin settings for the printed page. See Figure 7-32.

| Figure 7-32 | Document displayed in Web Layout view |

Trouble? Depending on the size of your monitor, the line breaks in your document may differ from those in Figure 7-32. This has to do with the fact that Web Layout view wraps text to fit the size of the screen, and is not a problem.

▶ **2.** Scroll through the document to review its appearance in Web Layout view.

▶ **3.** Save the document.

Next, you'll make some changes to the Green Fields Rev document that will improve its online appearance.

Applying a Background Effect

To make the document more visually interesting for online viewers, Zoe would like to add a background effect. You can apply one of the following background effects:

- Solid color
- Gradient—a single color or combination of colors that varies in intensity
- Texture—a design that mimics the look of various textured materials, including linen and marble
- Pattern—a repetitive design such as checks, polka dots, and stripes, in colors you specify
- Picture—a graphic image

Note that backgrounds do not appear in printed documents; they are visible only on the screen in Web Layout view and in documents saved as Web pages. After you apply a background color or texture, you should make sure your text is still readable. In poorly designed online documents, the background might be so dark or the pattern so obtrusive that the text is illegible. Zoe suggests you use an unobtrusive textured background.

To apply a background effect to a document:

1. Click the **Page Layout** tab, and then in the Page Background group, click the **Page Color** button. The Page Color palette opens, with a menu at the bottom. You could click a color in the palette to select it as a background color for the page. To select any other type of background effect, you need to click Fill Effects.

2. Click **Fill Effects**, and then click the **Texture** tab if necessary. The Texture list box displays a variety of textured backgrounds.

3. Click the gray box in the left column, fourth row down. An outline appears around the gray box, indicating that it is selected, and the name of the texture, "Newsprint," appears below the palette of tiles. See Figure 7-33.

Selecting a texture background ◄ **Figure 7-33**

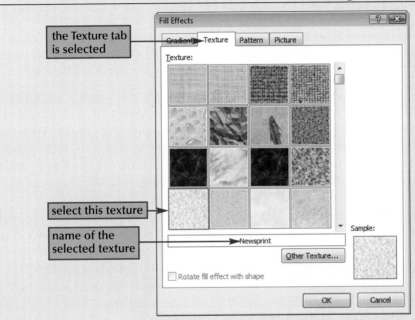

the Texture tab is selected

select this texture

name of the selected texture

4. Click the **OK** button. The gray texture fills the background of the Green Fields Rev document.

5. Save the document in Web Layout view.

The texture background is attractive and light enough to make the document text easy to read. Note that it's a good idea to make sure linked documents have a similar appearance. Later, Zoe plans to add a similar background to the Resume document. That way both of the linked documents will have a consistent look. She'll take care of that task, though. Instead, you can focus on saving the current document as a Web page.

Saving a Word Document as a Web Page

To create sophisticated Web pages (or a complete Web site), you'll probably want to use a dedicated HTML editor, such as Adobe Dreamweaver. But to create a simple Web page from an existing document, you can convert a document to a Web page from within Word.

So far, Zoe has created printed copies of her program description and an online version to e-mail to Alison. Next, she wants to convert her document to a Web page so she can make it available on the World Wide Web.

Another term for a Web page is **HTML document**. The acronym "HTML" is short for **Hypertext Markup Language**, a language that tells a Web browser how a Web page should look on the screen. When you save a Word document as a Web page, Word inserts HTML codes that tell the browser how to format the text and graphics. Fortunately, you don't have to learn the Hypertext Markup Language to create Web pages with Word. When you save the document as a Web page, Word creates all the necessary HTML codes (called markings, or tags). This process is transparent to you, so you won't actually see the HTML codes in your Web pages.

When you save a document as a Web page, Word saves the document as an HTML file and places the graphics that appear in the document in a separate folder. A group of smaller files travels across the Web faster than one large file, so this division of files makes it easier to share your documents on the Web.

You can choose from three different Web page file types in Word. The main differences among these file types are file size and the way special elements, such as WordArt, or embedded or linked objects, are treated when they are displayed in a browser:

- Single File Web Page—Saves the document as an MHTML file, which is slightly different from an HTML file. All graphics are stored in the file. When the Web page is open in Word, the linked and embedded objects continue to function as usual. When displayed in a browser, the file, including its linked or embedded objects, looks exactly as it did in Word. However, the linked and embedded objects do not function as embedded or linked objects when displayed in a browser. A Single File Web Page can be more than twice the size of the original Word document.

- Web Page—Saves the document as an HTML file, with all graphics stored in a separate folder. When the Web page is open in Word, the linked and embedded objects continue to function as usual. When displayed in a browser, the file, including its linked or embedded objects, looks exactly as it did in Word, but the linked and embedded objects no longer function as embedded or linked objects. A file saved using the Web Page file type might be 30 kilobytes, with 100 KB of accompanying files.

- Web Page, Filtered—Saves the document as an HTML file that contains only HTML codes, without any of the codes that ensure that special elements are displayed as they are in the Word document. Instead, these special elements are formatted by HTML codes. For example, the labels on an embedded Excel chart might look different than they did in the original Word document. Such formatting differences are apparent when you open the filtered Web page in a browser, or the next time you open the file in Word. A filtered Web page is very small, allowing it to travel quickly across the Web. A typical filtered Web page of a few hundred words might be about 4 KB, with 25 KB of accompanying files.

The Single File Web Page file type is a good choice when you plan to share your Web page only over a small network and not over the Internet. Having to manage only one file is more convenient than having to keep track of a group of files. But when you want to share your files over the Internet, it's better to use the Web Page, Filtered option. This will keep your overall file size as small as possible. Note that the folder Word creates to store the accompanying graphics files has the same name as your Web page, plus an underscore and the word "files." For instance, a Web page saved as "Finance Summary" would be accompanied by a folder named "Finance Summary_files."

Although saving a Word document as a Web page is easy, it's not foolproof, particularly when it comes to formatting. When you save your document as a Web page, some document formatting might be lost, or the formatting might look different. This is especially true if you use the Web Page, Filtered file type. Sometimes you might need to reapply formatting after a document has been saved as a Web page. As a general rule, once you save a document as a Web page, you'll want to modify it to make it more attractive for users of the Web. At the very least, you will probably need to reposition graphics.

Saving a Word Document as a Web Page | Reference Window

- Click the Office Button, and then click Save As.
- To save the Web page as a single file, click the Save as type list arrow, and then click Single File Web Page. To ensure that your Web page file is as small as possible, click the Save as type list arrow, and then click Web Page, Filtered.
- If desired, give the file a new filename. For files saved using the Single File Web Page type, Word automatically adds the .mht file extension. For files saved using the Web Page file type, Word automatically adds the .htm file extension. These extensions probably won't be visible in the Save As dialog box.
- Click the Change Title button, type a title for the Web page in the Set Page Title dialog box, and then click the OK button. This title will appear in the browser title bar.
- Click the Save button in the Save As dialog box.
- If you saved the document using the Web Page, Filtered option, click Yes in the warning dialog box.

To save the Green Fields Rev document as a Web page:

1. Close any Internet-related programs, such as e-mail editors and browsers.
2. Click the **Office Button**, and then click **Save As**. The Save As dialog box opens.
3. Click the **Save as type** list arrow, and then click **Web Page, Filtered**.
4. Change the filename to **Green Fields Web Page**.
5. Click the **Change Title** button to open the Set Page Title dialog box, and then type **Green Fields Fresh Lunch Program** in the Page title text box. This title will appear in the browser title bar.
6. Click the **OK** button in the Set Page Title dialog box.
7. Click the **Save** button in the Save As dialog box. A dialog box appears warning you that using the Web Page, Filtered file type will remove special codes, called tags, that control how the document is displayed in Word. That's fine, because you are concerned only with creating a file that is small enough to transmit quickly across the Web and that will be displayed properly in a Web browser.
8. Click the **Yes** button. The document is converted into a Web page, although it looks the same as it did before you saved it as a Web page. The revised filename, "Green Fields Web Page," appears in the Word title bar, as usual. The title you specified in Step 5 won't be visible until you open the Web page in a browser, at which point it will be displayed in the browser's title bar.

At this point, the new Green Fields Web page looks identical to the Green Fields Rev Word document when you displayed it in Web Layout view. Because you used the Web Page, Filtered file type, you might have expected the new Web page to look different. In particular, you might have expected the linked chart or the embedded worksheet to have changed appearance. Their appearance hasn't changed yet, because your computer's memory still retains the image of these elements with the proper Word formatting. Later, when you close the Web page file and open it in a browser, you will see some differences.

Although you can't see any visible change in the file, the file size has decreased from about 61 KB to only about 9 KB, plus about 29 KB of related files. Even though you are currently looking at the Web page in Word, the new HTML file is optimized for viewing in a Web browser such as Internet Explorer.

Formatting a Web Page

You can edit and format text and graphics in a Web page the same way you edit and format a normal Word document. After you have saved a Word document as a Web page, you need to format the Web page so that it is attractive when it is displayed in a browser—you need to format it for online viewing.

Inserting Horizontal Lines

Web pages sometimes include horizontal lines that separate sections of a document. These lines make it easy to see at a glance where one section ends and another begins. You can also add horizontal lines to Word documents that you plan to read in Web Layout view. If you don't like a horizontal line after you insert one into a document, you can delete it by clicking the line and then pressing the Delete key.

Zoe wants you to add a horizontal line below the title and at the end of each section except the last one.

To insert horizontal lines into the Web page:

1. Click at the beginning of the heading "Kids Are What They Eat."

2. Click the **Home** tab, if necessary, click the **Borders** button arrow ⊞ ▾, and then, at the bottom of the menu, click **Borders and Shading**. The Borders and Shading dialog box opens.

3. Click the **Borders** tab in the Borders and Shading dialog box if it is not already selected, and then click the **Horizontal Line** button. The Horizontal Line dialog box opens, displaying many styles of horizontal lines.

4. Click the line in the left column, second box from the top. The line is selected, as shown in Figure 7-34.

| Figure 7-34 | Selecting a horizontal line style |

5. Click the **OK** button. A black line with a small, black circle on each end is inserted into the Web page above the "Kids Are What They Eat" heading. Your Web page should look similar to Figure 7-35.

Newly inserted horizontal line   Figure 7-35

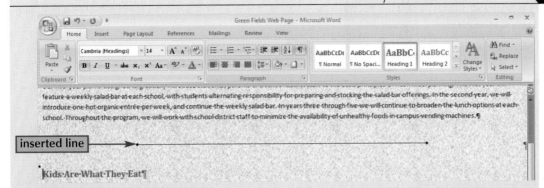

feature a weekly salad bar at each school, with students alternating responsibility for preparing and stocking the salad bar offerings. In the second year, we will introduce one hot organic entrée per week, and continue the weekly salad bar. In years three through five we will continue to broaden the lunch options at each school. Throughout the program, we will work with school district staff to minimize the availability of unhealthy foods in campus vending machines.¶

inserted line

Kids Are What They Eat¶

6. Scroll down, click to the left of the "B" in the Budget heading, and then insert the same style of horizontal line.

7. Insert the same style of horizontal line above the Program Director heading.

8. Scroll back to the top of the document and save your work. If you see the warning dialog box you saw earlier, click the **Yes** button.

> **Tip**
>
> You can use the F4 key to open the Horizontal Line dialog box after you complete Step 5.

Now that you've used horizontal lines to give shape to the document, you decide to improve the appearance of the document's text.

Modifying Text Size and Color

It's often helpful to format headings in a Web page in a larger size than you might use in a document that would be printed. Zoe wants you to increase the font size of the first heading in the document. She also wants you to center it.

To increase the font size for the first heading and center it:

1. Select the heading **Green Fields Fresh Lunch Program** at the beginning of the Web page.

2. In the Font group on the Home tab, click the **Grow Font** button [A˄] to increase the font size from 14-point to 16-point.

3. Continue clicking the [A˄] until the font size of the selected heading is **28-point**. Use the Font Size list box to see the current size of the selected text. If you increase the font size too much, use the Shrink Font button [A˅] to reduce the font size.

4. In the Paragraph group, click the **Center** button [≡] to center the heading at the top of the document, and then click anywhere in the document to deselect the heading.

5. Save your work. If you see the warning dialog box, click the **Yes** button.

You've formatted Zoe's document so that it will be visually appealing when displayed in a browser. Next, you'll create additional hypertext links and edit the existing link.

Creating and Editing Hyperlinks in a Web Page

As you looked through the HTML version of the program description, you probably noticed that it still contains two hyperlinks. The Alison Jorgenson link still jumps to the Program Director section at the end of the Web page, and the resume link still jumps to a Word document containing Alison's resume. Zoe wants to save the Resume document as a Web page and then format it to match the Green Fields Rev document. She also wants you to add a hyperlink in the resume that will jump back to the Green Fields Web page. Finally, because you'll save the Resume document with a new name, you have to edit the resume hyperlink (in the Green Fields Web page) to make sure it opens the right file.

In the following steps, you will convert the resume to a Web page, create a new link from the resume back to the Green Fields Web page, and then modify the hyperlink in the Green Fields Web page so that browsers can easily jump between the two documents.

To convert the resume to a Web page:

▶ 1. Open the file named **Resume** from the Tutorial.07\Tutorial folder included with your Data Files.

▶ 2. Click the **Office Button** ⊞ , click **Save As**, navigate to the Tutorial.07\Tutorial folder, select the **Web Page, Filtered** file type, use **Resume Web Page** as the file-name, and use **Alison Jorgenson's Resume** as the Web page title.

▶ 3. While the Save As dialog box is open, notice that Word has created a new folder, named "Green Fields Web Page_files," in which to store the files related to the Green Fields Web page. You should never save any other documents in this folder.

▶ 4. Click the **Save** button to save the file and close the Save As dialog box, and then click **Yes** in the warning dialog box. Word automatically switches to Web Layout view.

Next, you'll make some formatting changes to give the Resume Web page the same look as the Green Fields Web page. You'll use the procedures you learned earlier in this tutorial.

To format the resume Web page:

▶ 1. Click the **Page Layout** tab, click the **Page Color** button, click **Fill Effects**, click the **Texture** tab, and then apply the **Newsprint** style textured background.

▶ 2. Save your work. Click the **Yes** button in the warning dialog box.

The resume and the program description Web pages now have a similar appearance.

Inserting a Hyperlink to a Web Page

After users read Alison's resume, they most likely will want to return to the program description, so Zoe asks you to insert a hyperlink that jumps to the program description. You insert hyperlinks into Web pages just as you do in Word documents.

To insert a hyperlink in the Resume Web page:

▶ 1. Press the **Ctrl+End** keys to move the insertion point to the end of the Web page, press the **Enter** key to insert a blank paragraph, and then type **Return to Green Fields Web page.** (Include the period.)

▶ 2. Select the text **Return to Green Fields Web Page.**, click the **Insert** tab, click the **Hyperlink** button, and then, under Link to, click **Existing File or Web Page** if it is not already selected.

▶ 3. If necessary, navigate to the Tutorial.07\Tutorial folder included with your Data Files, click **Green Fields Web Page**, and then click the **OK** button. Word inserts the hyperlink to the program description.

▶ 4. Save the Resume Web page (clicking Yes in the warning dialog box), and then close the Web page. You return to the Green Fields Web Page.

The resume now contains a hyperlink that takes users back to the Green Fields Web page. You will test this hyperlink later in this tutorial, when you view both Web pages in a browser.

Editing a Hyperlink

The Green Fields Web page contains a hyperlink that targets the Resume document. You need to edit the hyperlink so that it targets the Web page version of the resume. Rather than deleting the hyperlink and reinserting a new one, you can edit the existing hyperlink to target the Resume Web Page document.

To edit a hyperlink:

▶ 1. Scroll to the end of the program description, and then position the pointer over the hyperlink. A ScreenTip appears indicating that the link will jump to a document named Resume.docx.

▶ 2. Right-click the **resume** hyperlink. A shortcut menu opens.

▶ 3. Click **Edit Hyperlink** in the shortcut menu. The Edit Hyperlink dialog box opens. This looks just like the Insert Hyperlink dialog box, which you have already used. To edit the hyperlink, you simply select a different target file.

▶ 4. Under Link to, verify that the **Existing File or Web Page** option is selected.

▶ 5. If necessary, navigate to the Tutorial.07\Tutorial folder.

▶ 6. Click **Resume Web Page** in the file list (you might have to scroll to see it), and then click the **OK** button. You return to the Green Fields Web page.

▶ 7. Place the mouse pointer over the resume hyperlink. A ScreenTip appears, indicating that the link will now jump to a Web page named Resume Web Page.htm.

▶ 8. Save your work, click the **Yes** button if you see a warning dialog box about the removal of Word tags, and then close Word.

The edited hyperlink in the program description Web page now correctly targets the Resume Web page. Note that if you move your Web page files to another folder or e-mail them to someone, the hyperlinks you created won't work because they refer to a specific location on your computer. Such links that refer to a specific location on a specific computer are known as absolute links. To avoid problems with absolute links, after moving a document, be sure to review all hyperlinks in the document, editing the hyperlinks as necessary to make sure they work correctly.

Breaking a Link Between Objects

When you convert a Word document to a Web page using the Single File Web Page file type or the Web Page file type, any embedded objects or linked objects continue to function as usual as long as the Web page is displayed in Word. That is, you can double-click them to display the tools of the source program. If you use the Web Page, Filtered file type, embedded and linked objects continue to function only as long as you don't close the Web page in Word. If you reopen the filtered Web page in Word, embedded and linked objects will no longer function. No matter what file type you use, when you display a Web page in a browser, the embedded or linked objects do not function. They are displayed in the Web page, but double-clicking them does not display the tools of the source program.

Even though the links to a source program continue to function in some types of Web pages when they are displayed in Word, they can be problematic. After all, the main reason to save a document as a Web page is to make transmitting it over the Web as easy as possible. You probably won't want to increase the total file size by transmitting the source file along with the Web page. Also, your readers will naturally open your Web page in a browser, not in Word, so even if the links were functional, the readers wouldn't notice them.

For these reasons, it's good idea to break any links between a Web page and a source file. When you **break a link**, the linked object becomes an embedded object, and any connection between the source file and the Web page is severed. Note that you can also break a link between a Word document and a source file. The steps are the same, whether you are working with a Word document or a Web page.

Reference Window | **Breaking the Link to a Source File**

- Click the Office Button, point to Prepare, and then click Edit Links to Files.
- Click the link that you want to break, and then click Break Link.
- To break all the links in a document, press the Ctrl+Shift+F9 keys.

Because you used the Web Page, Filtered file type, the link to the worksheet containing Alison's chart was broken automatically. There's no need to break the link now. Instead, you can proceed with viewing the new Web page in a browser.

Viewing the Web Page in a Browser

You're now ready to view the finished Web pages in a Web browser and to test the hyperlinks. In a browser, you don't have to press the Ctrl key to use a hyperlink. Instead, you simply click the link.

To view the Web page in a Web browser and test the links:

▶ 1. Click the **Start** button 🟢 on the taskbar, and then click **Internet Explorer**. If you are asked if you want to connect to the Internet, click No. If your browser automatically attempts to connect to the Internet, wait until the connection is established before proceeding to Step 2.

▶ 2. If you see a menu bar in Internet Explorer, click **File** on the Internet Explorer menu bar, and then click **Open** to display the Open dialog box. If you do not see a menu bar, press the **Ctrl+O** keys to display the Open dialog box.

▶ 3. Click the **Browse** button, navigate to the Tutorial.07\Tutorial folder included with your Data Files, click **Green Fields Web Page**, click the **Open** button, and then click the **OK** button. If you see a warning dialog box indicating that Internet Explorer needs to open a new window, click the **OK** button. The Green Fields Web Page file opens in Internet Explorer. See Figure 7-36.

Web page displayed in browser window | Figure 7-36

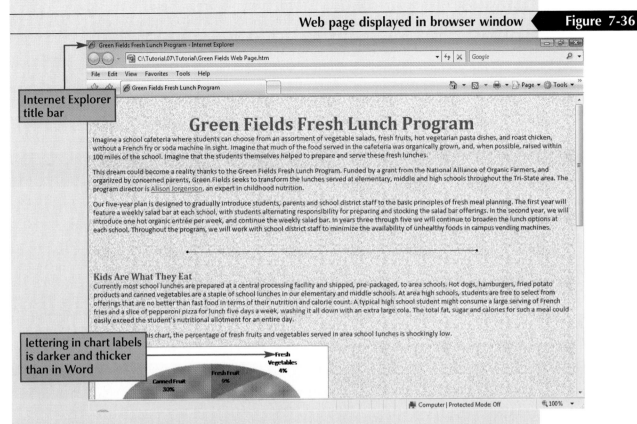

Internet Explorer title bar

Green Fields Fresh Lunch Program

Imagine a school cafeteria where students can choose from an assortment of vegetable salads, fresh fruits, hot vegetarian pasta dishes, and roast chicken, without a French fry or soda machine in sight. Imagine that much of the food served in the cafeteria was organically grown, and, when possible, raised within 100 miles of the school. Imagine that the students themselves helped to prepare and serve these fresh lunches.

This dream could become a reality thanks to the Green Fields Fresh Lunch Program. Funded by a grant from the National Alliance of Organic Farmers, and organized by concerned parents, Green Fields seeks to transform the lunches served at elementary, middle and high schools throughout the Tri-State area. The program director is Alison Jorgenson, an expert in childhood nutrition.

Our five-year plan is designed to gradually introduce students, parents and school district staff to the basic principles of fresh meal planning. The first year will feature a weekly salad bar at each school, with students alternating responsibility for preparing and stocking the salad bar offerings. In the second year, we will introduce one hot organic entrée per week, and continue the weekly salad bar. In years three through five we will continue to broaden the lunch options at each school. Throughout the program, we will work with school district staff to minimize the availability of unhealthy foods in campus vending machines.

Kids Are What They Eat

Currently most school lunches are prepared at a central processing facility and shipped, pre-packaged, to area schools. Hot dogs, hamburgers, fried potato products and canned vegetables are a staple of school lunches in our elementary and middle schools. At area high schools, students are free to select from offerings that are no better than fast food in terms of their nutrition and calorie count. A typical high school student might consume a large serving of French fries and a slice of pepperoni pizza for lunch five days a week, washing it all down with an extra large cola. The total fat, sugar and calories for such a meal could easily exceed the student's nutritional allotment for an entire day.

lettering in chart labels is darker and thicker than in Word

...is chart, the percentage of fresh fruits and vegetables served in area school lunches is shockingly low.

▶ **4.** Scroll down and review the Web page. Notice that the labels in the pie chart are darker and less elegant-looking than they appeared in Word. Likewise, the embedded worksheet is a bit harder to read. This decrease in visual quality is a disadvantage of choosing the Web Page, Filtered file type. Keep in mind, however, that this file type has the all-important advantage of very small files, which makes transmitting the Web page faster and easier. If you preferred a better-looking Web page, you could choose one of the other Web page file types. Zoe is primarily concerned with making sure the Green Fields members can easily retrieve the Web page over the Internet, so she prefers to stick with the small-sized files provided by the Web Page, Filtered file type, at the expense of readability.

▶ **5.** Near the beginning of the Web page, click the **Alison Jorgenson** hyperlink. The Program Director section is displayed in the browser window.

▶ **6.** In the last paragraph of the document, click the **resume** hyperlink. The browser opens the Resume Web page.

▶ **7.** Scroll through the resume. Notice that when you view the resume in the browser, the table format disappears and Alison's address information is left-aligned. In this case, the format is still acceptable, so you don't have to make any additional changes in Word. But in another type of document, such a change might necessitate another round of editing in Word.

▶ **8.** At the bottom of the resume, click the **Return to Green Fields Web page** hyperlink. The browser displays the Green Fields Web page.

Trouble? If any of the hyperlinks don't work properly, close the browser, return to Word, and then edit the hyperlinks so they link to the proper document.

▶ **9.** Close the browser window, start Word, open the **Green Fields Web Page** document from the Tutorial.07\Tutorial folder included with your Data Files, click the **Yes** button to update links, press the **Ctrl+End** keys to move the insertion point to the bottom of the Web page, press the **Enter** key twice, and insert the text **Prepared by** followed by your first and last name and a period.

▶ **10.** Save the Web page, print it, and close it. The printed Web page looks similar, but not identical, to the printed Word document.

Review | Session 7.2 Quick Check

1. True or False. A Web page is the same thing as an HTML document.
2. True or False. The Web Page file type results in the smallest possible total file size.
3. What's the difference between an intranet and the Internet?
4. What is the first step in creating a hyperlink to a location in the same document?
5. What term refers to the part of the Internet that transfers and displays Web pages?
6. Explain how to edit a hyperlink.
7. When saving a document as a Web page, which file type should you choose if you want to ensure that all OLE links to a source file are severed automatically?

Review | Tutorial Summary

In this tutorial, you turned on Track Changes in a document and inserted comments. Then you compared and combined documents, accepted and rejected changes, deleted comments, embedded an Excel file in a Word document, linked an Excel file with a Word document, edited an embedded Excel file, and edited a linked Excel file. You made a document suitable for online reading by adding hyperlinks, previewing the document in Web Layout view, and modifying the document's appearance to make it more interesting. Finally, you converted a Word document into a Web page, added additional hyperlinks, edited a hyperlink, and previewed the Web page in a browser.

Key Terms

bookmark	Internet	source file
balloons	intranet	source program
break a link	link	spreadsheet program
browser	linking	target
cell	merge	URL
combine	Microsoft Internet Explorer	Web
compare	Mozilla Firefox	Web address
destination file	object	Web Layout view
destination program	object linking and embedding (OLE)	Web page
embedding	online	Web server
HTML document	publish	Web site
home page	revision marks	worksheet
hyperlink		World Wide Web
Hypertext Markup Language (HTML)		

| Practice | **Review Assignments** |

Data Files needed for the Review Assignments: Expenses.xlsx, Menu.docx, Progress.docx, Progress HD.docx, Rates.xlsx

The first year of the Green Fields Fresh Lunch program was a success. Now Zoe and the staff of Rios Communication need to create a progress report to summarize the program's effectiveness. Zoe has written a draft of the progress report and e-mailed it to Henry. While Henry reviews it, she plans to turn on Track Changes and continue work on the document. Then she can combine her edited version of the document with Henry's, accepting or rejecting changes. Next, she needs to insert an Excel worksheet as an embedded object and insert an Excel chart as a linked object. She then wants to create an online version of the document with hyperlinks, format the document for online viewing, save it as a Web page, and view it in a browser. (Note: Text you need to type is shown in bold for ease of reference only; do not bold the text unless otherwise instructed.)

1. Open the file named **Progress** from the Tutorial.07\Review folder included with your Data Files. Save the file as **Progress Report** in the same folder.
2. Turn on Track Changes, and then edit the document by formatting the first two headings with the Heading 1 style. Delete "concerned" in the first main paragraph.
3. In the last line of the first main paragraph, insert the word **generous** before the word "grant," so the sentence reads "...by a generous grant...." In the middle line of the third main paragraph, select the word "thirty" and insert a comment that reads **Remember to verify this number**.
4. In the Current Membership section at the end of the document, replace "Marti Sundra" with your name. Save your work.
5. Combine the Progress Report document with Henry's edited version, named **Progress HD**. This file is in the Tutorial.07\Review folder included with your Data Files.
6. Close the Progress Report document (saving changes if necessary) and save the new document as **Progress Report Rev** in the Tutorial.07\Review folder included with your Data Files.
7. Turn off Track Changes, and then accept all the changes in the document except Henry's deletion of "extremely." Review the comments and then delete all comments in the document. Save your work.
8. Replace the placeholder [Insert Excel worksheet] with the budget in the Expenses.xlsx file in the Tutorial.07\Review folder included with your Data Files. Insert the budget as an embedded object, and then close Excel.
9. Center the embedded object, and then edit it to change the Parent Education value from $2,500 to **$3,000**.
10. Delete the placeholder [Insert Excel chart], make sure the insertion point is located in a blank paragraph between the two paragraphs of text, start Excel, open the workbook named **Rates.xlsx** file in the Tutorial.07\Review folder included with your Data Files, and then save it as **Rates Copy.xlsx**. Copy the chart and insert it as a linked object in the **Progress Report Rev** document at the insertion point. Save your work.
11. Return to Excel and change the Last Month participation rate for middle schools from 40% to **90%**. Save and close the **Rates Copy.xlsx** file and close Excel. Update the linked object in Word.
12. Print the **Progress Report Rev** document.

13. In the list of board members at the end of the document, select the word "Chair" and insert a bookmark named **Board**. At the end of the first main paragraph, insert the sentence **The Board of Directors is responsible for overseeing the grant.** Format "Board of Directors" as a hyperlink that targets the Board bookmark. Test the hyperlink to make sure it works.

14. In the paragraph below the heading "Year One: What Went Right?," click after the first sentence and insert the following: **(Click here for a typical salad bar menu.)** Select the word **here** and insert a hyperlink that targets the Word document named **Menu** in the Tutorial.07\Review folder included with your Data Files. Test the hyperlink to make sure it works, and then close the Menu document.

15. Switch to Web Layout view, and then format the report's background with the Newsprint texture.

16. Before every heading except the first, insert a black horizontal line with circles on each end.

17. Increase the font size for the first heading, "Green Fields Progress Report," to 28-point, and then center the heading. Save the document.

18. Save the report as a Web page in the Tutorial.07\Review folder using the Web Page, Filtered file type. Use **Progress Report Web Page** for the filename and **Green Fields First Year Progress** as the page title.

19. Use the hyperlink to open the **Menu** document, and save then save the Menu document in the Tutorial.07\Review folder as a Web Page using the Web Page, Filtered file type. Use **Menu Web Page** as the filename, and **Green Fields Typical Menu** as the page title. Format the menu's background with the Newsprint texture, and then save the close the file.

20. Close Word, open your browser, open the **Progress Report Web Page** from the Tutorial.07\Review folder, review the Web page in the browser, test the hyperlinks, and then close the browser.

21. Use your e-mail program to send the **Progress Report Rev** document to a fellow student. In most e-mail programs, you need to create a new message, and then attach the file to the message. Ask the recipient of the file to open it and test the various links. Can he or she access the source file for the Excel file? Why or why not? Do the other links in the document work? Why or why not?

22. Submit the documents to your instructor, in printed or electronic form, as requested.

Apply	**Case Problem 1**

Apply the skills you learned to create an investment statement.

Data Files needed for this Case Problem: Cook.docx, Statement.xlsx

KingFish Financial Planning   You have just started work as a certified financial planner at KingFish Financial Planning. At the end of every quarter, you need to send a letter to each client containing a statement that summarizes the client's investment portfolio. The letter is a Word document, and the investment data for each client is stored in an Excel file. You need to insert the Excel data in the Word document. Because your assistant updates this data every morning, you plan to insert the data as a linked object. That way, when you print and mail the statement at the end of the quarter, you can be sure that it will contain the most current data. In the following steps, you will create a statement for a client named Isabella Cook. You will also practice pasting copied worksheet data into a document as a Word table. (Note: Text you need to type is shown in bold for ease of reference only; do not bold the text unless otherwise instructed.)

1. Open the file named **Cook** from the Tutorial.07\Case1 folder included with your Data Files. Save the file as **Cook Letter** in the same folder. The letter is based on the Oriel Letter template.

2. Use the Date document control to select the current date. In the signature line, replace "Student Name" with your name.

3. Delete the placeholder "[Insert Excel worksheet.]."

4. Start Excel and open the file named **Statement** from the Tutorial.07\Case1 folder included with your Data Files. Save the file as **Cook Statement** in the same folder.

5. Copy the worksheet data to the Clipboard and insert it into the Word document in the blank paragraph that previously contained the placeholder text. Insert the data as a linked Microsoft Office Excel Worksheet Object.

6. Save and close the Word document.

7. Return to the **Cook Statement** worksheet and change the Year to Date value for the Roth IRA to **$28,000**. Save and close the Excel file.

8. Open the **Cook Letter** document in Word and verify that the Year to Date value for the Roth IRA has been updated to $28,000.

9. Save and print and the **Cook Letter** document.

10. Save the letter again as **Cook Letter** 2 in the same folder. Delete the worksheet object.

⊕ EXPLORE 11. Open the **Cook Statement** file in Excel again, and then copy the worksheet data to the Office Clipboard again. Return to the Word document, and this time simply paste the worksheet data into the document using the Paste button. Adjust column widths in the new table as necessary to make the statement easy to read.

12. Save and print the document.

13. Close Excel.

14. Submit the finished documents to your instructor, either in printed or electronic form, as requested.

Apply | **Case Problem 2**

Apply the skills you learned to create a Web page for an upscale dog kennel.

Data Files needed for this Case Problem: Kreelie.docx, Sun.docx

Kreelie Kennels Web Page   Brianna Kreelie is the owner of Kreelie Kennels, an upscale dog boarding facility in Knoxville, Kentucky. She would like your help in creating a Web page for her business. She has created a first draft and saved it as a Word document. In the document, she included some comments explaining the edits she would like you to make. After you edit the document and remove the comments, she would like you to format it for online viewing and save it as a Web page. (Note: Text you need to type is shown in bold for ease of reference only; do not bold the text unless otherwise instructed.)

1. Open the file **Kreelie** from the Tutorial.07\Case2 folder included with your Data Files, and then save it as **Kreelie Edits** in the same folder.

2. Turn on Track Changes, review the comments, and make the changes requested in the comments. When you are finished, delete the comments. At the end of the document, insert a comment that reads **I made all the changes you requested**.

⊕ EXPLORE 3. Save and print the document using the default print settings. Notice that the margin balloons and revision marks are printed by default.

4. Save the document as **Kreelie Final** in the Tutorial.07\Case2 folder.

5. Turn off Track Changes, and then accept all your changes in the document except for the deletion of the word "fleece," which you should reject. Delete your comment at the end of the document, and then save your work.

6. Open the document named **Sun** from the Tutorial.07\Case2 folder, save it as **Sundeck** in the same folder, and then close it.

7. In the **Kreelie Final** document, at the end of the "Fun in the Sun" section, format the word "here" as a hyperlink that opens the **Sundeck** document. For now, don't be concerned if the link is formatted in a color that is hard to see. Test the link, and then return to the **Kreelie Final** document.

8. Open the Theme Colors menu and preview the various color sets, noticing the different color applied to the hyperlink in each theme. Select the Technic theme colors.

⊕ EXPLORE 9. Format the page background for the **Kreelie Final** document and the **Sundeck** document using the yellow tile under Standard Colors in the Page Color menu.

10. Review the Kreelie Final document and the Sundeck document in Web Layout view. Save both documents in Web Layout view. Do not print the documents unless your instructor asks you to, because the yellow background could be problematic on some printers.

11. Save the Kreelie Final document as **Kreelie Web Page** in the Tutorial.07\Case2 folder, using the Web Page, Filtered file type. Use **Kreelie Kennels** as the page title. Save the Sundeck document as **Sundeck Web Page** in the same folder, using the same file type. Use **Kreelie Kennels Sundeck** as the page title.

12. Edit the hyperlink so it targets the correct file, and then save your work.

13. Close Word and open the **Kreelie Web Page** file in a browser. Test the hyperlink. Close the browser.

14. Submit the finished file to your instructor, either in printed or electronic form, as requested.

Create		**Case Problem 3**

Use your Web page skills to create the Web page shown in Figure 7-37.

Data Files needed for this Case Problem: Survey.xlsx

Seabird Optical Web Page   You have been asked to create a Web page for Seabird Optical, a supplier of high-quality eyeglasses in Bellingham, Washington. Perform the following steps to create the Web page shown in Figure 7-37.

Figure 7-37

Seabird Optical

3421 Island Way, Bellingham, Washington 98225

Think you don't need glasses? Think again. Our customer surveys show a surprising number of people don't discover they need glasses until they have an eye exam. The following chart prepared by Student Name summarizes our findings:

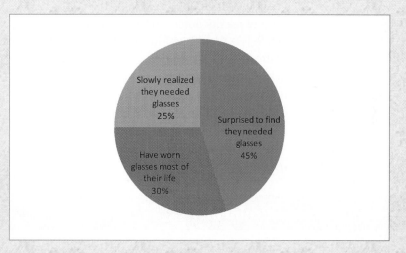

1. Open a new, blank document and save it as a document (not as a Web page) using the name **Sea** in the Tutorial.07\Case3 folder included with your Data Files. Insert two blank paragraphs.

⊕ EXPLORE

2. When creating Web pages and online documents, you might sometimes need to create simple graphics. To learn how, click the Start button on the taskbar, click All Programs, click Accessories, and then click Paint.

   a. Click Image on the menu bar, click Attributes, and then change the Width setting to 500 and the Height setting to 200.

b. Click the Brush button on the toolbar, click a blue box in the color palette, and draw the waves shown in Figure 7-37. Continue using these tools to draw the yellow sun and the black birds. (If you don't like your first attempt, use the Erase button to erase your work.) Don't expect to produce a perfect work of art; your goal is just to get familiar with using Paint.

c. Save the logo as a JPEG file named **Birds** in the Tutorial.07\Case3 folder, and then close Paint.

3. On the Insert tab, use the Insert Picture button to insert the **Birds** file into the first blank paragraph of the document. Center the picture at the top of the document.

4. In the second paragraph of the document, insert the company name as WordArt, as shown in Figure 7-37. Center the WordArt object.

5. Below the WordArt title, insert the text shown in Figure 7-37. Replace "Student Name" with your name. Format the text as shown in Figure 7-37.

6. Open the Excel file named **Survey** from the Tutorial.07\Case3 folder included with your Data Files, and then save it as **Survey Copy**.

7. Insert a linked copy of the chart from the Survey Copy file in the Word document. Close Excel.

8. From within Word, revise the linked chart to change the percentage for "Surprised to find they needed glasses" to 45%. Change the percentage for "Have worn glasses most of their life" to 30%. Update the link.

9. Format the page background with the Blue tissue paper texture. Insert a turquoise horizontal line as shown in Figure 7-37.

10. Break the link to the Excel file.

11. Review the document in Web Layout view, and then save it as a Web page using the Single File Web Page file type. Use **Seabird Web Page** as the filename and **Seabird Optical** as the page title.

12. In Web Layout view, resize the Excel chart to make it as wide as the last line of text in the paragraph above it, and then save your changes.

13. Close Word and open the Web page in a browser.

⊕ **EXPLORE** 14. Print the Web page from your browser, and then close your browser.

15. Submit the finished files to your instructor, either in printed or electronic form, as requested.

Challenge | Case Problem 4

Go beyond the skills you've learned to create a FAQ Web page.

Data File needed for this Case Problem: FAQ.docx

Great Falls Health Resource   Sebastian Morey is publications director at Great Falls Health Resource, a county agency in Great Falls, Montana, that helps county residents manage health and health insurance-related issues. Sebastian asks you to help create a FAQ (Frequently Asked Questions) page that answers some basic questions related to health insurance. So far, he has created the basic structure of the FAQ and inserted a few questions. He wants you to add the necessary hyperlinks.

1. Open the file named **FAQ** from the Tutorial.07\Case4 folder included with your Data Files, and then save it as a Word document using the name **Insurance FAQ** in the same folder.

2. At the bottom of the document, replace "Student Name" with your name. Replace "Date" with the current date.

⊕ EXPLORE

3. Create a system of hyperlinks that makes it possible for a user to click a topic in the Table of Contents and jump immediately to the relevant section in the Web page. Add hyperlinks to the "Back to top" text that jump to the "Table of Contents" heading at the beginning of the document. Use a heading as the target of each hyperlink rather than a bookmark.

4. At the bottom of page 1, delete the placeholder "[Insert chart here.]," and then verify that the insertion point is located in a blank paragraph between two other blank paragraphs.

⊕ EXPLORE

5. In the Illustrations group on the Insert tab, use the Chart button to insert the default type of column chart. Drag the mouse to select the bottom row of data and then delete it. In the same way, delete the data in columns C and D. Drag the border between the column headers for Columns A and B to the right to make Column A about four times wider than its default width. Replace the first three rows of data with the following data:
   - No employee contribution: 5%
   - Required for family coverage: 60%
   - Required for employee coverage: 80%

   Replace "Series1" with **Employee Contributions**. Locate the bottom-right corner of the selection box around the data, and drag it up and to the left so that it encloses the data you just typed. Close the Chart in Microsoft Office Word window. There's no need to save the chart in this window because it will be saved with the Word document.

⊕ EXPLORE

6. Double-click the chart in the Word document, and then examine the various Chart Tools tabs. Use a button on the Chart Tools Layout tab to turn off the chart legend. Use a button on the Design tab to edit the data, changing the percentage for "Required for family coverage" from 60% to 93%.

⊕ EXPLORE

7. Near the end of page 2, in the section on finding health insurance statistics on the Web, format the word "here" as a hyperlink that targets the Web site for the U.S. Census Bureau. In the Address box of the Insert Hyperlink dialog box, enter the following URL: **www.census.gov**. (Do not include the period at the end.) If your computer is connected to the Internet, test the hyperlink, and then close the browser.

8. Save the document and print it.

9. Save the document as a Web page using the file type that results in the lowest total file size. Use **Insurance FAQ Web Page** as the filename and **Insurance FAQ** as the page title.

10. Close Word and open the **Insurance FAQ Web Page** in a browser. Test all the table of contents and "Back to top" hyperlinks. If your computer is connected to the Internet, test the U.S. Census Bureau hyperlink.

11. Submit the finished files to your instructor, either in printed or electronic form, as requested.

Research | Internet Assignments

Go to the Web to find information you can use to create documents.

The purpose of the Internet Assignments is to challenge you to find information on the Internet that you can use to work effectively with this software. The actual assignments are updated and maintained on the Course Technology Web site. Log on to the Internet and use your Web browser to go to the Student Online Companion for New Perspectives Office 2007 at **www.course.com/np/office2007**. Then navigate to the Internet Assignments for this tutorial.

Assess | SAM Assessment and Training

If you have a SAM user profile, you may have access to hands-on instruction, practice, and assessment of the skills covered in this tutorial. Log in to your SAM account (**http://sam2007.course.com**) to launch any assigned training activities or exams that relate to the skills covered in this tutorial.

Review | Quick Check Answers

Session 7.1

1. Verify that the document is displayed in Print Layout view, click the Review tab, and then click the Track Changes button in the Tracking group. Verify that Final Showing Markup is displayed in the Display for Review list box in the Tracking group. Edit the document as you ordinarily would.
2. New Comment button on the Review tab
3. Combine
4. An embedded object is a copy of the original object; edits to an embedded object do not affect the original. A linked object is shortcut to the original object in the source file; edits to a linked object also affect the original object.
5. Object
6. Paste button arrow on the Home tab
7. True

Session 7.2

1. True
2. True
3. An intranet is a self-contained Web-based network that is owned by a single organization. The Internet is a worldwide network incorporating many organizations.
4. Create a bookmark
5. World Wide Web
6. Right-click the hyperlink, click Edit Hyperlink in the shortcut menu, and then select a different target file.
7. Web Page, Filtered

Ending Data Files

Tutorial.07 →

Tutorial
Green Fields Web Page_files (folder)
Resume Web Page_files (folder)
Chart Copy.xlsx
Green Fields.docx
Green Fields Rev.docx
Green Fields Web Page.htm
Resume.docx
Resume Web Page.htm

Review
Menu Web Page_files (folder)
Progress Report Web
   Page_files (folder)
Menu.docx
Menu Web Page.htm
Progress Report.docx
Progress Report Rev.docx
Progress Report Web Page.htm
Rates Copy.xlsx

Case1
Cook Letter.docx
Cook Letter 2.docx
Cook Statement.xlsx

Case2
Kreelie Web Page_files (folder)
Sundeck Web Page_files (folder)
Kreelie Edits.docx
Kreelie Final.docx
Kreelie Web Page.htm
Sundeck.docx
Sundeck Web Page.htm

Case3
Birds.jpg
Sea.docx
Seabird Web Page.mht
Survey Copy.xlsx

Case4
Insurance FAQ Web
   Page_files (folder)
Insurance FAQ.docx
Insurance FAQ
   Web Page.htm

Reality Check

At this point, you should feel confident that you have the word-processing skills to create, revise, and distribute polished, useful documents in the business world. But there's no need to wait to use your new word-processing skills. You can use them to create some practical documents right now. In the following exercise, you'll create documents using the Word skills and features presented in Tutorials 5 through 7.

Note: Please be sure *not* to include any personal information of a sensitive nature in the documents you create to be submitted to your instructor for this exercise. Later on, you can update the documents with such information for your own personal use.

1. Create a new report template to use for school reports or another type of report that you might have to create on a regular basis. Start with one of the templates installed with Word, delete or edit document controls as necessary, insert placeholder text as necessary, and customize the theme. Select an appropriate style set, and create at least one new style that will be useful in your report.

2. Use your template as the basis for a new report. Insert a file containing the text of a report you wrote for one of your classes, or insert appropriate text of your choosing, and then format the text using the template styles. Remember to include a table of contents in the report. At the end of the report, include a hyperlink that jumps to the beginning of the report.

3. If you are familiar with Excel, open a new workbook, enter some data that supports one of the points in your report, and then embed the worksheet data in your report. If you don't know how to enter data in Excel, you can embed the data from the Budget file in the Tutorial.07\Tutorial folder included with your Data Files, and then edit the data as necessary. Note that you can widen a column in Excel by dragging the right border of the column's header (the letter at the top of the column).

4. If possible, e-mail a copy of your report to a fellow student and have him or her edit the document with Track Changes turned on.

5. Turn on Track Changes in your copy of the report, and then edit it carefully for grammar, word choice, and punctuation. If you were able to ask a fellow student to edit another copy of the report, combine the two documents, and then accept or reject changes as necessary. Save the new, combined combined document with a new name.

6. Choose a type of information, such as e-mail addresses or birthdays, that you would like to organize in a single document. Create a Word table, and then enter fictitious versions of the information into the table. You can replace this with real information later for your personal use, after you've handed in your assignments. Sort the information based on one of the columns.

7. Create a main document for a directory that includes a dot leader. Use your Word table from Step 6 as the data source. Insert the necessary merge codes into the main document and complete the merge.

8. Format the merged document with a textured background and add a title. Format the title appropriately. Save the document as a Web page that consists of only one file.

9. Submit your documents to your instructor in electronic or printed form, as requested.

Glossary/Index

document control An on-screen element such as a text box that lets you select settings and other options for a document. WD 129

.docx file extension, WD 202

dot leader A row of dots or other characters separating tabbed text. WD 297

.dotx file extension, WD 202

drag and drop To move an item (either text or a graphic) by selecting it and then dragging it with the mouse. WD 54–57

drop cap A large, capital letter that highlights the beginning of the text of a newsletter, chapter, or some other document section. WD 170–171

E

editing
   hyperlinks, WD 363
   outlines, WD 241–242
   ScreenTip text, WD 351
   WordArt objects, WD 152

e-mailing Word documents, WD 347

embedding A technique that allows you to insert a copy of an existing object into a destination file. WD 333
   Excel worksheets, WD 336–339
   linking compared, WD 336
   modifying embedded worksheets, WD 336–339, WD 339–341

endnote An explanatory comment or reference that appears at the end of a document. WD 119–121

envelope, creating, WD 35–37

error correction, WD 20–25
   spelling and grammar errors, WD 21–24, WD 50–53

Excel. *See* Microsoft Office Excel 2007
exiting programs, OFF 28–29

F

field Placeholder that marks where dates, names, and other variable information will be inserted into a document. In Mail Merge, a field is called a merge field. WD 262. *See also* merge field
   names, organizing, WD 271

file. *See also* document
   closing, OFF 21
   earlier versions of Office, OFF 19

new, creating, OFF 22
open, switching between, OFF 5
opening, OFF 21–22
printing, OFF 27–28
saving, OFF 18–21

file extension A multi-character code that Office appends to a filename to identify the program in which that file was created. The default file extensions are .docx for Word, .xlsx for Excel, .pptx for PowerPoint, and .accdb for Access. OFF 19
   documents, WD 202
   templates, WD 202

filename The name you provide when you save a file and the name you associate with that file. OFF 19

Find and Replace dialog box A Word dialog box used to find a word or phrase in a document, replace the word or phrase with other text, or move directly to a specific part of a document. WD 61–64

Finish & Merge button, WD 183

first column The far-left column in a table. WD 112

floating graphic A graphic that can be moved independently of the surrounding text. WD 153

folder A container for your files. OFF 19

font A set of characters that uses the same typeface, style, and size. WD 9
   changing by changing theme, WD 84
   new, applying, WD 80–82
   themes, WD 209, WD 212–215

font color Text color. WD 99

Font dialog box
   applying italics, WD 220–221
   changing character spacing, WD 220

font size Determined by point size, which is a unit of measurement equal approximately to $\frac{1}{72}$ of an inch. WD 9, WD 82

footer Text printed at the bottom of every page in a document or at the bottom of every slide in a presentation. WD 128
   creating for entire document, WD 129–131
   methods for inserting, WD 129

footnote An explanatory comment or reference that appears at the bottom of a page. WD 119–121

format To change the way a document looks. WD 64
   aligning text, WD 69–71
   changing margins, WD 64–68
   character-level formatting, WD 100
   emphasizing text with bold and italics, WD 78–80
   fonts, WD 80–82
   Format Painter, WD 72–74
   formatting documents in sections, WD 122–124
   formatting headings with Quick Styles, WD 99–102
   formatting tables with styles, WD 112–115
   hidden formatting codes, WD 235
   indenting paragraphs, WD 71–72
   lists, bulleted and numbered, WD 74–78
   manually formatting tables, WD 115
   paragraph-level formatting, WD 100
   removing formatting, WD 224
   searching for formatting, WD 64
   themes, WD 80, WD 83–84
   Web pages, WD 360–361

Format Painter A button on the Ribbon that you can use to copy all the formatting features of one paragraph to other paragraphs. WD 72–74
form letter, WD 261

G

gallery A grid or menu that shows a visual representation of the options available for a command. OFF 12–13

GIF files, WD 161

grammar error, checking for, WD 50–53

graphic A drawing, painting, photograph, chart, table, design, or designed text such as WordArt. WD 124, WD 160
   aligning, WD 170
   anchored, WD 153
   clip art, WD 160
   cropping, WD 166–167
   desktop publishing. *See* desktop publishing
   detailed view, WD 124
   inline, WD 153
   inserting, WD 160–165
   moving, WD 169–170
   SmartArt, WD 124–128
   wrapping text around, WD 168

gridline Light gray line that defines the rows and columns of a table. WD 103

group A collection of buttons for related commands on the Ribbon. OFF 11

H

handle. *See* sizing handle

hanging indent A type of paragraph indentation in which all lines except the first line of the paragraph are indented from the left margin. WD 71

header Text that appears at the top of every page in a document or every slide in a presentation. WD 128

    methods for inserting, WD 129

    separating for sections, WD 131–134

Header and Footer view A Word view in which headers and footers are added or modified and the document text is dimmed. WD 128

header column A column on the left of a table that identifies the type of information in each row. WD 103

header row A row at the top of a table that identifies the type of information in each column. WD 103

heading

    formatting with Quick Styles, WD 99–102

    promoting and demoting in outlines, WD 241–242

Help (Office) Information in Office that you can use to find out how to perform a task or obtain more information about a feature. OFF 23–27

    Help window, OFF 23–27

    ScreenTips, OFF 12, OFF 23

Help window A window that provides access to all the Help topics, templates, and training installed on your computer with Office and available on Microsoft Office Online. OFF 23–27

hidden formatting codes, WD 235

home page The main Web page within a Web site (the one that is usually displayed first). WD 348

Home tab, Word window, WD 8

horizontal lines, inserting in Web pages, WD 360–361

HTML. *See* Hypertext Markup Language

HTML document Another term for a Web page. The acronym "HTML" is short for "Hypertext Markup Language." WD 358

hyperlink Specially formatted text and graphics that you can click to open, or "jump to," additional information in another Web page or document. WD 348–354

    to bookmark in same document, WD 348–352

    breaking, WD 364

    editing, WD 363

    keeping track of documents, WD 354

    to other documents, WD 352–354

    Web pages, WD 362–364

Hypertext Markup Language A programming language that tells a Web browser how a Web page should look on the screen. WD 358

I

Increase Indent button, WD 71–72

indent To move a line or paragraph to the right. WD 71–72

indent marker Mark on the horizontal ruler that indicates a paragraph's current indent setting. WD 71

inline graphic A graphic located in a specific position in a specific line of a document. WD 153

insertion point

    moving, WD 18–19

    Word window, WD 4, WD 5

integration The ability to share information between programs. OFF 3

Internet The largest, most widely used computer network in the world. WD 348

intranet A self-contained network, belonging to a single organization, which relies on Web servers and related technology. WD 347

italic type, WD 79, WD 220–221

J

JPEG files, WD 161

justified alignment A type of alignment in which full lines of text are spaced between both the left and the right margins and the text is not ragged. WD 69, WD 70–71

K

kerning The process of adjusting the spacing between characters to make them look like they are spaced evenly. WD 219

keyboard shortcut A combination of keys you press to perform a command. OFF 12, WD 79–80

keystroke, moving insertion point, WD 19

KeyTip An on-screen marker that indicates the keyboard shortcut for selecting a button or command; for example, Alt+H selects the Home tab on the Ribbon. WD 80

L

label, mailing, WD 291–296

Label Options dialog box, WD 292

landscape orientation A type of page orientation in which the page is wider than it is tall, so that text spans the widest part of the page. WD 122, WD 123–124

left alignment A type of alignment in which text aligns on the left margin and is ragged on the right. WD 69

letter, business. *See* business letter

letterhead, allowing space for, WD 68

line

    horizontal, inserting in Web pages, WD 360–361

    multiple, selecting, WD 30

    selecting, WD 30

line spacing The amount of vertical space between lines of text. WD 27

    adjusting, WD 33

    adjusting space in inside address, WD 183

link. *See* hyperlink

Task Reference

TASK	PAGE #	RECOMMENDED METHOD
Action, redo	WD 20	Click ↻
Action, undo	WD 20	Click ↺
AutoCorrect, set options	WD 21	Click 🏳, click Word Options, click Proofing, click AutoCorrect Options
Background, add textured	WD 357	Click Page Layout tab, click Page Color button in Page Background group, click Fill Effects, click Texture tab, click a texture, click OK
Boldface, add to text	WD 78	Select text, in Font group on Home tab click **B**
Bookmark, create	WD 349–350	Move insertion point to desired location, click Insert tab, click Bookmark button in Links group, type bookmark name, click Add
Border, insert around page	WD 174	Click Page Layout tab, click Page Borders button in Page Background group, click Page Border tab, click Box
Bullets, add to paragraph	WD 74	Select paragraph, in Paragraph group on Home tab click ☰
Character spacing, adjust	WD 219	*See* Reference Window: Adjusting Character Spacing
Clip art, crop	WD 166	Click clip art, click Format tab, click Crop button in Size group, drag picture border to crop
Clip art, find	WD 161	Click Insert tab, click Clip Art button in Illustrations group, type search criteria, click Go
Clip art, insert in document	WD 161–164	Click Insert tab, click Clip Art button in Illustrations group, click Organize clips, click picture, click Copy, click in document, press Ctrl+V
Clip art, resize	WD 165	Click clip art, drag sizing handle
Clipboard, use to cut, copy, and paste	WD 57	*See* Reference Window: Cutting (or Copying) and Pasting Text
Clipboard task pane, open	WD 57	In Clipboard group on Home tab, click Clipboard
Column, insert in table	WD 110	Click in column, click Table Tools Layout tab, click Insert Right or Insert Left button in Rows & Columns group
Column width, change in table	WD 112	Double-click or drag border between columns
Columns, balance	WD 173	Click end of rightmost column, click Page Layout tab, click Breaks button in Page Setup group, click Continuous
Columns, format text in	WD 158	Click where you want to insert columns, or select text to divide into columns, click Page Layout tab, click Columns button in Page Setup group, select options, click OK
Comments, delete	WD 329	*See* Reference Window: Accepting and Rejecting Changes and Deleting Comments
Comments, insert	WD 317	*See* Reference Window: Inserting Comments
Data source, create for mail merge	WD 269	*See* Reference Window: Creating A Data Source for a Mail Merge
Data source, edit in Word	WD 285	*See* Reference Window: Editing a Data Source in Word
Data source, sort	WD 288	*See* Reference Window: Sorting a Data Source
Date field, insert	WD 276	Click Insert tab, click Date & Time button in Text group, click a date format, select Update automatically checkbox if desired, click OK

TASK	PAGE #	RECOMMENDED METHOD
Date, insert with AutoComplete	WD 25	Start typing date, press Enter
Document, open	WD 46	Click 🔘, click Open, select drive and folder, click filename, click Open
Document, open new	WD 5–6	Click 🔘, click New
Document, preview	WD 34	Click 🔘, point to Print, click Print Preview
Document, save with same name	WD 17	On Quick Access Toolbar, click 🔳
Documents, compare or combine	WD 325	*See* Reference Window: Comparing and Combining Documents
Drop cap, insert	WD 170	Click in paragraph, click Insert tab, click Drop Cap button in Text group, select options
Embedded object, modify	WD 340	Double-click object, use commands and tools of source program to modify object, click outside embedded object
Endnotes, create	WD 119	*See* Reference Window: Working with Footnotes and Endnotes
Envelope, create	WD 36	*See* Reference Window: Creating an Envelope
File, close	OFF 21	Click 🔘, click Close
File, open	OFF 22	*See* Reference Window: Opening an Existing File or Creating a New File
File, print	OFF 27	*See* Reference Window: Printing a File
File, save	OFF 18	*See* Reference Window: Saving a File
Font, change typeface	WD 81	In Font group on Home tab, click Font arrow, click font
Font size, change	WD 82	In Font group on Home tab, click Font Size arrow, click point size
Footer, add	WD 129	Double-click in bottom margin, type footer text, select options on Header & Footer Tools Design tab
Footnotes, create	WD 119	*See* Reference Window: Working with Footnotes and Endnotes
Format, copy	WD 73	*See* Reference Window: Using the Format Painter
Graphic, crop	WD 166	Click graphic, click Format tab, click Crop button in Size group, drag to crop
Graphic, find	WD 161	Click Insert tab, click Clip Art button in Illustrations group, type search criteria, click Go
Graphic, resize	WD 165	Click graphic, drag sizing handle
Graphic, wrap text around	WD 168	Click graphic, click Format tab, click Text Wrapping button in Arrange group, click text wrapping option
Header, add	WD 129	Double-click top margin, type header text, select options on Header & Footer Tools Design tab
Help task pane, use	OFF 24	*See* Reference Window: Getting Help
Horizontal line, insert	WD 360	On Home tab in Paragraph group, click Borders and Shading list arrow, click Borders and Shading, click Horizontal Line, click a line style, click OK
Hyperlink, add type in document	WD 120	Type e-mail address or URL, press spacebar
Hyperlink, remove	WD 120	Right-click hyperlink, click Remove Hyperlink
Hyperlink, use	WD 120	Press Ctrl and click hyperlink
Hyperlink to a location in the current document, format text as	WD 149	*See* Reference Window: Linking to a Location in the Same Document
Hyperlink to an existing file or Web page, format text as	WD 353	*See* Reference Window: Creating a Hyperlink to Another Document
Italics, add to text	WD 79	Select text, in Font group on Home tab click 𝐼

TASK	PAGE #	RECOMMENDED METHOD
Line spacing, change	WD 32	Select text to change, in Paragraph group on Home tab click Line spacing button, click spacing option
Link, break	WD 364	*See* Reference Window: Breaking the Link to a Source File
Link, update	WD 344	In destination file, right-click linked object and then click Update Link
Mail Merge, perform	WD 264	Click Mailings tab, click Start Mail Merge in Start Mail Merge group, click Step by Step Mail Merge Wizard, follow steps in Mail Merge task pane
Mailing labels, create	WD 291	Click Mailings tab, click Start Mail Merge in Start Mail Merge group, click Step by Step Mail Merge Wizard, click Labels, click Next: Starting document, click Label options, select label type, click OK, click Next: Select Recipients, select or create data source, click Next: Arrange your labels, insert merge fields, click Update all labels, click Next: Preview your labels, click Next: Complete the merge
Margins, change	WD 65	*See* Reference Window: Changing Margins for a Document
Merge fields, insert in main document	WD 277	Click Mailings tab, click Insert Merge Field in Write & Insert Fields group, click a merge field
Nonprinting characters, show	WD 8	In Paragraph group on Home tab, click ¶
Numbering, add to paragraphs	WD 76	Select paragraphs, in Paragraph group on Home tab click ▤
Object, embed	WD 337	Select and copy object in source program, return to Word, click destination location, on Home tab in Clipboard group click the Paste button arrow, click Paste Special, select Paste option button if necessary, in As list box select option that will paste object as an Object, click OK
Object, link	WD 342	Select and copy object in source program, return to Word, click destination location, on Home tab in Clipboard group click Paste button arrow, click Paste Special, select Paste link option, in As list box select option that will paste object as an Object, click OK
Office program, start	OFF 3	*See* Reference Window: Starting Office Programs
Outline, create and edit	WD 238	*See* Reference Window: Creating and Editing Outlines
Page, view width	WD 10	Click Zoom level, click Page width, click OK
Page break, insert	WD 103	Click where you want to break page, click Insert tab, click Page Break button in Pages group
Page number, insert	WD 130	Open header or footer, on Header & Footer Tools Design tab, click Page Number button in Header & Footer group
Page orientation, change	WD 123	Click Page Layout tab, click Orientation button in Page Setup group, choose orientation type
Paragraph, decrease indent	WD 72	In Paragraph group on Home tab, click ▤
Paragraph, increase indent	WD 72	In Paragraph group on Home tab, click ▤
Paragraph spacing, adjust	WD 221	*See* Reference Window: Adjusting Spacing Between Paragraphs
Print Layout view, change to	WD 7	Click ▤ on status bar
Program, Office, exit	OFF 28	Click ✕ on title bar
Programs, Office, open	OFF 3	*See* Reference Window: Starting Office Programs
Research task pane, open	WD 249	Click Review tab, in Proofing group click Research button, Thesaurus button, or Translate button

TASK	PAGE #	RECOMMENDED METHOD
Research task pane, use	WD 248–249	Connect to the Internet if possible, open Research task pane, type term you want to research in Search for text box, click the list arrow and select a reference work, click [→]
Row, delete from table	WD 111	Click row, (or select multiple rows) click Delete button in Rows & Columns group on Table Tools Layout tab, click Delete Rows
Row height, change in table	WD 112	Drag divider between rows; to see measurements, press and hold Alt while dragging
Rulers, display	WD 7	See Reference Window: Displaying the Rulers
Section, insert in document	WD 122	Click where you want to insert a section break, click Page Layout tab, click Breaks button in Page Setup group, click a section break type
Shading, apply to table	WD 113	Click table, click Design tab, click More button in Table Styles group, click shading style
Special character, insert	WD 172	See Reference Window: Inserting Symbols and Special Characters
Spelling, correct individual word	WD 23	Right-click misspelled word (as indicated by a wavy red line), click correctly spelled word
Spelling and grammar, check	WD 50	See Reference Window: Checking a Document for Spelling and Grammar Errors
Style, apply from Quick Styles gallery	WD 100	Select text you want to format, in Styles group on Home tab click a style in Quick Styles gallery; if style you want is not visible in Quick Styles gallery, click the More button in Styles group, click style you want
Style, apply from Styles window	WD 224–225	Select text you want to format, click style in Styles window
Style, create a new	WD 227	See Reference Window: Creating a New Style
Style, modify	WD 223	See Reference Window: Modifying Styles
Styles window, open	WD 223	In Styles group on Home tab, click Styles Dialog Box Launcher
Symbol, insert	WD 172	See Reference Window: Inserting Symbols and Special Characters
Tab stop, set	WD 116	See Reference Window: Aligning Text with Tab Stops
Table, create in Word	WD 104	Click Insert tab, click Table button in Tables group, drag pointer to select columns and rows
Table, format	WD 113	See Reference Window: Formatting a Table with a Built-in Table Style
Table, sort	WD 108	See Reference Window: Sorting the Rows of a Table
Table of Contents, add text to	WD 233	See Reference Window: Working with a Table of Contents
Table of Contents, create	WD 233	See Reference Window: Working with a Table of Contents
Table of Contents, update	WD 233	See Reference Window: Working with a Table of Contents
Template, saving a document as	WD 233	See Reference Window: Saving a Document as a Template
Text, align	WD 69–71	Select text, click [≣], [≣], [≣], or [≣] on Mini toolbar
Text, copy and paste	WD 57	See Reference Window: Cutting (or Copying) and Pasting Text
Text, find and replace	WD 62	See Reference Window: Finding and Replacing Text
Text, move by drag and drop	WD 54	See Reference Window: Dragging and Dropping Text
Text, select entire document	WD 30	Press Ctrl and click in selection bar
Text, select multiple adjacent lines	WD 30	Click and drag in selection bar

Text, select multiple nonadjacent lines	WD 30	Select text, press and hold Ctrl, select additional lines of text
Text, select multiple paragraphs	WD 30	Click and drag in selection bar
Text, wrap around WordArt	WD 154	Click WordArt, click Format tab, click Text Wrapping button in Arrange group, click text wrap option
Theme, create a custom	WD 210	*See* Reference Window: Customizing the Document Theme
Theme colors, customize	WD 215	*See* Reference Window: Creating Custom Theme Colors and Theme Fonts
Theme fonts, customize	WD 215	*See* Reference Window: Creating Custom Theme Colors and Theme Fonts
Track Changes, use	WD 316	*See* Reference Window: Tracking Changes in a Document
Track Changes, accept and reject	WD 329	*See* Reference Window: Accepting and Rejecting Changes and Deleting Comments
Web page, save document as	WD 359	*See* Reference Window: Saving a Word Document as a Web Page
Web page, view in Web Layout view	WD 355	Click [icon]
Window, close	OFF 6	Click [icon] or click [icon]
Window, maximize	OFF 7	Click [icon] or click [icon]
Window, minimize	OFF 7	Click [icon] or click [icon]
Window, restore	OFF 7	Click [icon] or click [icon]
Word, start	WD 3	Click [icon], click All Programs, click Microsoft Office, click Microsoft Office Word 2007
WordArt, change shape	WD 153	Click WordArt, click [icon] in WordArt Styles group, click shape
WordArt, edit text	WD 152	Click WordArt, click Format tab, click Edit Text button in Text group, edit text, click OK
WordArt, insert	WD 149	*See* Reference Window: Creating WordArt
WordArt, wrap text	WD 154	Click WordArt, click Format tab, click Text Wrapping button in Arrange group, click text wrap option
Workspace, zoom	OFF 8	*See* Reference Window: Zooming the Workspace
Zoom setting, change	WD 10	Drag Zoom slider